PSYCHOLOGY and the
INTERNET

PSYCHOLOGY and the
INTERNET

INTRAPERSONAL,
INTERPERSONAL, AND
TRANSPERSONAL IMPLICATIONS
2nd Edition

Edited by
Jayne Gackenbach

Department of Psychology
Grant MacEwan College
Edmonton, Alberta, Canada

AMSTERDAM • BOSTON • HEIDELBERG • LONDON
NEW YORK • OXFORD • PARIS • SAN DIEGO
SAN FRANCISCO • SINGAPORE • SYDNEY • TOKYO

ELSEVIER   Academic press is an imprint of Elsevier

Academic Press is an imprint of Elsevier
30 Corporate Drive, Suite 400, Burlington, MA 01803, USA
525 B Street, Suite 1900, San Diego, California 92101-4495, USA
84 Theobald's Road, London WCIX 8RR, UK

Library of Congress Cataloging-in-Publication Data
Application submitted

British Library Cataloguing-in-Publication Data
A catalogue record for this book is available from the British Library.

ISBN 13: 978-0-12-369425-6
ISBN 10: 0-12-369425-6

For information on all Academic Press publications
visit our Web site at www.books.elsevier.com

Printed in the United States of America
06 07 08 09 10 9 8 7 6 5 4 3 2 1

CONTENTS

CHAPTER 1
The Internet in Context

Evelyn Ellerman

PART I
INTRAPERSONAL

CHAPTER 2
Children and the Internet
Connie Varnhagen

CHAPTER 3
Self Online: Personality and Demographic Implications
Jayne Gackenbach and Heather von Stackelberg

CHAPTER 4
Disinhibition and the Internet
Adam N. Joinson

CHAPTER 5
The Psychology of Sex: A Mirror from the Internet
Raymond J. Noonan

CHAPTER 6
Internet Addiction: Does It Really Exist? (Revisited)
Laura Widyanto and Mark Griffiths

PART II
INTERPERSONAL

CHAPTER 7
Revisiting Computer–Mediated Communication for Work, Community, and Learning
Caroline Haythornthwaite and Anna L. Nielsen

CHAPTER 8
The Virtual Society: Its Driving Forces, Arrangements, Practices, and Implications
Conrad Shayo, Lorne Olfman, Alicia Iriberri, and Magid Igbaria

CHAPTER 9
Internet Self-Help and Support Groups: The Pros and Cons of Text-Based Mutual Aid
Storm A. King and Danielle Moreggi

CHAPTER 10
Cyber Shrinks: Expanding the Paradigm
Joanie Farley Gillispie

PART III
TRANSPERSONAL

CHAPTER 11
From Mediated Environments to the Development of Consciousness II
Joan M. Preston

CHAPTER 12

World Wide Brain: Self-Organizing Internet Intelligence as the Actualization of the Collective Unconscious

Ben Goertzel

CHAPTER 13

The Internet and Higher States of Consciousness—A Transpersonal Perspective

Jayne Gackenbach and Jim Karpen

CONTRIBUTORS

Evelyn Ellerman, Centre for State and Legal Studies, Athabasca University, Athabasca, Alberta, Canada

Jayne Gackenbach, Department of Psychology, Grant MacEwan College, Edmonton, Alberta, Canada

Joanie Farley Gillispie, Department of Behavioral and Biological Sciences, University of California, Berkeley Extension, Mill Valley, California

Ben Goertzel, Applied Research Laboratory for National and Homeland Security, Virginia Tech, National Capital Region, Arlington, Virginia

Mark Griffiths, International Gaming Research Unit, Psychology Division, Nottingham Trent University, Nottingham, United Kingdom

Caroline Haythornthwaite, Graduate School of Library and Information Science, University of Illinois at Urbana-Champaign, Champaign, Illinois

Magid Igbaria, School of Information Systems and Technology, Claremont Graduate University, Claremont, California

Alicia Iriberri, School of Information Systems and Technology, Claremont Graduate University, Claremont, California

Adam N. Joinson, Institute of Educational Technology, The Open University, Milton Keynes, United Kingdom

Jim Karpen, Maharishi University of Management, Fairfield, Iowa

Storm A. King, 21 Redstone Dr., East Longmeadow, Massachusetts

Danielle Moreggi, PIR Psychology Department, University of New Haven, West Haven, Connecticut

Anna L. Nielsen, Graduate School of Library and Information Science, University of Illinois at Urbana-Champaign, Champaign, Illinois

Raymond J. Noonan, Health and Physical Education Department, Fashion Institute of Technology of the State University of New York, New York, New York

Lorne Olfman, School of Information Systems and Technology, Claremont Graduate University, Claremont, California

Joan M. Preston, Department of Psychology, Brock University, St. Catharines, Ontario, Canada

Conrad Shayo, Information and Decision Sciences Department, California State University, San Bernardino, San Bernardino, California

Connie Varnhagen, Department of Psychology, P217 Biological Sciences, University of Alberta, Edmonton, Alberta, Canada

Heather von Stackelberg, Faculty of Arts and Science, Grant MacEwan College, Edmonton, Alberta, Canada

Laura Widyanto, International Gaming Research Unit, Psychology Division, Nottingham Trent University, Nottingham, United Kingdom

ACKNOWLEDGMENTS

I would like to begin by thanking Grant MacEwan College (GMC) and especially the Department of Psychology and the Grant MacEwan Faculty Scholarly Activity Fund. This fund provided a grant for a research assistant to aid in editorial duties associated with this book. The grant recipient, Heather von Stackelberg, read and edited every chapter of this book as well as worked on the permissions clearances and other administrative duties. She has also offered insights from her communications background throughout this process, for which I am very grateful. Thanks to Syracuse University graduate students Jason Pattit and Caterina Snyder Lachel for reading and commenting on part of this book. I would also like to thank my editor at Academic Press, Nikki Levy, for her support of this second edition of this book.

Many others have contributed to and supported my interest in computers, the Internet, and video games, and they include colleagues (i.e., Russell Powell, Evelyn Ellerman, Brian Brookwell, Joan Preston, Storm King, David Lukoff, Steve Reiter, Harry Hunt, Richard Wilkerson, and Jill Fisher), students (i.e., Grant MacEwan College, Athabasca University, and Saybrook Graduate School), technical support staff (i.e., Grant MacEwan College, and Athabasca University), friends (i.e., Peter Thomas, Erik Schmidt, Wendy Pullin), and family (i.e., Mason Goodloe, Tony Lachel). Finally, I would like to acknowledge the eternal and special contributions of my children (Trina Snyder Lachel and Teace Snyder), mother (Agnes Gackenbach), and sister (Leslie Goodloe) without whose support and love no work could be accomplished.

Introduction

Jayne Gackenbach
Department of Psychology
Grant MacEwan College
Edmonton, Alberta, Canada

To say the Internet has exploded onto the media scene in the eight years since the publication of the first edition of this book is a bit of an understatement. While pundits had many forecasts for the impact this new media would have in the late 1990s, many are still surprised at the rapidity and breadth of the integration of the Internet into contemporary society. Today, the Internet is no longer a unique medium, but rather the basic structure of nearly all media as they increasingly change and merge. Thus, today when we think about the Internet it is not only something we access on our desktop home computer, but also on our cell phones, pagers, PDAs, televisions, video game consoles, MP3 players, and any number of portable laptop computers. We expect to find wireless access to the Internet in airports, coffee shops, and malls and recognize that wireless access will soon become part of the invisible communication sphere which surrounds us now, much like access to TV, radio, and cell phones.

But even the good old standbys of mass media, TV and radio, are changed due, in part, to the Internet. Now the late-night radio talk show we love but can not stay up for is available by podcast first thing the next morning when we turn on our laptop. Television shows are downloadable to our iPods and satellite radio can now be subscribed to and listened to in cars and online. So today when we talk about life online, the meaning of that is increasingly widespread across a variety of media vehicles.

In 1998, one might have pointed out that although the Internet is exciting and offers much potential, it is a relatively "local" phenomenon. That is, it's dominated by the United States. My, how times have changed in the eight years since the United States' early development and domination! According to Miniwatts International (2005), as of November 21, 2005, the North American usage of the Internet is only slightly less than a quarter (23%) of the overall usage worldwide. Another 29% of the usage comes, not surprisingly, from Europe, while Asia, with the largest segment of the world's population, also has the highest relative usage (34%). Since 2000, Miniwatts International statistics points out that although North America increased Internet use by about 100%, the rest of the world increased by almost 200%. But although usage is higher among the most populous area on the globe, penetration is still highest in North America at 68%. That is, most households in North America have Internet access. In other words, the merging of media just described is still largely a North American phenomenon.

The focus of the this book and its predecessor is psychological. We ask whether there are special psychological considerations both to using the Internet and to its effects upon the user. As before, answers to both of these questions are explored from three perspectives: intrapersonal, interpersonal, and transpersonal. The first chapter offers an overview from history, and is followed by several chapters in each of the three sections. Intrapersonal perspectives are addressed initially from a developmental perspective (Chapter 2), and then as a function of personality, gender, race, and culture (Chapter 3). The much puzzled-over phenomenon of disinhibition is revisited, followed by a chapter on online sex and Internet addiction. The interpersonal begins with an overview of the current status of computer-mediated communication research and then a look at virtual societies. The last two chapters in this section examine two online clinical concerns, self-help groups and therapy. The final section, unique to this book and rarely seen in other treatments of the psychology of the Internet, considers three transpersonal elements: virtual reality, the internet as Global Brain, and consciousness.

CONTRIBUTORS AND CHAPTER SUMMARIES

With the rapid growth of research into use of the Internet in all walks of life since 1998, this original groundbreaking book on the psychology of the Internet has a new chapter added on children, with two previous chapters on self and gender combined into a single chapter. Some of the chapters have either entirely new authors or added or lost previous coauthors. However, in general, the original contributors to this seminal book have become leading lights in the area of psychology and the Internet over the eight years since it was originally published. Several have their own books out about the Internet and all continue to work online as researchers, instructors, entrepreneurs, consultants, and clinicians. What follows is a brief look at each of the chapters and authors in this volume.

The first chapter, "The Internet in Context" is written by Evelyn Ellerman, chair of the Centre for State and Legal Studies and Program Director of Communication Studies at Athabasca University. She is interested in the effects of technological innovation on narrative and in the development of book culture in island nations of the South Pacific during decolonization. Ellerman offers a historical perspective for understanding the impact of the Internet in contemporary society. Relative to the first edition, Ellerman offers a more in-depth historical analysis with a cultural analysis of our relationship to machines. Not only does she draw a parallel between adoption of the Internet to the history of radio adoption as she did in the last edition, but she also examines how our society has come to understand and conceptualize the Internet by examining the metaphors used to describe it, and how they have changed over time.

INTRAPERSONAL CONSIDERATIONS

With this historical and cultural context, we examine the intrapersonal aspects of the Internet in the next five chapters. A developmental perspective is taken by Connie Varnhagen, who is a professor of Psychology at the University of Alberta. Her research is on how people interact with and learn from technology. Her recent work is on the search for and the critical appraisal of Web resources by children and adults. She is the author of *Making Sense of Psychology on the Web*, Worth Publisher, 2002, and numerous interactive Web resources and CD-ROM activities for learning about psychological principles and methods. Varnhagen examines various topics related to children being online. Following an examination of the use statistics, she considers how the Internet may be shaping children's social development. She focuses specifically on areas of concern, such as exposure to pornography and predators, as well as how children bully and are bullied online. Finally, she offers the reader some helpful hints for helping children to navigate life online.

The next chapter considers self and is written by this book's editor, Jayne Gackenbach, and Heather von Stackelberg. Gackenbach is a professor at Grant MacEwan College in the Department of Psychology and an instructor in the Department of Communication Studies at Athabasca University. Gackenbach has written several online courses in psychology and communications, offered various workshops and presentations at professional conferences on the psychology of Internet use, and hosted and co-wrote a three-part documentary on the Psychology of the Internet for Canadian Learning Television. She is a coauthor of the forthcoming "cyber.rules" with Joanie Farley Gillispie for Norton. Her coauthor on the self chapter is Heather von Stackelberg, a writer / researcher who has recently finished a Communication Studies degree from Athabasca University, to accompany her BSc in Botany. As a freelance writer, she has written about health, natural history, and technology, and finds people's varying reactions to change fascinating. She is currently a research assistant for the Associate Dean of Science at Grant MacEwan College.

Gackenbach and von Stackelberg follow Varnhagen's developmental chapter by considering how self online is affected by Internet use. They begin by briefly addressing how contemporary psychology thinks about self and turn then to a brief look at personality differences in online use, focusing especially on introversion and extroversion. Other personality characteristics are also considered. These Grant MacEwan College colleagues then examine self as a function of various demographics which have been shown in the developmental literature to contribute to the development of self: gender, race, culture, and socioeconomic status. Although the gaps between men and women, whites and people of color, industrialized and third-world countries, and rich and the poor are narrowing, the primary Internet use remains, to one degree or another, white men from the industrialized rich countries.

The next two chapters in the intrapersonal section consider specific aspects of the intrapersonal domain: disinhibition and sexuality. Dr. Adam Joinson is senior lecturer at the Institute of Educational Technology, the Open University, UK. He completed a BSc (Psychology) at the University of London (1991) and a PhD (Social Psychology) at the University of Hertfordshire (1996). His research interests include self-disclosure on the Internet, survey methodology, and educational technology. He is the author of *Understanding the Psychology of Internet Behavior* from Palgrave, which came out in 2003, as well as articles on computer-mediated communication, online research methods, personalization techniques, privacy, and e-learning. His webpage is http://www.joinson.com.

Joinson explains how disinhibition can lead to enhanced self-disclosure of both the positive and negative types. This author then considers several explanations for why disinhibition is observed so frequently online. The chapter serves as a cornerstone in understanding the psychology of Internet use, with the theme of disinhibition carried forward in many of the other chapters as well.

A far-reaching discussion of sex online is undertaken by Raymond J. Noonan, Ph.D., who is an Assistant Professor of Human Sexuality and Health Education at the Fashion Institute of Technology of the State University of New York (FIT-SUNY) in Manhattan. He is also director of SexQuest/The Sex Institute, providing educational consulting in human sexuality and educational content for the World Wide Web (http://www.SexQuest.com/). Noonan was coeditor of the award-winning *Continuum Complete International Encyclopedia of Sexuality* (Francoeur & Noonan, 2004), to which he contributed the chapter "Outer Space and Antarctica: Sexuality Factors in Extreme Environments," as well as numerous contributions to the chapters on United States, Brazil, and others. He was associate editor of volume four of the *International Encyclopedia of Sexuality* (Francoeur & Noonan, 2001), and contributed articles to Robert T. Francoeur's three-volume *International Encyclopedia of Sexuality* (Francoeur, 1997). He was also coeditor and author of *Does Anyone Still Remember When Sex Was Fun? Positive Sexuality in the Age of AIDS* (3rd Ed.) (Anderson, de Mauro, & Noonan, 1996).

After a rather extensive discussion from a systems approach of why sexuality is important to all levels of human activity, he focuses on its impact online. He surveys the history and diversity of sex online, followed by a consideration of online dating and blogs.

The last chapter in the intrapersonal section focuses on when online use goes wrong. "Internet Addiction: Does it Really Exist?" is written by Mark Griffiths, who is a Chartered Psychologist and Europe's only Professor of Gambling Studies (Nottingham Trent University). He specializes in technological addictions and has written extensively on Internet addiction and abuse. He has published over 155 refereed research papers in journals such as the *British Journal of Psychology, British Journal of Social Psychology, British Journal of Clinical Psychology, Journal of Community and Applied Social Psychology, Journal of Adolescence, Addictive Behaviors, British Journal of Addiction, Addiction Research, Journal of Psychology,* and extensively in the *Journal of Gambling Studies.* He has also published two books, numerous book chapters, and has over 400 other nonrefereed publications to his name.

In this chapter on Internet addiction, Griffiths updates his review of the research on Internet addiction. For the first edition of this book, his research had just begun. The reader will see that much has been done to identify the precursors, co-morbidity, and definitional issues. This author makes important distinctions among types of data collected and draws on case studies to distinguish between addiction and heavy use, with one being maladaptive and the other not.

INTERPERSONAL PERSPECTIVES

The next four chapters consider the interpersonal perspective. What happens when we meet or work with others online? The first two chapters in this section review previous research into computer-mediated communications, both in general and, more specifically, in work teams. The last two chapters consider clinical applications: self-help groups online and online therapy.

In "Revisiting Computer-Mediated Communication for Work, Community, and Learning," authors Caroline Haythornthwaite and Anna L. Nielsen offer a comprehensive overview of research and reviews of computer-mediated communication literature. Caroline Haythornthwaite is an Associate Professor in the Graduate School of Library and Information Science (GSLIS) at the University of Illinois at Urbana-Champaign. Her major works include *Learning, Culture, and Community in Online Education: Research and Practice* (2004) from Peter Lang Publishers coedited with Michelle M. Kazmer, and *The Internet in Everyday Life* (2002) from Blackwell, coedited with Barry Wellman. Dr. Haythornthwaite is an active and much published researcher in the area of computer-mediated communication. Anna Nielsen is a doctoral student at GSLIS, with an interest in computer-mediated communication and online learners.

Before psychologists "discovered" the Internet, communications scholars had been examining communications over computers for some years. This rich historical and contemporary overview is offered by these researchers with a focus on groups. They then consider how online and offline interactions can become better integrated, a particularly important point for online work groups.

Taking a broader view of the interpersonal elements online is the chapter by Conrad Shayo, Lorne Olfman, Alicia Iriberri, and Magid Igbaria entitled "The Virtual Society: Its Driving Forces, Arrangements, Practices, and Implications." The lead author on this chapter from 1998, Magid Igbaria, has passed away, but the coauthors agreed to update the chapter in his honor. The new first author is Conrad Shayo, who is a Professor of Information Science at California State University San Bernardino. Over the last 23 years, he has worked in various capacities as a university professor, consultant, and manager. He holds a Doctor of Philosophy degree and a Master of Science degree in Information Science from the Claremont Graduate University. He also holds an MBA in Management Science from the University of Nairobi, Kenya, and a Bachelor of Commerce degree in Finance from the University of Dar-Es-Salaam, Tanzania. His research interests are in the areas of IT assimilation, performance measurement, distributed learning, end-user computing, organizational memory, instructional design, organizational learning assessment, reusable learning objects, IT strategy, and "virtual societies." Dr. Shayo has published research on these and other topics in various books and journals. Currently, he is involved in developing reusable learning objects and web-based learning game simulations. He is also a coeditor (with Dr. Magid Igbaria) of the book *Strategies for Managing IS / IT Personnel*.

Lorne Olfman is the Dean of the School of Information Science and Fletcher Jones Chair in Technology Management at Claremont Graduate University. Lorne came to Claremont in 1987 after graduating with a PhD in Business (Management Information Systems) from Indiana University. Lorne also holds a Bachelors degree in Computing Science, a Masters degree in Economics (both from the University of Calgary), and a Masters of Business Administration degree from Indiana. Lorne's extensive work experience includes computer programming, economic analysis of government airport policy, and computer model development of financial plans for a telecommunications company. Lorne's research interests involve three main areas: how software can be learned and used in organizations, the impact of computer-based systems on knowledge management, and the design and adoption of systems used for collaboration and learning. He has published articles on these topics in journals including *MIS Quarterly*, *Journal of Management Information Systems*, and *Information Systems Journal*. Lorne has always taken an interest in using technology to support teaching and has been using the Internet to facilitate classes for more than a decade. A key component of Lorne's teaching is his involvement with doctoral students. Lorne has supervised 35 students to completion. Lorne is an active member of the Information Science community. He regularly reviews papers for journals and conferences, and was in consecutive years the program chair and general chair of the Association for Computing Machinery's Conference on Computer Personnel Research. He also coordinated mini-tracks of the Hawaii International Conference on System Sciences for 10 years. Alicia Iriberri is a Doctoral Student at the School of Information Science, Claremont Graduate University. Her research interests are User Interface Design, Computer Ethics and Virtual Communities. Currently, she is working on her dissertation and is involved in supporting various virtual communities in Claremont and Pomona.

These authors take a wide-ranging view of social life online ranging from politics and economic considerations to weblogs and virtual work teams. They then consider issues that are emerging for the new virtual society. They note that "in this chapter, we examine the driving forces behind the growth of virtual societies and discuss existing arrangements and practices at the individual, group, organization, and community levels. We also examine the implications of how people will live and work in societies where these arrangements and practices are widespread and mixed with face-to-face relationships."

The last two chapters in this section take a very different approach to interpersonal relationships online by examining two clinical issues, online self-help groups and online therapy. The authors of the first of these two chapters, "Internet Self-Help and Support Groups: The Pros and Cons," are Storm King and Danielle Moreggi. Storm A. King recently finished his doctoral degree in clinical psychology at Pacific Graduate School of Psychology. He has been researching the value of online self-help groups and the psychology of virtual communities, specifically, the therapeutic value perceived by members of e-mail groups that function as self-help groups, since 1993. He has proposed innovative ways for psychologists to use the Internet with clients and to gain new insights into a variety of disorders. His 1996 article, "Researching Internet communities, proposed ethical guidelines for the reporting of results," was one of the first articles to address the unique ethical dilemmas facing researchers who use Internet-archived text data to study the social impact of the Internet. He created and maintains a clearinghouse website for researchers interested in the psychology of virtual communities. Mr. King is a founding member and past president of The International Society for Mental Health Online. He has also published research on compulsivity in Internet gambling. His 1999 article, "Internet gambling and pornography: Illustrative examples of the psychological consequences of communication anarchy," published in *CyberPsychology and Behavior*, is considered by many to be a seminal article in that field. He coined the term "Internet Enabled Pathology," and introduced its use at the 2000 convention of the American Psychological Association and at the 1999 first annual convention of the Association of Internet Researchers. He is a member of the editorial board of the Mary Ann Leibert journal *CyberPsychology and Behavior*. He has coedited a special issue of that journal titled *The Internet and Sexuality*. His coauthor, Danielle Moreggi, is an Assistant Director of Counseling, PIR Psychology Department at the University of New Haven. After introducing the idea of self-help as actually mutual aid, they discuss its implication in a largely text-based environment. The authors then offer a list of pros and cons of both face-to-face and online self-help groups. They also consider distinctions between self-help groups and group therapy and its implications for the online environment.

The final chapter in this section on interpersonal aspects of life online is by Joanie Farley Gillispie. Gillispie holds a doctorate in clinical psychology from the Fielding Graduate Institute with an emphasis in Health Psychology. Dr. Gillispie works from a systems and individual perspective. She holds a Professional Postdoctoral Training Certificate from University of California, Berkeley in Neuropsychological Assessment Screening and advanced training in Strategic Depth Psychotherapy. Dr. Gillispie is an independent practitioner, an Area Chair for the Behavioral Health and Social Sciences Department at the University of Phoenix, regional trainer in HIV prevention for the American Psychological Association, and forensic evaluator for the Board of Prison Terms and Juvenile Justice Systems in Marin and San Francisco counties. Her clinical work includes forensic assessment of disability in court settings and cognitive–behavioral treatment with individuals and groups. Dr. Gillispie teaches at the University of California, Berkeley Extension. Postdoctoral courses for professional licensure and continuing education in the areas of behavioral health and ethical decision making are among her areas of focus. As Area Chair for the Bachelor of Science Program at the University of Phoenix, Dr. Gillispie teaches in the Behavioral Health undergraduate department and in the Masters in Teaching Program. In October 2002, she received a "Teacher of the Year" award for excellence in teaching at the University of Phoenix, Northern California Campus. She has recently finished a book with Jayne Gackenbach for clinicians and teachers for Norton Publishers called "cyber. rules" and her website is www.drjoaniegillispie.com.

In her chapter, Gillispie considers both professional and clinical issues with therapeutic online work. She points out that one does not have to do therapy online to be affected by this environment, as increasingly, clients are presenting with problems that are happening online or as a consequence of being online. Therefore, Gillispie argues that it is incumbent upon the clinician to become familiar with these issues.

TRANSPERSONAL ASPECTS

The final three chapters in this book consider the transpersonal perspective on the Internet. While the intrapersonal perspective focuses on self and the interpersonal perspective considers relationship to others, the transpersonal perspective views the sorts of human experiences that transcend or go beyond the ordinary ones taken up by most of psychology. The authors of all three chapters discuss the Internet in the most general form. This includes the notion of the Internet as a Global Brain to the Internet as one form of electronically mediated virtual world and its implications for the development of consciousness.

The author of the first of these three chapters is Joan M. Preston, who received her PhD from the University of Western Ontario and is a Professor of Psychology at Brock University. Her scholarly interests include visual and emotional processing in virtual reality, video games, and other media. Preston offers the reader a journey through Gibson's theory of perception as it applies to mediated virtual worlds. She then explains how the perception of mediated worlds offers many experiences that are of the natural world with potential to offer insights and experiences into altered states of consciousness. She uses the virtual art of Char Davies to illustrate these concepts.

The second of these three chapters is by Ben Goertzel, who writes of his work (personal communication, Dec. 30, 2005):

In the time since 1998, I have mostly been working in the software industry, focusing on AI, bioinformatics, and the Internet, and I have also been pursuing research in cognitive science and philosophy of mind. An example of my practical Internet work is the ArrayGenius software released by my company Biomind, which provides online analysis of bioinformatics data and has been used extensively by the Center for Disease Control and the National Institute of Health. I have also edited a book called *Artificial General Intelligence* for Springer-Verlag, which was released in 2005, and have been working on three other books on AI theory that are likely to appear in 2006 and early 2007. Finally, since September 2005 I have been working on natural language processing technology at Virginia Tech in their National Capital Region Operation.

Goertzel outlines the basic ideas behind Internet as a Global Brain by drawing upon complexity theory and the online Global Brain study group. He goes on to connect these ideas to Jung's notion of the collective unconscious.

The last chapter in the book is also written by this book's editor, Jayne Gackenbach, with Jim Karpen. Gackenbach's background in the psychology of the Internet was noted earlier in this introduction but most of her professional life has been in studying the development of consciousness with a focus on lucid dreaming. To this end, she has edited or written four books on dreaming with two on lucid dreaming and has authored numerous chapters and articles on the subject. As well as serving as a past president of the International Association for the Study of Dreams and editing for 10 years a semiprofessional journal on lucid dreaming, her career hallmark was an invitation to present research into lucid dreaming to the Tibetan Dalai Lama[1] at a conference in India on sleeping, dreaming, and dying. Her coauthor, Jim Karpen, is an Associate Professor of Professional Writing at Maharishi University of Management, Fairfield, Iowa. His 1984 dissertation focused on the "digitized word" and anticipated some of the developments being seen today with the Internet. Over the past 12 years, he's written hundreds of articles about the Internet that have appeared in newspapers and magazines and online. He holds an undergraduate degree from Maharishi International University, practices Transcendental Meditation, and has an ongoing interest in Maharishi Vedic Science and research on consciousness.

In this chapter, Gackenbach and Karpen first explain why consciousness develops, or perhaps evolves, by drawing on both historical literature and contemporary research. They then review research on how video game play is certainly affecting attention in heavy gamers, and possibly the potential development of consciousness, with their discussions drawing on studies done on this subject by Gackenbach and colleagues. They conclude that although interactive technologies may be affecting the expansion of consciousness in this way, it is not a substitute for a fully balanced life.

---

[1] Tibetan Buddhism considers the "lucid dream" a part of the process of the development of consciousness.

The broad perspectives of the authors in this book add up to more than the sum of their parts. The psychology of the Internet, how it changes us both as individuals and as a society, as well as how it reflects us, is a rapidly growing and fascinating field. It is the hope of the editor and the authors that this book will expand the view of its readers, teach them something, and inspire them.

CHAPTER 1

The Internet in Context

Evelyn Ellerman
Centre for State and Legal Studies
Athabasca University
Athabasca, Alberta, Canada

Introduction
Our Collective Love Affair with the New—
  Inventing the Self
Humans and Machines—An Ambivalent
  Relationship
The Ambivalence Deepens
And Now...the Internet
Take a Lesson from Radio
Studying the Net
Summary
References

INTRODUCTION

The Internet has changed considerably from its early adoption by business and the general public as a means of locating and exchanging information. These days it is increasingly difficult to name a communication function that our email programs, web browsers, cell phones, MP3 players, and Internet games cannot perform. We are daily "wow-ed" and often "cow-ed" by the seemingly endless shapes this technology is able to assume. But whether delighted or dismayed, our individual and collective responses to the Internet fall into recognizable patterns conditioned by our historical relations to technology. This chapter examines these responses, which are grounded in events that occurred over 500 years ago, but which continue to shape our attitudes to innovation, our belief in individual freedom, and our uneasy relations with the machine. It also suggests that any critical perspective on the functions that Internet technologies have played (or might play) in the new media landscape must be informed by a clear grasp of communication history.

Psychology and the Internet: Intrapersonal, Interpersonal, and Transpersonal Implications

OUR COLLECTIVE LOVE AFFAIR WITH THE NEW

Communication technology's well-known ability to focus our attention on the present actually relies on a very old motif in western society. Neil Postman (1985) alerts us to the prevalence of this motif in his critique of television, *Amusing Ourselves to Death*. Postman claims that the two most insidious words of the twentieth century are "Now...this." Among other things, he warns us about the way modern media emphasize the present in order to deny history, connectedness, and cause and effect. He feels this insistence on the present dangerously short-circuits our ability to evaluate both the media and the information they convey. In other words, in a technologically induced "dumbing-down," the mass media encourage us to absorb and react, but not to think.

Whether or not we agree with Postman's assessment of television as the *cause* and intellectual and social decay as the *effect*, most scholars in the field of communication would agree that the "now-ness" of the telegraph, the newspaper, the telephone, radio, television, and the Internet has indeed affected the way we think about and use them. Nobody, it seems, is interested in last night's news or yesterday's war. In fact, few can even remember last night's news. And we all want (or feel obliged) to keep current. Postman blames this psychology of the contemporary on television, but historians of communication technology recognize that, far from being the purview of technology, now-ness is a common cultural motif that predates television by at least 500 years.

Seeing "now" as a positive value and "then" as irrelevant is an important theme of European society that can be traced back to the close of the Middle Ages. It has its roots in medieval humanism, a rejection of the model for living that was developed by the Roman Catholic Church over a period of ten centuries. Humanists refused to live as though today were of no importance, as though the only goal of man should be the afterlife. In doing so, they opened the door to the study of contemporary society.

The Renaissance, or cultural "rebirth," that followed the Middle Ages fundamentally altered the way Europeans saw the world: their gaze changed. And when they focused on the world around them, the world of the now, they chose to see it as a break with the immediate past. They began to value not only the now, but the *new*. They thought of innovation as progress. This revolutionary emphasis on the life we know, rather than on the life we aspire to after death is the touchstone of the modern age.

Like many new ideas about the world and man's role in it, these ideas generated chaos. For the next two centuries, Europe suffered a devastating series of wars. People in Protestant and Catholic towns laid siege to one another; soldiers and mobs terrorized the countryside, blowing up and pulling down the symbols of power and belief belonging to the rival faith. Indeed, during this period, one can be excused for observing that it did not pay to own either a church or a castle; sooner or later, they were likely to be reduced to rubble.

The pyrotechnics of the Reformation and the counter-Reformation eventually generated an intense desire for law and order. Many people were obsessed with taking this desire for peace, order, and decorum with them to a "new" place. By the mid-seventeenth century, the notion of "pure and undefiled" places and peoples was gaining prominence as a social and cultural ideal. Some people fled religious warfare and persecution to the so-called New World, where they established ideal communities. Indeed, they frequently inscribed their settlements with the word "new," as if to ward off the excesses of the "old" world. Nova Scotia, New England, New France, New Orleans, New Norway, New Glasgow, New York ... it is a long and idealistic list. Far from representing an historical anachronism, this proclivity of the inhabitants of the new world to seek for and, indeed, to mythologize the "new" is crucial to understanding the development and reception of the Internet and all its technological progeny. When first made available to the public, it was presented as a new way to store and retrieve information, then as a "pure and undefiled" place for the expression of free thought and, more recently, as the purview of the young.

While thousands of people braved the vicissitudes of emigration to the clean and peaceful shores of the New World, thousands more stayed behind in the smelly, contentious "old" world, trying to improve it by rising above factional fighting. Taking part in the transnational exchange of "new" ideas was one way of doing this. The new sciences tried to find universal laws that would explain the natural phenomena of the observable world. New and more logical systems of thinking were developed. New and more natural ways of educating children were proposed. On the eve of the Industrial Revolution, then, notions of a better world had come to be associated with innovation and with knowledge.

INVENTING THE SELF

When medieval humanists argued for the value of lived experience, they were really arguing for the value of the human. Rather than concentrating on abstract theological discussions, they preferred to study humans as part of the natural world, because they believed that "man is the measure of all things." Their argument was given substance by the creation of the Protestant church, which formalized and gave authority to the concept of the individual. In effect, the Lutheran Church had eliminated a 1000-year-old function: the office of the priest. Individual believers could now communicate directly with God, without the intervention, or mediation, of a third party.

However, with individual freedom came individual responsibility. At first, this was understood as a spiritual task. Without the mediation of a priest, the individual needed to develop a personal relationship with the divine. The starting point was learning to read the Bible oneself. Humanism encouraged each person to seek truth everywhere, not just in sacred texts. Sophisticated methods were developed for recording observations of both the external world and humankind. Eventually, this way of knowing the natural world, and humans as part of that world, came to be called the scientific method. It reified nature as constructed (and therefore knowable) and the individual as part of that construction. For example, medical discoveries about the circulation of the blood, especially about the heart as a kind of pump, led philosophers and scientists to describe the human body as just another kind of machine.

Then, as now, people felt it necessary to define how humans differ from animals, indeed how humans differ from machines. Were humans just an assemblage of parts? Surely, animals lack a soul. Surely, machines lack the spark that makes humankind self-aware. When René Descartes proclaimed, "I think, therefore I am," he was addressing this very question. For Descartes and many others since, it was this ability to be self-aware that defines the human.

Indeed, it is a question that has persisted, as evidenced by the many fantasy and science fiction books, movies, and Internet games that continue to explore the interplay between the animal, the mechanical, and the human. We still worry, for example, about how much time we spend with certain machines—especially those that appear to think or communicate. Will the machine become self-aware as well? Will the human take on machine-like attributes and therefore become less human? Theories of the Internet as a global brain serve as catalysts for this centuries-old fear. Ever since the Renaissance, western society has explored the notion that awareness of self is, somehow, a human trait. Furthermore, it is a trait that must be tempered by some sort of self-control: conscience, for example. The eighteenth-century response to this question was that individuals could voluntarily impose moral obligations on themselves in the form of duty. In so doing, they demonstrated both their individual freedom from the mechanical laws of nature and their worthiness to partake in society. In other words, through self-awareness and self-control, humankind could transcend Nature.

By the late eighteenth century, the dialectic between individual freedom and personal self-control would resonate throughout European society and the New World. The notion that humankind could have freedom of thought generated the notion that freedom itself was a human right which political states ought to respect and support. Laws were considered morally defensible if they represented the will of the people. The good citizen was therefore the person who accepted a moral responsibility to obey the laws formed by the majority. In the best of all possible worlds, this balance between freedom and responsibility at the level of both the individual and the state would sustain an enlightened society.

These were the ideals that sustained both the American and French revolutions. But nowhere were they more finely tuned to the political than in the United States, where the coprinciples of individual freedom and collective responsibility were enshrined in a constitution. These ideals were associated with the printing press, the technology that helped to spread them throughout the American populace. A free and independent press became as much an ideal as that of the free individual. Today in the United States, this association between the technologies of thought and information and the intellectual and political freedom of the people is one of the most enduring conceptual links in the relations between humans and machines. When it works, it works very well indeed. The mythology of the Internet, for instance, echoes much of the mythology of America. Internet technologies are said to assist their users in maintaining personal and political freedoms, in seeking truth despite the obstruction of the powerful, in establishing and regulating their own democratic communities, and so on.

HUMANS AND MACHINES—AN AMBIVALENT RELATIONSHIP

The Renaissance invention of the "self" and the "new" supplies two components of the conceptual map for understanding society's contemporary responses to the Internet. Over the last five centuries, in the New World, novelty and individual freedom have become deeply ingrained social values which, despite their desirability, must be balanced against society's need for stability and control. Too much social change, too much individual freedom, can threaten social order. A consistent catalyst for tipping the balance between what society can accommodate and what it cannot is technological innovation.

The third component, then, of this conceptual map for understanding our relations with the Internet is the relationship of humans to the machine. Jessica Wolfe (2004) describes the deeply ambivalent attitude of western society to its machines. We believe that machines can improve many facets of our daily lives. The signature machine of the Middle Ages, the mechanical clock, is a good case in point. Like the computer, the clock at first seemed to offer many useful services to society. Gimpel (1977) describes the effects of the clock on medieval society. Astronomical clocks provided accurate measurements of the movement of the planets, the sun, and the moon. They allowed scientists and technicians (or mechanics) to collaborate in predicting the movements of tides. They served as complex calendars for saints' days and for movable feasts, such as Easter. As a secondary and somewhat revolutionary function, these clocks also told the time accurately and reliably. Mounted in towers situated in town squares, mechanical clocks ordered and dominated public and private lives just as the Church once had. The clock was a significant factor in facilitating the changed gaze of the Renaissance away from eternity toward the here and now.

However, over the next two centuries, the mechanical clock assumed an unprecedented control over the human body. La Mettrie's 1744 publication *L'Homme-Machine* compares the human body to an intricate machine that can be studied, controlled, and used as an instrument of power. In *Discipline and Punish*

(1977), Michel Foucault writes that, in eighteenth-century France, a new concept of discipline developed. It was modeled on monastic life, which was organized by the clock into seven offices or times of worship. This new mechanical model of social control manifested itself in the reorganization of armies into many ranks and subranks, using clockwork-like drills, in new methods of prison surveillance, and in new forms of keeping records on human activity.

Ordering and controlling soldiers and prisoners is one thing. But simulating God's creative power is another. Our own contemporary concerns about computer simulation of human intelligence and the real world mirror those of eighteenth-century Europe during the craze for automata, clockwork toys that simulated real human beings. Gaby Wood (2002) writes that these were no mere dolls, but life-sized humanoid machines mounted on stands and displayed to the general public in elegant showrooms. They were, in fact, precursors to the robot. The early dolls, such as the two "boys" created by Pierre Jaquet-Droz in Switzerland in 1774, played musical instruments, smoked pipes, sketched pictures, and wrote with quill pens. They rolled their eyes and appeared to breathe. The Droz dolls still perform once a month in Switzerland. At the end of each performance, their bodies are opened to reveal the mystery of life within—clockwork.

Makers of such automata were often obsessed with making their dolls as life-like as possible. De Vaucanson's chess player, for instance, challenged human beings to beat him at chess; the machine rarely lost. But while its maker was alive, he experimented in covering his mechanical creations with real skin, and in trying to construct automata that could bleed (that is, containing real veins and arteries). Naturally, these machines generated awe for the wonders that mankind could create, but they also created anxiety. When Droz exhibited his dolls in Spain, he was imprisoned by the Inquisition for heresy. What would the Inquisition make of computers that can talk or that beat humans at chess? Of internet servants that "remember" your preferences in order to search for the best insurance prices for you?

Never quite alive and yet never dead, eighteenth-century automata, or imitations of life, raised fundamental questions about what life was and about how it could be created. Could humans really create life from inanimate objects? And if they could, did they dare? Mary Shelley's *Frankenstein* (1818, 2003) was written in the early nineteenth century while she was visiting Switzerland. Whether she saw the Droz automata or not, her novel about the creation of artificial life must be understood within the context of popular concern about the nexus between the human, the mechanical, and the divine. It is a concern that has never left us.

Movies such as *Terminator* and *Blade Runner* and many other science-gone-wrong movies of the twentieth century are the direct inheritors of this latent mistrust of technologies that approximate the human. In the twenty-first century, we have been inundated by such movies. Increasingly, inspiration for such movies comes from Internet games, especially those that "learn" the players' moves in each round, so that the players "die" if they do not constantly learn how to "outwit" the game. Some movies, such as *Lara Croft: Tomb Raider,* simply make the game "come alive" by using flesh-and-blood actors to replace the computer-generated images of the game. Other movies ask complex questions about what is real and what is constructed. Will the virtual simulation become self-aware (*Virtualocity*)? Does the game really run through the bio-plug in a human's back (*Existenz*)? Are humans really the creation of the Internet, merely supplying it with energy (*The Matrix*)?

Such cultural products are a good barometer for social concerns. We may embrace Internet technologies, but we worry about how close we get to them and express our fears in cultural forms ranging from music to print to film. Nowhere is our ambivalence stronger than in the workplace. Ursula Franklin (1990) writes that the eighteenth-century fascination with regulating and controlling human bodies developed into "the factory system [which], with its mechanical devices and machines, only augmented the patterns of control. The machinery did not create them. The new patterns, with their minute description of detail, their divisions of labor, and their breakdown of processes into small prescriptive steps, extended quickly from manufacturing into commercial, administrative, and political areas." (p. 60)

The new division of labor in industrial society meant that people had less control over the product of their work and less control over their own bodies. The sense of individual power that had been generated by the notions of humanism had changed to one of powerlessness. It is common to lay the blame for this changing relationship between humans, progress, and technology on the Industrial Revolution. But, as Franklin points out, these changes were part of social patterns that had existed for centuries in Europe. She writes that, although "the eighteenth century exercised control and domination by regarding human bodies as machines, the nineteenth century began to use machines alone as instruments of control" (p. 62). To factory owners, machines seemed more predictable and controllable than people. They were therefore more than willing to eliminate those workers who could be replaced by machines and equally willing to force the remaining workers to work like machines.

THE AMBIVALENCE DEEPENS

From the nineteenth century onward, the relationship between progress, technology, and the individual has become increasingly problematic. Despite the speed of technological innovation in the twentieth century, western society is still in love with the idea of now-ness; our vocabulary is fairly littered with terms such as *breakthrough, groundbreaking,* and *cutting edge.* As a society, we still treat the new as a break from the past; we still equate it with progress, and we still act as though progress will bring us a better world. We feel both a financial and moral imperative to embrace the new. But we are also haunted by the effects of the technology on the individual and society as a whole. We feel it divorces us from nature, that it prevents us from knowing ourselves, that it controls our lives.

In *The Spirit of the Web: The Age of Information from Telegraph to Internet,* Wade Rowland (1997) writes that the more complex society becomes, the more necessary it is to develop methods of maintaining control. Communication and broadcast technologies are designed to do just that: they control people within a context of compliance. In all technologies of mass communication except the telephone, the Internet, and some forms of radio, the communication is organized in one direction, with only the illusion of contribution and control by the audience.

Franklin agrees that technology in general and communication technologies in particular are not neutral, but catalysts for control. She claims that technology is usually introduced to the general public in two stages. In the first stage, the technology is an option for the wealthy, the specialist, or the enthusiast. It often appears to be liberating; its promoters claim that it will free users in some way or make their jobs/lives easier. There is frequently an attempt to make the technology appear "user-friendly" in order to calm fear of the new. User communities such as clubs and specialist magazines are established. In this early phase, the users who have chosen the technology feel a strong degree of control. Franklin uses the introduction of a range of technologies as examples of this process: the automobile, TV dinners, the sewing machine, baby formula, and the computer.

The next phase in the introduction of new technologies is the introduction of infrastructure. As the new technology becomes more broadly accepted, its use becomes more necessary, if not mandatory. She points to the development of the sewing machine. In 1861, the sewing machine was advertised as a great liberator for women. No longer would they have to ruin their eyes handsewing their family's clothing. Once employers realized the speed at which these new machines could accomplish the task, a factory system was organized, operating a sewing machine became a requirement for the seamstress, and the slavelike conditions of the garment trade were the result. In the second stage, people become "captive supporters of both the technology and the infrastructures" (p. 97). The infrastructures themselves, she writes, are developed so that the technologies are easier to use and so that people will "develop a dependency on them" (p. 102). Freeways are an example of infrastructures that support a dependency on the automobile.

Franklin and Rowland remind us that the introduction of communication technologies has followed the general technological pattern outlined previously. From the telegraph to the radio to the Internet and CD-ROM, most communication technologies were developed first for military and then for commercial use. In most cases, governments have enabled, constructed, or maintained the distribution networks for these technologies in concert with a commercial monopoly (or at least a very restricted competitive field). They are therefore deeply implicated in the effects those technologies have on society, even though they may take pains to assume a neutral, or regulatory, distance from the technologies.

AND NOW … THE INTERNET

The introduction of the Internet seems to follow the two-phase pattern outlined by Ursula Franklin. It was developed in response to a strategic problem posed to an American think-tank, the Rand Corporation, during the 1960s. How could government keep informed and maintain order in the United States after a nuclear war if conventional communication technologies were destroyed? The answer was to create a networked system with no central control, which was so redundant that it would not matter if part of it were destroyed.

As a military response to the Cold War, Internet technology was the purview first of the army and then of the universities. In 1969, four universities with Defense Department contracts were connected to the network. By 1972, there were 37 nodes on the network. As the number of users multiplied, the network began to change. Originally designed as a computer-sharing network, the Advance Research Projects Agency, or ARPANET, had become a post office for personal messages and a conferencing center for researchers to discuss their work and collaborate on projects. The enthusiasm for this new system of long-distance communication was catching. People worked in their spare time to devise software that would make the Internet easier and faster to use. Since the early users were academics, their goal was to develop a free network with publicly shared information. Eventually, the network became so clogged with this university traffic that the military moved to a new network of its own.

Despite the enthusiasm of gifted "amateurs," the Internet remained a hobby of the philosopher-technicians of the universities until the 1990s, when its information-sharing and communicative functions attracted the interest of corporations and then of the general public. Now, most employees no longer have a choice in whether or not they use the Internet—it is a condition of work that they use e-mail and share files. As citizens, students, and customers seeking services from governments, schools, and corporations, they are increasingly directed first to online forms and resources. Paper alternatives are gradually being withdrawn. In short, if people do not participate in online activities, they feel excluded or powerless or, at the very least, out of date. Somehow, the revolution has passed them by.

How do we understand what has happened to us personally and culturally since the introduction of the Internet in the 1990s? How do we balance our culturally conditioned attraction to the novelty of the Internet against the seemingly never-ending newness of the thing? There's no rest from it: it continues to change. How do we measure the purported individual freedoms of the Internet against increasing external requirements to use it? Do we willingly embrace a technology that offers endless access to unorganized information, intimate psychological contact with millions of strangers, or health advice to technology addicts?

One way to gain perspective on technological innovation is to examine its cultural context. Another is to review the documented ways in which governments and corporations introduce and legitimate new technologies. A third way is to discover how the innovation has been incorporated into language and consciousness. Just as the mechanical clock became the principal metaphor for the modern age, the Internet seems to exhibit a powerful hold on the language and imagination of the postmodern age.

The degree to which a technology has affected the public imagination is evident in the kinds and numbers of stories that are told about it. They are an indication of its cultural strength. Legendary tales about early technicians and entrepreneurs are common to all technological innovation, but those about the "heroes" of the Internet are everywhere. Will they last? It is difficult to say. Among the many people involved in developing the printing press, we still remember Guttenberg; for the radio, Marconi; for the telephone, Bell. But who remembers the originators of television? We are all familiar, for example, with the success story of Bill Gates, who parlayed technical wizardry and ambition into a digital empire. Will his name be the one that remains? Perhaps.

Because the history of the Internet is so recent, we can still retrieve endearing lore about the nameless male graduate students, for whom the early Internet was full of limitless opportunity for exercising individual freedom. By 1986, Usenet (Unix User Network) was so large and unorganized that network administrators tried to restructure it, separating serious academic discussions from casual chat. Administrators proposed seven functional categories: *comp*uters; *misc*ellaneous; *news*; *rec*reation; *sci*ence; *soc*iety; and *talk*. "The last of the groups, 'talk,' was designed as a repository for all the unsavory, salacious, politically incorrect, and socially psychotic newsgroups that has appeared like banana slugs among the Usenet flora" (Rowland, 1997, p. 303). Gathering this activity into one spot on the Internet was an indirect attempt to manage or censor the Internet. It didn't work.

Rowland writes that the result of the "Great Renaming" was a flame war. Users felt that any attempt to organize and control the medium violated its democratic and nonjudgmental character. Their response was to subvert the attempted reorganization by proposing two new groups under the *rec* category: "rec.sex" and "rec.drugs." Although most users voted by e-mail to accept these two new groups, the Internet's volunteer administrators refused to create them. In answer to this refusal, the dissenting users created "alt.sex" and "alt.drugs" themselves and, just to round things off, "alt.rock-n-roll." It had become clear that no one had any real content control over this new medium. It's a wonderful story with a "Wild West" tone reminiscent of New World passions for the "new" and uncontaminated.

Will such stories survive in the popular imagination? How tied to American cultural ideals such as individual freedom and democracy are they? As the Internet loses its newness, as it matures into a regulated and somewhat tarnished vehicle for any number of private and public interests, will these narratives seem irrelevant? Will utility overcome idealism?

There is no doubt that the Internet has produced its own heroic culture. But most of its users are not part of the privileged inner circle. How does the multiplicity of the Internet's users understand the new technology in their midst? Language often holds the clue. New technologies borrow words and phrases from other aspects of daily life in order to describe their own character and function. When airplanes were invented, for instance, they were first understood as "airships." This is the reason that planes are flown by "pilots" and "co-pilots." It is why they have "captains," "pursers," "steward-esses," and "navigators." And it is why, when a plane rolls to a stop at an airport gate, it has "docked."

The Internet began by appropriating existing terms from other paradigms. Until the Internet, for instance, a word association game might have yielded the results contained in Table I.

As a technology becomes more widely used and more culturally entrenched, it can become its own paradigm. Had we added the word "google" to our pre-Internet word association game, the audience response would likely have been "What?" Had we added "connectivity," the response might have been, "Do you mean 'connection'? 'Connectivity' isn't a word."

Such lexical indicators can point the way to more general, guiding ideas about what a technology is and what it does. Once more, metaphor points the way.

TABLE I

Pre-Internet Word Association

Word	Word Association
net	fishing
browser	shopper
navigate	ship
web	spider
Jeeves	butler
yahoo	hooray
mail	letter
link	chain
server	waiter
virus	disease
provider	husband
site	place
worm	earth
crash	plane

The Internet is too new to have had the clear metaphorical impact on society that the mechanical clock had in Renaissance Europe. But we can discover how society has been trying to understand the Internet by analyzing the metaphorical hats proposed for it during its introduction to the general public.

The first of these, and probably the most widely remembered, is that the Internet is a kind of highway that carries information. The life of this initial metaphor can be quickly and informally followed by employing the search term "Information Highway" AND "Internet." For the purposes of this essay, the academic database, Expanded Academic ASAP was used. This particular database contains articles and chapters from newspapers and popular magazines as well as from scholarly journals and books across many disciplines, so it provides a broad range of public and professional perceptions of the new technology.

The first published article addressing the Internet as an information highway appeared in this database in 1992. The following year there were 6 articles; in 1994, 114 articles; in 1995, 73 articles; then 40, in 1996. By 1999 (only seven years after its first appearance), the articles had dwindled to fewer than 6 per year, which remained the trend into 2004.

Clearly, an initial use that had been envisioned for the technology was almost immediately rejected as inadequate. Nevertheless, "highway" was a metaphor that was easily understood. Titles from these articles play artfully on what a highway is: open road, busy signal, access, exits, gutter, trip, online lane, bypass, way station, maps, lights dim, fast lane, cyber-route. Articles located using this metaphor also muse on what the human experience of a highway might be: lurking danger, hitch-hiking, roadblocks, death en route, potholes, new frontier, roadkill, blazing trails, stay off the highway, student drivers. Evidently, the information highway was perceived as an adventurous, yet likely dangerous, place to be.

Most of the articles from 1994 address issues of capacity-building. They ask whether governments could raise the necessary money to build infrastructure and whether schools could keep up with the technology. In other words, the information highway metaphor seems to have been of most interest to institutions. It fit the parameters of their concerns over policy and program. It seems that, once the logistical problem of actually building the information highway had been solved, the term died.

A second metaphor, that of "cyberspace," coexisted with and outstripped "information highway" in its frequency of use. But it suffered an equally meteoric rise and fall in popularity. Beginning in 1993 with 13 articles and rising quickly to 97 in 1994, "cyberspace" balloons in popularity for the next 3 years, with 246 articles in 1995, 260 in 1996, and 183 in 1997. By 2004, the use of this metaphor had dwindled to 28 articles. Unlike "information highway," which had its genesis in the administration of American president, Bill Clinton, the term "cyberspace" was the invention of novelist William Gibson. The term first appeared in *The Neuromancer* (1984, 1995). Heir to MIT experiments of the 1940s in cybernetics, the term "cyberspace" is evocative of an early reaction to the potential dangers of the Internet. In Greek, *cyber* means "control" and "space" provided a description of where the Internet might be found. In fact, the term "cyberspace" makes the highway metaphor look positively antiquated.

Controlling this new space, where many unforeseen things were occurring, was a new concept. After the heady Wild West show of the early Internet, control seemed like a good idea. And control could be exercised across the full range of its users. Unlike "information highway," the "cyber-" adjective is applied to almost every aspect of online activity: education, business, personal relationships, citizenship. On a grammatical level, the term can be widely applied *because* it is an adjective. However, it works as a metaphor because of widespread contemporary fear about the effects of the new technology. Every society needs to establish its level of comfort with individual freedoms, and early on in the history of the Internet, concerns were being voiced about how wild and free society could allow the Internet to be.

The titles of the cyberspace articles indicate strong concerns with impending social and moral chaos: dissent, kiddie porn, losing souls, computer gambling, hack attacks, exposure. And they are redolent with phrases that indicate what to do about that chaos: crack down on dissent, First Amendment in cyberspace, disinfect computer bugs, self-appointed cops, intelligent decisions, regulating cyberspace. A preponderance of the titles contain the words "law," "control," "order," and "regulation."

The third early metaphor for the Internet is "virtual." The notion of the Internet as a technology that imitates reality seems to have occurred later than the first two. The number of articles on the "information highway" peaks in 1994–1995; and those on "cyberspace" in 1995–1996. Articles found using "virtual" AND "Internet" reach their peak in 1997–1998, although they surface in the early 1990s as do the other two. Even so, by 2004 the number of articles employing the "virtual" metaphor dwindles to 72.

"Virtual" seems to have appealed to yet another need in the community of Internet users and with differing intensity. A total of 187 articles appears at the height of interest in the "information highway"; slightly more than twice that amount, 506, appear at the height of popularity for "cyberspace." But, nearly double that number, 964, can be found at the apex of popularity for "virtual." Which seems odd, since "virtual" is an unlikely candidate for a borrowed metaphor. By definition, it does not call up any associations at all. It may be that, with "virtual," writers were beginning to find a metaphor that more cleanly described what the technology was actually like. This seems a reasonable assumption, since the overwhelming use of the metaphor in the database articles was for communication. That is, "virtual" connoted the ability of the Internet to provide "real-seeming" communication. Most of these articles concern themselves with the need for safe, effective communication and focus on such technical aspects of Internet communication as bandwidth and encryption.

Prior to 2002, an interesting subset of these articles employs "virtual" to simulate the visual. Art galleries, museums, libraries, publishers, and schools use "virtual" in order to represent cultural artifacts or to guide students through visual experiences. After 2002, a number of education- and health-related articles appear but, by then, the metaphor was on the wane.

Clearly, these three Internet metaphors had run their course by 2004 and no others seem to have taken their place. This is significant for the history of the Internet. Metaphors for technical innovation come and go. Their use indicates a need to understand a new and dynamic event. They remain in use until they feel outdated or inappropriate, or until the technology has become so familiar that it no longer requires perceptual aids to understanding. The history of communication technologies suggests that this "new" technology has taken its place in the long chain of innovation that stretches from the Renaissance to the present day.

TAKE A LESSON FROM RADIO

The speed at which the Internet has developed has taken us by surprise. But it shouldn't have; it has all happened before, with radio. We have forgotten, because we were too focused on the now-ness of computer technology. So, although Wade Rowland writes that the Internet is a "technology without precedent," he actually devotes six chapters each to the radio and the Internet, making clear allusions to the parallel ways they have affected us as individuals and as social beings. By drawing our attention to the historical connections between radio and the Internet, Rowland tries to remedy the effects of now-ness. He argues that when we study the mass media, we must pay attention to the past, or seriously risk misunderstanding the social role of each new medium that comes along. If we look at the Internet, then, as a two-way, long-distance communication technology that is readily available to the general public, radio provides the first model of how such technology affects society.[1] But when we study the early history of radio (when it was actually a two-way interactive medium), we discover an interesting fact: within 20 years of the invention of radio, infrastructures had been set in place to take control out of the hands of the average person. It had become the one-way technology that we know today. Although it is the boast of Internet users that they have so far resisted such attempts by government and industry and that, technologically, such control is impossible, the history of communication technology argues otherwise.

Like the Internet, radio began as a communication tool for military use that soon attracted the interest of both commerce and highly trained enthusiastic amateurs. In Europe and North America, radio was used by the navy and the shipping industry for long-distance maritime communication. As with the Internet, the first users of this new

---

[1] We will not consider the telephone here because long-distance telephone use was, for many years, both difficult and expensive for the average person. In addition, after the first few years of its existence, the telephone carried only personal and business messages, a much more restricted range than those carried by radio and by the Internet.

technology were highly skilled young men working in privileged positions. And, also as with the Internet, the new technology soon developed a cachet. By 1908, it had become a subculture for boys and young men, complete with its own legends and heroes, its own jargon and conventions. Unlike the Internet, two-way radios were cheap to buy and easy to build for any young man with a little expertise and a few dollars. But otherwise, the parallels are remarkably similar. Radio clubs and magazines sprang up. Radio was seen as an adventure. In 1909, when the S. S. Republic was making its way along the American Atlantic coastline, it hit the S. S. Florida and began to sink; it was the ship's wireless operator, Jack Binns, whose emergency signal saved the day. Jack Binns became an instant hero.

The virtual nature of both media is important to note. At the turn of the twentieth century, the airwaves offered young boys and men an unlimited virtual land for exploration and adventure. When they tuned in, they never knew where they would be, what exciting discovery they would make, who they would meet, what strange events they would witness. They never knew when their turn would come to save lives. As with the Internet, the use of pseudonyms and the mode of delivery was a great leveler. Radio reduced age, race, and class (but not gender)[2] to the one important qualification: enthusiasm. A community of worldwide radio users developed very quickly. But, almost as quickly, the airwaves became chaotic and crowded, even dangerous. It was difficult to ask anyone monopolizing the ether to give way to others. Each user felt he had the right to speak out as a citizen of the radio world.

Whereas the Internet was originally meant to maintain government control after the disaster of nuclear war, radio was originally meant as a life-saving device after disaster at sea. But the irresponsible and uncontrolled use of it was often blamed for disasters like the sinking of the Titanic. Navies and shipping companies demanded that the airwaves be regulated and that the technology be forbidden to the general public. Bit by bit, regulations were imposed. Interestingly enough, the first blow to the independence of radio was struck with the declaration of war. During World War I, governments in Europe and North America reasserted their power over long-distance communication technology by forcing all civilian users to turn in their equipment as a security measure.

After World War I, governments began to realize the commercial gain and political control that could be achieved by using radio. They worried about who could use the powerful medium and to what purpose, because radio also had considerable subversive potential. Then, as now, attempts to censor radio through government control varied. In Britain, private radio was outlawed and the responsibility for radio was passed to the post office, which regulated the telegraph and telephone systems. In Canada, private radio stations and networks were operated by newspapers, universities, railroads, and other commercial companies. The distribution system generally followed that developed by the telegraph companies and was therefore largely controlled by American firms. After the War, the Canadian

---

[2] As with most technological innovation in communication, early development and use was a male pursuit.

government became increasingly concerned about the threat to Canadian culture from predominantly American programming; so it instituted the Canadian Broadcasting Corporation (the CBC), a public broadcasting system similar to the British Broadcasting Corporation (BBC), but in competition with private radio.

By the late 1920s, the twin forces of commercial greed and politics had turned radio into a one-way, heavily regulated voice of authority where the former users/operators had become listeners/customers (for private radio) and listeners/citizens (for public radio). Time will tell whether the users of the Internet will suffer the same fate. But the social tensions between individual and corporate and governmental interests are already apparent. The now famous shutdown of Napster and the subsequent (re)negotiation of music rights on the Internet is a case in point.

The exponential growth of the Internet amazes us, as though it were a single event in social history. But such rapid growth also has happened before. Despite governmental control over the use of two-way radio, ordinary people remained profoundly optimistic about the new medium. In the United States alone, 100,000 sets were sold in 1922; the next year, a *half million* (Babe, 1989, pp. 69–70). Like the Internet, radio was felt to represent the voice of the people. Radio became the main way that most people received their news. It was simply the fastest method of transmitting the news to the greatest number of people. (It probably still is.) What is more, people believed the news they heard on the radio. Radio news reports were often read right off the telegraph wire service, without the interpretation or editorializing that was common to newspapers. The medium began with small local stations employing young reporters, whose voices radiated enthusiasm and sincerity. When the airship *Hindenburg* crashed in 1937, the sobbing reporter cried, "Oh, the humanity!" as he broadcast live from the scene, and this had the immediacy of lived experience with which no newspaper could compete. Radio gave people in urban and rural areas equal access to information. Women could listen to it without leaving the home. Children could tune in after supper. People felt they had power in their ability to "surf" the airwaves, changing from one channel to the next. Radio felt like the "people's medium" long after local stations had been gobbled up into national networks and long after the invention of television. The strong attachment that many people now feel toward their involvement in Instant Messaging and MSN communities is a latter-day incarnation of this vox populi.

The personal connection that people felt with radio was generated partly from the nature of the medium itself. The invisible "waves" were magical and frightening at the same time. Our reactions to the Internet today are not dissimilar. There is about the Internet, as there was about radio, an aura of the unknown and the forbidden. The virtual connections made between people and ideas impart an almost spiritual quality to both media. The many sites on the Internet devoted to religious and spiritual concerns are a testament to how strong this aspect of the Internet experience is. With both the Internet and radio, our imaginations are seduced by the notion of the intangible; we can reach out into the "ether" and construct any reality we want. Churches recognized this aspect of radio from the outset and were quick to broadcast sermons, educational shows, children's hours, and choral music. To this day, churches have extensive radio networks around the world and are now equally active on the Internet. But, although radio might provide spiritual comfort to some, it was profoundly disturbing, even thrilling, to others. In the 1920s and '30s, the virtual nature of radio complemented a strong parochial interest in spiritualism and the otherworldly. So, radio became a natural companion to the ouija board, the séance, and the substantial book trade in science fiction.

Popular magazines in the 1920s are filled with articles about the frightening possibilities of radio. The comments sound remarkably contemporary. When we ask ourselves whether the Internet has become some sort of "global brain," we participate in an intellectual paradigm that is nearly a century old. "We are playing on the shores of the infinite," wrote Joseph K. Hart in 1922. "Man has his fingers on the triggers of the universe. He doesn't understand all he is doing. He can turn strange energies loose. He may turn loose more than he figured on; more than he can control" (p. 949). Waldemar Kaempffert was equally in awe of the possibilities of radio: "You look at the cold stars overhead, at the infinite void around you. It is almost incredible that all this emptiness is vibrant with human thought and emotion" (1924, p. 772).

Radio was connecting humankind to the cosmos. What if there were other voices out there besides our own? In 1919, Marconi himself had announced that his operators were picking up signals that did not originate on earth. Nicola Tesla and other scientists thought that signals might be coming from Mars. Articles such as "That Prospective Communication with Another Planet" (Tesla, 1919) in *Current Opinion*, "Those Martian Radio Signals" in *Scientific American* (1920), and "Can We Radio a Message to Mars?" in *Illustrated World* (Walker, 1920) give some indication of how radio was changing perceptions of the relationship between humans and the cosmos.

The panic caused in the eastern United States by the 1938 Orson Welles' broadcast of the "War of the Worlds," a dramatized invasion of earth by Martians, was the culmination of radio's two-decade flirtation with the ineffable. But this broadcast was also a turning point in the credibility of radio as a medium of truth. Welles had deliberately misrepresented science fiction as though it were a news report. Americans had been conditioned to listen to "news flashes" about invasions in Europe; some of them, therefore, *believed* the news flash about a Martian invasion. Welles had broken a truth convention and the ensuing public outcry revealed how betrayed the public felt. Today, we are ambivalent about the new people's medium, the "Net." When someone tells us, "I found it on the Net," we are still powerfully compelled to accept and believe. On the other hand, we know that there are no guarantors of truth value for anything on the Net. In both cases, this diminution of truth value has affected the power of the medium to stand against "official" truths.

But we can define "people's medium" in other ways. When we link mass media with notions of democracy, we link the people with the notion of official truth. In Britain and Canada, and in the early days of state-supported RCA (Radio Corporation of America) in the United States, radio was welcomed as a tool for educating citizens in the liberal arts, in matters of health and hygiene, in history and politics. Radio presented its listeners with opera, folk music, popular music, and symphonies; documentaries, readings from history; short stories, poetry, and children's literature; forums, speeches, sermons, and debates; fine drama and comedy; helpful hints and advice. In short, governments saw public radio as a cheap, effective tool for educating its citizens; in many remote locations, children and adults took their schooling over the airwaves. For governments, radio was also an excellent tool for strengthening both nationalism and acceptance of regional diversity; at home, radio could create a sense of solidarity against the foreign; abroad, it could bolster an empire. In Britain and in Canada, the BBC and CBC, respectively, were used for exactly those purposes from the 1930s onward. Today, governments *share* the Internet with individual citizens in providing useful information about its programs and services, in promoting national ideals, and so on. But there is no way of really knowing who has created any of the sites we encounter.

In the U. S., where commercial radio quickly outmaneuvered public radio, the educational function of the technology was soon lost. Radio became little more than a medium of entertainment. This shift worried educators and government officials alike. Radio, after all, was in every home and no one could actually control what came over the airwaves. Now that more and more homes are connected to the Internet, similar concerns are being voiced about this new technology, especially about violent, pornographic, and hate sites that might affect young children. Educators then and now were worried that communication technology was producing an illiterate public who would rather give themselves over to mindless enjoyment than read a good book.

In a 1924 article that could have been written yesterday about the Internet, an enthusiastic parent wrote "It's Great to Be a Radio Maniac." In it, he claimed that radio had made his son more informed and more manually dexterous. Radio "gave everyone the chance and the impulse to learn to use his brains." Eventually, it would "level the class distinctions, which depend so largely on the opportunity for information and culture" (O'Brien, p. 16). In our own times, we are daily presented with the notion that the Internet will eliminate the traditional classroom and the need for teachers. Like so much in the history of communication technology, this prediction has a familiar ring. In *Radiating Culture*, Joseph Hart (1922) envisioned students galvanized "by a single inspiring teacher who speaks to the thousands of revived students through a central radio-phone. A whole nation of students might thus come under the stimulating touch of some great teacher" (p. 949).

But the uncritical enthusiasm with which society first greeted radio soon gave way to grave doubts about its negative effects. After the rise of private radio in the United States, dozens of scholarly books were written, from the late 1920s into the 1940s, studying the ways in which the new technology was reshaping personal relationships, the structure of the family, the literacy of children, and the ability of people to think critically and express themselves clearly. We have only to pass by the shelves of any bookstore to see this whole process repeating itself with respect to the Internet.

Belief in the ability of radio to improve political life was also short-lived. At first, people thought that a better informed public would demand that its politicians be sensible and accountable. In *How Radio is Remaking Our World*, Bruce Bliven (1924) argued that it was easy for a politician to take advantage of a crowd by appealing to its emotions instead of its intellect. But, the new medium of radio would prevent that, since people listened to radio as individuals. Listeners would therefore take the time to reflect. And since radio had so many channels, it was possible for people to hear many more politicians than they would in person; this would give them the chance to compare and contrast the messages before deciding with which they agreed. This opportunity to encounter information individually (and asynchronously) from multiple sites is also an argument for the democratic power of the Internet, if the medium remains as a free forum for all ideas.

Even with these assurances, governments in the 1940s were nervous about the power radio seemed to have in swaying people's voting patterns and about the access radio gave to unprincipled politicians and foreign powers. Could radio reshape its audience into an uncultured, unthinking mob that could be easily manipulated? In his book, *Radio and the Printed Page* (1940), Paul Lazarsfeld, one of the leading communication scholars of the day, outlines the real fear for American authorities. Nazi radio propaganda had essentially put Hitler into power during the 1930s in Germany; Nazi sympathizers were broadcasting from within the United States, and the American government was regretting its loss of control over radio at home.

"By the grace of history, this country has been left time to solve some of the problems which have precipitated chaos in Europe. We ought to use this time to understand what social forces are operating and to adapt our thinking and our way of life to a greatly changed situation." (p. xvii–xviii)

Lazarsfeld's observations are as salient today as they were during World War II. Examples of terrorist use of the Internet in the 1990s demonstrate yet again that anyone with an agenda can use communication technologies for subversive purposes. But, what is interesting to note about Lazarsfeld's comments is that radio did *not* produce a nation of illiterate zombies who could be easily controlled by those in charge of the communication medium.

Radio historian Susan Douglas (1999) writes that radio "is arguably the most important invention of the [twentieth] century" (p. 9). She makes this claim, in part, because of the way in which radio prepared its audience for the technologies that were to follow. But her contention is based on a fundamental belief that radio is the ultimate interactive technology that has never stopped adapting to its cultural and political contexts.

"Because radio has taken so many forms over the century and is such a flexible, adaptable, and relatively inexpensive technology, it has been used both to buttress and to challenge the economic, political, and cultural status quo in America. It has been neither the particular technical qualities of the device nor the people's goals and ambitions but rather the often unstable, unpredictable marriage between the two that has determined radio's relationship to social change." (pp. 20–21)

STUDYING THE NET

As a society, we pay a price for devoting so little attention to our own technological history. Part of that price is that we regularly confuse the difference between one-way and two-way communication technology. And in so doing, we misunderstand the dynamics between people and new technologies. So, the now-ness of the Internet is part of an historical trend that prevents us from connecting it to similar developments and effects in the recent past. This is especially the case because, unlike other communication technologies, the Internet has developed like magic before our very eyes. The speed and nature of this metamorphosis is both fascinating and terrifying, depending on how we situate ourselves with respect to change and computer technology. If we are not rhapsodizing daily about each new Internet application, we are worrying about its effects on us as individuals and as a society.

When we do turn from wonder to analysis, we are often most concerned with the effects of communication technology on society. In general, such analysis takes three broad theoretical approaches. The first falls under the heading of technological determinism, which examines the ways in which technology shapes society. The second approach tries to counter the first by looking at how people use the technology. The third analyzes the historical contexts in which technology develops.

If we look at the Internet from the standpoint of technological determinism, we assume that technology affects all patterns of human activity and that changes to technology constitute the single most important changes in society. Each technology has certain inherent characteristics that direct its use. In fact, any given period of history can be defined by the technology in use at the time. The two communication theorists most often associated with technological determinism were Harold Innis (1950) and Marshall McLuhan (1967). Innis is best remembered for his original observation that each technology alters the relationship that its users have with time and space. McLuhan's work first explored the notion that the form of technology is more significant than its content.

When studying the relations between society and the Internet, a determinist perspective might lead us to claim that ours is now a digital society; that the ways we think, act, and interact are governed by the ways we communicate using networked digital technology. Certain words and phrases from the technology make their way into our vocabulary, reshaping the way we see the world. Certain modes of communication are opened to us and others are closed because of the dominant technology. Extreme points of view on technological determinism, like that taken by Jacques Ellul (1964), would argue that technology has even taken on a life of its own apart from human agency. Ellul is perhaps the most important proponent of the notion that technology is out of control. He would claim that the technological creations of humankind have a willful, self-determining quality of their own. "At the present time, technology has arrived at such a point in its evolution that it is being transformed and is progressing without decisive intervention by man" (p. 85). Many would make similar claims about the Internet.

Technological determinism takes little account of social context or individual action. So, a second way of analyzing the effects of communication technology is to take a "uses and gratifications" approach. Social psychologists and communications scholars often employ this theoretical framework as a means of balancing technological determinism with human agency. Uses and gratifications adopts the stance that people can choose to use technology or not, or even to adapt it to their own needs. This way of examining the relations between technology and society explores first the types and levels of human needs and then the ways in which we try to satisfy them. Scholars who use this approach to study the Internet might argue that the technology is a useful tool for increasing the amount and kinds of personal interactions we have all enjoyed using, for example, telephone technology: that it saves us time, or that it allows previously disadvantaged individuals to have personal relationships that are otherwise not possible.

Joe Walther's "Social Information Processing Theory," first formulated in 1992, is a good example of early attempts to understand interpersonal communication on the Internet. He developed the theory in rejection of the determinist stance that claimed such communication was inferior to face-to-face communication. In the years since he proposed the SIP framework, Walther (Walther & Parks, 2002) has discovered that computer-mediated communication is far more complex than he first assumed; he is now reexamining his original framework to accommodate a decade of research. Walther's case is not unusual. Theories addressing the uses and effects of communication technologies must remain supple enough to incorporate new knowledge. In fact, he now calls his framework a *perspective* rather than a *theory*, partly because our psychosocial experience of the Internet is changing too rapidly for theory to be reliably predictive.

Other theorists have been more concerned with the uses that specific groups make of the Internet. In recent years, Cheris Kramarae has extended to the Internet the notions of "Muted Group Theory," which examines how women are disadvantaged because language (and its technologies) are male-dominated. According to Kramarae (Taylor & Kramarae, 2004), the Internet is still the purview of men and of those women who can afford to be online. The true potential of cyberspace will not be realized for women until computer terminals are readily available in shelters for the homeless, in laundromats, daycare centers, and so on.

A third approach to studying new technologies focuses on the various contexts in which the technology is introduced and employed. Both Franklin (1990) and Rowland (1997) take this approach when studying technology. They maintain that technology does not fall from the sky fully formed. It is developed by individual societies for particular reasons. Once it is in use, it has a complex relationship with that society: technology affects and is, in turn, affected by the social, technological, and political context in which it is used. This approach sees the Internet as a participant in the history of technological developments, rather than as a sudden and inexplicable arrival.

Since the Internet is such a recent arrival on the technological scene, appears to incorporate so many previous technologies, and continues to evolve, communication theorists have been slow to construct frameworks that describe and explain this new phenomenon. The starting point must be to situate the Internet within the history of communication technologies. One useful such attempt is that of Jay Bolter and Richard Grusin in *Remediation: Understanding New Media* (1999). Like Ursula Franklin, these authors argue that the new media are best understood not as unique technologies, but as developments from older media. Their theory of new media claims that all communication technologies refashion, or "remediate," previous forms, while negotiating space in the existing technological landscape. But the "landscape" is not passive. Their theory also explains how preexisting media resist, imitate, or accommodate the new.

Although all three of these approaches may be used separately, we frequently combine them, especially when trying to account for the introduction of a new technology as complex as the Internet.

SUMMARY

Internet technologies seem to have taken linguistic and narrative hold in western society. The myths of origin are in place. An Internet-specific lexicon has developed. The metaphors that bridged old and new technologies have served their purpose and been discarded. The second phase of technological innovation outlined by Ursula Franklin (1990) seems to have been achieved: infrastructures have been constructed and Internet use has become more or less compulsory. Remediation, as posited by Bolter and Grusin (1999), seems to be ongoing. Internet technologies have adopted the shape and functions of several preexisting technologies; radio is one example. And other technologies have taken on attributes of the Internet in order to survive; television comes to mind.

The tentativeness of theory-making with respect to the Internet reflects its relative youth and continuing growth. Joe Walther's (2002) reluctance to use the word "theory" for his own attempts to develop predictive mechanisms for the Internet is indicative of the historical moment we all occupy with respect to this particular technology. His is an honest admission that our intellectual engagement with Internet technologies needs to be as open and fluid as the technologies now are.

REFERENCES

Babe, R. (1989). Emergence and development of Canadian communication: Dispelling the myths. In R. Lorimer & D. Wilson (Eds.), *Communication in Canada: Issues in broadcasting and new technologies* (pp. 58–79). Toronto: Kagan and Woo.

Bliven, B. (1924, April). How radio is remaking our world. *Century Magazine, 108*, 149.

Bolter, J., & Grusin, R. (1999). *Remediation: Understanding new media.* Cambridge: MIT Press, 1999.

Douglas, S. (1999). *Listening: Radio and the American imagination.* Minneapolis: University of Minnesota Press.

Ellul, J. (1964). *The technological society.* New York: Vintage Books.

Foucault, M. (1977). *Discipline and punish: The birth of the prison.* London: Allen Lane.

Franklin, U. (1990). *Real world of technology.* Toronto: CBC Enterprises.

Gibson, William (1984, 1995). *Neuromancer.* HarperCollins, 1995.

Gimpel, J. (1977). *The medieval machine: The industrial revolution of the Middle Ages.* New York: Penguin.

Hart, J. K. (1922). Radiating culture. *Survey*, Mar. 18, 1969.

Innis, H. (1950). *Empire and communications.* Toronto: University of Toronto Press.

Innis, H. (1950). *The bias of communication.* Toronto: University of Toronto Press.

Kaempffert, W. (1924, June). The social density of radio. *Forum, 71*, 772.

La Mettrie, J. O. de. (1744). *L'Homme machine.* Leyde, Netherlands: E. Luzac.

Lazarsfeld, P. (1940). *Radio and the printed page.* New York: Duell, Sloan and Pearce.

McLuhan, M. (1967). *The medium is the message.* New York: Bantam.

O'Brien, H.V. (1924, Sept. 13). It's great to be a radio maniac. *Collier's, 74*, 16.

Postman, N. (1985). *Amusing ourselves to death: Public discourse in the age of show business.* New York: Viking.

Rowland, W. (1997). *Spirit of the web: The age of information from telegraph to Internet.* Toronto: Somerville House.

Shelley, Mary (2003). *Frankenstein.* Harmondsworth, UK: Penguin Classics.

Taylor, H. J., & Kramarae, C. (2004). Creating cybertrust: Illustrations and guidelines. In O.V. Burton (Ed.). *Computing in the social sciences and humanities*, (pp. 141–158). University of Illinois Press, Urbana.

Tesla, N. (1919, March). That prospective communication with another planet. *Current Opinion, 66*, 170.

Walker, T. (1920, April). Can we radio a message to Mars? *Illustrated World, 33*, 242.

Walther, J. B., & Parks, M. R. (2002). Cues filtered out, cues filtered in: Computer-mediated communication and relationships. In M. Knapp & J. A. Daly (Eds.), *Handbook of interpersonal communication*, 3rd ed. (pp. 529–561). Sage: Thousand Oaks, CA.

Wolfe, J. (2004). *Humanism, machinery, and renaissance literature.* Cambridge: Cambridge University Press.

Wood, G. (2002). *Edison's Eve: A magical history of the quest for mechanical life.* New York: Knopf.

PART I

Intrapersonal

CHAPTER 2

Children and the Internet

Connie K. Varnhagen
Department of Psychology
University of Alberta
Alberta, Canada

INTRODUCTION

The Internet is a vast virtual environment. Children can access a wealth of information on subjects ranging from acne to zebras. They can communicate with others from around the world, sharing their experiences and interests while breaking down cultural barriers. They can listen to music from around the world, watch awardwinning public service announcements, and play games that test their skill and coordination. Children can also access pornography, hate, and terrorism. In addition, children are vulnerable to sexual solicitation and predation and cyber-bullying and harassment. How do we help them access the cognitively and culturally enhancing aspects of the Internet while, at the same time, protecting them from the dark side of the Internet?

Although the news media is quick to report on any situations where children are adversely affected by the Internet, we are only beginning to learn about children's use of the Internet, their exposure to unwanted or undesirable resources, and how these exposures affect their development. We need a principled approach to understanding this new environment and children's dynamic interactions with it. Critics of the Internet claim that children's social development is arrested through interactions with the Internet, that children are victimized by unwanted exposure to pornography and hate, and that they are easy targets for sexual predators and cyber-bullies. Although the most dire predictions of critics of the Internet have not been borne out by the research literature, there are risks for children online. Just as we empower our children with shrewd awareness of the possible dangers around

Psychology and the Internet: Intrapersonal, Interpersonal, and Transpersonal Implications

them as they explore the physical environment, we need to empower them with critical appraisal of information and opportunities they encounter as they explore the virtual environment of the Internet.

WHAT ARE CHILDREN DOING ON THE INTERNET?

The vast majority of children in the United States and Canada have accessed the Internet; over 95% had been online by 2003 (Kaiser Family Foundation, 2004; Environics Research Group, 2001) and close to 75% had Internet access in their homes (Kaiser Family Foundation, 2004; Statistics Canada, 2003). Internet use is comparable or slightly lower in other developed countries (e.g., Livingstone and Bober, 2005; Nielsen ratings). Many children access the Internet at least once a week from school, home, or libraries; surveys from the past few years indicate that up to one-half of children spend more than one hour on the Internet per day (Environics Research Group, 2001; Roberts *et al.*, 2005).

Moreover, children access the Internet from a very early age. In a 2001 Canadian survey for the Media Awareness Network (Environics Research Group, 2001), 15% of youth under the age of 18 years recalled learning to use the Internet at 7 years of age or younger. In a 2003 United States survey of parents, Rideout *et al.* (2003; see also Calvert *et al.*, 2005) found that children started looking for Web sites without parental supervision at 4 years of age and sent an e-mail by themselves as early as 3 years of age. Clearly, children are immersed in the Internet environment in increasing numbers for increasing lengths of time.

Children mainly access the Internet through the World Wide Web. Children use the Web to access information resources through Web searches and browsing preferred Web sites; communicate using e-mail, instant messaging, and discussion; and access music, video, and computer games (Environics Research Group, 2001; Rideout *et al.*, 2003; Roberts *et al.*, 2005). Children as young as second grade have an e-mail address through their classrooms. These e-mail accounts are used as part of the language arts curriculum for developing reading and writing skills and as part of the social studies curriculum for communication with children from other cultures. Young children may also have an e-mail account to communicate with family members. Children also use instant messaging to communicate with friends, often in parallel with playing computer games or doing homework (Shiu & Lenhart, 2004). Children most often surf the Web for games and music but they also search for information for school reports and personal interest (Environics Research Group, 2001; Lenhart *et al.*, 2001).

Specialized children's Internet resources have become increasingly popular— among parents and educators, at least—and are marketed as providing children with safe and secure access to the Internet. For example, although many children use

Hotmail (http://hotmail.com) or Yahoo (http://mail.yahoo.com) accounts available to everyone, specialized children's e-mail services such as KidMail (http://kidmail. net) and Surf Buddies (http://www.surfbuddies.com) provide spam-free, secure e-mail for a small fee. These resources allow parents to limit children's e-mail contacts and the programs automatically filter out questionable content and spam. Almost all other e-mail services allow setup of filters but these childsafe resources appeal to parents who do not feel confident modifying program preferences and options.

Child versions of search programs have also become popular. Yahooligans (http://yahooligans.com) and Ask Jeeves for Kids (http://www.ajkids.com/) are search directories designed specifically for children. All resources that can be searched or browsed from the home pages have been verified as appropriate for children by a team of educational consultants. These directories are quite limited, however, and don't include information on many topics children might be investigating for school or personal interest, such as specialized information on dinosaurs found in Canada or adoption resources for searching for biological parents.

Many entertainment resources have been developed specifically for children. A number of media companies, such as the Public Broadcasting Corporation (http://pbskids.org/), Warner Brothers (e.g., http://harrypotter.com), and Scholastic (e.g., http://scholastic.com/kids/) have developed information and game resources for their child audiences. Most of these resources are completely self-contained and contain no off-site links; those that do include off-site links provide a warning before the child clicks to an off-site link.

Finally, children's Internet access can be controlled through the use of filtering programs, such as Net Nanny (http://netnanny.com/) or Cyber Sitter (http://www.cybersitter.com/), and children's browsers, such as zExplorer (http://www.zxplorer.com/). These commercial programs limit children's access to the Internet, filtering spam, advertising, and content determined inappropriate for children. Because it is difficult to define spam and inappropriate content, these programs necessarily provide very restrictive access to the Internet.

Although these child-oriented Internet resources are increasing in number and popularity, given the unorganized and unregulated nature of the Internet, they are not foolproof and children may still be exposed inadvertently to objectionable content. Also, most of these resources are overly restrictive; for example, because of "adult" content of some encyclopedia articles, children are unable to access such ubiquitous resources as the World Book Encyclopedia through many of the resources. Finally, and possibly most importantly, by passively limiting children's access to possibly unseemly information and resources on the Internet, children may not learn to actively appraise and evaluate Internet information.

CONCERNS

Historically, parents, teachers, policymakers, and the press have been concerned about the adverse effects of new media on children (Gackenbach & Ellerman, 1998; Paik, 2001; Wartella & Jennings, 2000). Movies, radio, and television were all seen initially as potentially harmful for children's development. Computers are seen as depriving children of important social and physical development opportunities. Critics warn that important social contact and physical activities are displaced by time spent socially isolated in front of a computer screen—these are much the same concerns that were expressed when televisions began to appear in living rooms. Because the Internet is freely accessible, critics are also concerned about children being exposed to issues they cannot comprehend or cope with, such as pornography and hate. Finally, given the anonymity of the Internet, critics are now becoming increasingly concerned about children being victimized by sexual predators and cyber-bullies.

SOCIAL DEVELOPMENT

Children develop a sense of who they are and how they fit into their family, school, and community. They learn to critically evaluate the characteristics that define themselves and they learn to control their behavior to adapt to society's norms and values. These aspects of social development require children to interact with others in order to differentiate themselves from others, compare characteristics that define themselves with those that define others, and develop self-control.

Critics have complained that computer use leads to social isolation, which often leads to depression and other mental disorders. Given that many children have access to the Internet in their bedrooms (Kaiser Family Foundation, 2004), this concern may be valid. There is some evidence to suggest a correlation between social isolation and depression and computer use. Kraut *et al.* (1998) reported results of a survey of first time Internet users as part of the HomeNet longitudinal study conducted 1995–1998 regarding the impact of the Internet on social interactions. These first-time Internet users reported a decline in social interaction and an increase in depressive symptoms over their first months of Internet use; in addition, the correlations between Internet use and isolation and depression measures were slightly higher for the adolescents in the sample than those for adults. These effects were short-lived, however; Kraut *et al.* (2002) followed the HomeNet participants over a longer period of time (three years as opposed to 12–18 months) and the negative effects of Internet use had disappeared. In a second study, Kraut *et al.* (2002) found that extroverted children and adults reported greater increases in social interaction and self-esteem as a function of increased use of the Internet.

Gross (2004) argued that, as more children use the Internet, more of their friends will as well, and the Internet will simply become one more form of communication and interaction.

Other research indicates that the Internet may have positive effects on social development. Stern (2002) analyzed teenage girls' personal Web sites. She found that the girls' self-expressions were consistent with theories of social development. Stern argued that the Internet provides an excellent opportunity for children to express themselves as they develop socially and sexually.

Several studies have examined the relationships between social well-being and Internet instant message use. Instant messaging is becoming the most common form of communication on the Internet (Environics Research Group, 2001; Ipsos-Reid, 2004; Law, 2004). In a study of the relationship between self-concept and instant messaging use, Law surveyed adolescents between the ages of 11 and 19 years and found no correlation between self-concept and instant messaging use. However, consistent with the statistics on increasing use of instant messaging, over three-quarters of Law's adolescent participants used instant messaging daily. Similarly, Gross (2004) surveyed adolescents aged 11 to 16 years and found no relationship between amount of time spent online and measures of loneliness, social anxiety, depression, or daily life satisfaction.

Gross *et al.* (2002) examined relationships between well-being and closeness of instant message partners in adolescents aged 11–13 years. Among adolescents who used instant messaging, those who reported feeling comfortable in their social interactions reported communicating primarily with school friends whereas adolescents who reported feeling socially isolated also communicated with people they did not know well. Ybarra *et al.* (2005) found that children aged 10–17 who reported significant depressive symptoms (e.g., experiencing functional impairments in school, personal hygiene, and/or self-efficacy) spent more time on the Internet at school and used e-mail more often for social communications than those reporting fewer or no depressive symptoms. Their sample came from a large United States study, the Youth Internet Safety Survey, conducted in 1999–2000 with children aged 10 to 17 years (Finkelhor *et al.*, 2000). Wolak *et al.* (2002, 2003), using the same sample as Ybarra *et al.*, found that children who reported depressive symptoms and having been victimized in some way had more close personal relationships with people they had met on the Internet than did children who were not as troubled. Rather than remaining socially isolated and alone, troubled and depressed children and adolescents appear to reach out to online friends.

Indeed, online communication may help children develop a sense of self in an anonymous and supportive environment. Turkle (1995) argued that multi-user dungeon games provide an important opportunity for people to experiment with different selves and, in so doing, refine their own self-concept. Subrahmanyam *et al.*

(2004) analyzed a 30-minute transcript from a teen chat room which included 52 different participants. Topics discussed in the time period included sports, sex, and parental concerns. The participants openly discussed their feelings and, when a participant expressed a personal concern, the others quickly supported the participant. Subrahmanyam *et al.* concluded that the Internet can provide a socially safe environment in which adolescents can discuss embarrassing topics and practice social relationships.

Suzuki and Calzo (2004) examined postings to teen general issues and sexuality discussion boards over a one-month period and found postings similar to those found by Subrahmanyam *et al.* (2004). Postings to the general board predominately dealt with romantic issues and posting to the sexuality board predominately considered sexual health. As well, topics dealing with personally relevant issues, such as body image and working out, received more viewings by others than did basic factual topics, such as pregnancy prevention. Suzuki and Calzo argued that the boards allowed the children to candidly discuss and receive social support for embarrassing adolescent issues. Other researchers have similarly argued that the Internet can be an important source of information and support for embarrassing or social taboo topics (Boies *et al.*, 2004; Gray *et al.* 2005; Longo *et al.*, 2002).

Greenfield (2004a), however, cautioned that free expression in chat rooms may not always be developmentally positive. She explored children's use of various forms of Internet communication (e.g., unmoderated and moderated chat, instant messaging) and identified many communications promoting sexual infidelity, racism, and prejudice. Although acknowledging that none of her concerns was unique to the Internet, she argued that the anonymity of the Internet may lead children to engage in more degrading communications and therefore amplify the potentially negative effects of such communications.

Taken together, and recognizing the cautions expressed by Greenfield (2004a), the research on social development and the Internet conducted to date indicates that, rather than leading children into social isolation and deprivation, the Internet can provide a *positive* environment for social development. Children continue their face-to-face relationships when separated, possibly in much the same way as they would on a telephone. Indeed, Internet technologies provide children with more opportunities for social interaction than possible with a telephone; children can simultaneously communicate with a large number of peers on a large number of topics through e-mail, chat, and instant messaging. Children who feel socially isolated in a face-to-face setting, are depressed, and/or lack self-confidence are able to communicate in a socially safe environment rather than keeping their concerns to themselves. Furthermore, children are able to "try out" different personal identities, discuss personal concerns, and obtain personally relevant information without embarrassment or disclosure.

UNWANTED EXPOSURE TO PORNOGRAPHY AND HATE

Very little research has been conducted on the effect on children of pornography and hate sites on the Internet. Pornography is prevalent throughout the Internet; pornographic images are available on millions of Web sites and through hundreds of thousands of Internet sources. While pornographic material is generally quite obvious and easily agreed upon, hate is more insidious; hate can be difficult to find and define.

Children access pornography in many ways, some intentional and many unintentional. Children can intentionally access pornography though Web searches (e.g., searching for *sex* on Google) or typing in possible URLs (e.g. http://www.sex.com). Children are much more likely to access pornography unintentionally, however. This may occur through innocent combinations of multiple meaning keyword searches (e.g. *boy toy*) and through techniques used by pornographic distributors to recruit new customers. Pornographic distributors may send spam e-mails with pornographic content or inviting recipients to access pornography. Many times, the invitation is innocuous, such as an invitation to compete for a laptop computer or learn about livestock. Pornographers also acquire or use common-sounding Web domain names (http://whitehouse.com used to be a hard core pornography site—the correct URL for the White House is http://whitehouse.gov). Pornographers also manipulate spelling of URLs to introduce children to pornography (several common misspellings of http://Disney.com once led to pornographic Web sites). More recently, pornographic distributors have invaded peer-to-peer transfers so that a child downloading the latest Britney Spears audio file from a less than reputable peer-to-peer network might receive a hardcore pornographic video instead. Although many of these techniques are no longer used—regulators have shut down many distributors of pornography and other distributors have developed fee-based Web sites and peer-to-peer Internet downloads—children still can inadvertently access pornography.

Mitchell *et al.* (2003a) analyzed data from the Youth Internet Safety Survey (Finkelhor *et al.*, 2000). Phone interview questions included inadvertent access to pornography on a Web site, in e-mail, or instant message as well as whether the child was distressed by the exposure. One-quarter of interviewed children indicated they had been inadvertently exposed to pornography, 75% through a Web site and 25% through e-mail or instant messaging. Older children were more likely to have been inadvertently exposed to pornography than were younger children; however, the older children engaged in more Internet activities, including entering chat rooms and engaging in risky Internet behavior, such as chatting with people they had never met offline. Although a quarter of children who had experienced inadvertent exposure indicated they were very or extremely upset by the exposure (this represented 6% of the total survey sample), very few mentioned the incident to anyone and few revisited the offending material. Although some children were distressed by their exposure, most children simply dismissed the pornographic material.

Children are exposed to sexuality in other media, including music videos, movies, magazines, and television. A large body of research does suggest a relationship for adolescents and young adults between viewing pornography and engaging in risky and/or deviant behavior (cf. Greenfield, 2004b) but this research is correlational in nature. No causal link has been firmly established to indicate that viewing pornography—on or off the Internet—has adverse consequences on children or adolescents. Ultimately, concerns about adverse consequences of inadvertent or purposeful exposure to pornography on the Internet may be simply an urban myth (Potter & Potter, 2001).

Hate, possibly because it is so insidious, is more difficult to understand and investigate. Gerstenfeld *et al.* (2003) conducted a content analysis of Internet sites hosted by white nationalist, neo-Nazi, skinheads, Ku Klux Klan, Christian identity, Holocaust denial, and other hate groups. Only one-half of the sites included identifiable hate symbols such as swastikas or burning crosses. One-quarter of these extremist sites claimed their group did not espouse hate or racism and over 80% either made no mention of violence or claimed they were opposed to violence. Many of these sites had contradictory language, such as denying racism but exclaiming Whites as the "only" race. Although few sites included resources for children (one notable exception is http://martinlutherking.org/, which is designed expressly for children), the lack of identifiable symbols as well as claims of nonracism and nonviolence or contradictory language regarding racism and violence may lead to confusion among children.

Although Turpin-Petrosino (2002) found that very few high school students reported contact with a hate group through the Internet, Gerstenfeld *et al.* (2003) argued that the Internet presence of these groups is too subtle for most children and adolescents to understand. This premise is supported by Lee and Leets' (2002) research on the persuasiveness of hate sites with adolescents. Adolescents, aged 13–17 years, viewed Web pages modified from actual extremist Web resources, then completed a survey immediately following viewing the pages and two weeks later to examine the persuasiveness of the different pages. In some conditions, the Web page was presented as a narrative, with characters and a plot. Other Web pages had less of a narrative structure. In some conditions, the pages concluded with an explicit message and, in others, with an implicit message. Web pages presenting information in narrative form with an implicit message were initially perceived by adolescents as very persuasive. However, the persuasiveness dissipated over time, while pages with low narrative content and explicit messages remained relatively stable over time. In addition, the adolescents' receptivity interacted with the persuasiveness of the messages. Young people who were originally neutral with regard to the views expressed by the Web pages were initially more influenced by the implicit messages.

Lee and Leets' findings regarding the persuasive effects of implicit messages on naïve adolescents are particularly important considering that extremist groups use the Internet for recruiting new members (Turpin-Petrosino, 2002). Young adolescents, because they are seeking an in-group with which to identify but lack important critical appraisal skills, may be particularly influenced by the recruitment strategies used by extremist groups on the Internet.

PREDATION AND BULLYING

Increasingly, news reports of children being lured into cars seem to be replaced by reports of children being lured on the Internet. Similarly, schoolyard bullying seems to be moving into the Internet. Just as parents historically became concerned as their children began to venture further and further from home, they now become concerned as their children venture further and further into the Internet environment.

Finkelhor et al. (2000; Mitchell et al., 2001) analyzed questions on sexual solicitation from the 1999–2000 Youth Internet Safety Survey. Almost 20% of the respondents aged 10–17 reported receiving an unwanted sexual solicitation through e-mail or chat. Almost all of the solicitations came from someone encountered only on the Internet. Few of the solicitations were direct requests for face-to-face meetings; the solicitations included asking a girl about her bra size, asking a boy to engage in cybersex, and sending sexually explicit drawings.

Older children, aged 14–17 years, in the Finkelhor et al. (2000; Mitchell et al., 2001) study reported solicitation more often than younger children, aged 10–13 years, and twice as many girls reported solicitation than boys. Risk for receiving sexual solicitation was higher for "troubled" children (based on a composite reporting of depressive symptoms, victimization, and family instability). Risk was also higher for children reporting more frequent use of the Internet and engaging in potentially risky behaviors on the Internet, such as posting personal information, using sexually suggestive aliases in chat rooms, talking about sex with someone met solely online, and visiting pornographic Web sites. The characteristics of troubled family and personal life and risky behavior that Mitchell et al. found in relation to Internet predation also characterize children and adolescents targeted by offline sexual predators (cf. Dombrowski et al., 2004). Although the Internet can bring predators into easier contact with children, it does not necessarily alter the children who are targeted.

Finkelhor et al. (2000; Mitchell et al., 2001) also found that controls such as parental rules and filtering software were not related to reports of sexual solicitation. These tools may also not be sufficient to guard against approaches used by predators to monitor a victim. Commonly, Internet predators use a variety of sophisticated techniques to gather information about and eavesdrop on a potential victim (Dombrowski *et al.*, 2004; McGrath & Casey, 2002). At the technologically simplest level, a predator may search the Web for information about the victim, reading personal Web pages and blogs to gather personal information on the potential victim. Increasingly technologically advanced approaches include using "sniffer" software to eavesdrop on a child's communications and infiltrating the child's computer through Trojan and worm viruses. Thus, even if a child attends to and obeys a parent's rules not to give out personal information, an ingenious Internet predator may be able to obtain that information through nefarious and clandestine means.

Only one-half of the children who reported sexual solicitation in the Finkelhor *et al.* (2000, Mitchell *et al.*, 2001) study reported the incident to someone and only half of these were reported to a parent. In part, the lack of reporting could have been due to few children being concerned about the solicitation; only 25% of the children reported being upset about the solicitation and these were mainly the younger children in the study. Although organizations such as CyberTipline and Cybertip.ca did not exist at the time of the Youth Internet Safety Survey, few parents or children reported knowing they should report upsetting Internet episodes to their Internet Service Provider or to a law enforcement agency.

Recently, law enforcers have begun masquerading on the Internet as children to combat sexual solicitation crimes. Wolak *et al.* (2003a) analyzed arrests made in the United States during 2000–2001 for Internet sex crimes involving children and found 508 cases in which an alleged predator used the Internet to lure the child and a further 644 undercover cases in which an alleged predator used the Internet to lure a law enforcement agent posing as a child. Mitchell *et al.* (2005) investigated a sample of these arrests and found many were successfully prosecuted or led to a guilty plea. Although the characteristics of actual cases and undercover cases differed slightly (e.g., the victim was stated to be slightly younger, more contacts were made in sexually oriented chat rooms, and less time elapsed before the "meeting" in undercover as opposed to actual cases) as did the characteristics of the alleged predator (e.g., the alleged perpetrator was slightly older, more likely to be employed full time, and had a slightly higher mean income in undercover as opposed to actual cases), Mitchell *et al.* (2005) concluded that the Internet has improved the ability of law enforcement agencies to detect and prevent crimes against children.

Particularly because of its anonymous nature, Internet harassment can be psychologically devastating. In 2002, Ghyslain Raza, an overweight adolescent, used school equipment to videotape himself acting out a *Star Wars* scene with a golf ball retriever as an imaginary light saber. Several months later, some students found the tape in a locked cabinet and uploaded the recording to a peer-to-peer network and encouraged viewers to post insulting comments about the youth. In 2004, Gary Brolsma created a Flash video while lip-syncing and dancing in his chair in front of his Web cam and posted it on the Web.

Although he originally meant only to share it with his friends, the clip quickly spread across the Web and he became embarrassed and upset by the widespread media attention and comparisons with "the *Star Wars* kid." These events focused attention on cyber-bullying and harassment.

The Youth Internet Safety Survey also asked children about online harassment and bullying. Finkelhor *et al.* (2000) reported that 6% of respondents indicated they had been harassed on the Internet, with older children being more likely targets of harassment. Episodes of harassment ranged from harassing instant messages, chat communications, and e-mails to posting a hate Web site about a 17-year-old. As with sexual solicitation, only half of the children told a parent about the incident.

Ybarra *et al.* (2004a) analyzed characteristics associated with victims of Internet harassment from the Youth Internet Safety Survey. One-third of the children who reported having been harassed indicated they were very or extremely upset by the harassing incident. Males who reported more depressive symptoms (e.g., decreased feelings of self-efficacy, difficulty completing schoolwork, difficulty engaging in personal hygiene) were more likely to report harassment than were males who reported few depressive symptoms—this relationship was not found with females who reported harassment. Ybarra argued that the relationship between depression and harassment makes Internet harassment an important mental health issues.

A number of children who reported being victims of Internet harassment also reported being perpetrators of harassment. Ybarra and Mitchell (2004b) analyzed characteristics of children from the Youth Internet Safety Survey who reported harassing another on the Internet. Ybarra and Mitchell found that 15% of respondents to the Youth Internet Safety Survey indicated they had made rude or nasty comments to another and 1% used the Internet to embarrass or harass someone in the past year. Consistent with offline bullies, Internet harassers tended to have poor family bonds and engage in risky behaviors such as substance abuse and delinquency—characteristics that, according to Ybarra and Mitchell, are common to offline bullying and harassment. Ybarra and Mitchell (2004a) found that while much Internet harassment may be an extension of schoolyard bullying, some aggressors appear to harass others only on the Internet. Based on their results, and consistent with Greenfield's (2004a) concern, Ybarra and Mitchell argued that the anonymity of the Internet may allow some children to adopt a more aggressive persona than they express in real life.

In summary, the research on Internet predation and bullying closely resembles that of offline predation and bullying. The Internet provides greater access to children and a larger environment in which to engage in bullying and harassment, however, so the effects of such events can be more devastating to the victimized child.

BECOMING "INTERNET-WISE"

Three approaches have been used to protect children from the damaging effects of the Internet. One approach is to legislate what materials can be distributed across the Internet. The Child Online Protection Act (COPA) was passed by the United States Congress in 1998, prohibiting commercial Internet service providers from distributing content objectionable to minors. Although this law has never taken effect due to court challenges that the law violates the First Amendment right to free speech, many states have enacted similar laws. In response to the potential law, many pornography sites shut down, only to reappear on other domains hosted outside the United States.

As noted earlier, another approach to protecting children from the dangers of the Internet has been the development of software to filter out or block children's access to offensive resources. In part, this comes from legislation. The Children's Internet Protection Act (CIPA), passed by the United States Congress in 2000, requires schools and public libraries to install filtering software on all computers in order to be eligible for federal funding. Although CIPA has been partially struck down by the Supreme Court, various states have enacted similar legislation. Many schools and libraries have installed filtering software and commercial companies such as Net Nanny and Cyber Sitter engage in extensive marketing of their filtering programs to parents.

Both of these approaches, legislating content and blocking content, do appear to protect children by attempting to prevent access to objectionable content. Neither is completely successful, however. The Internet is simply too vast to police all the objectionable resources; as one site shuts down another opens up, often in another country that is immune to legislation. Filtering software cannot block objectionable content without severely limiting accessible content. Richardson et al. (2002) found that filtering software significantly blocks access to many health topics important to children and adolescents, ranging from condoms and sexually transmitted diseases to dieting and depression. Similarly, a Consumer Reports ("Filtering Software," 2005) study of filtering software found that most software blocked pornography very well but also blocked sex education and gender issue sites. The software also blocked hate poorly, allowing results on terrorism, weapons-making, and violence, while blocking drug education resources. Use of filtering software also does not appear to prevent unwanted sexual solicitation (Mitchell et al., 2001). Furthermore, neither legislation nor filtering software credits children with the capacity to appraise and filter objectionable content on their own.

A third, and likely most successful, approach is to teach children to critically appraise on their own. Critical thinking skills underlie almost all decision making tasks and need to be taught and generalized across a wide range of domains, from making healthy eating choices, to making appropriate decisions about sexual behavior, purchasing, and information gathering.

Children do become more critical of information they find on the Internet as they develop yet they still rely on the Internet as an important source of information. As part of a larger study (Varnhagen, unpublished data), we asked students in eighth and eleventh grade and first year of university which of three sources, an encyclopedia article, the newspaper, or the Web, was most likely to provide credible information. Almost three-quarters of the eighth-grade children indicated that the Web was the most credible source of information whereas fewer than half of the eleventh graders and one-fifth of the university students rated information from the Web to be most credible. Regardless of their beliefs about credibility, however, almost all students indicated they used information from the Web in writing school reports.

Critical appraisal as it regards the Internet requires children to appraise the author and host of the Internet resource; the purpose and target audience for the resource; the accuracy, objectivity, comprehensiveness, and currency of any information; and relevance of the Internet resource to their needs (Varnhagen, 2002). For example, an early adolescent seeking information on the Web about acne will need to appraise the author: is the author knowledgeable? If the author is knowledgeable, the information is likely overall to be more credible than if the author has limited knowledge of acne.

The adolescent will also need to determine the purpose and target of the resource: Is the resource a product advertisement? A source of medical information? An old wives' tale? Someone's personal belief? Product advertisements are biased toward influencing and purchasing decisions. A resource with a purpose of providing medical information is more likely to be credible than are resources designed to sell or persuade. Related to the purpose, the child will also need to appraise the authenticity of the information: How accurate is the advice? Is the information based on objective medical information? Is it complete? Is it up-to-date? Acne information has changed over the past several years; the latest medical research shows that drying agents are more likely to excoriate skin and lead to scarring. Also, the child must determine whether the resource is relevant to his or her needs.

Needless to say, children are very unlikely to perform such an extensive appraisal of many of the millions of resources resulting from a search for information about acne. Indeed, Brem *et al.*, (2001) found that adolescents evaluating scientifically valid and hoax Web sites were very uncritical of the information they found. For example, the students relied more on surface features, such as number of links to other sites, in their evaluation of the information. Even though they acknowledged that some authors had an ulterior motive, such as to sell or persuade, the authors' motives were unlikely to influence accurate reporting of information.

Children may be even less likely to consider critically appraising other types of Internet resources, such as games, chat, instant messaging, music, and videos. For example, children may be more likely to be drawn to an Internet game based on visual and auditory appeal than they are to appraise the host for potential to download viruses or accuracy of the feedback given on performance. They are unlikely to assume a new buddy met in a chat room who expresses shared interests is anyone other than a peer. They are likely to download immediately the latest bootlegged music video than consider what viruses that video might bring with it.

Children need to learn to critically appraise the resources and communications they encounter on the Internet. Librarians and schoolteachers have developed a number of information literacy resources to help children learn to critically appraise informational resources (Schrock, 2001). For example, "Kathy Schrock's Guide for Educators" (http://school.discovery.com/schrockguide/eval.html), one of the oldest and best known resources, provides a set of yes/no questions for children of different ages to use as they find and evaluate information Web resources. Younger, early elementary-aged children are encouraged to consider whether they agree or disagree with the information; older, high school-aged adolescents are encouraged to critically appraise the content and authority of the information.

Many child safety organizations provide guides and resources for parents and children. WebAware (http://www.bewebaware.ca/english/default.aspx) includes general Internet checklists for children of different ages. In addition to content appraisal, WebAware encourages children to consider whether they are writing rude messages or providing personal information on the Internet. WebAware also includes safety tips for parents of children of different ages, such as using child-friendly search engines with 5- to 7-year-old children and encouraging teens to enter only moderated chat rooms. SafeKids.com (http://safekids.com) and SafeTeens.com (http://www.safeteens.com) provide similar resources for children and parents. CyberAngels (http://www.cyberangels.org/) provides a wide range of resources on various Internet crimes (e.g., child pornography, identity theft) for parents and educators as well as an online form for reporting suspected cases of child pornography.

Some organizations include safety games and quizzes for children. In *ID the Creep* (http://www.idthecreep.com/), developed by the National Center for Missing and Exploited Children, children engage in simulated e-mail, chat, and instant messaging and identify potentially risky situations and predators. The Media Awareness Network (http://www.media-awareness.ca/english/special_initiatives/games/index.cfm) has developed a number of games available for children, ranging from *Privacy Playground: The First Adventure of the Three Little CyberPigs*, a game for children, aged 8–10 years, about marketing techniques and protection of privacy, to *Joe Cool/Joe Fool*, quizzes for adolescents about safe Web surfing.

NetSmartz (http://netsmartz.org), developed by a joint initiative of the National Center for Missing and Exploited Children and the Boys and Girls Clubs of America, is an online training resource that includes evaluation checklists, tips, parental resources, games, and quizzes. In an evaluation of the resource (Branch Associates, 2002), children from ages 6 to 18 improved their knowledge of Internet safety through interacting with the resource and over three-quarters of adolescents indicated they would change their behavior on the Internet as a result of what they had learned through NetSmartz.

The relationship between intentions and actual behavior is complex (cf. Ajzen, 2001), however, and children may not translate their new knowledge of and attitudes toward the Internet to safe behavior on the Internet. Software solutions may help children learn to control their behavior on the Internet by forcing them to critically appraise Internet resources before using them. Just as caregivers teach children to cross the street safely, intelligent software solutions could be created to help children navigate the Internet. Rather than simply blocking resources, new versions of filtering software could allow access to a portion of a resource and require the child to correctly answer a series of critical appraisal questions before continuing to the entire resource. An intelligent chat "buddy" application could point our hurtful posts or potentially unsafe communications. Until intelligent software solutions are developed, simple checklist applications can be created to float over an Internet browser and pose critical appraisal questions that help children stop and think as they explore the Internet. Tools such as these will help children learn to apply what they have learned from checklists, teaching resources, and Internet safety activities and games to the real virtual world of the Internet.

The Internet is a limitless virtual environment with many possibilities for positive child development and exploration. Children can visit many places, explore many cultures, try out many technologies, and communicate with many different people. These experiences help children develop cognitively and socially. The Internet also has a seamy side. Children can be exposed to pornography and hate, harassed, stalked, and kidnapped. By empowering our children to gain critical appraisal skills and to become Internet-wise, we can help them expand their minds and worlds safely through the Internet.

REFERENCES

Boies, S. C, Knudson, G., & Young, J. (2004). The Internet, sex, and youths: Implications for sexual development. *Sexual Addiction & Compulsivity, 11,* 343–363.

Branch Associates. (2002). *NetSmartz Evaluation Project: Internet Safety Training for Children and Youth Ages 6 to 18.* Atlanta, GA: Boys & Girls Clubs of America and National Center for Missing & Exploited Children. Retrieved August 1, 2005, from (http://www.netsmartz.org/pdf/evalstathigh.pdf)

Brem, S. K., Russell, J., & Weems, L. (2001). Science on the Web: Student evaluations of scientific arguments. *Discourse Processes, 32,* 191–213.

Calvert, S., Rideout ,V. J., Woolard, J. L., Barr, R. F., & Strouse, G. A. (2005). Age, ethnicity, and socioeconomic patterns in early computer use: A national survey. *American Behavioral Scientist, 48*, 590–607.

Dombrowski, S. C., LeMasney, J.W., Ahia, C. E., & Dickson, S.A. (2004). Protecting children from online sexual predators: Technological, psychoeducational, and legal considerations. *Professional Psychology: Research & Practice, 35*, 65–73.

Environics Research Group (2001). *Young Canadians in a wired world.* Retrieved August 1, 2005, from (http://www.mediaawareness.ca/english/resources/special_initiatives/survey_resources/students_survey/yciww_students_view_2001.pdf)

Filtering software: Better but still fallible. (2005). *Consumer Reports.* Retrieved August 1, 2005, from (http://www.consumerreports.org/main/content/display_report.jsp?FOLDER%3C%3Efolder_id=597365)

Finkelhor, D., Mitchell, K. J., & Wolak, J. (2000). Online victimization: A report of the nation's youth. Alexandria, VA: National Center for Missing and Exploited Children. Retrieved August 1, 2005, from (http://www.missingkids.com/en_US/publications/NC62.pdf)

Gackenbach, J. I., & Ellerman, E. (1998). Introduction to psychological aspects of Internet use. In J. I. Gackenbach (Ed.), *Psychology and the Internet* (pp. 1–26). San Diego: Academic Press.

Gerstenfeld, P. B., Grant, S. R., & Chiang, C-P. (2003). Hate online: A content analysis of extremist Internet sites. *Analyses of Social Issues and Public Policy, 3, 29–44.*

Gray, N. J., Klein, J. D., Noyce, P. R., Sesselberg, T. S, & Cantrill, J. A. (2005). Health information-seeking behaviour in adolescence: The place of the internet. *Social Science & Medicine, 60,* 1467–1478.

Greenfield, P. M. (2004a). Developmental considerations for determining appropriate Internet use guidelines for children and adolescents. *Journal of Applied Developmental Psychology, 25,* 751–762.

Greenfield, P. M. (2004b). Inadvertent exposure to pornography on the Internet: Implications of peer-to-peer file-sharing networks for child development and families. *Journal of Applied Developmental Psychology, 25,* 741–750.

Gross, E. F. (2004). Adolescent Internet use: What we expect, what teens report. *Journal of Applied Developmental Psychology, 25,* 633–649.

Gross, E. F., Juvonen, J., & Gable, S. L. (2002). Internet use and well-being in adolescence. *Journal of Social Issues, 58,* 75–90.

Ipsos-Reid (2004). The Internet is changing the way in which teens socialize in Canada: Instant messaging, e-mail and online gaming the most common weekly online activities for teens. Ottawa, ON: Ipsos-Reid.

Kaiser Family Foundation (2004, September) Children, the digital divide, and federal policy. Retrieved August 1, 2005 from (http://www.kff.org/entmedia/loader.cfm?url=/commonspot/security/getfile.cfm&PageID=46360)

Kraut, R., Patterson, M., Lundmark, V., Kiesler, S., Mukophadhyay, T., & Scherlis, W. (1998). Internet paradox: A social technology that reduces social involvement and psychological well-being? American Psychologist, 53, 1017–1031.

Kraut, R., Kiesler, S., Boneva, B., Cummings, J. N, Helgeson, V., & Crawford, A. M. (2002). Internet paradox revisited. Journal of Social Issues, 58, 49–74.

Law, D. (2004). Participation in online environments: Its relationship to adolescent self-concept. Unpublished Masters thesis, University of British Columbia.

Lee, E., & Leets, L. (2002). Persuasive storytelling by hate groups online: Examining its effects on adolescents. American Behavioral Scientist, 45, 927–957.

Lenhart, A., Rainie, L, & Lewis, O. (2001). Teenage life online: The rise of the instant-message generation and the Internet's impact on friendships and family relationships. Washington, DC: Pew Internet & American Life Project. Retrieved August 1, 2005, from (http://www.pewinternet.org/pdfs/PIP_Teens_Report.pdf)

Livingstone, S., & Bober, M. (2005). UK children go online: Final report of key project findings. Retrieved August 1, 2005, from (http://www.lse.ac.uk/collections/children-go-online/UKCGOfinalReport. pdf)

Longo, R. E., Brown, S. M., & Orcutt, D. P. (2002). Effects of Internet sexuality on children and adolescents. In A. Cooper (Ed.), Sex and the Internet: A guidebook for clinicians (pp. 87–105). New York: Brunner-Rutledge.

McGrath, M. G., & Casey, E. (2002). Forensic psychiatry and the Internet: Practical perspectives on sexual predators and obsessional harassers in cyberspace. Journal of the American Academy of Psychiatry & the Law, 30, 81–94.

Mitchell, K. J, Finkelhor, D., & Wolak, J. (2001) Risk factors for and impact of online sexual solicitation of youth. Journal of the American Medical Association, 285, 3011–3014.

Mitchell, K. J, Finkelhor, D., & Wolak, J. (2003a). The exposure of youth to unwanted sexual material on the Internet: A national survey of risk, impact, and prevention. Youth & Society, 34, 330–358.

Mitchell, K. J, Finkelhor, D., & Wolak, J. (2003b). Victimization of youths on the Internet. Journal of Aggression, Maltreatment, & Trauma, 8, 1–39.

Mitchell, K. J, Wolak, J., & Finkelhor, D. (2005). Police posing as juveniles online to catch sex offenders: Is it working? Sexual Abuse: A Journal of Research and Treatment, 17, 241–267.

Paik, H. J (2001). The history of children's use of electronic media. In D. G. Singer & J. L. Singer (Eds.), Handbook of children and the media (pp. 7–27). Thousand Oaks, CA: Sage Publications.

Potter, R. H., & Potter, L. A. (2001). The Internet, cyber porn, and sexual exploitation of children: Media moral panics and urban myths for middle-class parents? Sexuality & Culture: An Interdisciplinary Quarterly, 5(3), 31–48.

Richardson, C. R., Resnick, P. J., Hansen, D. L., Derry, H. A., & Rideout, V. J. (2002). Does pornography-blocking software block access to health information on the Internet? Journal of the American Medical Association, 288, 2887–2894.

Rideout, V. J., Vandewater, E. A., & Wartella, E. A. (2003). Zero to six: Electronic media in the lives of infants, toddlers, and preschoolers. Menlo Park, CA: The Henry J. Kaiser Family Foundation.

Roberts, D. F., Foehr, U. G., & Rideout, V. (2005). Generation M: Media in the lives of 8 to 18 year olds. Menlo Park, CA: The Henry J. Kaiser Family Foundation.

Schrock, K. (2001). Tapping the Internet for classroom use: Information literacy skills pave the way. MultiMedia Schools, 8(2), 38–43.

Shiu, E., & Lenhart, A. (2004). How Americans use instant messaging. Pew Internet & American Life Project. Retrieved August 1, 2005, from (http://www.pewinternet.org/pdfs/PIP_Instantmessage_ Report.pdf)

Statistics Canada (2003). Household Internet use survey. Retrieved August 1, 2005, from (http://www. statcan.ca/Daily/English/040708/d040708a.htm)

Stern, S. (2002). Sexual selves on the World Wide Web: Adolescent girls' home pages as sites for sexual self-expression. In J. D. Brown, J. E. Steele, & K. Walsh-Childers (Eds.), Sexual teens, sexual media: Investigating media's influence on adolescent sexuality (pp. 265–285). Mahwah, NJ: Lawrence Erlbaum Associates.

Subrahmanyam, K., Greenfield, P. M., & Tynes, B. (2004). Constructing sexuality and identity in an online teen chat room. Journal of Applied Developmental Psychology, 25, 651–666.

Suzuki, L. K., & Calzo, J. P. (2004) The search for peer advice in cyberspace: An examination of online teen bulletin boards about health and sexuality. Journal of Applied Developmental Psychology, 25, 685–698.

Turkle, S. (1995). Life on the Screen: Identity in the Age of the Internet. New York: Simon and Schuster.

Turpin-Petrosino, C. (2002). Hateful sirens... Who hears their song?: An examination of student attitudes toward hate groups and affiliation potential. Journal of Social Issues, 58, 281–301.

Varnhagen, C. K. (2002). Making sense of psychology on the Web: A guide for research and critical thinking. New York, NY: Worth Publishers.

Wartella, E. A., & Jennings, N. (2000) Children and computers: New technology—Old concerns. Future of Children, 10(2), 31–43.

Wolak, J., Finkelhor, D., & Mitchell, K. J. (2003a). Internet sex crimes against minors: The response of law enforcement. Alexandria, VA: National Center for Missing and Exploited Children. Retrieved August 1, 2005, from (http://www.missingkids.com/en_US/publications/NC132.pdf)

Wolak, J., Mitchell, K. J., & Finkelhor, D. (2002). Close online relationships in a national sample of adolescents. Adolescence, 37, 441–455.

Wolak, J., Mitchell, K. J., & Finkelhor, D. (2003b). Escaping or connecting? Characteristics of youth who form close online relationships. Journal of Adolescence, 26, 105–119.

Ybarra, M. L. (2004). Linkages between depressive symptomatology and Internet harassment among young regular Internet users. CyberPsychology and Behavior, 7, 247–257.

Ybarra, M. L., Alexander, C., & Mitchell, K. J. (2005). Depressive symptomatology, youth Internet use, and online interactions: A national survey. Journal of Adolescent Health, 36, 9–18.

Ybarra, M. L., & Mitchell, K. J. (2004a). Online aggressor/targets, aggressors, and targets: A comparison of associated youth characteristics. Journal of Child Psychology and Psychiatry, 45, 1308–1316.

Ybarra, M. L., & Mitchell, K. J. (2004b). Youth engaging in online harassment: Associations with caregiver–child relationships, Internet use, and personal characteristics. Journal of Adolescence, 27, 319–336.

CHAPTER 3

Self Online: Personality and Demographic Implications

Jayne Gackenbach and Heather von Stackelberg
Grant MacEwan College
Edmonton, Alberta, Canada

INTRODUCTION

Like all other communications technologies, the advent of the Internet has changed our culture profoundly, but it has also had a strong influence on how we relate to ourselves as well as to each other. It has allowed us to be authentically ourselves or to try on and try out different identities and personalities in ways that are just not possible in face-to-face reality, with both positive and negative effects. The narrow bandwidth of communication, including the lack of visual cues, allows us to relate to others without the judgments of their physical presence which happens in face-to-face communication, but also allows disinhibition, in the form of greater disclosure, sexual content, and aggression. The Internet can create greater self-awareness and become a catalyst for positive change, or it can reinforce maladaptive facets of ourselves.

Identity isn't only in our heads; it is also part of a larger context, including our gender, race, or ethnic heritage, and our socioeconomic status. These have an effect on how we relate to the Internet and how it affects us. Like all new communication technologies, the Internet was initially dominated by those in power, in this case, by relatively wealthy white males. Though this is changing, the effects are still resonating throughout society. In this chapter, we briefly examine self online from our private inner worlds to how demographic identifiers differ online.

NEW WAYS OF THINKING ABOUT IDENTITY

Psychologists believe that we have an identity that is made up of different facets reflecting different aspects of self, depending on our psychological and biological history and our current situation. Although we do not "split off" parts of our personalities in everyday life, as is the case in Dissociative Identity Disorder, we frequently shift who is "on stage," depending on the situation. Our capacity to integrate various aspects of the self into one identity has long been considered the developmental marker of adulthood. However, postmodern thinking views the notion of multiple selves, rather than one discrete self, as a healthy adaptation to the complexity of modern lives. In contemporary society, alternative lifestyles, types of family structures, and cultural models of identity have become increasingly visible, so the various projections of self online, depending on context, may no longer be seen as inherently maladaptive but rather as an example of explorations of the self.

There are many opportunities for deepening one's awareness of self online, both consciously, by meaningful discourse with individuals you may never have the chance to meet in person, such as distant family members, and unconsciously, by getting emotionally engaging with someone in ways that rarely occur in face-to-face interactions. For instance, the large numbers of immigrants in North America, as well as their children, can "meet" online relatives in their country of origin and connect, or reconnect, with their ethnic heritage. This contact can make the ethnic facet of identity easier to grow and maintain than would normally be possible in a western mainstream culture.

The Internet can also allow a young gay man to explore his gay identity and become comfortable with it in relative anonymity before coming out to friends and family. Someone who is shy or self-conscious about their physical appearance can open up and explore emotional intimacy in an environment in which physical appearance is, for the most part, irrelevant.

However, the Internet also allows easy access to many potential addictions, including pornography and fantasy role-playing. The Internet also offers a broad stage and easy access to victims for those who engage in predatory behaviors.

Even when a person's behavior online doesn't cause direct harm to themselves or others, if the person projected online is radically different from one's offline personality, it may cause psychological distress, not only to self but to others as well. A prank initiated in fun, such as a woman pretending to be a man online, and leading on a female friend, can lead to hurt feelings and ruptured friendships. These sorts of actions affect not only the initiator.

ONE SELF OR MANY: ADOLESCENT EXPLORATIONS

We all have many aspects of self, in addition to the experience that we are a unified whole. We see the fluidity between these possible selves initially in adolescence when the uncertainty of establishing one's identity dominates. Teens sometimes explore radically different identities as a way to assert their independence, often annoying their parents or other adults. They push the limits as a way to be able to leave the comfort of the nest. Blue hair, nose rings, and food fetishes are bodily ways to be unique. The Goth, Skater, Grunge, and Stoner cultures allow kids to explore different selves. However, when children try out different personalities in the offline world, they are limited to only a few realistic choices. Some of these are healthy explorations of the self (like vegetarianism or political activism) while others can be harmful (engaging in illegal activities with peers).

Online, opportunities to explore different identities may be easy, exponential, and unregulateable but they are also becoming increasingly the norm. This has been found by Valkenburg *et al.* (2005) who surveyed 600 18-year-olds in classroom settings, asking if they had explored their identity online using chat rooms or instant messaging. The social scientists found that "50 percent indicated that they had engaged in Internet-based identity experiments. The most important motive for such experiments was self-exploration (to investigate how others react), followed by social compensation (to overcome shyness) and social facilitation (to facilitate relationship formation)" (p. 383).

Who did the students in the Valkenburg *et al.* study pretend to be? Most presented themselves as someone older than they were in real life (50%), with other variations including presenting themselves as a real-life acquaintance, an elaborated fantasy person, or a more flirtatious person. A few presented themselves as more beautiful or more macho. These fantasy self-presentations differed as a function of the adolescent's age, gender, and personality. So that extroverts more than introverts presented themselves as older online than they actually were as did younger adolescents and girls. The real-life acquaintance online alternative self was more common among boys, as was presenting themselves as a fantasy person. These findings are consistent with most adolescent identity theories but point to the important role that the Internet has come to play in such explorations.online versus offline selves.

Identity can be viewed in terms of "self-focusing" or "self-awareness"—the degree to which our attention is focused on the self. This perspective on self is closely tied to memory and thinking. Not surprisingly, if we focus on our self, we gain insight into who we are. But mood affects self-focusing: In a negative mood, we are more likely to attend to negative information about self, while the opposite is true if we are feeling positive. Developmentally, our ability to gain insight increases as we move from childhood through adolescence to adulthood. So just as mood regulates what shows we choose to watch on TV, so too it regulates what sites we visit online. Clinicians know that their depressed patients tend to be less physically active and watch too much television. Now, lonely and isolated individuals can reach out to cyberfriends and interact in meaningful ways.

Psychological research comparing online versus offline identities suggests that some of the processes of creating those online and offline identities are similar. Krantz *et al.* (1997) compared results from identical experiments on men's perception of attractiveness of females conducted on- and offline. They point out that "if the same psychological variables drive the results of both data sets, the trends in data should be similar" (p. 264). This is exactly what they found. In other words, how one rated a female in terms of her physical attractiveness did not differ whether done online, or in a more traditional face-to-face (F2F) laboratory setting. How we perceive personal attractiveness as well as various other psychological elements is likely to be the same online or offline. Conducting psychological research online has now become a widespread and accepted practice in the scientific communities, with methodological procedures and caveats noted (Kraut *et al.*, 2004). But there are aspects of the online world which result in a unique experience of self as well.

SELF EXPANSION OR DISINHIBITION ONLINE

If our psychological processes are similar online and offline, how come we hear so many stories of people being different or at least projecting very different parts of themselves into cyberspace? Many individuals find themselves acting in uncharacteristic ways online, due to the phenomenon called *disinhibition*. Disinhibition is defined as the inability to control impulsive behaviors, thoughts, or feelings, and manifests online as people communicating in ways that they would not ordinarily do offline. These communication patterns can be positive or negative. An example of disinhibition online is the propensity for self-revelation that results in people feeling more intimate. This self-disclosure can be either positive and appropriate, allowing for a deepening connection, or negative and inappropriate, such as angry comments or lack of honestly in disclosure. For a discussion of other aspects of disinhibition, see the chapter in this book by Adam Joinson, called "Disinhibition and the Internet."

Even researchers studying disinhibition can be surprised by the disconnect people seem to manifest after having behaved in a disinhibited manner online. Niederhoffer and Pennebaker (2002) were amazed when, in post-experimental interviews, students who had just engaged online in "overt invitations for sex, explicit sexual language, or discussion of graphic sexual escapades" (p. 14) were demure and shy.

Suler (2004) argues that "rather than thinking of disinhibition as revealing an underlying 'true self,' we can conceptualize it as a shift to a constellation within self-structure, involving clusters of affect and cognition that differ from the in-person constellation" (p. 321). In other words, it is still us online, but it's a part of ourselves that we generally keep fairly hidden. In a detailed analysis of the disinhibition effect, Suler highlights six reasons why people extend their emotional expression of the self while online.

1. *Dissociative Anonymity*: Although not a formal pathology, the sense of self while online becomes compartmentalized into an "online self," which is perceived as alone and anonymous, and an offline self that is different

and separate. Because the Internet feels so virtual and boundaryless, it is tempting to perceive "the other" as not real.

2. *Invisibility*: You don't have to worry about how you look when chatting with someone online. One need not worry, am I smiling enough, was that sigh of exasperation heard? What you have to write then takes on deeper meaning. Analyzing the textual clues of communication, without the nonverbal, leans heavily on one's thinking . . . as thoughts can be the precursor to the written word.

3. *Asynchronicity*: For many online communications, one can respond at one's leisure, and the pressure of an immediate response is gone. Here, Suler talks about "emotional hit and run," where a scathing message can be left on a message board and the poster never returns to check on the responses or repercussions of their words.

4. *Solipsistic Introjection*: As absorption in an online exchange increases, some experience the online companion as a "voice within one's head" (Suler, 2004; p. 323). The online friend becomes incorporated into one's intrapsychic world. Like a character in our dreams, our waking thoughts include stories about various people. Some of these interactions are real and immediate, while others are somewhat less so, such as an imagined comeback to your boss. The boss is real but the exchange is not. The online friend can take on a special status in our imagined internal dialogues, which can result in a felt sense of special closeness existing outside the boundaries of time and space.

But this can result in the opposite effect, too. With the lack of cues such as tone, expression, and body language, additional meanings are read into a message based on the reader's assumptions, insecurities, and mood, often without the person even realizing that they are doing it. The result can be a fairly neutral or innocently meant statement or question being taken as a deadly insult by a person with low self-esteem or someone who is in a bad mood that day.

5. *Dissociative Imagination*: Some people keep careful boundaries between their online fictional selves and their real-world offline selves. So, for instance, in online role-playing games such as Everquest, when the computer is turned off, the online self as wizard is gone. The online world and the self that inhabits it become a separate realm of being. This provides the online self the freedom to do things which the offline self very likely wouldn't do, such as flirt outrageously or act aggressively.

6. *Minimization of Status and Authority*: Although you know your boss has a different status from you at work, when responding to his e-mails, that gap minimizes. The playing field seems level when online; thus, authority differences are minimized, and it becomes easy to make a nasty or sarcastic comment by e-mail that would never have been spoken face to face.

These various facets of ourselves which can be revealed through interactions on the Internet, once out, don't necessarily stay compartmentalized, but can become integrated into our whole selves. Turkle (1995) has argued that rehearsals of unexpressed behaviors can generalize from the virtual world into the real world. She discusses how experiences of multiple user domains (MUDs) can dramatically help or hinder self. Turkle argues that "[t]he Internet has become a significant social laboratory for experimenting with the constructions and reconstructions of self that characterize postmodern life" (1995, p. 180). This media researcher maintains that by interacting in these mostly text-based virtual communities, some people have found unparalleled opportunities to explore self through experiences hard to come by in real life. These range from pretending to be a member of the opposite sex to slaying a dragon. Turkle asks the question: Is MUD play psychotherapy or addiction? She points out that MUDs offer a rich place to act out or work through psychological issues, but notes that when used by someone who has a fragmented self in face-to-face reality, MUDs can be problematic. In some sense, however, all interactions online constitute one massive multiple user domain.

Straus (1997) suggests that Internet culture is "delivering new kinds of blows to our narcissism or self absorption because it generates questions we cannot answer without immersing ourselves in a crisis of representation in time and space" (p. 96). So now the new media user is not only sitting on a chair in front of their computer, but is simultaneously in another "space," such as Everquest *Kera's Island Quest* at another "time," a thousand years in the future. Perhaps our new cultural obsession with the Internet offers yet another way to explore our identities in both positive and negative ways. Urban historian Boyer (1996) warns that:

> the computer is to contemporary society what the machine was to modernism, and that this metaphor profoundly affects the way we ultimately grasp reality. But there is … an inherent danger here: as cyberspace pulls us into its electronic grasp, we withdraw from the world and risk becoming incapable of action in a real city plagued by crime, hatred, disease, unemployment, and under-education.

Many of us, adults and kids alike, know others who have pushed the boundaries between online and offline identity. The Internet's ability to generate powerful examples of disinhibition and self-disclosure has generated a new breed of concerns that counselors, parents, and teachers are struggling to understand. Some of the new ways of "being" online are exciting, allowing us to develop parts of our personalities that deepen our potential. But other projections of cyber self are more troubling.

PERSONALITY ONLINE

The ability to get to know people who are on the Internet is deeply reinforcing. We are social beings and we thrive on feeling connected to others who are like us. In Yuen and Lavin's (2004) recent study of college students' vulnerability to Internet dependence, the authors found that shy students were more likely to use the Internet compulsively, leading to failing classes and eventually leaving school. Evidently, because shy students preferred online interactions over F2F, their offline social skills suffered. "The Internet provided a safe haven where feelings of social discomfort are alleviated" (p. 382). These shy students cut morning classes because they would surf the web all night. They preferred to sit at their computers rather than participate in F2F social events to make friends. The authors admit that colleges and universities have inadvertently laid the groundwork for unhealthy online behaviors; most college dorm rooms are wired with T-3 lines and even have e-mail accounts, home pages. Ethernet ports can be found among the grass and trees in the quad. The authors propose that "as students enter the collegiate population it is necessary to address the binge drinking, date rape, and the dangers of compulsive Internet use" (p. 382).

Children and teenagers are not the only ones who are vulnerable to online/offline identity issues. As we age, we certainly get a clearer sense of self, but that does not mean that our adult perspective of who we are remains static throughout our lives. Although there are a variety of traits we might use to describe ourselves, researchers have identified some major personality constructs that are relatively enduring for most of us to some degree throughout our lifespans. Called the "Big 5," the primary personality characteristics are introversion/extroversion, agreeableness, conscientiousness, emotional stability, and openness to experience (Larsen & Buss, 2005). Few of us think of ourselves only in these ways, however; there are other personality characteristics that may emerge as a result of life events. Not surprisingly, given the empirical importance in the personality literature of these constructs, it is the characteristics of introversion and extroversion that have been studied quite a lot in terms of Internet effects.

INTROVERTS AND EXTROVERTS ONLINE

The most controversial study on the self as a function of life online was done by Kraut *et al.*, (1998). Called the "Internet Paradox Study," these researchers initially found that Internet use increased loneliness and depression in a sample of people who received free computers and Internet access in the early days of the Internet. Their results, which are now considered almost outdated by Internet research standards, seemed paradoxical given other studies pointing to positive social and personal impacts of Internet use. This study resulted in a lot of dialogue among psychologists interested in this new media, as well as feature articles in *Psychology Today* and the *APA Monitor*. Some pointed to various methodological flaws in the Internet Paradox Study as well as noting that statistical difference is not always the same as clinical difference. In other words, statistics may not be accurate when attempting to explain the subtleties of human behavior.

In a 3-year followup study, this same group examined introvert/extrovert personality styles. Kraut *et al.* (2002) found positive effects for communication, social involvement, and psychological well-being, depending on personality type. They found that in line with their personalities, extroverts increased their social contacts by being online, while introverts who used the Internet extensively decreased social contact. The same result was found with loneliness; extroverts became less lonely with extensive Internet use and introverts became lonelier.

Internet usage is often suggested as a way to practice social exchanges for shy individuals but the research just cited does not seem to support that suggestion.

But extroversion is related to being online as Yang and Lester (2003) examined. A question in their research was the relationship between extroversion and neuroticism and Internet usage for citizens from 18 industrialized nations. These researchers found that extroversion was positively associated with Internet usage while neuroticism was negatively associated. That is, extroverts but not neurotics use the Internet across cultures in the industrialized nations.

However, the findings of the Kraut group are not equivocal since some others have replicated their investigations in part and obtained some different results (Wastlund *et al.*, 2001). Engelberg and Sjoberg (2004) found that "use of the Internet was related to loneliness and adherence to idiosyncratic values (strong effects), and also to poorer balance between work and leisure and emotional intelligence (weaker effects)" (p. 41). However, they did not find any relationship to the Big 5 personality traits.

OTHER PERSONALITY TYPES ONLINE

Needless to say, people differ in the degree to which they are susceptible to the disinhibition effect, just as online situations vary as to how likely they are to elicit this effect. Morgan and Cotton (2003) found that depressiveness was associated with Internet use but depended on the *type* of use. Specifically, they found that e-mail, chat, and instant messaging were associated with *decreased* depressive symptoms while shopping, playing games, or information seeking were associated with *increased* depressive symptoms. The basic difference between the sets of activities is that chatting involves others, while activities that are solitary appear to increase isolation and thus lower mood. In personality research, it has also become clear that the parts of your personality you choose to project into cyberspace are reflected in what you are doing online (e.g., in face-to-face reality, churches or bars elicit very different aspects of self). Morgan and Cotton's (2003) research also shows that the emotional openness evident in chat rooms can be therapeutic because we feel able to express ourselves and be understood (see the King and Moreggi chapter in this book for an extended discussion of this point). In contrast, no such response typically occurs while shopping or gambling online, since these are solo activities.

Morahan-Martin and Schumacher (2003) found that lonely college students were more likely to report Internet use for emotional support than were nonlonely students. However, such research on individual differences in Internet use is not entirely consistent. Hills and Argyle (2003) found no association between personality type and overall Internet use while Jackson *et al.* (2003) found an association between personality and Internet use for the first three months of having access to the Internet but no difference thereafter.

In an interesting study on empathy, researchers hypothesized and found that those high in empathy were more able to experience a sense of reality (called *telepresence*) in the virtual world (Nicovich *et al.*, 2005). This differed as a function of gender, with empathic men using the interactions of the virtual world to become increasingly engaged while empathic women simply watched the environment for the same effect. Given that empathy is the ability to identify with another's experience, this is not surprising. It appears that men need more direct engagement to experience empathic presence than do women.

Various studies have examined personality variables as related to problem behaviors online. One study dealt with personal use of the Internet at work (Everton *et al.*, 2005) while another examined misuse of the Internet by children (Harman *et al.*, 2005). Everton *et al.* (2005) found that "people who use their computers in unproductive ways tend to be men, younger, more impulsive, and less conscientious" (p. 143). They also noted that sensation seekers were more likely to use their computers/Internet to view sexual material at work. Personality and children's misuse of the Internet was the focus of the work by Harman *et al.* (2005), who were particularly interested in faking behavior online. Children between 11 and 16 who were more likely to do this "had poorer social skills, lower levels of self-esteem, higher levels of social anxiety, and higher levels of aggression" (p. 1). When one considers that half of children in the study by Valkenburg and colleagues (2005) faked their identities online, this finding is of concern, if perhaps not surprising. Adolescence, the focus of both studies, is a time of growth and change regarding the self. What is also interesting about this finding of Harman and colleagues was that it was not the amount of time children spent online that was associated with these problems in personality but rather what they did online. In this case, they were faking who they were.

Finally, Engelberg and Sjoberg (2004) report no specific personality differences nor did Hills and Argyle (2003). The latter, however, point out that while "gender and age significantly influenced patterns of use, ... there were remarkably few significant associations with individual differences in personality when gender and age were controlled for" (p. 59). Thus we'll turn our examination of self online to various demographics, including gender and age, which may be a clearer way of determining how self influences and is influenced by the Internet experience.

THE SELF AS A DEMOGRAPHIC ONLINE

Developmental psychologists have shown us that one of the earliest elements in the construction of our sense of self is gender. Also important in developing self are elements of age, race, culture, and socioeconomic status. So, too, online these elements of self inform our experience. It is this view of self that we will consider in the remainder of this chapter.

In 1998, Morahan-Martin noted:

> There is a gender gap in Internet use ... from childhood on, males are more experienced with computers and have more favorable attitudes towards computers than females. These gender differences in computer experiences and attitudes as well as the masculinization of the computer culture may be transferred to Internet use and attitudes. In fact, the Internet culture was developed by its earliest users, primarily male scientists, mathematicians, and technologically sophisticated computer hackers. This culture can be discomforting and alien to females.

While Morahan-Martin argues that this gap continues today, at least in terms of use patterns (personal communication, April 26, 2005), the UCLA group (Cole et al., 2003) reported that the majority of both men and women are now online (73.1% of men and 69% of women).

In this respect, this gendered pattern of Internet usage is not new. The telephone was originally the province of white businessmen, but as women gained comfort and familiarity with the medium, it became increasingly used for female social purposes. A report by Williamson in eMarketer (May 2005) shows that as of 2004, women have become the majority of United States Internet users (51.6%) and that trend is expected to continue. Women have embraced the Internet for use in online games, health content, and music, but increasingly are shifting consumer spending to online.

GENDER AND INTERNET USE

It might be suggested that the origins of male interest in video games, and thus their earlier use of computers and the Internet, may be found in sex-related differences in abilities such as spatial skills. It is probable that the decline of these differences is a result, in part, of the increasing invisibility of the computer as a medium of access to the Internet. After all, women use all the other communication media as much as or more than men, once the use of the medium is demystified. This is happening with the Internet as well.

As the Internet increases its penetration into contemporary society, the social skills once typically the province of women are increasingly necessary for effective Internet usage. This social skills need is especially evident in the incidence of disinhibition, more commonly called "flaming," seen in some Internet communications.

This sort of rude behavior is less likely to occur when women are part of the communication cycle. Some suggest that the introduction of "netiquette" can be in part attributed to the increase in numbers of women online.

As research mounts addressing gender issues in Internet usage, some trends have been identified. Ono and Zavodny (2003) reviewed several surveys of gender differences in Internet usage from 1997 through 2000. They found that when controlling for socioeconomic differences, "women were significantly less likely than men to use the Internet at all in the mid-1990s, but this gender gap in being online disappeared by 2000. However, once online, women remain less frequent and less intense users of the Internet" (p. 111). Since this report, others have continued to note a consistent, if small, difference in gender use of the Internet worldwide (Cole et al., 2003; Lebo & Wolpert, 2004). Additionally, gender differences in types of usage have been reported by several groups including the Pew group (Rainie & Kohot, 2000). They note:

- 55% of Internet users say their email exchanges have improved their connections to family members—60% of women assert that; 51% of men say that
- 59% of those who email family members report they communicate more often with significant family members now that they use email—61% of women say that; 56% of men say that
- 66% of Internet users say email has improved their connections with significant friends—71% of women assert that; 61% of men say that
- 60% of those who email friends report they communicate with significant friends more often now that they use email—63% of women assert that; 54% of men say that
- 49% of email users say they would miss email a lot if they could no longer use it—56% of women say that; 43% of men say that (p. 7)

One might conclude that women may not use the Internet as much overall as men, but when they do, it's more for communication. However, these absolute differences are so small that likely they are disappearing.

GENDER AND GAME PLAY

Research has shown that video game play is a strong predictor of later computer and Internet use (Morahan-Martin, 1998). Furthermore, such game play has increasingly has moved online. Meunier (1996) pointed out that males tend to be more interested in computers than are females, but makes some clear statements that this phenomenon stems from socialization both in and outside the schools and different play preferences in video gaming. A 2001 report from the NUA Internet

Survey indicates that the female audience does indeed seek a different gaming experience:

- Women now constitute 50.4% of online gamers, although males represent 55% of total gamers.
- The "Spotlight on Games: Categories and Hardware" study found that men and women prefer different types of games. Women were less likely to play first-person shooter games (12 %) compared to men (38%).
- Women preferred board or card games, with 78% having played such games, in contrast to 51% of males. Quiz, trivia, and gambling-oriented games were also more popular with women.

Although females are less likely to play most forms of electronic games, there are some that they play more often. Jones *et al.* (2003) report that women are more likely to play computer (32%) and Internet (15%) games than are males (19 and 12%, respectively) but less likely to play video games (17% of females versus 53% of males). So, too, reasons for playing differ as a function of gender. Jones *et al.* note that women were more likely to report playing because they were bored while men played for fun. Also, women were "much less likely to believe that gaming improved their relationship with friends than men believed" (Jones *et al.*, 2003; p. 11).

This is illustrated by a recent Nielsen/NetRatings (2004) study which found that for online gamers 35 or older, it was women and not men who dominated. However, some online games still show the male preference. For instance, Griffiths *et al.* (2003) report on two very large surveys from online role playing games (*Everquest* and *Allakhazam*). With almost 18,000 respondents on a question about gender, about 85% were male.

Goldstein (2003), in a review of the gaming literature, notes that this confound of gender with playing frequency has misled researchers in some of their conclusions about the results of gaming. Results may have more to do with gender differences than game playing frequency differences. This is illustrated in another study about online role playing games. "Boys in same-sex pairs interacted with one another through action, rapid changes, and playful exchanges. Girls in same-sex pairs interacted primarily through written dialogue. In mixed pairs, boys wrote more and engaged in less playful exchanges, and girls wrote less and increased their actions." (Calvert *et al.*, 2003; p. 627). These are play behaviors that are typical of gender and not necessarily of online play per se.

That said, it has been suggested that "female gaming is the last frontier; 2006 is going to be a milestone year" (Dickey & Summers, 2005). In a recent *Newsweek* story interviewing industry spokespersons, it was pointed out that although 50% of game purchases are made by women, no one really knows the exact percentage of women playing games. It is widely thought that most of the purchases are for males in their lives. The overlooked potential of women as gamers was discovered by the surprising popularity of *Sims* among women. Fully half of players online and off are women who enjoy the relationship and the creative aspects. In *Sims*, the players can make their own home and engage in various social interactions. But also, to the surprise of the industry, "girls and women started flocking to the fantasy landscapes of sword-and-sorcery universes like World of Warcraft" (Dickey & Summers, 2005). These, as well as other newer online role-playing games like *Fascade* and *Second Life*, are bringing in female gamers.

In a related study and contrary to common assumptions, Anderson *et al.* (2003) found few gender effects on how violent media affects aggression. They note that previous research revealed strong gender differences, with boys more affected by violent content in games than girls. Boys were found to enjoy violent video games more than do girls. However, we know that game designers cater to male characters and interests, with the heroes and action characters always male. Research now shows an interesting gender difference: girls generally prefer fantasy violence, while boys prefer human violence. These are, of course, in line with traditional sex role play preferences and consistent with the gender differences in online role playing games noted earlier in this chapter.

THE INFLUENCE OF AGE, ETHNICITY, CULTURE, AND POVERTY

As noted earlier, when age and gender were controlled for, personality seemed to make less difference in determining Internet use. This is because self is also informed by one's age, ethnicity, culture, and socioeconomic status. In this section, we consider these variables in terms of Internet use. The chapter in this book by Varnhagen on children and the Internet covers an important component of how age influences people's engagement of the Internet with self. Here, we first take a brief look at the elderly and the Internet.

Elderly

The segment of the population least represented among users of the Internet is the elderly. They represent only 18% of households with Internet access, according to the U. S. Census of 2000 (Newburger, 2001). By 2003, the UCLA report (Cole *et al.*, 2003) says that the 65+ group has 34% users. Clearly, Internet usage among the elderly is growing. Noel and Epstein (2003) report upon an online survey of use of the Internet by those 50 years of age or older. They note that "In a comparison of highly social Internet users versus low-social users, we found that high-social users spent more time on-line and reported more physical and mental health problems. However, the groups did not differ in amount of or satisfaction with social support they received" (p. 35).

In a recent report from the Pew Internet and American Life Project (Fox, 2004), 436 seniors who use the Internet were interviewed by telephone. The author reports these highlights:

There have been big increases since 2000 in the number of online seniors doing several key activities. It is important to stress, though, that even with these high growth rates, it is usually the case that online seniors have done these online activities at *lower rates* that younger Internet users.

- 66% of wired seniors had looked for health or medical information online at some point in their online life by the end of 2003. That is a 13-point jump since 2000, and a growth rate of 25%. And online seniors are much more likely than other Internet users to have logged on to get information about Medicare and Medicaid.
- 66% of wired seniors had done product research online by the end of 2003. That is an 18-point jump since 2000 and a growth rate of 38%.
- 47% of online seniors had bought something on the Internet by the end of 2003. That is an 11-point increase since 2000 and a growth rate of 31%.
- 41% had made travel reservations online by the end of 2003. That is a 16-point increase since 2000 and a growth rate of 64%.
- 60% of wired seniors had visited government Web sites by the end of 2003. That is a 20-point jump since 2000 and a growth rate of 50%.
- 26% of wired seniors had looked for religious and spiritual information by the end of 2003. That is a 15-point jump since 2000 and a growth rate of 136%.
- 20% of online seniors had done banking on the Internet by the end of 2003. That is a 12-point increase since 2000 and a growth rate of 150%. (p. ii)

Despite these advances, the elderly are still the least likely to go online among various demographic groupings (Madden & Rainie, 2003). Although it may be a steep learning curve, as the baby boom generation ages, it is likely that more and more will be online.

Socioeconomic Status and Culture

It is not surprising that Internet technology is proving to be the province of the North American middle class, (and, until recently, the *male* middle-class), which by world standards is well-to-do. Historically in Western culture, new communication technology has always been controlled by the economic and social elite.

Enthusiasm about the potential of the Internet to bring the world's peoples together must be tempered by sobering statistics. Norris, in her book *The Digital Divide* (2000), points out that the areas of the world with more money are the areas with more Internet usage. In addition to financial differences, it reflects a general cultural difference. Psychologists point out that the world's cultures can be conceptualized along the dimension of collectivism versus individualism (Larsen & Buss, 2005). Some emphasize the individual's rights while others emphasize group responsibilities. Western, industrial, and Internet-connected cultures, in general, tend to be wealthy and individualistic while Asian, Middle Eastern, South American, and African cultures, which have much lower percentages of Internet connections, tend to be collectivist. The most extreme individualist culture is the United States, with one of the highest levels of Internet connections. Thus, the Internet reflects to a large extent the primacy of self.

Relative to other mass media, worldwide, radios have the widest dissemination, but only 40% of the world's population have radios. Thus, Internet users represent a very small, if influential, segment of the world's population. The Internet is another mass communication technology that may be perpetuating the gap between the haves and the have-nots. Thus, the question of socioeconomic class as well as gender, which has historically related to the power and well-being of an individual, becomes crucial to our understanding of the psychology of the Internet.

On a hopeful note, some data in the early days suggested that Internet use by disadvantaged populations allows them to access electronic mail and information services that can mediate some of the negative circumstances of their lives (Bier, 1997). More recently, Spooner and Rainie (2004) of the Pew Internet and American Life Project reported that the digital divide for African-Americans, who are one of the largest poverty groups in the U. S., is narrowing. There are other places as well where Internet usage among the poor is relatively high, including Sweden and Korea (Lebo & Wolpert, 2004). By relatively high, we mean between 40 and 50% of the poorest individuals in these countries go online. In most other countries, the figure is lower, according to this Pew Project report.

Ethnicity

The ethnicity of online users is also changing, as the following results from NUA Internet Surveys (2001) indicate:

- The number of home Internet users in the U. S. increased by 33% in 2000, with African Americans leading the online growth.
- According to figures from Nielsen/NetRatings (2004), the African American online population increased by 44% to 8.1 million between December 1999 and December 2000.
- Internet use among Hispanics grew by 19% to more than 4.7 million people, while the number of Asian American Internet users reached 2.1 million, an increase of 18%.
- Caucasians remain the largest ethnic group online, currently accounting for 87.5 million of America's home Internet users.

- NetRatings attributed the growth in Internet use across ethnic groups to the lowering cost of PCs and cheaper Internet access. (www.NUA.ie)

In spite of these improvements, the Internet remains a relatively privileged environment, with ethnicity, class, and gender linked to Internet usage in our society.

For example, Badagliacco (1990) has shown that ethnicity affects computer access, use, and attitudes. She found that, just as men have had more computer experience and more favorable attitudes toward computers than have women, so whites have had the most and Hispanics the fewest years of computer experience. Coley notes (1997):

> For college-bound seniors from the class of 1996, word processing exposure was the most frequent type of coursework or experience. Minority group seniors were less likely to have courses or experience in word processing and computer literacy and less likely to use computers in English courses and to solve problems in math and science.

While 85% of U. S. schools surveyed for the study had multimedia computers and 64% had Internet access, Coley found that poor and minority schools had less access. In addition to the economic disadvantage often experienced by nonwhites in getting access to communication technology, the content of the Internet can be a factor. Because it is unregulated, the Internet provides unprecedented opportunity for the distribution of pornographic and racist texts. Such material may, perhaps, cause a person to avoid the medium or to pause before revealing his or her ethnic background. In this way, the Internet may indeed provide an opportunity for blacks and other minorities to reaffirm their rights in Western society.

In a more recent report by the Pew group (Spooner & Rainie, 2004), the racial difference between blacks and whites in the U. S. was examined. Similar to the results shown in previous studies, blacks (36%) do not use the Internet as much as whites do (50%; data from 2000) but when they do, they report higher incidence of usage across a broad band of activities. Specifically, these authors say:

- Online blacks are 69% more likely than online whites to have listened to music on the Web.
- Online blacks are 65% more likely than online whites to have sought religious information on the Web.
- Online blacks are 45% more likely than online whites to have played a game on the Web.
- Online blacks are 38% more likely than online whites to have downloaded music files from the Web.
- Online blacks are 38% more likely than online whites to have sought information about jobs on the Web.
- Online blacks are 30% more likely than online whites to have sought information about a place to live on the Web.
- Online blacks are 20% more likely than online whites to have conducted school research or gotten job training on the Web. (p. 2)

SOCIAL ROLES AND INEQUALITY ONLINE

For nearly 400 years after the invention of the printing press, most Europeans were illiterate. It was only after the advent of compulsory primary education in the mid-nineteenth century that the ability to read became a psychological, social, and economic value. Until very recently, computer literacy was ancillary to individual success in Western society.

However, on a global level, the social ground has shifted. The ability to operate computers and access the Internet has acquired an economic and moral force. As a society, we are beginning to feel that we ought to know how to use these technologies, and that we are somehow intellectually lax if we do not; intellectual slowness has taken on an almost moral overtone. In this climate, traditionally disadvantaged groups (such as women, minorities, and the poor) have a doubly difficult task—mastering a new technology that has been developed for and is still controlled by the gender, cohort, race, and social class that has traditionally controlled everything else.

Many forms of communication technology have been associated with a particular sociopolitical organization. In the history of Western communication technology, the alphabet and the printing press have been lauded as harbingers of democracy and free speech. Many people make similar claims about the Internet; there is a wild and woolly "everyman" aura about the Internet that some people find very inviting. Its seemingly chaotic environment is especially appealing to a young computer-literate generation.

Yet, there is a paradox. The virtual land of free speech and personal freedom has restricted access. The Internet is a racially, sexually, economically coded technology that can prove daunting to many members of society at large. Access to the technology for these people requires a heavy psychoemotional investment that some people may not be able to afford. The payoff for those who do manage to push past the doors of privilege and prejudice is access to a certain kind of power to change their own environment.

REFERENCES

Anderson, C. A. Berkowitz, L., Donnerstein, E., Huesmann, L. R., Johnson, J. D., Linz, D. *et al.* (2003). The influence of media violence on youth. *Psychological Science in the Public Interest, 4(3)*, 81–110.

Badagliacco, J. (1990). Gender and race differences in computing attitudes and experience. Special Issue: Computing: Social and policy issues. *Social Science Computer Review, 8* (1): 42–63.

Bier, M. (1997). *Assessing the effect of unrestricted home Internet access on the underserved community: A case study of four east central Florida families.* Unpublished dissertation from Florida Institute of Technology.

Boyer, M. (1996). *Cybercities: Visual perception in the age of electronic communication.* Princeton: Princeton Architectural Press.

Calvert, S., Mahler, B., Zehnder, S., Jenkins, A., & Less, M. (2003). Gender differences in preadolescent children's online interactions: Symbolic modes of self-presentation and self-expression. *Applied Developmental Psychology, 24*, 627–644.

Cole, J., Suman, M., Schramm, P., Lunn, R., Aquino, J-S., Firth, D. *et al.* (2003). *The UCLA Internet report: Surveying the digital future: Year three.* Los Angeles: UCLA Center for Communications Policy, Retrieved July 21, 2004 from (http://www.ccp.ucla.edu)

Coley, R. (1997). *Computer access lags for minority students.* Retrieved March 17, 2001, from http://www.usatoday.com/life/cyber/tech/cta505.htm.

Dickey, C., & Summers, N. (2005). A female sensibility. *Newsweek International Edition.* Retrieved Oct. 4, 2005, from http://www.msnbc.msn.com/id/9378641/site/newsweek/.

Engelberg, E., & Sjoberg, L. (2004). Internet use, social skills, and adjustment. *CyberPsychology & Behavior. 7(1),* 41–47.

Everton, R. W., Mastrangelo, P. M., & Jolton, J. A. (2005). Personality correlates of employees' personal use of work computers. *CyberPsychology & Behavior, 8(2),* 143–153.

Fox, S. (2004). *Older Americans and the Internet.* Washington, DC: Pew Internet & American Life Project. Retrieved July 19, 2004, from http://www.pewinternet.org/pdfs/PIP_Seniors_Online_2004.pdf.

Goldstein, J. (2003). People @ play: Electronic games. In H. van Oostendorp (Ed.), *Cognition in a digital world* (pp. 25–45). Mahwah, NJ: Lawrence Erlbaum Associates.

Griffiths, M. D., Davies, M. N. O., & Chappell, D. (2003). Breaking the stereotype: The case of online gaming. *CyberPsychology & Behavior, 6(1),* 81–91.

Harman, J. P., Hansen, C. E., Cochran, M. E., & Lindsey, C. R. (2005). Liar, liar: Internet faking but not frequency of use affects social skills, self-esteem, social anxiety, and aggression. *CyberPsychology & Behavior, 8(1),* 1–6.

Hills, P., & Argyle, M. (2003). Uses of the Internet and their relationships with individual differences in personality. *Computers in Human Behavior, 19(1),* 59–70.

Jackson, L., von Eye, A., Biocca, F., Barbatsis, G., Fitzgerald, H., & Zhao, Y. (2003). Personality, cognitive style, demographic characteristics, and Internet use—Findings from the HomeNetToo project. *Swiss Journal of Psychology, 62(2),* 79–90.

Joinson, A. I. (in press). Disinhibition and the Internet. In J. I. Gackenbach (Ed.), *Psychology and the Internet: Intrapersonal, interpersonal, and transpersonal implications* (2nd ed.), San Diego: Academic Press.

Jones, S., Clarke, L. N., Cornish, S., Gonzales, M., Johnson, C., Lawson, J. N. *et al.* (2003, July 6). *Let the games begin: Gaming technology and entertainment among college students.* Washington, DC: Pew Internet and American Life Project.

Krantz, J. H., Ballard, J., & Scher, J. (1997). Comparing the results of laboratory and World-Wide Web samples on the determinants of female attractiveness. *Behavior Research Methods, Instruments & Computers, 29(2),* 264–269.

Kraut, R., Kiesler, S., & Boneva, B. (2002). Internet paradox revisited. *Journal of Social Issues, 58(1),* 49–74.

Kraut, R., Olson, J., Banaji, M., Bruckman, A., Cohen, J., & Couper, M. (2004). Psychological research online: Report of board of scientific affairs' advisory group on the conduct of research on the Internet. *American Psychologist, 59(2),* 105–117.

Kraut, R., Patterson, M., Lundmark, V., Kiesler, S., & Scherlis, W. (1998). Internet paradox: A social technology that reduces social involvement and psychological well-being? *American Psychologist, 53,* 1017–1031.

Larsen, R. J., & Buss, D. M. (2005). *Personality psychology: Domains of knowledge about human nature* (2nd ed.). New York: McGraw Hill.

Lebo, H., & Wolpert, S. (2004, January 14). First release of findings from the UCLA world internet project shows significant "digital gender gap" in many countries. *UCLANEWS.*

Madden, M., & Rainie, L. (2003). America's online pursuits: The changing picture of who's online and what they do. Pew Internet and American Life Project. Retrieved Dec. 31, 2005, from http://www.pewinternet.org/pdfs/PIP_Online_Pursuits_Final.PDF.

Meunier, L. (1996). *Computer background of men and women.* Retrieved May 1998 from http://lists.cmhc.com/research/1997/0626.html. (Note: This item was no longer available online on March 17, 2001.)

Morahan-Martin, J. (1998). Chapter 8: Males, females, and the Internet. *In* J. I. Gackenbach (Ed.), *Psychology and the Internet: Intrapersonal, interpersonal and transpersonal implications* (pp. 169–196). San Diego: Academic Press.

Morahan-Martin, J., & Schumacher, P. (2003). Loneliness and social uses of the Internet. *Computers in Human Behavior, 19(6)*, 659–671.

Morgan, C., & Cotton, S. (2003). The relationship between Internet activities and depressive symptoms in a sample of college freshmen. *Cyberpsychology & Behavior, 6(2)*, 133–142.

Newburger, Eric C. (2001) *Home Computer Use and Internet Use in the United States: August 2000.* U.S. Census Bureau, Current Population Reports, Series P23-207. Washington, DC: U. S. Government Printing Office.

Niederhoffer K. G., & Pennebaker, J. W. (2002). Linguistic synchrony in social interaction *Journal of Language and Social Psychology, 21(4)*, 337–360.

Nicovich, S. G., Boller, G. W., & Cornwell, T. B. (2005). Experienced presence within computer-mediated communications: Initial explorations on the effects of gender with respect to empathy and immersion. *Journal of Computer-Mediated Communications, 10(2)*, Retrieved Oct 12, 2005, from (http://jcmc.indiana.edu/vol10/issue2/nicovich.html)

Nielsen//NetRatings (2004). Online games claim stickiest web sites, according to Nielsen//NetRatings. Retrieved Oct. 4, 2005, from (http://www.internetadsales.com/modules/news/article.php?storyid=1470)

Noel, J., & Epstein, J. (2003). Social support and health among senior internet users: Results of an online survey. *Journal of Technology and Human Services, 21(3)*, 35–54.

Norris, P. (2000). *Digital divide? Civic engagement, information poverty, and the Internet worldwide.* Cambridge: Cambridge University Press. Retrieved July 20, 2004, from (http://ksghome.harvard.edu/.pnorris.shorenstein.ksg/Books/Digital%20Divide.htm)

NUA Internet Surveys. (2001, February 27). *Yahoo: African Americans lead in U.S. Internet growth.* Retrieved March 17, 2001, from (http://www.nua.ie/surveys/?f=VS&art_id=905356501&rel=true)

Ono, H., & Zavodny, M. (2003). Gender and the Internet. *Social Science Quarterly, 84(1)*, 111–121.

Rainie, L., & Kohot, L. (2000). *Tracking online life: How women use the Internet to cultivate relationships with family and friends.* Washington, DC: Pew Internet and American Life Project. Retrieved July 19, 2004, from http://www.pewinternet.org/pdfs/Report1.pdf.

Spooner, T., & Rainie, L. (2004). African-Americans and the Internet. *Pew Online Life Report.* Retrieved July 21, 2004, from http://www.pewinternet.org.

Straus, N. (1997). The fourth blow to narcissism and the Internet. *Literature and Psychology, 43(1–2)*, 96–109.

Suler, J. (2004). The online disinhibition effect. *CyberPsychology & Behavior, 7(3)*, 321–326.

Turkle, S. (1995). Chapter 7: Aspects of the self. From *Life on the Screen: Identity in the age of the Internet* (pp. 177–209, 310–312). New York: Simon and Schuster.

Valkenburg, P. M., Schouten, A. P., & Peter, J. (2005). Adolescents' identity experiments on the internet. *New Media & Society, 7(3)*, 383–402.

Wastlund, E., Norlander, T., & Archer, T. (2001). Internet blues revisited: Replication and extension of an internet paradox study. *CyberPsychology & Behavior, 4(3)*, 385–391.

Williamson, D.A. (2005) *Women online in the U.S.: A growing majority.* e-Marketer Reports; retrieved Dec 27, 2005, from: www.emarketer.com/Report.aspx?women_may05.

Yang, B., & Lester, D. (2003). National character and Internet use. *Psychological Reports. 93(3–1)*, 940.

Yuen, N., & Lavin, M. (2004). Internet dependence and shyness. *CyberPsychology & Behavior, 7(4)*, 379–383.

CHAPTER 4

Disinhibition and the Internet

Adam N. Joinson
The Open University
Milton Keynes, United Kingdom

> **Evidence for Disinhibition**
> **Internet Pornography**
> **Explanations of Disinhibition on the Internet**
> **Conclusions**
> **References**

Over the last ten years of research on psychology and the Internet, there has been a general recognition that people often behave differently when online than in roughly equivalent offline situations (e.g., Joinson, 2003; Suler, 2004). For instance, they might be an outrageous flirt online, while being painfully shy offline. They might gossip and forward others' e-mails online, when they would usually act with discretion. Or, they might seek information online (such as health information or pornography) that they wouldn't dream of doing offline. This general difference has been termed "disinhibition" (Joinson, 1998) or an "online disinhibition effect" (Suler, 2004).

In the definition of disinhibition online provided in the first edition of this book, Joinson (1998), argued that "if inhibition is when behavior is constrained or restrained through self consciousness, anxiety about social situations, worries about public evaluation and so on (Zimbardo, 1977), then disinhibition can be characterized by an absence or reversal of these same factors ... disinhibition on the Internet ... is seen as any behavior that is characterized by an apparent reduction in concerns for self-presentation and the judgement of others" (p. 44).

One advantage (and problem) of the this definition is its vagueness—the use of the word "apparent" allows subsequent explanations to treat reduced concern for self-presentation as a dependent variable with no explanatory effect, or as an independent variable that in some way explains online behavior. Moreover, reduced self-presentation is obviously in the eye of the beholder, allowing researchers to apply their own views of what is "abnormal" to the behavior of those they study. However, disinhibition among computer users has proved to be a difficult term to define (Lea *et al.*, 1992). As a word, it is often used interchangeably with "flaming" (Lea *et al.*, 1992) and has encompassed behaviors ranging from being impolite

Psychology and the Internet: Intrapersonal, Interpersonal, and Transpersonal Implications

(Kiesler *et al.*, 1985) to the use of capital letters or exclamation marks (Sproull & Kiesler, 1986) and expressions of personal feelings toward another person using a computer network (Kiesler *et al.*, 1985).

Others (e.g., Suler, 2004) have avoided providing a definition of disinhibition, but instead have focused on possible causes of an effect. Such explanations usually rely on aspects of the online environment, for instance, anonymity or asynchronicity, to explain disinhibitory effects. In the present chapter, I argue that explanations that rely simply on aspects of the media (e.g., anonymity) and their presumed psychological impact (e.g., reduced concern for impression management) are doomed to fail to fully explain disinhibited behavior online. This is because behavior online does not occur in a vacuum—people have a variety of media to choose from much of the time, and the choice of an online alternative may be due to the expectation that its attributes can be appropriated to satisfy their own needs. So, what looks at first glance to be a disinhibition effect of a media may, in fact, be a strategic choice by the user (Joinson, 2004).

The present chapter focuses on evidence of disinhibition online in two main areas: communication (in the form of self-disclosure and flaming) and information seeking (in the form of the seeking of pornography). There are, of course, many other example of disinhibited behavior (e.g., inappropriate forwarding of e-mail messages), but for the purposes of the present chapter, these will suffice.

EVIDENCE FOR DISINHIBITION

SELF-DISCLOSURE AND THE INTERNET

A large body of experimental and anecdotal evidence suggests that computer-mediated communication (CMC) and general Internet-based behavior can be characterized as containing high levels of self-disclosure. For instance, Rheingold (1993) claims that new, meaningful relationships can be formed in cyberspace because of, not despite, its limitations. He further argues that "the medium will, by its nature ... be a place where people often end up revealing themselves far more intimately than they would be inclined to do without the intermediation of screens and pseudonyms." Similarly, Wallace (1999) argues that, "The tendency to disclose more to a computer ... is an important ingredient of what seems to be happening on the Internet" (p. 151). Self-disclosure has been studied in a number of different settings using computers. For instance, Parks and Floyd (1996) studied the relationships formed by Internet users and found high levels of self-reported disclosure within online relationships. Rosson (1999) analyzed 133 stories posted by Internet users on a resource called "Web Storybase." Overall, 81 of the stories contained personal information of some sort. Rosson concludes that: "users seem to be quite comfortable revealing personal—even quite intimate—details about their lives in this very public forum" (p. 8). Similarly, McKenna and Bargh (1998) argue that participation in online newsgroups gives people the benefit of "disclosing a long secret part of one's self" (p. 682). McKenna and Bargh also found that self-disclosure online had powerful repercussions for "real life":

> As a direct result of Internet newsgroup membership and participation, over 37% of participants in Study 2, and 63% of those in Study 3 revealed to others what had been an embarrassing secret about themselves (p. 691).

More recently, Chesney (2005), in a small scale study of online diaries, reported high levels of disclosure of sensitive information, with half of his participants claiming to never withhold information from their diaries.

In the series of studies reported by Joinson (2001), the level of self-disclosure was measured using content analysis of transcripts of face-to-face (FtF) and synchronous CMC discussions (study one), and in conditions of visual anonymity and video links during CMC (study two). In keeping with the predicted effect, self-disclosure was significantly higher when participants chatted using a CMC system as opposed to FtF. In the second study, incorporating a video link while the participants chatted using the CMC program led to levels of self-disclosure similar to the FtF levels, while the comparison condition (no video link) led to significantly higher levels of self-disclosure.

These two studies together provide empirical support that visually anonymous CMC tends to lead to higher levels of self-disclosure. The results of these studies also suggest that high levels of self-disclosure can effectively be designed out of an Internet interaction (e.g., through the use of a video link or accountability cues (Joinson, 2001, study 3), as well as encouraged.

Further empirical confirmation of increased self-disclosure during CMC comes from the work of Tidwell and Walther (2002). They proposed that heightened self-disclosure during CMC may be due to people's motivation to reduce uncertainty. According to Uncertainty Reduction Theory (URT; Berger & Calabrese, 1975), people are motivated to reduce uncertainty in an interaction to increase predictability. In FtF interaction, uncertainty can be reduced through both verbal and nonverbal communication and cues. Tidwell and Walther hypothesize that during CMC, uncertainty-reducing behaviors are text-based only, including increased levels of self-disclosure and question asking. To test this, Tidwell and Walther recruited 158 students to hold a discussion in opposite sex pairs with an unknown partner using a CMC system or FtF. The subsequent conversations were content analyzed for disclosure using the breadth and depth of self-disclosure indices developed by Altman and Taylor (1973).

Tidwell and Walther found that those in the CMC condition displayed higher levels of both question asking and self-disclosure compared with the FtF condition. The questions asked by CMC discussants were also more probing and intimate than those asked by those talking FtF, while both the questions and disclosure by FtF interactants tended to be more peripheral than those in the CMC condition. Tidwell and Walther conclude that the limitations of CMC encourage people to adapt their uncertainty-reducing behaviors—they skip the usual asking of peripheral questions and minor disclosure and instead opt for more direct, intimate questioning and self-disclosure.

Surveys and research administered via the Internet, rather than using paper methodologies, have also been associated with reductions in socially desirable responding (Frick *et al.*, 2001; Joinson, 1999), higher levels of self-disclosure (Weisband & Kiesler, 1996) and an increased willingness to answer sensitive questions (see Tourangeau, 2004).

In a similar vein, survey methodology techniques that tend to reduce human involvement in question administration also increase responses to sensitive personal questions. For instance, compared to other research methods, when data collection is conducted via computer-aided self-interviews (where participants type their answers on to a laptop), people report more health-related problems (Epstein *et al.*, 2001), more HIV risk behaviors (Des Jarlais *et al.*, 1999), more drug use (Lessler *et al.*, 2000), and men report fewer sexual partners and women more (Tourangeau & Smith, 1996). Medical patients tend to report more symptoms and undesirable behaviors when interviewed by computer rather than FtF (Greist *et al.*, 1973). Clients at a STD clinic report more sexual partners, more previous visits, and more symptoms to a computer than to a doctor (Robinson & West, 1992). Ferriter (1993) found that preclinical psychiatric interviews conducted using CMC compared to FtF yielded more honest, candid answers. Similarly, automated or computerized telephone interviews, compared to other forms of telephone interviewing, led to higher levels of reporting of sensitive information (see Lau *et al.*, 2003; Tourangeau, 2004).

Conversely, methods that increase the social presence of the surveyor (e.g., by using photographs of the researcher) have been predicted to lead to a reduced willingness to answer sensitive questions (Tourangeau *et al.*, 2003), although the findings of Tourangeau *et al.* were equivocal. However, Sproull *et al.*(1996) found that participants "present themselves in a more positive light to the talking-face displays" (p. 116) than to text-only interfaces. Joinson *et al.* (in press) reports that although personalizing the research experience leads to higher response rates to a self-administered survey, it also reduces self-disclosure. Given the need for high response rates to reduce sampling error in surveys, and the need for candid disclosure to maintain data quality, this potential tradeoff between response rates and disclosure is important. Joinson *et al.* suggests that the provision of "I prefer not to say" options may well provide one route to manage the tradeoff because respondents with compromised anonymity can still complete the survey without a subsequent loss of privacy.

FLAMING AND ANTI-SOCIAL BEHAVIOR

In its original format, "flaming" referred to incessant talking or pointless chatter. However, it came to be generally seen as negative or antisocial behavior on computer networks. When such antagonistic or aggressive messages are traded between people, it becomes a "flame war." Academic research into flaming has been hampered by a lack of clarity in the definitions used to measure it in laboratory research.

For instance, Kiesler *et al.* (1985) operationalized flaming as:

- impolite statements
- swearing/flirting
- exclamations
- expressions of personal feelings toward another
- the use of superlatives

Other operationalizations of flaming include items such as profanity, "typographic energy" (e.g., exclamation marks), name calling, swearing, and general negative affect. When the focus of a research project moves from flaming to "uninhibited" communication, the definition widens to include even non-task-based messages and conveying bad news.

A further problem with the definition and operationalization of flaming is its *a priori* link to computer-mediated communication (Lea *et al.*, 1992). In many instances, flaming is, by definition, something that either only occurs on computer networks, is unique to computer networks, or is more evident on computer networks than face-to-face.

EMPIRICAL EVIDENCE FOR FLAMING

According to Selfe and Meyer (1991), "heated, emotional, sometimes anonymous, venting ... is a common, if not universal, feature of computer-based conferences" (p. 170).

In three early studies outlined in Kiesler *et al.* (1984) the levels of uninhibited verbal behavior were compared in four conditions: face-to-face communication, anonymous computer conferencing (one-to-many), non-anonymous computer conferencing (one-to-many), and e-mail. In the experiments, groups of three people were asked to reach a consensus using a choice–dilemma task (a dilemma where groups weigh up two possible choices, often a risky and cautious option, and come to a joint decision). The researchers also found higher levels of uninhibited verbal behavior (defined in this instance as hostile comments such as swearing, name calling, and insults) in each experiment when people used computers to communicate.

The highest levels of uninhibited behavior were recorded when people discussed anonymously using a real time (synchronous) computer-conferencing system.

Castellá *et al.* (2000) compared levels of flaming between groups discussing a dilemma using e-mail, video-conferencing, or face-to-face. They categorized flaming into "informal speech" (including "ironic comments" and "expressions which try to endow the written speech with certain characteristics of oral speech" (p. 148)) and flaming (aggressive and overtly hostile comments). They found that flaming occurred 94 times in the text-based discussions (4.72% of remarks), compared to 8 times (0.21%) and 16 times (0.39) in face-to-face and video conferencing conditions, respectively.

So, although flaming was rare, it was significantly more likely to occur in the text-based discussions than face-to-face or video conferencing. In further analyses of the data, Castellá *et al.* found no links between an individual's assertiveness or the familiarity of the group and flaming, although being more familiar with the other group members did predict levels of informal speech.

Aiken and Waller (2000) studied two groups of business students who discussed the impeachment of President Clinton and parking problems on campus (both judged as reasonably controversial issues). They found that flaming comments were written by a small but consistent group of people, who were all male. In one group, 20% of the individuals wrote flaming messages for the parking discussion, and 50% for the president discussion. All participants who wrote flaming messages in the first discussion also wrote them in the second. But, they found no links between the controversy or perceived importance of the topic and flaming, suggesting that "flames are probably due to the characteristics (such as gender, level of maturity, hostility, etc.) of the individual writing them" (p. 99). Indeed, Smolensky *et al.* (1990) found that uninhibited communication was related to an individual's level of extroversion, as well as the level of familiarity within the group.

Coleman *et al.* (1999) examined the discussions of 58 face-to-face and 59 CMC participants discussing a set topic in groups of 3–7 people. The subsequent discussions were rated on (among other things), negativity. Positive or neutral statements were scored as 1; statements containing overt disagreement or criticism scored 2; and profanity, hostility, and name-calling were scored as 3. The level of negativity between the two groups did not differ: For the CMC groups, it was 1.24, while for the FtF groups, it was 1.21. However. Coleman *et al.* do note that all cases of "level 3" negativity, while rare, occurred in the CMC condition.

A second type of study into flaming involves asking Internet users to report post hoc the number of flames they see FtF and during CMC. One such study was conducted by Sproull and Kiesler (1986) when they studied the e-mail communications of 96 staff working for a large organization in the United States. They studied the e-mail communication of 96 staff, as well as collecting questionnaire responses. In accordance with their predictions, Sproull and Kiesler found that their participants reported seeing 33 flames on e-mail in a month, and just 4 in face-to-face interaction.

In summary, then, although flaming is relatively rare, there is evidence that it is more likely to occur in CMC than FtF encounters. However, part of the problem is the archival nature of much CMC—a single flame can be forwarded, saved, and reread online. This might introduce a bias in favor of CMC as a location of flaming, because flames are more likely to be recalled under these circumstances.

DISINHIBITION AND THE WORLD WIDE WEB (WWW)

Throughout this discussion, the focus of attention has been communication. However, there is also considerable evidence that behavior on the World Wide Web, while not necessary "deviant," can be seen (at least at times) as disinhibited. Psychological studies of the WWW tend to focus on three main areas: the use of the WWW for conducting psychological research (e.g., Birnbaum, 2004); interaction with WWW interfaces and usability; and psychological processes involved in WWW behavior.

However, despite its importance in popularizing the Internet outside academic and military circles, the psychological processes associated with information seeking (or "browsing") on the World Wide Web has received scant attention from psychological researchers. Of the few studies published that do not deal exclusively with its use as a research tool, the majority deal with the evaluation of WWW sites, or in rare cases, the use of search engines and/or navigation strategies from a human–computer interaction perspective. This pattern is repeated in medical research, with the majority of work that deals with the WWW focusing almost exclusively on the content of the Web sites rather than users' behavior in accessing information.

The omission of the WWW from the body of developing knowledge of social behavior on the Internet is problematic because the WWW drove much of the development on the Internet in terms of usage and application/innovation. While the almost limitless amount of information available on the WWW is often touted as one of the main reasons to access the Internet, little is known about the psychological processes that underpin the seeking of that information.

INTERNET PORNOGRAPHY

One area of WWW behavior that has received some research attention is the accessing of pornographic material. Pornography is considerably more accessible on the Internet than on paper. This increase in accessibility not only circumvents any locally held laws on obscenity (effectively reducing what is acceptable to the lowest common denominator because that is where Web sites will be hosted), but it also removes many of the psychological inhibitions associated with, say, purchasing pornography in one's local shop.

It is commonly alleged that pornography has been at the forefront of technological developments on the WWW. To be sure, pornographers have been quick to use new technologies—the invention of photography, the telephone and telegraph, cinema and 8mm film, and VHS video has quickly been followed by the use of the technology for pornography. Moreover, as different technologies have been adopted, the consumption of pornography has become increasingly a private affair. The cost of producing and distributing cinema-quality film meant that, until the advent of video, most pornography was viewed by groups. The development of peep shows (where individuals watch pornography in a small booth relatively anonymously) served to privatize pornography (and was a massive success before the advent and widespread adoption of video in the mid to late 1970s). Indeed, back in the 1980s, it was similarly argued that pornography and horror movies were the "killer app" of video—and video "nasties" were implicated in negative social outcomes in the same way the Internet is today.

However, the content and quantity of pornography on the Internet has been under-researched by cyberpsychologists. In part, this is due to the controversy that followed the publication and ensuing publicity of a study by Rimm in 1995. Rimm, a researcher at Carnegie Mellon University, surveyed sexually explicit images available on Usenet and pay-to-view subscription services. The report was picked up by *Time* magazine, which ran a cover story on "CYBERPORN!" Based in part on the study by Rimm, the *Time* magazine story claimed that 83.5% of images on Usenet are pornographic in nature, and that trading in pornography is one of the most popular, if not the most popular, activity on the Internet. However, the data collected by Rimm didn't support this at all. Of the 900,000 occurrences of sexually explicit material collected, less than 1% came from Usenet—the rest from the subscription servers (that generally require credit card details). Following the ensuing outcry from Internet users who felt tarred by this allegation, independent investigations were conducted by both Carnegie Mellon and Georgetown University (who had originally published the study in their *Law Review*). *Time* magazine posted a partial retraction of their story. But, the idea that the Internet is awash with pornography still persists.

FORMATS OF PORNOGRAPHY ON THE INTERNET

Rimm's study of pornographic images attempted to analyze them for content by automatically collecting the descriptions of the images. As the description of the images is likely to be more linked to advertising than necessarily the actual content, it is likely that this method inflated the level of obscenity.

To counter this inflation of obscenity, Mehta and Plaza (1997) analyzed 150 sexually explicit images taken from 17 newsgroups on a single day in 1994. A majority of the images posted were by anonymous noncommercial Usenet users (65%). The main themes that emerged from the analysis were closeups of human genitalia (43%), erect penises (35%), fetishes (33%), and masturbation (21%). The amount of material most likely to be deemed illegal in most countries was also high: 15% of the images either contained children or adolescents or signified youth in the image or text. Other paraphelias were noted, including bondage and discipline (10%), the insertion of foreign objects (17%), bestiality (10%), incest (1%), and urination (3%). Mehta and Plaza note that the distribution of types of images is similar to that found by Rimm in his study of bulletin boards.

Mehta and Plaza also note that the content of Internet pornography seems to differ from that of magazines and videos. For instance, fellatio, homosexuality, and group sex were more often found on Internet sites (15, 18, and 11%, respectively) than in comparable studies of traditional media (8.1, 2–4, and 1–3%, respectively). Compared to the anonymous, noncommercial users, commercial users (i.e., those effectively posting advertisements) were significantly more likely to post explicit material (use of a foreign object, fellatio, and children/adolescents).

Mehta and Plaza (1997) conclude that the amount of explicit/illegal material posted by commercial users reflects an unregulated, fiercely competitive market where pay-to-view bulletin board and Web sites need to offer something different (i.e., increasingly explicit or unusual images). They also note that many of the images of children or adolescents gave the illusion of youth, but may well have been a model aged over 18. None of the images involving children or adolescents were sexually explicit—"the vast majority of the small number of images depicting children and adolescents probably come from nudist magazines.... We never came across an image depicting a sexual act between an adult and a child/adolescent, or acts between children." (Mehta & Plaza, 1997, p. 64). They further note that most of the images uploaded by users seemed to be scanned directly from magazines.

Manning et al. (1997) presented some early evidence from the HomeNet study that suggests that although many Internet users might have once looked at sexually explicit material on the Internet, few return to do so again. Curiosity, then, rather than any other variable would seem to drive many initial visits to Internet pornography sites.

However, the perception of anonymity of Web browsing may well make the accessing of pornographic images socially and psychologically safer online than offline. Of course, it is also considerably more convenient, as well as providing, at least for home users, privacy of consumption (something pornography distributors aim for much of the time).

Anonymity, or at least the perception of anonymity, is the usual explanation for disinhibited Web behavior (e.g., Joinson, 1998). However, to fully understand the impact of anonymity on Web behavior, we need to take into account the various types of anonymity and differential impact on behavior. So, perhaps a home user with an anonymous ISP account or direct dial in to a bulletin board will feel anonymous when seeking online pornography. But, for the vast majority of users, anonymity is also associated with the recognition that their privacy is an illusion when online.

When we talk about anonymity, we need to think of to whom the user is anonymous. Not the Web site, to be sure, which may have not only his or her credit card details, but also details of their IP address or at least their ISP.

In this case, the user may well be seeking information or images away from the gaze of friends, family, or local community, and willingly accepts (or ignores) other privacy concerns. The perception of anonymity is something to be designed into systems, rather than something that the Internet provides as a birthright. Sites that design in a clear lack of anonymity (e.g., compulsory registration procedures) are effectively entering a negotiation with potential users that may well limit the potential benefits of anonymity on Internet behavior. When we think about anonymity and Web behavior, we also need to factor in the actual content sought and, as such, the users' concern about how willing they are to suspend privacy concerns in seeking information. For someone browsing health information sites, perhaps the balance between relative anonymity (compared to, say, picking up leaflets in a local medical center) and privacy concerns wins out. For someone seeking potentially illegal or vulnerable material, privacy and anonymity concerns need to be addressed through the design of systems or protocols that address these concerns before we see a disinhibitory effect.

EXPLANATIONS OF DISINHIBITION ON THE INTERNET

DEINDIVIDUATION

The concept of deindividuation can be traced to French researcher Gustave Le Bon in 1895. Le Bon argued that being a member of a crowd led to submergence, a state where the normal constraints on individual behavior are removed. Within modern experimental social psychology, the term deindividuation was coined by Festinger et al. (1952) to explain why males who remember less individuating information show more hostility toward their parents. According to Festinger et al., when a person is not individuated in a group, "there is likely to occur for the member a reduction of inner constraints" (p. 382). This approach was extended by the research of Zimbardo (1969). According to Zimbardo, anonymity, arousal, sensory overload, mind-altering drugs, and a reduction in self-focus lead to deindividuation and thence to disinhibited, hostile behavior. During the 1970s and early 1980s, deindividuation theory was subjected to a series of reformulations, variously taking into account the role of reduced internal focus (Diener, 1980) and reduced awareness of the public component of one's own behavior (Prentice-Dunn & Rogers, 1982). Prentice-Dunn and Rogers suggest that deindividuation is caused by two factors: a reduction in accountability cues (e.g., anonymity or membership of a group leads to reduced concern about others' reactions) and reduced private self-awareness (and therefore decreased self-regulation and use of internal standards). According to some CMC researchers, people communicating via computers may be deindividuated. For instance, Kiesler *et al.* (1984) argue that when a CMC user is anonymous, and perhaps he or she is focused on the task at hand, rather than the recipient of their internal standards, then he or she is deindividuated. However, this view of the average CMC user as deindividuated has been strongly criticized (Lea *et al.*, 1992; Postmes & Spears, 1998; Reicher *et al.*, 1995). Lea *et al.* (1992) argue that CMC is not antinormative (as suggested by the deindividuation explanation), but rather is sometimes under the control of norms derived from an active social identity.

Reduced Social Cues

An associated explanation of disinhibited online behavior comes from the limited bandwidth of CMC networks, and an alleged subsequent reduction in social cues during interaction. This, according to the reduced social cues approach, leads to a reduction in the influence of social norms and constraints (Kiesler *et al.*, 1984;) and thus leads to antinormative and deregulated behavior.

According to the reduced social cues (RSC) model, lower social and contextual cues leads to (a) an attentional shift toward the task rather than the recipient, (b) a reduction in the normal hierarchy by removing status cues, leadership cues, and so on, and (c) deindividuation, caused by a combination of anonymity, lack of self- and other-focus, and lowered self-regulation (see Spears & Lea, 1992, for a summary of this approach).

However, the RSC approach has been strongly criticized for taking the "socialness" out of CMC (see Spears & Lea, 1992). According to the RSC model, social influence in CMC will be primarily based on the balance of information exchanged (Kiesler *et al.*, 1984). However, Spears and Lea (1992) summarize group polarization research that suggests that CMC, in certain circumstances, adheres to normative influence rather than lending itself to antinormative behavior.

However, the development of online relationships, alongside the development of interpersonal social cues (e.g., smilies, action signs) and category cues contained in e-mail headers and signatures (e.g., gender, location, occupation), suggests that CMC does not lack "socialness" (Spears & Lea, 1992).

Two-Component Self-Awareness Model

It has also been argued that the disinhibition often seen in studies of CMC may be due to higher rather than lower self-focus (Joinson, 2001; Matheson & Zanna, 1988). According to Duval and Wicklund (1972), conscious attention can be directed toward the environment (termed "public" self-awareness) or toward the self (termed "private" self-awareness). Public self-awareness is induced by situations in which an individual is aware of the possibility of being evaluated (e.g., when being videotaped or assessed) or when they are socially distinctive (e.g., when they are a minority in a group). Private self-awareness is when the person is aware of their inner motives, attitudes, goals, and so on, and can be induced, for instance, by having people look into a mirror. Being privately self-aware should lead to behavior's being regulated by individual goals, needs, and standards (Carver & Scheier, 1981). According to Matheson and Zanna, private and public self-awareness are considered to be "relatively orthogonal" (p. 222), that is, one can be aware of "both, one or neither aspect of the self" (p. 222).

Matheson and Zanna argue that evidence from CMC suggests that people may have increased private self-awareness, and reduced public self-awareness, during CMC. As greater self-disclosure is associated with heightened private self-consciousness (Franzoi & Davis, 1985), this would suggest that computer users experience increased private self-awareness since we see increased self-disclosure online. Furthermore, people tend to respond in less socially desirable ways when communicating via a computer compared to pen-and-paper tests (Kiesler & Sproull, 1986), regardless of their level of anonymity (Joinson, 1999). This suggests that an increase in private self-awareness is likely to be linked with a decrease in concerns for evaluation, or public self-awareness.

Matheson and Zanna (1988) tested this notion in a study comparing the levels of self-awareness of 27 introductory psychology students discussing a topic using computers and 28 students discussing the same topic FtF. They found that "users of computer-mediated communication reported greater private self-awareness and marginally lower public self-awareness than subjects communicating face-to-face" (p. 228).

This suggests that while self-presentation concerns are reduced (via lower public self-awareness), self-regulation and focus on internal states and standards may be enhanced (via higher private self-awareness). Matheson and Zanna themselves raise the two main criticisms of this study: First, participants only discussed for 15 minutes; second, the two items comprising the measure of private self-awareness seem to lack internal reliability.

Joinson (2001, Study 3), rather than relying on measures, instead manipulated private and public self-awareness while dyads talked using a CMC system. Private self-awareness was increased by using a video feed of the participant onto their own screen as an equivalent of a mirror. It was reduced by replacing this video feed with a cartoon. Public self-awareness was reduced by stressing anonymity and increased by increasing accountability cues. The results showed that the condition in which high private and low public self-awareness were combined led to high levels of self-disclosure, similar to those seen in naturalistic CMC environments.

Sassenberg *et al.* (2005) examined the role of private self-awareness in attitude change during CMC. They found that the impact of media (CMC versus FtF) on attitude change was mediated by private self-awareness—that is, reduced attitude change during CMC compared to FtF was dependent upon increases in private self-awareness during CMC. In a second study, they also found evidence that trait private self-awareness moderated the impact of medium on attitude change. Together, these studies confirm the role of self-awareness in understanding the impact of CMC on behavior.

The work of both Joinson and Sassenberg *et al.* suggests that online behavior can be understood in an interpersonal sense. That is, our focus on ourselves relative to other people explains (some) aspects of online behavior. However, in common with the next model (SIDE), the self-awareness approach suggests that online behavior is regulated—by either our own attitudes and beliefs (through increased private self-awareness) or our group memberships and associated attitudes (through salient social identities).

SOCIAL IDENTITY EXPLANATION OF DEINDIVIDUATION EFFECTS (SIDE)

A further explanation of CMC behavior comes from a SIDE model (Reicher *et al.*, 1995). According to this model, most deindividuation effects, from those reported by Zimbardo (1969) onward, can be explained without recourse to deindividuation. Anonymity, because of the lack of focus on the self as an individual, tends to lead to the activation of social identities rather than the activation of personal identities (Reicher *et al.*, 1995). This leads to the regulation of behavior based on the norms associated with the salient social group. For instance, Reicher *et al.* (1995) report a study on group polarization in which the salience of a group membership (in this case, as a psychology student) and the anonymity of the participants was manipulated. Group polarization is the tendency for a group's attitudes to become more extreme (in the direction of the average attitude) following group discussion. Reicher *et al.* predicted that there would be an interaction between group salience and anonymity. In other words, when participants were visually anonymous and their group membership was salient, there would be greater polarization of attitudes following group discussion. This is because the participants are using group norms to direct their behavior. When they are identifiable and the group membership is salient, it was predicted that no group polarization would occur. This is indeed what they found, suggesting that "the combination of psychological group membership and anonymity in the group results in enhanced conformity to group norms, rather than anti-normative behavior" (Reicher *et al.*, 1995, p. 182).

The SIDE model has slightly more difficulty explaining general disinhibition, rather than group polarization, during CMC. One explanation is to discount the existence of uninhibited verbal behavior, and argue that it may be both context-dependent and normative within CMC (e.g., Lea *et al.*, 1992). However, this requires a social identity to be salient, and that the norms associated with that social identity are toward disinhibition. Certainly, that disinhibition in CMC can be characterized by both flaming and excessive self-disclosure suggests that the SIDE model is right in predicting that behavior on computer networks is context dependent. However, that it exists when the user is non-anonymous, and that much of the information is self-relevant, suggests that it might not always be caused by the activation of a social identity.

MULTI-FACTOR EXPLANATIONS AND DISINHIBITION

Suler (2004) identifies six main factors that lead to an "online disinhibition effect," some previously well established, others based on psychoanalytic theory. These are dissociative anonymity, invisibility, asynchronicity, solipsistic introjection, dissociative imagination, and minimization of authority. Suler argues that anonymity online allows people to compartmentalize their online selves and rationalize that their online behaviors 'aren't really me at all" (p. 322). Invisibility, according to Suler, is visual anonymity (as used by the SIDE researchers)—that is, although many online interactants know each other, visual anonymity leads to a situation akin to the traditional psychotherapist sitting behind the client to encourage disclosure. Asynchronicity enables people to engage in "emotional hit and run"; they don't need to face the immediate reaction to their behavior. Meanwhile, solipsistic introjection is due to the lack of visual or verbal cues—Internet users read e-mail messages in their own voice in their head, leading to processes of merging and possibly transference. When combined with dissociative imagination—that we can leave imaginary world of the Internet behind when we switch off the computer—according to Suler, we can also leave behind any responsibility for our behavior in this different realm. Finally, Suler claims that the Internet causes the minimization of authority, again encouraging disinhibited behavior.

A PRIVACY-BASED APPROACH TO UNDERSTANDING DISINHIBITION

Joinson and Paine (in press) have argued that the increased surveillance of Internet activities renders explanations based solely on anonymity unviable. Instead, they have argued that we need to ask to whom is a user non-anonymous, and in what form? For instance, the Internet, and new media in general, have tended to erode privacy through, among other methods, data mining, cookies, and data footprints. Often, the impression of privacy is a mirage; high levels of personal information are held by a number of gatekeepers through the processes of registration, caches, and logs kept on various servers or even locally based records. It therefore becomes critical to grasp the role of these gatekeepers to understand fully disinhibition online. Joinson and Paine (in press) propose that as well as looking at the micro-level impacts of the media environment on disclosure, one also needs to look at the macro-level—the wider context in which the micro-level behavior is enacted. Specifically, Joinson and Paine identify trust, control, and costs and benefits as critical to understanding any disinhibitory effect. Specifically, they point out that often we "purchase" access to an environment in which we can act in a disinhibited manner by leaving our personal information with a trusted gatekeeper (e.g., a website owner via a registration form). Joinson and Paine argue that this enables users to purchase pseudonymity, for instance, through the use of nicknames on a chat server. A second process that Joinson and Paine identify relates to the costs and benefits of an activity. Many "disinhibited" activities conducted online (e.g., cybersex, self-disclosure, accessing pornography) carry a cost in real life. Self-disclosure can make the discloser vulnerable to others, while accessing pornography can be a cause of embarrassment or shame. The Internet may well address this balance of costs and benefits by reducing the likely cost of a behavior—disclosing secrets is easier if the recipient doesn't know who you are. Finally, Joinson and Paine argue that control is also a critical issue. Walther (1996) argues that hyperpersonal social interaction online occurs, at least in part, because of the increased control afforded by asynchronous, visually anonymous CMC. For instance, we can control what information we choose to disclose, in what manner, and how we disclose it. By removing control from CMC (for instance, by introducing video or synchronicity), we also remove control, and thus compromise privacy. Clearly then, according to this approach, we need to fully appreciate not only the aspects of the media that enable disinhibited behavior, but also the motivations and psychological processes of the individual users and their particular social context.

CONCLUSIONS

Disinhibition is one of the few widely reported and noted media effects of online interaction. However, despite the evidence that disinhibition occurs in a number of different contexts online, including CMC, Web-logs and submission of Web forms, most approaches to understanding the phenomenon confine themselves to considering the impact of a single factor—anonymity. I would argue that by focusing solely on this micro-level media effect, the wider context in which the behavior is conducted is ignored—and that ignoring this context limits how we can conceptualize online behavior. By considering the wider context, and in particular, its implications for privacy, it is possible to develop a more nuanced picture of disinhibited online behavior across situations.

REFERENCES

Aiken, M., & Waller, B. (2000). Flaming among first-time group support system users. *Information and Management, 37*, 95–100.

Altman, I., & Taylor, D. (1973) *Social penetration: The development of interpersonal relationships.* New York: Holt, Rinehart and Winston.

Berger, C. R., & Calabrese, R. J. (1975) Some explorations in initial interaction and beyond: Toward a developmental theory of interpersonal communication. *Human Communication Theory, 1*, 99–112

Birnbaum, M. H. (2004). Human research and data collection via the Internet. *Annual Review of Psychology, 55*, 803–832.

Carver, C. S., & Scheier, M. F. (1981). *Attention and self-regulation: A control theory approach to human behavior.* New York: Springer Verlag.

Castellá, V.O., Abad, A. M. Z., Alonso, F. P., & Silla, J. M. P. (2000). The influence of familiarity among group members, group atmosphere, and assertiveness on uninhibited behaviour through three different communication media. *Computers in Human Behavior, 16*, 141–159.

Chesney, T. (March, 2005). *Online self disclosure in diaries and its implications for knowledge managers.* UKAIS Conference, Northumbria University, United Kingdom.

Coleman, L. H., Paternite, C. E., & Sherman, R. C. (1999). A reexamination of deindividuation in synchronous computer-mediated communication. *Computers in Human Behavior, 15*, 51–65.

Diener, E. (1980). Deindividuation: The absence of self-awareness and self-regulation in group members, In P. Paulus (Ed.), *The psychology of group influence* (pp. 209–242). Hillsdale, NJ: Lawrence Erlbaum.

Des Jarlais, D. C., Paone, D., Milliken, J., Turner, C. F., Miller, H., Gribble, J., Shi, Q., Hagan, H., & Friedman, S. (1999) Audio-computer interviewing to measure risk behaviour for HIV among injecting drug users: A quasi-randomised trial. *The Lancet 353* (9165): 1657–1661.

Duval, S., & Wicklund, R. A. (1972). *A theory of objective self-awareness.* New York: Academic Press.

Epstein, J. F., Barker, P. R., & Kroutil, L. A. (2001) Mode effects in self-reported mental health data. *Public Opinion Quarterly, 65*, 529–550.

Ferriter, M. (1993). Computer aided interviewing and the psychiatric social history. *Social Work and Social Sciences Review, 4*, 255–263.

Festinger, L., Pepitone, A., & Newcomb, T. (1952). Some consequences of deindividuation in a group. *Journal of Abnormal and Social Psychology, 47*, 382–389.

Franzoi, S. L., and Davis, M. H. (1985). Adolescent self-disclosure and loneliness: Private self-consciousness and parental influences. *Journal of Personality and Social Psychology, 48*, 768–780.

Frick, A., Bächtiger, M. T., & Reips, U. D. (2001) Financial incentives, personal information and dropout in online studies. In U. D. Reips & M. Bosnjak (Eds.), *Dimensions of Internet Science,* (pp. 209–219). Lengerich: Pabst: Germany.

Greist, J. H., Klein, M. H., & VanCura, L. J. (1973) A computer interview by psychiatric patient target symptoms. *Archives of General Psychiatry, 29*, 247–253

Joinson, A. N. (1998). Causes and effects of disinhibition on the Internet. In J. Gackenbach (Ed.) *The psychology of the Internet* (pp. 43–60). New York: Academic Press.

Joinson, A. N. (1999) Anonymity, disinhibition, and social desirability on the Internet. *Behaviour Research Methods, Instruments and Computers, 31*, 433–438.

Joinson, A. N. (2001) Self-disclosure in computer-mediated communication: The role of self-awareness and visual anonymity. *European Journal of Social Psychology, 31,* 177–192

Joinson, A.N. (2003) *Understanding the psychology of Internet behaviour: Virtual worlds, real lives.* Basingstoke and New York: Palgrave Macmillan.

Joinson, A.N. (2004). Self-esteem, interpersonal risk and preference for e-mail to face-to-face communication. *CyberPsychology and Behaviour,* 7 (4), 472–478.

Joinson, A. N., and Paine, C. B. (in press). Self-disclosure, privacy and the Internet. In A. N. Joinson, K. Y. A. McKenna T. Postmes, T., and U.-R. Reips (Eds). *Oxford Handbook of Internet Psychology.* Oxford: Oxford University Press.

Joinson, A.N., Woodley, A., & Reips, U.-R. (in press). Personalization, authentication, and self-disclosure in self-administered Internet surveys. *Computers in Human Behavior.*

Kiesler, S., & Sproull, L. S. (1986). Response effects in the electronic survey. *Public Opinion Quarterly, 50,* 402–413.

Kiesler, S., Siegal, J., & McGuire, T. W. (1984). Social psychological aspects of computer mediated communication. *American Psychologist,* 39, 1123–1134.

Kiesler, S., Zubrow, D., Moses, A. M., & Geller, V. (1985). Affect in computer mediated communication: An experiment in synchronous terminal-to-terminal discussion. *Human Computer Interaction, 1,* 77–104.

Lau, J. T. F., Tsui, H. Y., & Wang, Q. S. (2003) Effects of two telephone survey methods on the level of reported risk behaviours. *Sexually Transmitted Infections, 79,* 325–331.

Lea, M., O'Shea, T., Fung, P., & Spears, R. (1992). "Flaming" in computer-mediated communication. In M. Lea (Ed.). *Contexts in computer-mediated communication* (pp. 89–112). London: Harvester Wheatsheaf.

Lessler, J.T., Caspar, R.A., Penne, M.A., and Barker, P.R. (2000) Developing computer assisted interviewing (CAI) for the National Household Survey on Drug Abuse. *Journal of Drug Issues,* 30, 19–34

Le Bon, G. (1995). *The crowd: A study of the popular mind.* London: Transaction Publishers. (Original published 1895).

Manning, J., Scherlis, W., Kiesler, S., Kraut, R., & Mukhopadhyay, T. (1997). Erotica on the Internet: Early evidence from the HomeNet trial. In S. Kiesler (Ed.), *Culture of the Internet* (pp. 68–69). Nahwah, NJ: Lawrence Erlbaum.

Matheson, K., and Zanna, M. P. (1988). The impact of computer-mediated communication on self-awareness. *Computers in Human Behaviour, 4,* 221–233.

McKenna, K.Y.A., & Bargh, J. (1998). Coming out in the age of the Internet: Identity demarginalization through virtual group participation. *Journal of Personality and Social Psychology,* 75, 681–694.

Mehta, M. D., & Plaza, D. E. (1997). Pornography in cyberspace: An exploration of what's in USENET. In S. Kiesler (Ed.), *Culture of the Internet* (pp. 53–67). Nahwah, NJ: Lawrence Erlbaum.

Parks, M. R., and Floyd, K. (1996) Making friends in cyberspace. *Journal of Communication, 46,* 80–97.

Prentice-Dunn, S., & Rogers, R. W. (1982). Effects of public and private self-awareness on deindividuation and aggression. *Journal of Personality and Social Psychology, 43,* 503–513.

Postmes, T., & Spears, R. (1998). Deindividuation and anti-normative behavior: A meta-analysis. *Psychological Bulletin, 123,* 238–259.

Reicher, S. D., Spears, R., & Postmes, T. (1995). A social identity model of deindividuation phenomena. In W. Stroebe & M. Hewstone (Eds.), *European Review of Social Psychology,* (Vol. *6,* pp. 161–198). Chichester: Wiley.

Rheingold, H. (1993) *The virtual community (rev. edn).* London: MIT Press.

Rimm, M. (1995). Marketing pornography on the information superhighway. *Georgetown Law Review, 83,* 1839–1934.

Robinson, R., & West, R. (1992) A comparison of computer and questionnaire methods of history-taking in a genito-urinary clinic. *Psychology and Health, 6,* 77–84.

Rosson, M. B. (1999). I get by with a little help from my cyber-friends: Sharing stories of good and bad times on the Web. *Journal of Computer-Mediated Communication, 4* (4). Available at http://jcmc. indiana.edu/vol4/issue4/rosson.html. Accessed 10 December 2005.

Sassenberg, K., Boos, M., & Rabung, S. (2005). Attitude change in face to face and computer-mediated communication: Private self-awareness as mediator and moderator. *European Journal of Social Psychology, 35,* 361-374.

Selfe, C. L., & Meyer, P. R. (1991). Testing claims for on-line conferences. *Written Communication, 8,* 163–192.

Smolensky, M. W., Carmody, M. A., & Halcomb, C. G. (1990). The influence of task type, group structure, and extroversion on uninhibited speech in computer-mediated communication. *Computers in Human Behavior, 6,* 261–272.

Spears, R., & Lea, M. (1992). Social influence and the influence of the "social" in computer-mediated communication. In M. Lea (Ed.). *Contexts in computer-mediated communication* (pp. 30–64). London: Harvester Wheatsheaf.

Sproull, L., & Kiesler, S. (1986). Reducing social context cues: Electronic mail in organizational communication. *Management Science, 32,* 1492–1512.

Sproull, L., Subramani, M., Kiesler, S., Walker, J. H., & Waters, K. (1996). When the interface is a face. *Human-Computer Interaction, 11,* 97–124.

Suler, J. (2004). The online disinhibition effect. *CyberPsychology and Behavior, 7,* 321–326.

Tidwell, L. C., & Walther, J. B. (2002). Computer-mediated communication effects on disclosure, impressions, and interpersonal evaluations: Getting to know one another a bit at a time. *Human Communication Research, 28,* 317–348.

Tourangeau, R. (2004). Survey research and societal change. *Annual Review of Psychology, 55,* 775–801.

Tourangeau, R., & Smith, T. W. (1996). Asking sensitive questions: The impact of data collection mode, question format, and question context. *Public Opinion Quarterly, 60,* 275–304.

Tourangeau, R., Couper, M. P., & Steiger, D. M. (2003). Humanizing self administered surveys: Experiments on social presence in Web and IVR surveys. *Computers in Human Behaviour, 19,* 1–24.

Wallace, P. (1999). *The psychology of the Internet.* Cambridge, UK: Cambridge University Press.

Walther, J. B. (1996). Computer-mediated communication: Impersonal, interpersonal, and hyperpersonal interaction. *Communication Research, 23,* 3–43.

Weisband, S., & Kiesler, S. (1996) Self-disclosure on computer forms: Meta-analysis and implications. *Proceedings of CHI96.* Retrieved June 20, 2005 from (http://www.acm.org/sigchi/chi96/proceedings/papers/Weisband/sw_txt.htm)

Zimbardo, P. G. (1969). The human choice: Individuation, reason, and order vs. deindividuation, impulse, and chaos. In W. J. Arnold & D. Levine (Eds.). *Nebraska Symposium on Motivation* (pp. 237–307). Lincoln: Univ. of Nebraska Press.

Zimbardo, P. G. (1977). *Shyness: What is it and what to do about it.* London: Pan Books.

CHAPTER 5

The Psychology of Sex: A Mirror
from the Internet

Raymond J. Noonan
Health and Physical Education Department
Fashion Institute of Technology of the State University of New York
New York, New York

GENERAL TRENDS

Sex on the Internet is, at once, a compendium of the good, the bad, the beautiful, and the ugly. As such, one could argue that it is reflective of sex in real life, with the bad and the ugly often being the chief focal points for many people in the United States and elsewhere. Yet, the good and the beautiful are well represented in both arenas. The problem, of course, is distinguishing between the two groupings, because, for too many people, there simply are no such distinctions. As a result, on the Internet, as in real life, it is left to the individual to navigate her or his own way through the dizzying array of sex information and services available. As a result, too, there are those who seek to impose their own agendas and viewpoints on what others may view or the services to which others may have access. Therein lie the daunting qualities of the Internet and efforts to bring sanity to the sexual global village.

Sexuality is inextricably linked with the Internet, the World Wide Web, and the Usenet newsgroups in the minds of both many professionals and the general public. This should not be surprising, because sexuality *is* inextricably linked with virtually every imaginable discipline in some way, making it one of

Psychology and the Internet: Intrapersonal, Interpersonal, and Transpersonal Implications

the most interdisciplinary of subjects. These aspects, in turn, influence society's attitudes—and hence, the directions of scientific research and public policy in those domains (Noonan, 1998a). Yet, sex-related Web sites and other areas of the Internet represent only a small portion of each part of the global computer network, as they have since its inception. Nevertheless, like the medium itself, the role that sexuality online plays in all of our lives has the potential to affect us as individuals and as a society in profound ways, both positive and negative. In fact, the Internet reflects the sexuality of its users and the global society of which they are a part as much as, or perhaps more than, it has the potential to influence sexual attitudes and behavior. This chapter surveys the major segments of the Internet in which sexual content resides and conjectures about their psychological significance. Inherently, I also suggest avenues for further research to clarify some of the unknowns that remain since the first iteration of this chapter (Noonan, 1998d), in contrast to the rapid and incredible technological advances and social changes that have occurred in the meantime.

For health professionals and students in sexuality, psychology, education, and other allied disciplines, this chapter uses the Web to enhance our teaching, learning, and understanding by supplementing our writings, practice, and instruction via complementary Web sites. For example, *The Continuum Complete International Encyclopedia of Sexuality* by Francoeur and Noonan (2004) provides additional avenues at http://www.SexQuest.com/ccies/that readers might use in applying the concepts in this chapter to different cultures. This chapter also has its own companion Web site, *The Psychology of Sex: A Mirror from the Internet Companion Page* at http://www.SexQuest.com/SexualHealth/psychsexmirror.html (Noonan, 2006), with annotated links and updates to the Web resources cited in this chapter. I hope this site will extend the chapter's usefulness by keeping its links up-to-date and in providing additional insights for our readers in the realm of sexual health and the role that the Internet can play therein.

SEXUALITY ON THE INTERNET: ROOTS AND CONTROVERSIES

Sex has been a controversial topic on the Internet since before the implementation of the first alt.sex newsgroup on April 3, 1988. It was at that time that an alternative network was begun in response to the refusal of the Usenet hierarchy at the time to include a recreational sexuality group. Hardy (1993), who wrote that the early history of the Internet has yet to be adequately documented, described in his brief history the events that surrounded these early developments. He noted that the abdication of these early administrators in providing these types of forums, despite the expressed desire for them, established what might be called the cooperative anarchy that largely characterized the newsgroups for many years. Clearly, they provided the impetus for other "alternative" communications, both inside and outside the realm of sex, to find their way to interested communities participating in the Usenet newsgroups.

In fact, according to Stefanac (1993), it is likely that the dissemination of sexually oriented materials began early on in the development of the Internet with the informal exchange of text (and later images) via email (the popularity of which, itself, had been unanticipated by the original designers, as noted by Hardy (1993), Moore (1994), and others). These communications probably included both suggestive and explicit erotica and pornography (if I may use a common linguistic distinction between those that are "good" and those that are "bad," although many people use the terms interchangeably in the positive sense, given the subjective nature of such judgments). Later, private informal and early commercial bulletin board services (BBSs) allowed members to dial in directly to access computer-based pornography, although BBSs were technically on the fringe of what would be considered the Internet since they were usually not connected to the global network and were merely accessed by modem. As such, the sexual content available via the Internet reflects the wide range of such material in "adult" videos, magazines, and other media. What had become new by the mid-1990s was the extent of the commercialization of such materials, long established in other media, to this medium. It was especially the World Wide Web, the graphical environment of the Internet, that enabled explicit material to be more fully exploited for commerce and that continues to enjoy the most popularity after email. In addition, the Web continues to offer—now more than ever, not only in the United States, but around the world—the means to provide much-needed sexuality information and services to underserved and inaccessible populations who may not otherwise have them available locally, thus giving those groups the opportunity to realize their sexual potential and to enhance the overall quality of their sexual lives (Francoeur & Noonan, 2004; Noonan, 1997b; Noonan & Britton, 1996).

Unfortunately, this availability of diverse sex information and entertainment is not without controversy in the United States, both on the Internet and outside it. In that regard, former U. S. Surgeon General David Satcher noted in his July 2005 address at the 17th World Congress of Sexology in Montréal, Canada, that the United States is a third-world country in the realm of sexuality in many ways, by which he meant we are far behind many other nations in how appropriately we deal with sexual health issues. His address provided a followup on efforts being made to find "common ground" on these issues among Americans, which was at the heart of *The Surgeon General's Call to Action to Promote Sexual Health and Responsible Sexual Behavior 2001*, released by the Office of the Surgeon General (2001) in the first year of the presidency of George W. Bush. The president and his team, for their part, rejected it. Certainly, no nation is perfect in its ways of addressing sex and gender issues, but virtually all have some of the answers if we care to look (Noonan, 2005a). Add to that the role that sexuality plays as a motivator in how and why some fundamentalist Christian and Islamic factions seek to impose their beliefs and to influence local and world politics (Noonan, 2004d), and one can readily envision the clash of cultures that often surrounds sexuality on the Internet today. For additional insights into sexuality in the international arena, the reader is referred to Francoeur and Noonan (2004, 2006, 2007).

The Influence of Sexuality on New Communications Media

The notion that any new communications medium is soon used for sexual purposes is by now well known (Lyman, 2005; Morford, 2005; Stefanac, 1993; USA Today Tech Report, 1997; Weber, 1997). Only in the not-too-distant past did VCRs and video cameras experience a boom in which consumers voted with their pocketbooks their approval of the availability of sexually explicit films for their private use at home and participation in creating their own amateur productions for their own enjoyment. Similarly, writers in the media have noted that erotic imagery was depicted in cave drawings from 5000 B.C., ancient Greek and Egyptian art, as well as daguerreotype photographs during the American Civil War and libraries of images and interactive erotic multimedia on compact disks (CDs) today. Likewise, Gutenberg's invention of movable type was soon used to produce erotic books, after his press was first used to print the Bible; and from the technology of silent films, and later those with sound, soon emerged those of the erotic variety. In addition, early cable and pay-per-view television services depended on sexual material to launch these industries, and some services, such as the 1-900 telephone lines used for phone sex, have been virtual gold mines for the telecommunications industry, although this appears to have slowed somewhat as a result of free erotic chatrooms on the Web. As the USA Today Tech Report observed, then, sex on the Internet is just history repeating itself.

That dynamic continues to be felt as new technology has emerged, such as digital versatile disks (DVDs), high definition television (HDTV), and camera cell phones (leading to bans on their use, in this latter case, in some gyms and public bathrooms). Most recently, news reports surfaced that indicated that Apple's new video iPod, Sony's PlayStation Portable (PSP), newer cell phones, and similar portable devices would likely benefit from the availability of miniature erotic films, much to the (at least publicly expressed) chagrin of Apple Computer, Inc., and others (Hansen, 2004; Lyman, 2005; Tharp, 2005). Yet, it is difficult to imagine that they would eschew a significant stimulus for sales. As one report noted:

> "The degree to which the adult industry adopts iPod or PSP content is going to be an important factor in how the market grows for mobile video," Yankee Group senior analyst Mike Goodman told *MacNewsWorld*. "The porn industry makes new markets— entirely new markets, time and time again. When they adopt it, that market grows."
> (Lyman, 2005)

Podcasting, the process of downloading audio and video content to such devices from various Web sites, which has become hugely popular, will also be a likely source of "live" portable sexual content in the near future. At the same time, sex has begun to make its way into another recently popularized technology, blogging (from *Web logs*), which often documents in online diaries (blogs) the writers' public and private lives and ideas in this newest form of journaling that often become online conversations of interested communities, which will be discussed in a later section. In my article on the sexual roots of terrorism (Noonan, 2004d), I wrote, "*Cherchez le sexe* to determine the level of intensity with which terrorists will act to impose their visions on others" (p. 1139). Perhaps the same could be said with respect to gauging the potential future of any new technology as well, since popular culture is often driven or shaped by sexuality factors, which in turn shape its technology and the political and psychosocial responses to both (Noonan, 2004c).

Thus, we could say that two of humanity's apparently primal urges, war and sex, have been important to the Internet, both having been crucial in the initial and continuing development of its technology. War, or at least the fear surrounding the potential devastating effects of the Cold War going hot (an idea perhaps fostered by a 1964 RAND study, but now questioned, according to a discussion at Wikipedia, 2005), led in the 1960s to the perceived need to develop a communications system that could "intelligently" bypass possible catastrophic breaks in the system (or individual component failures) by rerouting information through other nodes of the system—hence, the "web" and "net" metaphors for the network by analogy to the web of a spider or a fishing net. As a result, what was to become the Internet was born, as the ARPANET was initiated by the U.S. Defense Department's Advanced Research Projects Agency (ARPA) (Hardy, 1993; Moore, 1994). ARPANET was the first wide-scale network using a packet-switched protocol that allowed discrete units of data (packets) to be routed through other computers on the network by whatever path was available to their final destination, where the packets were reassembled to form the complete message. Hardy noted that the original intent of the ARPANET to function in the face of catastrophic damage at any point in its path was clearly shown by the Internet's continued availability following the 1989 San Francisco earthquake, although telephone and other communications services in that area were disrupted. Similarly, the network has since continued to function following other catastrophic events, including the terrorist attack on the World Trade Center in New York City in 2001, the regional blackout of 2003 affecting several northeastern states in the U. S. and neighboring parts of Canada, and the devastating floods of New Orleans following Hurricane Katrina in 2005, which destroyed or shut down huge chunks of the network in those areas. Indeed, the "wireless revolution," still in its infancy, with cell phones and the Web using distant towers and satellites, promises to further enable these technologies in all spheres, as the process of convergence continues to meld the multifunctionality of these various devices. And sex will be there to help facilitate (and fund) the process.

Much as war and defense organizations were instrumental in funding the development of the early Internet at both the hardware and software levels, sexuality fueled many of the more recent developments of the Internet, particularly on the World Wide Web, as it became commercialized in the 1990s. The "adult entertainment" industry, another euphemism for sex-related services intended to stimulate erotic fantasies and sexual arousal, either masturbatory or couple-oriented, has been cited as one of the primary investors in extending the technology of the Internet ("An Adult Affair," 1997; Hirsh, 2002; USA Today Tech Report, 1997; Weber, 1997). Sex helps to generate the revenues that both dictate and refine the emerging technologies that allow more compelling ways for the product to be delivered, often methods designed to more effectively involve the viewer/participant. Other innovations aim at improving online commercial transactions. Among all these technologies have been videoconferencing, real-time streaming audio and video, online credit-card verification and billing systems, digital compression techniques for interactive multimedia data, increasing broadband access, and so on. Many of these developments have become essential components in mainstream commerce on the Internet, as well as in the delivery of other services online.

Tracking down usage statistics of sexuality sites on the Web remains tricky at this time. Data published in 1995 might be relevant in a static marketplace or even in demographic studies, where supply and demand or population data might fluctuate with some regularity and stability over many years. But the World Wide Web, which debuted in the early 1990s, was only starting to become popular in 1995 (Pike, 1995). By the closing years of the twentieth century, with both the market and the technology changing so rapidly, the Web had become a vastly different place, as it has become so in the first few years of the new millennium, and as it will likely be even more different as time passes. And, as in most histories of the Internet or the Web, the role that sex has played tends be politely ignored. Nevertheless, some data are available, but keep in mind that reports of such data are often out of date even before they are published; thus, here they provide a glimpse of just a brief period of time from which to make future comparisons.

According to one report (Simons, 1996), adult entertainment sites accounted for about 10% of the merchant sites on the Web in 1996; only computer products and travel services accounted for more, about 27% and 24%, respectively. Forrester Research of Cambridge, Massachusetts, one of the few market research firms in the technology arena that even acknowledged the impact of sex-related factors, whose data were cited in the 1996 report, predicted that by the year 2000, adult-entertainment revenues would account for about 4% of all sales on the Internet. It would be influenced strongly, they said, by the increase in female and senior-citizen users in the coming years. Women, in particular, were expected to access fewer sex-related sites, although, as I anticipated, this proved to be true only with respect to many of the types of explicit sites available in 1996 that were targeted to the 60% of users who were male. The emergence of erotica designed for female audiences outside the Web around that time suggested that women might enjoy a different kind of pornography, so its nature on the Internet would probably shift to include their interests, while not excluding those that many men seemed to prefer. Davis and Bauserman's (1993) review of research findings regarding sex differences in viewing sexually explicit materials would also tend to add support for this premise, since sexual explicitness in itself is not necessarily an issue for many women. I cited as an example, Candida Royalle's Femme Productions (http://www.royalle.com/), which continues to produce such films and has had great success in targeting the women's market; it has also been hailed by some sexologists for promoting positive sexual role models. Today, more and more informational Web sites on sexual health are also often addressed to women specifically, and there is no indication that these sites are not also popular for both women and men in search of such services. Nevertheless, more sites are being addressed specifically toward men's issues, as generic Web sites have become less associated primarily with men, and as men have emerged as a distinct marketing target beyond their traditional boundaries.

The following year, a comprehensive report in *Wired* magazine (Rose, 1997) helped to put a better perspective on the entertainment aspects of sex on the Internet compared to entertainment products in other venues. They noted that the sex industry generated about $9 billion in revenues in the United States during 1996, more than the $8.15 billion and $5.9 billion garnered by the sale of prerecorded music and movie box-office revenues, respectively, and less than the $11.18 billion spent by consumers on magazines and $26.1 billion on new books. Of the $9 billion spent for sex-related products and services (apparently, only those legally available were considered), a majority (more than $5 billion) was spent on video sales and rentals; $925 million was spent at online sex sites. In fact, sex sites were among the few Web offerings that were making a profit, according to many observers during those early years, although specific data were often lacking because these sites tended to be private, as opposed to public, ventures. And much of this profit, according to the *Wired* and other reports, was being used to advance further developments of both the Internet's infrastructure and the software being used to deliver information and entertainment.

Unfortunately, by 2002, most market research firms, including Forrester, cited in the Simon (1996) report, no longer covered the adult entertainment industry, according to Hirsh (2002). Thus, it is difficult to clarify how the figures have changed. However, CBS News' *60 Minutes*, in September 2004, estimated that Americans were spending about $10 billion a year on adult entertainment, noting further that it was as much as they were spending on professional sports events, buying music, or going out to movies. Thus, we might estimate that maybe there was a 10% increase over the previous eight years. Greenspan (2003) reported that online pornography accounted for $2.5 billion of the $57 billion market worldwide in 2003 (about 4%), and that the number of Web pages had increased over 1,850%, from 14 million in 1998 to about 260 million in 2003. Hansen (2004) noted that the research group Visiongain has predicted that "wireless porn" profits will hit \$4 billion by 2006, reflecting the burgeoning interest in wireless services in general, including wireless Internet. No research shows us a comparable picture of how many sex-related informational and educational Web sites exist and how many people use them, although one could probably safely assume they are nowhere near as prevalent as the entertainment ones. Here, we might observe that sexual arousal is more potent as entertainment or motivator, which is also a reflection of life in the real world, than educational pursuits are in general.

THE MEANINGS OF SEXUALITY FOR HUMAN BEINGS: A CHAOTIC SYSTEMS APPROACH

Human sexuality, however, is more than just erotic mental stimulation designed for sexual arousal, which is as legitimate as any other aspect of our sexuality. Sexuality is also more than just sexual activity, no matter how valuable we humans find that activity to be. In fact, sex ranges at once from the trivial to the profound. Human sexuality encompasses almost all of life's endeavors, as noted earlier, making it among the most interdisciplinary of subjects. It involves both biomedical (physical) aspects and psychosocial and cultural ones, all of which interact. I have termed this interplay of the various dimensions of our sexuality the *human sexuality complex* (Noonan, 1998a, 2004b) to emphasize both the unified and interconnected nature of the various facets, adopting an open systems perspective to help us better understand its complexities and improve people's sexual and overall lives. Specifically, I have defined the human sexuality complex as the constellation of factors in which sexual functions, processes, or structures are involved in the biological, psychosocial, emotional, political, and other aspects of the lives of human beings. It is an open dynamic multiple complex systems approach that incorporates the recent application of chaos theory to psychological phenomena (Blackerby, 1993; Masterpasqua & Perna, 1997). Chaos theory involves the study of apparently random behavior in complex dynamic systems, and chaotic behavior is sometimes described as the result of extreme sensitivity to initial conditions (e.g., the butterfly effect; see Bender *et al.*, 2004). Thus, the human sexuality complex conceptualizes its various dimensions as being a unified system of various subsystems in the lives of human beings in any society. In this context, paradoxically, sexuality is a chaotic organizing principle that both derives meaning and gives meaning to people in complex ways, with a multiplicity of feedback options available that mediate the expression of its various facets in a given environment over a given period of time. Indeed, human beings are themselves chaotic systems. Yet, we have a confounding factor—self-directed intention—that can alter the course of behavior and related events. Then, we might consider intention as being a subsystem of chaotic behavior itself, with its own subtly defined chaotic characteristics.

There are many aspects of the human sexuality complex that have been resistant to a clear understanding, because of the complex ways in which they are understood and the ways in which they function in everyday life. Because of my phenomenological and intellectual experience with it, I intuitively understand human sexuality to be a complex of chaotic happenings that probably have subtle deterministic properties that define its expression in many different, yet bounded, ways, but whose mechanisms are presently indescribable in the sense of attractors, strange or otherwise. (Still, my experience and interpretations may or may not correspond with those of others.) Similarly, the Internet could be viewed as a chaotic complex environment, a premise on which Ben Goertzel elaborates in his chapter in the present volume. The intersection of the two domains, while exciting for just these reasons, is open to discovery using such an expanded systems perspective. This perspective, of course, is radically opposed to the simplistic notions we currently see in addressing sexual issues of any kind, often in a prescribed dualistic manner, such as "good" and "bad" or "nature" and "nurture." This approach is now most noticeably seen in many of our approaches to sex in cyberspace, just as many health educators criticize the abstinence-until-marriage "sexuality education" programs for young people that fail to teach about condoms (Satcher, 2005). Sexology will not advance, and public policy will not evolve, until we can break the bonds of prescriptive sexology—what ought to be—with descriptive sexology—what is—and apply these principles to promoting sexual health. Religious imperatives are rightly the domain of sexosophy rather than sexology, including the U. S. secular versions, that is, politically correct postmodernist discourse. Still, elements of prescriptive sexology have their place in sex therapy and counseling, as well as in education (Noonan, 2005a, 2005b).

It is likely that all systems are chaotic systems. Indeed, as the brief "Beyond the Movie" extra on the DVD of the popular 2004 film, *The Butterfly Effect*, has noted, "Now that science is looking, chaos seems to be everywhere," citing Gleick's 1988 book *Chaos: Making a New Science*. Does this mean, then, that we should abandon traditional systems theory, or, for that matter, traditional family systems theory? Probably not, given the success we have in using them as engineering, treatment, or predictive tools. However, perhaps *constrained systems theory* might be a more accurate characterization of such perspectives. Systems that appear to rigidly follow Newtonian laws, such as, for example, a car's ignition system, therefore, might be more properly called constrained systems, if only because *we* apply constraints (even if only in our minds, as in the sex education example already cited, that appear to force the system into rigid conformity with our conception of nature's laws by counterbalancing the chaotic path with our "gentle" nudging toward our desired outcome). Living systems theory (Miller, 1991), another useful systems framework that has been used to characterize complex systems as metaphorically living organisms with analogous characteristics, such as the Internet and spaceflight missions (Noonan, 1998a, 2004b), is inherently a chaotic systems approach, although I do not believe it has ever been characterized as such. Jayne Gackenbach and Jim Karpen in their chapter in the present volume apply chaos and complexity theory to the coevolution of technology and consciousness and their inherent interconnections and provide additional valuable insights.

For the most part, up to the present, explicit systems perspectives have not typically been enunciated in most sexological writing or research. A remarkable exception is in the work of Schnarch (1991), who has been extending the systems work used in family interactions and the family systems approach to family therapy (Glick *et al.*, 1987). Schnarch has been primarily concerned with sex therapy for married couples, although he began laying the groundwork for applying systemic thinking to broader sexual issues, such as the nature of intimacy and partner involvement. In fact, Schnarch (1997) has begun to look at these issues with respect to the Internet, with some significant psychological insights. Yet, one can see glimmers of systems awareness in the writings of such earlier authors as O'Neill and O'Neill (1972), Macklin and Rubin (1983), and the futuristic work of Kirkendall (1984), all of whom sought to more fully integrate individual and couple sexual concerns into their biopsychosocial milieu and the surrounding environment. I find the possibility of extending the systems approach with chaos theory to be an intellectually exciting tool for future investigations of the human sexuality complex in various environments, including cyberspace. Chaos theory gives us new ways to think about the data gathered that might not otherwise be apparent. The value of chaos theory is that it provides a framework within which to interpret data that appear to be disordered and without reason, and to seek patterns in that data that are affected by the multiple systems that might impinge on or interact with it.

Perna and Masterpasqua (1997) considered the contradictions implicit in understanding that there is meaning in chaos, and these contradictions clearly extend to sexuality in cyberspace. They occur because of our modernist assumptions about linearity and reductionism and our comfort with these modes of thinking. Nevertheless, these authors noted, "chaos and self-organization are inextricably linked in the dynamic development of living systems" (p. 1). Thus, understanding the sciences of complexity and chaos is the next step in the evolution of knowledge about metaphorically "living" things in this new era of science in which these concepts can be discerned. In this context, the Internet might now be viewed as a living system about which we have much to learn. We will probably find that the certainty that has been so facilely applied to its various components in probably all societies on Earth will give way to a more natural uncertainty that seems to characterize our age. Perna and Masterpasqua noted that this uncertainty began at the start of this century with the discovery in quantum physics that particles, at least at the subatomic level, could never be measured with any certainty. Soon afterward, Freud's proposition that irrationality was at the core of human dynamics extended the concept of uncertainty to human behavior.

Fogel and Lyra (1997) applied the ideas of complexity and chaos to the development of relationships. They noted, "Relationships, like individuals, have a coherence over time and a particular character that develops as a result of the continuing engagement of the participants" (p. 75). As such, they considered that interpersonal relationships are driven by change that defines the developing dynamic systems of verbal and nonverbal communication, which, in turn, creates the meanings of the relationship. The relationship changes in stages as the various meanings change over the history of the relationship. Although they focused on dyadic relationships, they believed the principles could be applied to groups of any size. Thus, a foundation exists on which to apply these concepts to sexuality issues in cyberspace and the behavior of individuals and the online relationships that develop. Such a perspective can also help to explain the range of meanings that sexuality has for so many people. Online, relationships are initiated through written verbal communication and are maintained through the interpretations of meaning ascribed to them. Emotional content in the sexual arena is felt by the participants and determines the directions the relationship might take, either in the cyberspace experience itself or in any real-world manifestation that might develop (see the discussion on online dating later in this chapter).

It can certainly be said that people create their own meanings in their lives; individuals determine what is important to them, to what they voluntarily devote their energy. It may be religion, work, or sexuality, among other endeavors, or combinations thereof. We might ask, then, what is the nature of human sexuality? Certainly, it is one of the most complex aspects of human life. As an activity, the expression of different aspects of sexuality may be conceptualized as procreational, recreational, and relational (or affiliative), all of which project teleological explanations on its phenomenological manifestations. Bolton (1995, pp. 294–295) has enumerated some of these manifestations: sex as play; stress-seeking; adventure; transcendence; fun; fantasy; interaction and connectedness; pleasure; time-out, as a break from everyday reality; ritual; self-testing of one's limits; growth; a source of community; giving; sharing; ecstatic experience; theater; an endorphin-induced high; spirituality; expression of emotions; a source of meaning; power; aesthetics; sacrifice; beauty; and love. As Bolton said, "The list could continue; it is far from exhaustive of the richness and complexity of sexuality, not only in the forms it takes but in its meanings" (p. 295). Sexuality online illustrates this richness, if only in the sense that many of these manifestations may be played out through the Internet. They can also provide tangible expressions in the form of words or images that can be printed or saved as computer files to be reflected upon later or relived in the imagination.

The foregoing can aptly be described as generally positive manifestations of the human sexuality complex in a world typically focused on the negative. As such, it properly belongs in the realm of sexual health. Although many Americans in their "official" public personas tend to focus on sexual risk and pathology, recent efforts have been accelerated to highlight the more widely experienced positive aspects of sex since this author and a group of fellow doctoral students and faculty at NYU first published *Does Anyone Still Remember When Sex Was Fun? Positive Sexuality in the Age of AIDS* in 1990 (Anderson *et al.*, 1996). At the same time, generally negative approaches have not provided the impetus for innovative changes in other realms of public policy, and sometimes even among academics and in the sexual and health sciences (see Francoeur & Noonan, 2004; Money, 1995; Noonan, 1998a; see also di Mauro, 1995a,b). For example, Bolton (1995), an anthropologist, has criticized those anthropologists and AIDS researchers who "have focused almost exclusively on the dangers of sex, thereby contributing to the right-wing, eroto-phobic agenda....We have become part of the machinery for turning sex into a dangerous and despicable activity" (p. 294).

In the realm of sexual expression and the Internet, countless writers have highlighted the Internet as a dangerous place, both psychologically in terms of compulsive behavior and socially in terms of predatory behavior, especially for young people. Cooper (2002) and Cooper and Griffin-Shelley (2004) have described various online sexual problems and cite numerous reports on both sexual addiction and Internet addiction, along with financial, workplace, relationship, and family consequences, among other problems. Many of these problems are sensa-tionalized in articles in the popular press as well as some research reports, although Cooper and Griffin-Shelley (2004) acknowledge that the majority of online sexual activity does not lead to such problems. Nevertheless, the sexual addiction model of sexual behavior, although simply a metaphor lacking any substantive evidence as to its existence (Fienberg, 2000; Henkin, 1991, 1996; Klein, 2000), is accepted as fact by many professionals and laypersons. Addictions have traditionally referred to external substances that alter the brain chemistry of an individual and cause various physiological and psychological problems, with nicotine and heroin as typi-cal examples, with physical reactions to withdrawing the stimuli. Some substances later came to be imbued with psychologically addictive properties (e.g., marijuana), from which a conceptual jump led to behaviors and the natural body chemistry that accompanied them being similarly labeled. Naturally occurring endorphins are produced by the body during certain physical activities, such as orgasm and exercise, resulting in pleasurable feelings in the brain and the body as a whole, toward which some individuals may focus much of their attention in their day-to-day lives. Although this behavior may certainly be characterized as compulsive, it is not addictive, except in a metaphorical sense. Bancroft and Vukadinovic (2004), in fact, in their quest for a better theoretical model, posit that both sexual compulsiv-ity and sexual addiction are conceptually of uncertain scientific value with respect to sexual behavior that is out-of-control with problematic consequences. Similar arguments can be made for so-called Internet addiction and cybersex addiction as well as other behaviors, yet these metaphorical constructs are gaining consider-able support among many psychologists and laypeople (see the chapter by Mark

Griffiths in this book for additional perspectives on this question). If they were truly addictions, one could probably argue that these are simply pleasure addictions, with any good feelings thus pathologized if they are done "too much," compulsively, or inappropriately. Little is gained except neat media sound bytes and logically fuzzy scientific reasoning, which often have little impact on minimizing any actual harm to either children or adults.

In contrast, Prescott's (1977, 1983) writings on sexuality and touch and their relationship to intolerance and interpersonal violence provide useful theories for considering the possible effects of somatosensory/sexual deprivation. His research has generally been ignored, possibly because his conclusions about the importance of body pleasure and sexual touch in healthy personality development, and the devastating effects of their lack on adult violence, made erotophobic and antisexual conservatives, politicians, and social critics particularly uncomfortable. As Bolton (1995) wrote:

> Our goal should be the elaboration of healthy sexualities, which may be a prime ingredient in being able to reduce problems in other domains of culture as well, such as violence. A repressive sexual counterrevolution will not solve the problems of AIDS, but it will definitely contribute to other problems as a manifestation of increased unhappiness and frustration. (p. 301)

Sex also has symbolic value in the lives of human beings. For the young, it often signifies becoming an adult, which may partly account for the rush to begin a sexual relationship or sexual activity; for those who are older, it often signifies youth and attempts to reclaim it, which may account for some child pornography and for many fantasies. In the West, in our evolutionary and agrarian past, sex started at younger ages, a pattern that was disrupted by the Industrial Revolution and other societal changes (Murstein, 1974). Bolton (1995, p. 293) noted that sex is both rational and irrational; social and cultural conditions provide the context for behavior. Thus, again, the Internet provides a context, with its own social and cultural environments, for individuals to privately explore their own inner meanings and to find a community that may not exist in their geographic location.

For some people, sex symbolizes freedom and independence or rebellion; for others, it symbolizes oppression and subjugation, restrictions, and the lack of freedom. Clatts (1995) has identified what he calls *survival sex* among some sex workers, such as those in prostitution, who use it as a way to earn a living. Sex can be an indication of status within a social group, as well as a source of self-validation, self-esteem, self-worth, and self-empowerment. It can also be a symbol of ownership of the partner and of the ability to control a small part of the world. In addition, one's sexuality can provide a source of community or be a political statement in an us-versus-them power struggle (e.g., some feminist, gay, transgender, alternative-lifestyle, military, or religious groups), all of which have found expression on the Internet, helping to express and solidify community bonds.

The variety of sexual meanings is reflected in the lifestyle choices available, including celibacy, monogamous marriage and open marriage for heterosexual people, relationships analogous to these marriage patterns for unmarried heterosexual, bisexual, and homosexual people, uncommitted sexual relationships, and secret extramarital affairs, among many others. The trend toward legalizing gay marriages in the United States and in other countries is a further indication of how this variety of meanings is being extended to more people. Libby and Whitehurst (1977), Macklin and Rubin (1983), Noonan (1979), and others have explored the broad scenarios within relationship possibilities that began to flourish with the various heterosexual alternative-lifestyle movements in the 1970s that continue to be of relevance in polyamory groups in 2005. As we will see in later sections, all of these meanings and expressions have found voices (and often opponents) on the Internet.

Because the social possibilities of the global village made possible by the Internet extend to romantic possibilities made real as a result of the mainstreaming of online dating, much as in any other worldly community, it is imperative to emphasize the benefits of sexual expression to counterbalance the daunting power of the overemphasis on the potential harms. It is not enough to simply say that most potential harms do not materialize in cyberspace or in real life, as many have attempted in the past. Planned Parenthood Federation of America (2003) has published a compendium of research studies, *The Health Benefits of Sexual Expression*, that summarizes how sexual activity and orgasm benefit the biopsychosocial systems of human beings. It is known, for example, that such activity can have an ameliorative effect on suicidal ideation and depression, preventing many suicides, as well as reducing stress. It can enhance longevity, self-esteem, and fitness, and is correlated with overall quality of life. Physiologically, it can bolster the immune system, promote sleep, alleviate pain, and reduce the risk of breast cancer, heart disease, and stroke. Recognizing the more positive aspects of sex also led the World Association for Sexual Health (WAS, after its former name, the World Association for Sexology) to issue its historic Montreal Declaration "Sexual Health for the Millennium" at the 17th World Congress of Sexology in July 2005 to promote sexual health around the world throughout the lifespan (see text available at http://www.worldsexology.org/ or http://www.worldsexualhealth.com/). The goal of the Declaration is to encourage governments, international agencies, the private sector, and academic institutions to prioritize and integrate sexual health into any and all sustainable development goals and international agreements and to fully integrate sexual health and sexual rights into the work aimed at achieving the landmark Millennium Development Goals of the United Nations. As will be noted in a later section, these goals may well be achieved through the sexual empowerment of individuals that is increasingly becoming accessible to more people worldwide because of the Internet.

RELIGIOUS AND CULTURAL INFLUENCES

Francoeur (1984; Francoeur & Perper, 1997, 2004) has theorized that people's overall sexual attitudes are mainly influenced by their *Weltanschauungen* or worldviews. Although religion plays a major role in such conceptualizations, variations in these religious philosophies are much more important, according to Francoeur. He has posited dichotomous poles on a continuum that he believes define and characterize these points of view: the fixed versus the process worldview. Each worldview has adherents within virtually every religious tradition—both Western and Eastern. Francoeur suggested that believers in any given religion are more likely to take similar approaches to sexual issues as those people whose worldview is most closely aligned with theirs in other religions than they would with people whose worldview is opposed to theirs within their own religion. The nature of the conflict can be briefly summarized in the following paragraphs:

> At one end of the spectrum are fundamentalist, evangelical, charismatic factions that accept as word-for-word truth the writings of the Bible as the word of God, and advocate the establishment of the United States as a Christian nation. For them, living under God's rule would be evidenced by the man firmly established as the head of each family ... and the woman in her God-given role as submissive and bearer of children for the Kingdom of Heaven. Similar fundamentalist strains in the United States are apparent among ultra-orthodox Jews and radical Muslims.... These embody an absolutist/natural law/fixed worldview. (Francoeur & Perper, 2004, p. 1140)

These perspectives would be contrasted at the other end of the continuum as those of the "various mainstream Protestants, Catholics, Jews, and Muslims who accept a processual/evolutionary worldview," in which, for example in the Roman Catholic tradition, the divinely revealed sacred texts are respected as

> the record of the response to the word of God addressed to the Church throughout centuries of changing social, historical, and cultural traditions. The Faithful responded with the realities of their particular situation, guided by the direction of previous revelation, but not captive to it. (Thayer *et al.*, 1987, cited in Francoeur & Perper, 2004, p. 1140)

Thus, moral and other interpretations evolve according to the ongoing evolution taking place in each society. This way of thinking might be represented by, for example, the more secularly oriented approach of situation ethics, in which context is considered in judging various actions. The conflict is manifested in both American and other societies in the debates that occur within various denominations and in the world-at-large. These, in turn, may take the form of formal pronouncements (as from the Vatican or other church, synagogue, or mosque officials), reports of study groups by local committees, and attempts and successes by politicians at legislating specific moral and religious points of view surrounding issues involving sexuality and gender. Many of these perspectives about sexuality are available on the Internet. Links to some of these Web sites can be found at *SexQuest's Web Index for Sexual Health: The SexQuest WISH List* at http://www.SexQuest.com/ SexQuest.html, which was compiled by this author. *The JSR Website Review Companion Page* at http://www.sexquest.com/SexualHealth/JSRwebsite-reviews.html, written to accompany a review of Web resources for sex researchers that appeared in the *Journal of Sex Research* (Noonan, 2001a,b), includes additional links.

As is often the case, in what might be described as life imitating pornography, the media tends to exaggerate matters having to do with sex, because it increases revenues. Politicians jump on the bandwagon because they know it generates interest, and, given Americans' deep ambivalence toward sexuality, try to exploit both the unsubstantiated fears and the legitimate concerns that people have about sex-related issues (Noonan, 1996a, 1998b). Wilkins (1997) offered a description of the sociological concept of *moral panic*, which aptly describes much of the current timeworn responses we continue to see in sexual arenas:

> A moral panic is characterized by a wave of public concern, anxiety, and fervor about something, usually perceived as a threat to society. The distinguishing factors are a level of interest totally out of proportion to the real importance of the subject, some individuals building personal careers from the pursuit and magnification of the issue, and the replacement of reasoned debate with witchhunts and hysteria.

Certainly, moral panic is an apt description for much of our collective responses to sex on the Internet. From the introductory section of this chapter, one could surmise that there is little justification for it—but only if one looks at the bigger picture objectively—yet these moral panics persist regarding sex on the Internet and other aspects of sexual expression. So what then is on the Internet about this embarrassing, contentious, delightful, ugly, beautiful, confusing world of sex? What are its dynamics and why is it important for us to integrate this new medium into our consciousness of sexuality? A look at some key issues in modern sexology should help to put some of the possibilities into perspective, as well as to provide guideposts for future action. Later sections address the sex-related content and possible motivations and ramifications of the various responses to it.

NEW INSIGHTS FROM THE SCIENCE OF SEXOLOGY

Sexology today has vastly broadened its scope beyond its earliest roots in psychoanalytic theory and the biology of sex. Profoundly interdisciplinary in nature as has been noted, it has borrowed concepts from the other sciences and the humanities, even as it has given them some of its own principles. Many of the most important sexological ideas of the latter half of the twentieth century have come from the writings of John Money (1985 et seq.), considered by many to be one of the most important contemporary theoreticians, who has vigorously criticized the rampant antisexualism in American society. Money's pioneering work in gender identity/role, sexual rehearsal play, and in the paraphilias, for example, is at the foundation of much of today's scientific understanding of sexuality and gender, although not without controversy. *Paraphilia*, which is now an established part of the psychological lexicon, for example, is the scientific terminology popularized by Money for those sexual behaviors that are often called perversions in the legal system and kinky practices or fetishes colloquially. In fact, the word *gender* itself, was Money's contribution to sexological theory to distinguish between the socio-cultural manifestations of masculinity, femininity, and androgyny and the biological aspects of being male, female, or intersexed. Money (1995) has since come to somewhat regret that invention, which he borrowed from linguistics, because it has since been misused by some social scientists as distinguishing between the "clean" part of the "dirty" world of the genitals: Gender is above the belt and sex is below. In other contexts, such as surveys, gender and sex have become synonymous where the mere mention of *sex* might be held as suspect.

Nevertheless, the impact of sexologists' potential contributions to understanding the role of sex on the Internet is confounded by a lack of respect generated by their failure, for the most part, to clarify some of the muddy waters of subjects currently in their domain—often compounded by a similar failure in their predominant disciplines of psychology, sociology, medicine, or otherwise. Salient examples include some of today's critical issues defined by so-called political correctness, such as child sexual abuse and recovered memories, sexual harassment and date rape, and misconceptions about AIDS. Many sexologists appear to have uncritically accepted, as have many other social scientists, some of the popular myths surrounding these issues without looking more closely at their ramifications. In addition, sexologists have failed to wrest moral authority on other sexual issues, such as monogamy and premarital sex, from the traditional religionists, despite the prevalence of alternative moral systems that have evolved in today's world (e.g., Lawrence, 1989). The problem in both instances lies in the misuse of science either to promote personal biases while excluding conflicting facts or to disguise moral precepts as scientific assertions. Scientists (and sexologists) can and do have moral positions that are influenced by scientific understanding, but it is not within the realm of science to broadly dictate such moral positions. For example, I would argue that mental health professionals should do more to emphasize that using mental erotic stimulation to enhance sexual arousal is a normative and generally healthy aspect of sexual expression; yet, this is in marked contrast to some professionals' moral position that it may not be so. It is, perhaps, in the context of such clashes that the difficulty in dealing with sex on the Internet becomes exceedingly clear. We can understand politicians' usurpation of morality for political gain, but many of us have a difficult time excusing it in mental health professionals.

Dysfunctional behavior, both specifically sexual and more generally psychological and social, may be thought of as resulting from an individual's system failure in response to internalized conflicts because of his or her metaphorically separating the genitals from the rest of the body. This may also be conceptualized as compartmentalizing the genital experience as distinct from and/or incompatible with the experience of the whole person in the process. Money (1986a,b) has described paraphilias, the possible manifestations of such unfortunate responses, as the turning of the tragedy of such distortions of one's sexuality and the self into the triumph of the survival of eroticism itself, albeit distorted in its mode of expression or object choice. The lovemap was posited as the locus in which they operated.

Money (1986a) coined the term *lovemap* to describe the highly individualized mental representation a person has of the idealized lover and the idealized program of sexual and erotic activity or imagery that arouses him or her. Such lovemaps may be normophilic or paraphilic, depending on their congruence with the statistically normal incidence of the arousing object or activity in the relevant culture. A lovemap is said to be vandalized if a sexually traumatic experience occurs during early psychosexual development, which results in its paraphilic expression (Money & Lamacz, 1989). Later, Money (1995) coined the extended term *gendermap* to describe the mental representation of one's gender identity/role. The gendermap encompasses the lovemap and codes it as masculine, feminine, or androgynous, as well as endows it with whatever is gender-encoded socially, culturally, vocationally, and so on. In defining both terms, Money stressed that the locus of each representation was in both the mind and the brain. As the reader will see in the next section, the paraphilias are well represented on the Internet—and, in some respects, have attained a status of near-uncritical acceptance not afforded to some normophilic sexual behavior.

Several issues are on the horizon that also may impact the ways professional sexologists approach their science—and these will affect how we approach sex on the Internet as well. Among the issues is continuing research on biological entities such as pheromones and their role in sexual attraction (Kohl & Francoeur, 1995) and the biology of sexual orientation. In addition, professionals in the social sciences are seeking new paradigms to counteract repressive trends that threaten to undo some of the social gains made in the past. In addition, technology holds a promise of future gains, as in the treatment of sexual dysfunctions such as impotence, although not without controversy. The Working Group on a New View of Women's Sexual Problems (2000), for example, has reconceptualized the sexual "difficulties" of women that diverges from the "medicalization" of sex that is inherent in technology. Many men, too, have begun to rethink their relationships with women in light of the insights they have gained from various aspects of the women's movement—and all of these changes have found voice on the Internet.

The most noteworthy aspect of some of the ongoing work in sexology is the often-predominant focus on some of the potentially and distinctly negative aspects of sexuality. Such poorly supported notions as sexual addiction (Fienberg, 2000; Henkin, 1991, 1996; Klein, 2000) or the risk of heterosexually transmitted AIDS in the absence of the IV-drug vector (Fumento, 1990; National Research Council,

1993) are good examples. The generally sex-negative perspectives inherent in the promotion of these unwarranted beliefs may be another reflection of the conservative trends that have dominated American society over the past three decades, which will, in all likelihood, continue in some form for several more decades as a result of recent Supreme Court nominations by the Bush administration in the United States. It definitely has been felt in the approach to sexuality on the Internet by various government and private bodies, such as the continuing efforts to limit access to various types of materials in certain venues or to conduct Internet sting operations against sexual predators, although some of it may well be justified. Fortunately, however, this focus is one that appears to be cyclical. Reiss (1990) has outlined how American society has experienced two major sexual revolutions in the twentieth century alone, and he argued for taking a proactive stand with respect to shaping the next one, the seeds of which he predicted would be sown in the field of the 1990s. Others might argue that there have been several smaller revolutions, including those dealing with expansion of women's rights and gay rights in the sexual arena, but their work is not yet complete. And much work remains—and is being undertaken in various venues on the Internet—on some of the neglected rights of men and heterosexuals, particularly with respect to interactions in which various rights are in apparent conflict (see, e.g., http://www.SexQuest.com/alt.sex. conference/).

Within the arena of sexual politics, for example, heterophobia has only been recognized in the past two decades (Noonan, 1996a, 1998c; Patai, 1996, 1998; see Noonan, 2004a, for the most comprehensive examination of this topic), although it does not yet have the popular recognition that its sibling, homophobia, has. (Both are good examples, as well, of the blurring of political and psychological sensitivities that often confound our understanding of sexual issues—in this case, the suffix *-phobia* implies something that may or may not be accurate. I have encouraged the use of *homonegativity* and *heteronegativity* as more exact alternatives where appropriate in Noonan, 2004a, after Weis, 2004a). Heterophobia has been defined in various ways, from a fear of things different (such as other cultures) to the reverse of homophobia, only with heterosexuals as the target. Because I believe it is primarily enabled by the general antisexualism of American culture, I have broadened it and used it more as a synonym for this generalized sex-negativity that has crystallized around heterosexual behavior—particularly against heterosexual males—and especially against heterosexual intercourse (see Noonan, 1996a, 1997a, 1998b, 2004a). Internalized heterophobia, then, becomes the mechanism by which such distortions of normophilic behavior becomes normalized. As such, recognition of its impact on sexual health, research, and education in American culture is on the cutting edge of contemporary sexology. In effect, heterophobia has become an unacknowledged—and often unmentionable—force that influences public policy, and, in silent alliance with conservative religious and other social forces, determines how sexual issues as a whole are addressed or not in important domains of human living, both in real life and in cyberspace. Patai (1998), for example, applied the concept to contemporary sexual harassment theory and what she called the Sexual Harassment Industry (SHI), which was being used, she argued, to separate men and women for often personal or political gain or self-interest. She defined heterophobia as the "fear of, and antagonism toward, the Other—in the present context men in general—and toward heterosexuality in particular" (p. 5). She went on to document how this hostility, which "is not limited to the lunatic feminist fringe where it originated in the late 1960s" (p. 14), was being implemented by the expansion of sexual harassment indoctrination sessions and laws.

Some of this emerging consciousness, to be sure, may be nothing more than a backlash to some of the excesses of the feminist and gay movements that have rippled through American society since the 1990s and before (Noonan, 2004a; cf. Patai & Koertge, 1994; Patai, 1998). Money (1995) has referred to some of those excesses as a sexual counterreformation and has criticized the concurrent development of the false science of victimology, with recovered memories and the like as their pseudoscientific tools. Yet, some of it is clearly the awareness that sexual pluralism, to use Reiss's (1990) paradigm, ought to be the ideal for which we as a society strive. By extension, it will help to sort out the crosscurrents that continue to confound our responses to sex in cyberspace.

Feminist contributions have been important in this respect because they highlight the need for alternative interpretations of personal perspectives and social interactions in the study of human sexuality. Such social constructionist theories have undoubtedly advanced our understanding of many aspects of the human sexuality complex, and have become an essential part of social science research. Yet, some social scientists appear to have adopted uncritically some of the more radical ideological rhetoric of contemporary feminist, gay, and other minority discourse, which illustrates the political aspects of sexuality in which some responsible debate is beginning to be heard because of the Internet. Too often, proponents of these radical views seem more interested in promoting the limited self-interests of their particular group or of themselves personally. Often allied with others who believe their perspectives and needs are also not being heeded, they often seek to create a political movement that would place their group as the one that defines social norms and entitlements *in opposition to* the groups perceived as the dominant enemies. The well-known alliance between antipornography feminists and ultraconservative political and religious groups is a prime example, the influence of which has the potential to undermine sexual expression on the Internet by limiting other sexual discourse and perspectives. Although they each oppose pornography for different reasons, their agendas are often centered on other sex-related and unrelated concerns (Klein, 1990/1992). Thus, information on abortion, sex education, and gay and lesbian rights, for example, could be restricted, as the now-defunct Communications Decency Act (CDA) demonstrated. It is likely that these dynamics, along with the common association of heteronegativity with feminists in the popular mind, are part of the reason that so many of today's young women refuse to be identified with feminism, although they typically recognize the opportunities that they have because of its gains.

Although this purpose of promoting primarily self-interest and one's own position of political power and authority has typically not been explicitly acknowledged (although it has been occasionally recognized), the end result, nevertheless, has been the paradox that these groups are often seeking to establish a social order for themselves that they want to wrest from others. Discourse then becomes a means to justify their existence, and so false dichotomies, with the opposition set up as straw figures ready to be knocked down, are created. Money (1995) has noted it, for example, with respect to the resurgence of the nature/nurture debate that is inherent in how strict social constructionists posit a picture of biological determinism that many of its proponents would not recognize. The centrality of the political positioning of these various social constructionist ideas is buried in Tiefer's (1995) critique of naturalism in sex. Tiefer found that the use of arguing that sex is natural was a defense of sexology rooted in seventeenth- and eighteenth-century political philosophy defending the revolutionary movements of the day. She did not, however, make the conceptual jump to recognizing that today's social constructionists are, in effect, often doing the same things they criticized in their opponents—seeking only to change those who were in control. Thus, efforts at eliminating such destructive attitudes as racism, sexism, and heterosexism have often had more success in stimulating counterbigotry, only more broadly based in its targets, than in eliminating or reducing them. This is reflected in some commonly held myths, such as that minorities who have been traditionally oppressed cannot be racist and that women cannot engage in sexual harassment. On the Internet, such arguments become open debates in which all interested parties can participate and contribute.

SEXUAL EXPRESSION AND INFORMATION ON THE INTERNET

Sexual content exists on the Internet in probably all forums. Aside from e-mail, the most generally accessible areas are the Usenet newsgroups and World Wide Web. In addition to the informal sexual messages that may be exchanged between two specific individuals via email, there are the scattershot "spam" messages (the unwanted ubiquitous advertisements that are the blight of the Internet) and the more-targeted listservs, email discussion lists to which one typically subscribes if the topic is of interest. The content may be for sexual products or services, as in the case of spam, or may be professionally oriented (or otherwise) discussions and announcements. Examples of the latter include the Academic Sexual Correctness list (ASC-L) out of California State University, Long Beach (http://www.csulb.

edu/asc/asc.htm and http://groups.yahoo.com/group/asc-l/), which focuses on "all aspects of university sexual control issues," and the SEXNET listserv, a small academic discussion list for serious sex researchers of every stripe, including sexologists, biologists, psychologists, psychiatrists, sociologists, and others (for more information, see *The Psychology of Sex: A Mirror from the Internet Companion Page* at http://www.SexQuest.com/SexualHealth/psychsexmirror.html) (Noonan, 2006). SSTARGAZE, the listserv of the Society for Sex Therapy and Research (SSTAR), is an example of one maintained by an organization solely for its members, in this case, professionals who have clinical or research interests in sex (http://www.sstarnet.org/). Another is the listserv of the American Association of Sex Educators, Counselors, and Therapists (AASECT), also a restricted list for current members of AASECT (http://www.aasect.org/). Others exist for virtually every academic profession, political cause, special interest, and so on related to sexuality and gender issues, as well as those that intersect across these lines (revealing how the personal really is the political for most of us in these professions). Many of these lists can be found in the various indexes that exist on the Web, such as http://www-unix.umbc.edu/korenman/wmst/f_sex.html, which focuses on a wide range of sexual orientation, feminist, and other issues (some highly specific) of interest to some women. Similar to what we will see in the following sections with respect to the highly traveled, more accessible areas of the Internet, such sexuality-oriented material is a small proportion of the volume in these venues as well, since most listservs (or spam, for that matter) are not specifically about sexual topics.

USENET NEWSGROUPS AND THE PSYCHOLOGY OF SEX

Sexual expression takes many forms on the Internet. The most explicit open forums for various sexual practices and interests are to be found in the Usenet newsgroups, which one accesses with a newsreader, now often integrated with email programs, or directly on the Web. Because of their openness and availability virtually worldwide, newsgroups provide the most explicit of the sexual offerings, with the highest proportion of erotic imagery on the Internet (other than the commercial sex sites on the Web)—and they are free. These offerings occur in both story form and digitized images. Considerable discussion can take place as well, either about particular postings or about issues that are generally relevant to some of the participants. Because nobody owns or, for the most part, controls the newsgroups, they are what their readers and those who post to them make them, although the spam messages have effectively rendered many sex-related newsgroups almost useless for their original purpose. By design, theoretically, they most clearly reflect the sexual interests of their users. However, many Internet Service Providers (ISPs) do not carry some or all of the most sexually explicit groups, or they require a specific request to gain access to some of the groups. Therefore, the universal easy access to sexually explicit material that is often attributed to these groups is more myth than fact for millions of subscribers, although it can sometimes occur. As a result, various premium news services have arisen that allow subscribers to access more complete, uncensored newsgroups, with postings that do not "expire" (become unavailable and disappear) as quickly as normal because of space limitations on most ISPs' news servers.

The names of sex-related newsgroups usually contain the strings "alt.sex," "alt.binaries.pictures.erotica," or variants of those themes, although others exist that typically discuss sex topics that are less recreational in nature (see *Harley Hahn's Master List of Usenet Newsgroups* at http://www.harley.com/usenet/index.html for a comprehensive general listing of newsgroups). Binaries, usually encoded to facilitate transmission within text-based messages, are digital file formats that are typically programs, images, video clips, or sounds and so on, as opposed to text files, which contain only ordinary alphanumeric characters, such as those that make up plain-text email, newsgroup postings, or most Web pages. The keywords in these strings are mostly *sex* and *erotic(a)*, and several searches for these terms in the names of newsgroups using an older newsreader on my uncensored ISP's news (or groups) server over a six-month period in 1997 showed a figure that represented a little over 4% of all newsgroups available. When the first edition of this chapter (Noonan, 1998d) was being written from about mid-1997 to February 1998, 593 out of 24,704 newsgroups contained the word *sex* and 431 contained the word *erotic*, for a total of 1,024 (with about a dozen that contained both terms), a little over 4% of the total. Clearly, there had been a proliferation of alt.sex newsgroups in less than a decade from the single one started in 1988, although, for comparison, it should be noted that in 1997 there were 7,798 alt-hierarchy newsgroups in total, which began with just three (alt.drugs and alt.rock-n-roll being the other two) (Hardy, 1993).

It seems that it is no longer as easy to get a snapshot of the sex-related newsgroups as it was in 1997–1998, perhaps because they became unwieldy some years ago because of the spam as well as the changes in newsreaders, and so became more difficult for the occasional researcher in this area of the Internet. Around mid-2005, Google released its beta newsgroup site on the Web at http://groups.google.com/. Their intent is to provide an archive of most textual newsgroups from 1981 to the present (according to their FAQ (Frequently Asked Questions page) at http://www.google.com/googlegroups/help.html). Because it does not contain binary files (photos, etc.), one could arguably say that it is somewhat censored, although with its claim of archiving about 845 million (searchable) posts over the past 20-plus years, one can readily see that including binaries would take an enormous amount of storage space on the server, given that individual binary files are significantly larger than text files. Thus, Google Groups reports that there are about 54,000 newsgroups archived at the site, as of November 2005. Going back to my own uncensored ISP used in the figures in the previous paragraph, I found there are about 1,900 newsgroups that contained the word *sex*, and about 400 that contained the word *erotic*—for a total almost double what it was in 1997—giving about 4% of the total again, as in 1997, although I cannot be sure what the margin of error is, given that the calculations involve two different sets of data with no sure way to compare them. A serious limitation, of course, is that Google Groups does not have any of the binary listings. Another limitation is that the historical nature of the Google site means that it includes groups that no longer exist, as they die out in time if no one posts to them.

In addition, I did not delve deeply into the apparently relevant alt.binaries. erotica posts on my ISP, given the child-pornography stings reported to be scattered across the Internet in recent years. I did notice that the more obvious names for such material no longer existed on the news server of my ISP, perhaps reflecting the reported efforts by law enforcement to take down such groups, although it has also been reported that some individuals would post them again under new names. I did not feel it prudent to "take one for science," as it were, to ascertain its prevalence, nor did I have the time to sift through the maze of newsgroup permutations to ascertain what kind of content actually was there, although, as Weis (2004b) has noted, such material has always been an extremely small proportion of pornographic imagery (p. 1186). Nevertheless, I did decide to look into one I thought might be a "safe" representative group (in case "they" were watching), alt.binaries.erotica.amateur.female, to try to get a sense of how a group purporting to be postings of real amateur (i.e., not staged) people might look today. It revealed about 221,000 postings from just the past two months or so; the preponderance of images were relatively high quality and clearly professionally produced and posted as advertisements for various commercial pornography sites on the Web (i.e., spam), much of it whole sets of images that seemed to be repetitively posted every so often. Almost all were on-topic, in that they were images of women (or in couples and groups) clearly aimed at heterosexual men (targeted marketing); it also included a handful of possibly "real" amateurs and a few of what would be classified as child pornography in the United States. Still, my reluctance to take the risk to update this chapter points to a real problem that social scientists face when addressing ultracontroversial issues. It seems that we just do not really want to know how to solve these problems, if legitimate researchers cannot even ask the right questions nor be allowed to find out and state what the real answers are (cf. Rind *et al.,* 2000, 2001a; Rind & Tromovitch, 1997; Rind *et al.,* 1998, 2001b).

With the foregoing in mind, it became just as apparent that the number of sex-related newsgroups is a small proportion of all groups that cater to different interests. This should not be surprising since sexuality, in one or more of its many manifestations, is one of those topics that are relevant to probably all populations. Further research uncovered additional Usenet statistics that showed that sex-related newsgroups are among the most popular (http://www.newsadmin.com/). For example, during one week (from November 12–18, 2005), when I was updating this section, I found that an average of 75 specific sites of the top 100 sites accessed each day that week were obviously groups that had sexual images or videos posted, and they accounted for 53.9% of the total sites accessed that week. Nevertheless, the time it takes to download pictures (transfer the files from the news server to one's own local computer), not to mention the far larger files that contain video data, can be considerable, although that has become much less often the case with cable and DSL connections becoming so widespread. Such a time investment generally can make it impractical for all but the most dedicated aficionados. Besides, there are the countless CDs containing sexual material available for the computer, the contents of many of which were culled from newsgroups, that can probably still be purchased online or in stores, which eliminates the time involved in downloading them—not to mention the now ubiquitous use of DVDs for video and interactive content. In fact, as one report (Stefanac, 1993) noted, erotic multimedia CDs may have encouraged computer users to purchase CD-ROM drives, sound cards, and high-resolution displays in the same way that sex-oriented videotapes drove the VCR market in the 1980s, with the same more recently holding true for DVDs. Still, the Usenet appears to now have the highest proportion of sexually explicit material available of any area of the Internet, with the exception of commercial sites on the Web, as has been noted. Because listservs and blogs have increasingly taken over many of the original "democratic access" and announcement and discussion functions of the Usenet (Caslon Analytics, 2005), it is likely that its recreational-sex orientation will become stronger.

In accordance with the general premise of this chapter, then, taking the limitations already noted into account, the material available in the Usenet newsgroups still appears to be quite diverse, again reflecting the breadth and depth of sexual expression. Even a cursory glance through just the names of the newsgroups demonstrates the vast diversity of human sexuality online. Sampling some of the pictures throughout these newsgroups would probably confirm that this was still the case, although the overwhelming amount of spam certainly skews the true picture. When I did this in the past, I was immediately struck by what some individuals find erotic. Some were limited in scope, to be sure; many might find that most of it was not particularly sexually arousing. Yet, even in some of the subjects that did not correspond with one's own lovemap, one might be surprised to find stimulating pictures. Among the spam used to be notices for sex tours to Thailand, Cuba, and elsewhere, and advertisements for phone sex, escort services, and videos and CD-ROMs of sexually oriented materials (which appears to have diminished), as well as advertisements and links to sex sites on the World Wide Web (which have definitely increased).

Otherwise, the quality of the visual material ranged from beautiful, artistic, high-quality scans and digital photographs (mostly commercial, often repetitively posted), to amateurish low-quality scans and less-than-cell-phone-quality digital photographs and video frame captures (at this point, it seems, mostly "professional amateurs"), to digital video clips of varying quality and length on every imaginable subject. They included traditional "glamour" shots and masturbatory exhibitions to straightforward heterosexual, homosexual, and bisexual activity—especially anal intercourse and "facials" (ejaculation on women's faces) to many of the paraphilias and fetishes, especially bondage and discipline and sadomasochistic scenarios. Transsexualism ("she-males") and heterosexually oriented lesbianism appear to be still well represented. Condoms appear to be used more often now than in the past. Fantasies as well as depictions of actual rape and sexual abuse also still seem to be available. Almost every racial and many ethnic groups in the world appear to be represented, with a heavy representation of Asian individuals, couples, and groups. Many of the individuals depicted appeared to be having fun while others were decidedly not—while still others appeared to be far away from the activity in which they were participating. Idyllic scenery and ordinary studio sets were used, as well as actual home sites. All body types were represented, as well as, though to a much lesser extent, women with stretch marks or pregnant, and people with obvious physical disabilities. Nevertheless, youth is still probably as greatly valued as it was a decade ago—as it is still in much of the "real" world—although it appears from the group names that elderly individuals are more represented than in the past, perhaps because more of the baby-boomer generation has become more comfortable with computers, at the same time as they have begun to retire. Certainly, the psychology of beauty is a realm that has not been studied, but could have revealing insights for normative development as well as for therapy if studied from the chaotic systems perspective previously noted.

Some of the materials were obviously likely to be sexually arousing to the typical person, women included. However, much of it would not be arousing beyond those whose specific lovemap incorporates that imagery. Some of the material was definitely obscene, if only because it was censored with masking blocks and other devices to cover the genitals. Misrepresented photos were there, such as fake celebrity and other adult nudes, as well as child pornography digitally created by superimposing parts of different nonsexual photos with sexual ones or by digital artistic manipulation. Of particular note, because it represents a different industrial society from that of the United States (which produces most of the world's sex-oriented material, according to Rose, 1997), was that which originated in Japan, including numerous bondage and "Lolita" images. Among the oddities reflecting local laws in Japan were pixelated digital distortions of the pubic areas of both men and women (and children) in what was, thereby, presumably legal material, although the law and customs have changed in Japan in the meantime. (For additional information on sex in Japanese and other international cultures, see *Archive for Sexology* (online), 2005; Francoeur, 1997; Francoeur & Noonan, 2001, 2004.)

In many of the sexually oriented newsgroups, established American, Japanese, and other international "porn" stars are often highlighted, as are a wealth of copyright violations from published magazines. Many of the people depicted are stereotypically attractive, although many are not. Heterosexually oriented depictions of women are predominant, probably reflecting the overall majority of heterosexuals in the population and the early use of the Internet predominantly by men. Nevertheless, significant libraries of lesbian and gay material exist, as well as bisexual and transgender/transsexual material and groups on bondage and other paraphilias across all sexual orientations. Pictures may, using the familiar film-rating system for analogy, be R-rated, X-rated, or even G-rated, i.e., photos of models from mainstream shopping catalogs for women and children, and can include celebrity nudes gleaned from various sources both private and public. There are also depictions of relatively atypical activities such as heterosexual fisting, bestiality, pedophilia, and other less common paraphilias. At the same time that the supply of images appears limitless, the role that this saturation may play on its users as a result has yet to be elucidated, as is the role of satiation. Boredom is a likely result, which may trigger the search for variety, although it is unlikely that the search would extend beyond one's lovemap into, say, the realm of child pornography.

An important question—and one that has not been addressed to any extent yet—arises in the event that someone comes across a photo, or even several photos, that he or she finds erotic, but which is not congruent with his or her identified lovemap. For example, if a gay scene or a pedophilic scene causes unexpected sexual arousal, does that mean that one is gay—or worse, a pedophile or one who is likely to sexually molest children? Unfortunately, today such questions are rarely asked. But, combined with technophobic reactions to the once new, still evolving, and, in some senses, still largely unknown medium of the Internet, these issues provide the fuel for promoting fears—of pedophiles, stalkers, and other sexual predators—that are disproportionate to their actual occurrences online. A possible explanation of this phenomenon is what I have termed *self-defined lovemap-inappropriate sexual arousal* (*SDLISA*). It may include pedophilic, sadomasochistic, homosexual, heterosexual, or whatever imagery or ideas are incongruent or conflict with one's perception of one's own ideal sexual persona, yet which may be sexually arousing, often in a way that troubles the individual. A common manifestation of it may be seen in the adolescent—who may or may not be gay—who fears he may be gay because a same-sex encounter, sexual or nonsexual, was arousing. The concept of SDLISA and its implications (as well as other psychological or behavioral mechanisms that may be involved) are poorly understood at this time and require further investigation.

With regard to child pornography, one might be surprised that children in shopping catalogues may be held to be erotic by some individuals. Some artistic photographs are clearly not pornographic, yet would be considered child pornography under current U. S. laws. One would have to wonder whether such draconian laws might not be merely guilt reactions to society's general lack of help for many of our children in other domains, such as education, healthcare, and parenting skills (cf. Leach, 1994). Some depict obvious sexual abuse, but many appear not to be so, except by definition. In others, the children clearly appear to be aware of the power of their sexuality. The complexity of the various situations depicted makes it easy to understand why merely defining all of it as sexual abuse is such a common response—until we realize the many ways in which we are failing our children overall. Yet, many countries with more abysmal records of overall child neglect are adopting many of these arguably warped American standards of sexuality and nudity. I often view such a focus on sex as merely a powerful distraction to allow political and social leaders to avoid addressing effectively the root causes of the real injuries, inequities, and injustices in their societies, much as it is in the United States.

It is open to debate what may cause some observers to participate in such illegal newsgroups as those that display sexual activities of adults with children or of children with other children. However, the number of such photographs appears to be small and has tended to be material that has been available for decades, including much of it that was once legal in the United States and other countries. Also, the likelihood that children will meet pedophiles through the Internet is extremely low, although the media coverage of these events when they do occur very accurately exhibits the characteristics of moral panic described earlier. There has yet to be any research that truthfully examines the far greater likelihood that children will be abused, sexually or otherwise, in venues that have nothing to do with the online world, and that most sexual predators lurk offline. Instead, sensationalistic panaceas, such as the ubiquitous Megan's Laws, help to give the public the illusion that politicians are doing something about sexual abuse by focusing on that initiated by strangers. In fact, most data indicate that the majority of sexual abuse is perpetrated by parents (56%, according to Laudan, 1994), with another significant percentage committed by relatives and known friends. Still, I suspect that emotional abuse of children is far more common and far more damaging to more children than is otherwise acknowledged. Similarly, controversy arose over the publication of a meta-analytic research report of a study reanalyzing the data from 59 previous studies of college students that found that child sexual abuse may not be traumatizing to all individuals, and that it was different for girls than for boys, among other findings (Rind *et al.*, 2000, 2001a; Rind & Tromovitch, 1997; Rind *et al.*, 1998, 2001b). The original study published in 1998 in *Psychological Bulletin* created a public furor that resulted in its official condemnation by the U. S. Congress, and a call by the American Psychological Association (APA) for researchers to consider the public-policy ramifications of any future research.

With regard to online access to sexual imagery, little is typically said of the fact that young people, if they decide to do it, can often find a way to acquire sexually explicit materials offline, despite the great efforts to prevent it. A *New York Magazine* article, for example, indicated that 65% of teenagers in four Manhattan high schools had watched an X-rated movie, while parents in the same demographic as the teens had estimated that only 25% of *their* children had done so (Thiel, 2005). This gap between children's sexual activities and their parents' knowledge of what they were doing occurred to varying degrees across every one of the 36 sexual activities mentioned without exception. It seems that many adults forget that they were able to find such materials when they were younger, and that they appear to believe that they are unique in the fact that such materials did not cause them any apparent harm. In fact, in their review of the research literature over the previous two decades on the effects of exposure to such materials, Davis and Bauserman (1993) wrote:

> We have seen that people exposed to [sexually explicit materials] can be influenced, but are not necessarily influenced, by that exposure. The effects are a complex, interactive function of the predispositions of the person being exposed and the various aspects of the exposure situation, including, especially, the nature of the stimuli and the amount of exposure. In the language of the attitude theorists used here, the effect will be a function of the motivational demands of the situation, the ability to respond to processing requirements of the situation, the content characteristics of the stimuli, and the other persuasion cues in the situation. (p. 197)

Thus, with an implicit awareness of complex systems perspectives, Davis and Bauserman showed that a variety of circumstances tend to mediate the effects that pornography has on people. The most pronounced response is typically short-term sexual arousal and a tendency to accept a variety of normophilic sexual behaviors. A predisposition to having stereotypical, callous, adversarial beliefs and myths with regard to women were more indicative of actual sexual aggression, and then usually only in certain instances in which the men were prone to violent behavior. They noted that men's strong socialization (in Western countries) against sexual aggression toward women tends not to be countermanded by viewing even the relatively small percentage of pornography that depicted it. Further, Diamond and Uchiyama (1999) found that the legalization of sexually explicit materials in Japan was correlated with a reduction of rapes and other sex crimes over a 20-year period, as had been the case in other countries.

Despite the findings, moreover, that the vast majority of sexual crimes are not linked to sexual materials, a large number of people refuse to believe the data. This has resulted, in part, in the ongoing legal fad in the United States of equating even the most innocuous use of women's photos in some situations with sexual harassment. Whether the findings with regard to sexually explicit content in other media apply equally to the interactive multimedia erotica available on CDs, DVDs, or the World Wide Web has yet to be explored. Computer simulations, when enhanced to their fullest, such as in aerospace flight simulators, for example, are now regularly being used to train pilots and others to perform complex tasks, and the possibility that such interactive technologies used for erotic entertainment might foster antisocial behaviors must be considered. The element of directing or controlling the sexual actions of others in virtual environments, without regard to their desires, may have a detrimental effect on some users who are simultaneously not being shown how to consider the rights and feelings of others, itself a general trend in conservative American society that seems to be increasing in the nonsexual realm as well.

Curiosity and the allure of what might be called "forbidden treasures" are also factors that have not been considered in the appeal of either illegal or more typical erotic newsgroups. Although it has been noted that an X or other adult rating can be detrimental to the economic success of some films, similar ratings indicating explicit sexual content, say, of music or multimedia CDs, can significantly increase sales (Stefanac, 1993). The phenomenon that causes an attraction to such things as pornography, particularly child pornography, in the newsgroups may be that, by forbidding them, the government sets up an interest in and compulsion for obtaining this material. Although they probably are not savvy enough to be intentionally manipulating this to provide jobs for law enforcement and the legal industry or to provide free advertising that helps to distinguish what may be otherwise nondescript products from others, the government, nevertheless, draws attention to them. (Recall the marketing adage that even negative publicity can be good for a product or idea.) This can stimulate curiosity, which can simply encourage looking for it. Once there is the interest and the roadmap, as it were, there is also likely to be the intermittent reinforcement of finding treasures among the chaff, such as the occasional erotically appealing image among the advertisements in the newsgroups. Although we now have the concept of the lovemap to help us understand what makes something sexually appealing to a given individual, the etiology of what makes the lovemap more versus less encompassing in terms of the imagery that is attractive continues to be elusive, as is the role of restricting access to it. Still, sex on the newsgroups might be conceptualized as a metaphor for life: looking for love in all the wrong places or so many men/women, so little time.

THE SEXUAL DIVERSITY OF THE WORLD WIDE WEB

Over the past several years, numerous writers have noted that sex is the most searched-for topic on the Internet (Cooper, 1997b, 2002; Cooper & Griffin-Shelley, 2004), a claim that still appears to be true. We are referring here, of course, to the World Wide Web, which offers a much wider array of information and services beyond those that are sexually explicit, although they, too, are certainly available, usually for a fee requiring a credit card to prove legal age. Most such Web sites also require an affirmative response to questions that ask, for example, whether one is of legal age in his or her locale and whether viewing such material is legal there, and to affirm that one is not a law enforcement officer seeking to entrap the operators. Ample warning is almost always given, particularly at the commercial sites, whose operators appear to be sincerely interested, if only for economic and legal reasons, in restricting their clientele to adults. Hypertext links, for example to the Disney Web site, are usually available for those who indicate they do not wish (or are not legally permitted) to view sexually explicit material. An implicit trust that the viewer is being truthful is assumed, if only, presumably, to exercise due diligence and to avoid legal liability. Among the libraries of explicit photos that often make their way back and forth between the Usenet and some of these Web sites (although, at this point, most appear to have been commissioned, bought, and/or produced by the sites themselves) are the cutting-edge technologies, such as live video and audio feeds that allow the viewers to interact with models stripping or dancing or performing various sexual acts. Again, as noted earlier, the impact that this directing of the performers' actions might have on these viewers' attitudes toward sexuality (and toward women and men in particular) in everyday social interactions is something that still needs to be assessed. Appropriate countermeasures (which should not include simply banning them) might be warranted that might then become part of a general socialization program to foster respect and consideration between and among the sexes, a practice that is similarly lacking today in many interpersonal interactions in the nonsexual realm in American society at large. It is important to remember that pleasure and eroticization should not preclude such respect, despite the often explicit message in some "sex education" programs that experiencing these feelings is a *de facto* indication of a lack of respect—particularly self-respect—and particularly for girls. It is incumbent on parents, educators, mental health professionals, the media, and society-at-large to reject such messages that more often set the stage for lifelong internal conflict and defeat.

The Web also offers the technology for individuals to interact in "real time" using chat rooms (or simply chat) and instant messaging (IM)—textual messages typed on the keyboard with conferencing software, such as the AOL (America Online), MSN (Microsoft Network), or Yahoo Instant Messengers (or via the older but still somewhat available technologies called ICQ or Internet Relay Chat, IRC). Many of the newer technologies also offer audio chatting, and AOL Instant Messenger, like the older CU-SeeMe videoconferencing software, offers chats with sound and video using a video camera (or webcam). Chats may occur in a variety of venues on the Internet and frequently take the form of noted authors, athletes, or celebrities "conversing," usually using just textual messages, but more frequently using simultaneous video and audio with their audience. Often, too, are chats taking place more informally, which involve just the audience-as-participants in a discussion about almost anything. Whereas the Usenet newsgroups are more archival in nature, being more like newspapers in a library that one accesses when one chooses, chats are more involving and occur in synchronous real time: One must be there when it occurs to participate. Instant messaging is similar, in that one "converses" with one's "buddy list" when they are online, of which one is automatically notified by the program after the user configures the list of friends. In contrast, the newsgroups, listservs, and online discussion boards are asynchronous: One posts a message that others may read and respond to at any time after the original poster has gone offline.

Out of these capabilities grew the popular practice of cybersex. Cybersex involves suggestive or explicit erotic messages or sexual fantasies exchanged via the computer connected with others who are online at the same time. Although the term is no longer new, in fact, as van der Leun (1995) noted, "Cybersex has been going on since humans received the gift of imagination.... [It is] simply old sexual fantasies in a new electronic bottle." Worthington (1996) noted a survey on Prodigy (one of the original proprietary networks similar to but predating AOL) in which 52% of the respondents said they had had cybersex, of whom 36% said they had reached orgasm and 25% said they had faked it. More recently, Cooper and Griffin-Shelley (2004) have noted that between 20% and 33% of people have used the Internet for online sexual activity. This highlights the fact that, as in many if not most sexual fantasies, the glands of the participants are involved, if not the bodies. As Worthington described it online, "And where endorphins go, attachment follows." It also highlights the fact that masturbatory activities—still a very difficult subject for many Americans to publicly acknowledge—are very much a part of cybersex, just as they are closely associated with many sexual fantasies, particularly when enhanced with sexually explicit materials. For some people, reading the intimate confessions of others can serve to initiate sexual fantasies and arousal, much as romance novels are often considered to be women-oriented pornography.

Cybersex, like phone sex, is a metaphorical term for sexual talk between two or more individuals that may or may not include simultaneous or subsequent masturbatory activities for one or more of them, as previously noted. There is some support in the literature for considering it another form of "having sex," although there is little evidence to support that interpretation. "Real sex" itself remains a controversial issue among sexologists and others, many of whom insist on including all types of sexual behavior, most often oral sex, as "having sex." Certainly, these activities are sexual behaviors, but the common expression "having sex" is typically understood to mean having sexual intercourse, although some confusion will persist with respect to some activities, such as anal sex. The incidence of cybersex flirtation raises the question among the public, as well as mental health and legal professionals, of whether such activity is adultery or cheating, with one such case reaching the courts as early as 1996 amid much media coverage (e.g., Worthington, 1996). Although I would be hard pressed to define cybersex (or even phone sex) as having sex, others use this metaphor as an apt description of what they are doing. In fact, during one guest appearance on MSN that I did, one of the questions asked of me and the members who participated in the chat was, "Is cybersex better than real sex?" That question arises often enough still, with members debating among themselves that one is superior to the other. What is perhaps clarified is the nature of jealousy, that imagined dalliances—virtual intimacy—could have as much of an impact as actual sexual intimacy with an outside lover. Ephemeral relationships may occur, although one might ask if this is all that different, too, from many relationships offline. Much has been written as well on the many marriages and other committed relationships that developed as a result of meeting online (Miller, 1998). The marriage-oriented dating site eHarmony.com, for example, states that more marriages occur from their matches than from those on any other service, with numerous testimonials attesting to their claim appearing on their website.

Many psychologists, too, have delved into the world of cybersex and have conjectured as to its impact on the participants and their partners, including elucidating treatment options for compulsive online sexual behavior. Cooper (2002) and Cooper and Griffin-Shelley (2004), who have probably written the most comprehensive treatments on sex and the Internet, have broadly defined the concept of online sexual activity (OSA) as the "use of the Internet for any activity (including text, audio, and graphic files) that involves sexuality, whether for purposes of recreation, entertainment, exploration, support, education, commerce, efforts to attain and secure sexual or romantic partners, and so on" (Cooper & Griffin-Shelley, 2004, p. 1290). They included cybersex ("cybering") as a subset of online sexual activity. They also defined two problematic aspects of online sexual behavior: online sexual problems (OSP) and online sexual compulsivity (OSC), a subset of the former. Online sexual problems include all of the difficulties that people can have from online sexuality, including its "negative financial, legal, occupational, relational, and/or personal repercussions" (p. 1290). Online sexual compulsivity refers to the "excessive" online sexual behaviors "that interfere with the work, social, and/or recreational dimensions of the person's life. In addition, there are indications of a 'loss of control' of the ability to regulate the activity and/or to minimize adverse consequences" (p. 1291). They hypothesized that these activities and problems were powered by what they called the "Triple-A Engine" of the Internet: accessibility, affordability, and anonymity (or, more correctly, the perception of anonymity by many people). They believed that online sexuality was the "next sexual revolution" (Cooper & Griffin-Shelley, 2002, 2004, p. 1290), a claim with which this author agrees.

The appeal of cybersex is understandable in some ways. Communicating via the Internet is easy, accessible, safe, relatively inexpensive, and can be exciting. The emotional content of the interaction is controllable, versus a face-to-face encounter, and some people prefer masturbatory activities because they avoid what are perceived as the hassles of in-person relationships. Anonymity is often important in this context, although it leaves open the possibility—or, often enough, the probability—that certain aspects of the individuals' physical appearance, social characteristics or standing, or other details will be omitted, exaggerated, or falsified, such as age and gender. Suler (2005) offers a brief overview of this "disinhibiting" effect of the perceived anonymity that many users feel as a probable contributor to the tendency of some people to do or say things they might not otherwise do (for a more detailed look at this phenomenon, see Adam Joinson's chapter in the present volume). Goldsborough (1996) has noted that there is some evidence that the personal computer is regarded by some people as an extension of themselves, in effect, expanding McLuhan's (1964) thesis that the media are extensions of our senses (see also Norden, 1969). It is interesting to note that it was McLuhan who coined the term *global village*, and that some of his ideas are beginning to be reconsidered as

communications theorists have begun to recognize the validity of many of his predictions that are now being validated with respect to the Internet. McLuhan's ideas
had already been applied to sexual styles of relating by Francoeur and Francoeur
(1974). Along similar lines, Hamman (1996) used cyborg theory to consider the
computer as a sexual prosthesis in people's experimentation with multiple selves in
his study of cybersex in AOL's online chatrooms.

Typically, masturbation has been the sexual behavior most closely associated
with Internet use in a sexual context, whether viewing erotic imagery, reading erotic
stories, or participating in cybersex. Masturbation, of course, is a highly problematic
behavior for a significant number of Americans, particularly many of those individuals who closely identify with the more orthodox flavors of various religious traditions (cf. the discussion by Francoeur and Perper, 1997, 2004) of fixed versus process
worldviews, which comprise a continuum of attitudes and values, and the behaviors—sexual and nonsexual—often congruent with them, as noted earlier). I have
long held the belief that it is the erotic component of sex that triggers the most
intense negative feelings in some people, probably because of the powerlessness that
many people feel when they experience it. Masturbation in both sexes may be con-
taminated because of this association with eroticism, probably as much as its negation
of the procreative potential. Masturbation also has the added baggage of being more
closely associated with male sexuality, at once exalted and denigrated in postmodern
American culture as well as in some social science circles. The fear of masturbation, as
well as moral objections to it, may have some of its etiology in these factors, although
Money (1985) has clearly noted the antisexualism of some prominent early American
health practitioners who opposed it because of the harm they believed it caused.

In addition to these activities that are geared to sexual entertainment on the
Web, the "serious" side of sex, both sex-positive and sex-negative, is more fully
represented than in the newsgroups. These include an enormous amount of information about such things as contraception and abortion, sexuality and disability,
religious views of sexual morality, sexual health statistics, and heterosexual, homosexual, bisexual, and intersexual interests and lifestyles. Some are oriented to professional interests; others are addressed to the informed public or to both. True to
part of the Internet's initial purpose of facilitating communication and collaboration between researchers worldwide, the Web is also a vast repository of research
and scholarly and media reports on sex-related topics. Virtually every major sexual
health organization has a presence on the Web, such as the Planned Parenthood
Federation of America (http://www.plannedparenthood.org/) and many of its local
affiliates, the Sexuality Information and Education Council of the United States
(http://www.siecus.org/), and many others. In addition, major sexuality resources,
such as *The Magnus Hirschfeld Archive for Sexology at Humboldt University in Berlin*
(http://www2.hu-berlin.de/sexology/), provides copious online documents of use
to sex researchers, counselors, and public policymakers, including the complete text
of several standard reference books. In fact, by the time this volume is published, the

author's award-winning *Continuum Complete International Encyclopedia of Sexuality* will have begun to be posted in its entirety on the website of the Kinsey Institute (http://www.kinseyinstitute.org/ccies/), covering sexual attitudes and behaviors in 62 countries and places. Links can be found to these and many more sexuality-related websites at http://www.SexQuest.com/SexQuest.html.

POLITICAL, PERSONAL, AND COMMUNITY ASPECTS OF SEX ON THE INTERNET

Earlier, I discussed some of the meanings that sexuality has for human beings and the ways that the dissemination of cultural values, and conflicts about sexual expression, occur in human societies. An important difference with the Internet, however, from these more traditional organizational activities is the emergence of the individual as a potential force in the promotion of both established and opposing ideas. Given the relatively inexpensive means available at the present time in the United States to publish one's own personal "home page" on the Web, as well as the emergence of blogs of every conceivable nature, it is possible for individuals to empower themselves to express opinions and offer new insights about virtually any topic. On the Internet, all such sites are roughly equal, supported only by the power of the words and arguments expressed by the person presenting them, and, with respect to blogs, the community that develops around them. Certainly, as in any medium employing words, written or spoken, the clarity, sense, internal logic, and external support of the ideas are called upon to bolster the views promoted. It is then left to the readers or listeners, based on their own experience, education, temperament, and so on, to evaluate the persuasiveness of the arguments and either reject or accept them, and, again with respect to blogs (and to a lesser extent, list-servs) to offer one's opinions. There are typically no editors or censors mediating the process or telling us only what we are supposed to hear or read.

This, of course, can cause some problems, particularly for authoritarian organizations and personalities. Anyone can believe that what she or he has to say is worthwhile, which can result in support for truths that threaten existing power structures. Power tends to relinquish itself reluctantly, because power is an advantage in today's competitive world where rights seem to be considered scarce commodities gained only at the expense of taking comparable rights from others. This faulty thinking is maintained because it fragments political opposition, thus maintaining the status quo, in which the needs of the majority of people are often either ignored or manipulated in the interests of those already controlling society or important subsections of it (see Noonan, 1998a, for insights to how this might affect public policy, including the direction of research on sex-related issues). Others have noted that censoring sexual content, thereby controlling people's sexuality, helps to control them in other ways. The Beat poet, Allan Ginsberg, for example, whose poem *Howl* was banned from the public airwaves by the Federal Communications Commission (FCC), said:

> Censorship of sexual discourse or public communication about sex is one way of keeping the populace under control. If you can censor the seat of one of the greater emotions, then you've got the other varieties under control. In a sense, metaphorically, once you get people by the balls, then you've got them. (Quoted in Stefanac, 1993, p. 39)

In the national and international political arenas, participatory democracy is often seen as a value that may find its ultimate expression via the immediacy of the anticipated ubiquitous Internet (see Katz, 1997). Yet, similar conflicts are often seen in the territorial disputes among various professionals who lay claim to particular areas of expertise or specific ideologies that have developed within them, such as those referred to today as "politically correct." In most arenas, communities have developed on the Internet that challenge or support—or simply supply information about the subject involved. These may involve Web sites or blogs devoted to a singular passion, newsgroups focused on a specific cause, or listservs via email in which "subscribers" debate and support each other in their various viewpoints about an issue. In the sexual arena, the Academic Sexual Correctness listserv mentioned earlier, for example, has generated much discussion among college educators on false accusations of sexual harassment and similar abuses in academia. Similar debates among proponents of various men's and women's issues—as well as varying viewpoints about all sorts of sexual health issues—exist on the Web, which are highlighted with links at http://www.SexQuest.com/SexQuest.html.

Meanwhile, sexologists, like psychologists and other social scientists, have begun to look seriously at the sexual issues raised by the Internet and communicating online (Cooper, 1997a). Cooper (2002) has provided the first manual for psychologists and others who are encountering the various sexual problems related to Internet use in his *Sex and the Internet: A Guidebook for Clinicians*. The achievement of sexual health has been illustrated as well by various studies over the past few years that have shown some potential for reaching the sex partners of individuals infected with HIV or STDs through email and Internet chat rooms and referring them for testing and treatment (CDC, 2003, 2004a, b).

MEETING POTENTIAL PARTNERS AT ONLINE DATING SITES

If sex can be said to have driven the technological development of the Internet, then we might say that sex has been driving the expansion of online dating sites that have exploded on the Web. Sex in this sense would be in its broadest interpretation, from those seeking partners for pure erotic pleasure and release, to marriage and babies, to social and interpersonal connectedness, to alleviating loneliness or boredom, among others—with or without love of whatever sexual orientation. Ross (2005) has provided a useful framework for researchers to explore Internet-mediated sexuality. He focuses on social theory and sexual scripts, among other perspectives, that he hopes will help us to better understand the diversity of sexual interactions on the Internet as a part of sexual culture at large. Delmonico (2003) highlights some of the challenges that online daters face:

> On the Internet, relationships are virtual—that is, not based in the same reality on which we have created relationships for thousands of years. Our five senses are often lost or distorted during Internet interactions. I usually cannot see, hear, touch, smell, or "taste" the individual with whom I am trying to form a relationship. There are attempts to approximate these senses; however, efforts at videoconferencing and voice chatting are far from replacing the "real world." Even more difficult is that sixth sense that we tap into when forming relationships—that inner instinct when our senses combine with our history, expectations, and desires which results [in] that internal feeling of "good" or "bad" about a relationship. Granted, these first impressions about relationships can be wrong, but as most of us know, if we trust these feelings, they are typically good cues about the future of that relationship. Perhaps this is what the Internet will never replace. (p. 259)

Most online dating services, such as the very popular Match.com, appear to start with the premise that similar interests and other factors that the two individuals share contribute greatly to the potential for success. Prospective members fill out online profiles when they subscribe to the service that detail one's self-description and that of the ideal mate across various parameters. These sites seem to meet the needs of millions of subscriber-members. Specialized niche services exist as well that cater to people with very focused interests. One such organization, eHarmony.com, seems to have the most comprehensive enrollment process that statistically matches members based on an extensive sophisticated questionnaire which subscribers complete online. The instrument, according to the website, was developed based on research done by Dr. Neil Clark Warren, eHarmony's founder, into various compatibility traits that he believes contribute to successful marriages. A key factor is that the site is strongly oriented toward traditional marriage and is clearly marketed to an audience seeking that. They subscribe to the popular belief that they can help one find her or his soul mate. Research conducted by eHarmony indicates that marriages that resulted from matches made there had higher scores on marital satisfaction than comparison couples who had met elsewhere (Carter & Snow, 2004). Some specialized niche services cater to racial or ethnic populations, activities or special interests, such as exercising or pets, just casual dating or sex, or a host of other variables. Of particular note are the sites that exist for individuals who are afflicted with herpes, HPV, HIV/AIDS, or other STDs. One of the most popular is PositiveSingles.com, which allows one to connect with other singles who understand the problems with potential rejection that having such infections can cause. As such, they can encourage honesty in relationships, as many people sometimes refrain from disclosing that they have certain diseases, such as herpes and HPV. These individuals can then enjoy the intimacy that they want, with the full knowledge that their partner will understand the need for certain restrictions. They can thus enhance their self-esteem and the general satisfaction with life that intimacy brings, to which everyone is entitled.

In the summer of 2005, television viewers were given a glimpse of the world of online dating in *Hooking Up* (Taylor, 2005), a "reality TV" documentary from ABC News following the online dating adventures of several New York City women as they searched for "Mr. Right." It was revealing in that it clearly demonstrated that the trials and tribulations of online dating were not substantively different from those of traditional forms of dating. The women—and to a lesser extent, the men—still appeared to cling to unrealistic notions that there existed "out there somewhere" their one-and-only soul mate, their Mr. or Ms. Right, if only they could find them. According to the program, there are 40 million online daters in the United States, all searching for someone. It was apparent that high-tech involvement in the initial meeting process did not mediate the insecurities, the need for approval, the desperation, the vulnerabilities, the fear or experience of rejection and failure, and so on, that real people with real bodies and minds have in negotiating a potential intimate relationship. Several dynamics of relationships were highlighted, including the observation by some of the women that "women have the upper hand" in the online dating experience, at least in the screening process. They enjoyed the fact that they can be independent and the pursuer and be in control and have power. Sex was often seen as a commodity and a bargaining chip in the dating game, which gave the women power. "Dating deception" was also highlighted, as were lies and manipulation on the part of both the women and the men, which counterbalanced some of the shifting power dynamics within the couples, much as often happens in traditional dating scenarios. Most of this deception did not seem malevolent, but rather attempts to allow the other person to see how they "really" were beyond aspects of their true identities and professions. Still, the bottom line, as in traditional first meetings, was that chemistry and spark (the sexual component, although it was rarely articulated as such), along with shared interests, were what everyone seemed to be seeking.

The first national survey on online dating took place in the fall of 2005 conducted by the Pew Internet & American Life Project (Madden & Lenhart, 2006; summary: http://www.pewinternet.org/PPF/r/177/report_display.asp), which revealed some interesting insights into the rising popularity of online dating in recent years. A preliminary report was also published based on the same data (Rainie & Madden, 2006; summary: http://www.pewinternet.org/PPF/r/173/report_display.asp), which presented some additional insights into romantic pairings in contemporary America. Of particular note was the discovery that actively looking for romantic partners was not a high priority for most young singles, and that significant numbers of those seeking relationships were not even dating very frequently. The reader is referred to these online reports for statistics on current committed-relationship and partner-seeking status among Internet users, as well as comparison data on where first meetings took place among those who are married or in committed relationships (only 3% met through the Internet). Yet, online dating sites have been affecting how we date early in the 21st century, according to these reports.

Among the major findings relative to online dating itself, Madden and Lenhart (2006) found that roughly two-thirds of those who are currently single and looking have used the Internet in some way, including online dating, to further their romantic interests. They also found that significant numbers of Americans personally know people who have tried online dating and succeeded at it, resulting in a major shift in public attitudes toward it in recent years. Yet they found that most Internet users believe that online dating is dangerous because of posting personal information online. Still, among those who have actually tried it, a slight majority feels it is not dangerous, although many others believe it involves some risk. Yahoo! Personals and Match.com were found to be the most popular dating sites among those who took part in the survey. More than half of the respondents said they had mostly positive experiences with online dating, while less than a third reported mostly negative experiences. (I know of no comparable data with respect to offline dating with which to compare their experiences, although anecdotal stories suggest that it might be similar.) The young seemed to have the most favorable responses in general. The authors noted that, although deception is certainly a possibility as in offline encounters, it "seems to be the exception rather than the rule" (p. 2), despite the fact that most people said they believed that a lot of people lie about their marital status. On social attitudes in general, there were statistically significant differences between online daters and both Internet users and Americans in general. An interesting highlight was the finding that 15% of American adults and 43% or online daters personally knew someone who found a long-term partner online.

All of this, of course, raises the question as to the role that psychologists or commentators might play in improving the dynamics of couples' relationships, if they themselves believe in such concepts as Mr. and Ms. Right, one-and-only soul mates, and similar mythologies. It appears that the lifecycle of relationships follows the same path as that in offline relationships. Thus, Internet dating is just another way to meet people. Is it a hit-or-miss proposition as much as random meetings with new people are? After all, we only get intimately involved with people with whom we come in contact; if we do not meet them, we will not have a relationship. And what of the failures that will likely ensue? It has long been my contention that if we told young people that most relationships do not last, we would help inoculate them from the self-blame or fear of failure that often results from failed relationships. Certainly, we still have much to learn about creating successful relationships.

BLOGGING: SEXUAL EMPOWERMENT VIA ONLINE CONVERSATIONS

Blogs are a recent form of online journaling, as noted earlier, which have become increasingly important in the online world and which are having an impact on the real world. Their importance as instant news reporting and commentary forums really made their power known during the 2004 U. S. presidential national conventions, as word from the inside began to regularly scoop national television and other media coverage of significant events at the grassroots level. Sexuality and other mental health professionals have been relatively slow at adopting this new technology, although that began to change in 2005. The value that blogging has for sexual health and expression lies in the empowerment that is achieved by both individuals and communities on the Web. Another new technology that seems to have been necessitated by rapidly emerging posts on blogsites is that of RSS (Really Simple Syndication) newsfeeds, which work with programs called news aggregators to automatically go out on the Web and collect headlines from blogs (and websites so configured) soon after new articles or comments are posted. This empowers users to scan headlines as they scroll across their screen on their computer's desktop or in customized lists of headlines and abstracts also accessible on the desktop or on the Web. As noted earlier in this section with respect to the political aspects of sex on the Internet, power dynamics can shift as information that is privileged to the select few can now be published to interested communities on a global scale. Although blogs can be similar to any other page on the Web, the power comes from the ability that is built into the technology for the community to publicly respond to the ideas and events made known in the posting, and to engage in multiple dialogues to maybe influence some outcome. In the sexuality arena, this can have multiple uses—in political advocacy and community building to education and counseling to erotic stimulation. The following blogsites illustrate these personally and socially empowering uses that have the potential to provide "insignificant" input to the chaotic systems that comprise Internet sexuality by perhaps influencing the "extreme sensitivity to initial conditions" that drives sexual attitudes and behavior online and offline to different outcomes at various levels as noted earlier with respect to the butterfly effect. These effects have the potential to be triggered by both experts and the educated lay public who have a specialized interest.

Yahoo's health expert blogs include *Real & Revealing* (http://blogs.health. yahoo.com/experts/sexlevine), which deals with enhancing sexual well-being. It is written by Deborah Levine, a syndicated columnist on the Web who is the founder and director of Internet Sexuality Information Services, Inc. (ISIS), a nonprofit organization that focuses on online sexual health promotion and disease prevention using high-tech solutions (http://www.isis-inc.org/). Yahoo also offers Dr. Leonard DeRogatis's *Rx for Your Sexual Health* (http://blogs.health. yahoo.com/experts/sexderogatis), dealing with various medical issues. WebMD's expert blog, *Sexual Health: Sex Matters* (http://blogs.webmd.com/sexual-health-sex-matters/) by Dr. Louanne Cole-Weston provides authoritative information along with commentary on many health aspects of sexuality for the general public, often linking to articles published at WebMD.com. WebMD also has a number of other sex-related blogs, including Terri Warren's blog, *Genital Herpes: Intimate Conversations* (http://blogs.webmd.com/genital-herpes-intimate-conversations/) with information on all aspects of the disease, among others on men's health, pregnancy, and other general health topics. The Sexual Health Network Experts' blog, *Sex and Meaning* (http://sexualhealth.com/blog/) provides commentaries on current issues focusing on media reports. One of their contributors, Dr. Marty Klein, also publishes a monthly electronic newsletter, *Sexual Intelligence*, which is also online (http://www.sexualintelligence.org/), providing news, media critiques, social commentary, and political insight from a sex-positive point-of-view, although it is technically not a blog in that readers cannot directly comment on the postings. This author's *SexQuest Blog: International Trends, Chaotic Systems, and Alternative Futures in Sexuality* (http://www.SexQuest.com/blog) began publishing in mid 2006.

Daze Reader's more erotically explicit blog (http://www.dazereader.com/weblog. htm) focuses on news and commentaries on sexual culture from various angles, including links to numerous sex-oriented blogs, many about personal erotic adventures and musings or pornographic websites and the sex industry. Rachyl's *Dating and Romance Blog* (http://www.caije.com/dating-romance-blog/), dealing with mostly sexual issues for singles, is an example of a grassroots layperson's blog offering advice related to these issues. Another is the *Kiss & Blog* (http://www.kissnblog.com/) site providing insights to issues related to singles with humorous banter between a man and a woman, both anonymous. C. D. Oldenburg's blog (http://www.bycdoldenburg.com/) focuses on gay, lesbian, bisexual, and transgender (GLBT) news and issues. *Best Gay Blogs* (http://www. bestgayblogs.net/) provides links to rated blogs of interest to the GLBT community, from the political to the personal. Similarly, *Feminist Blogs: Independent Alternatives to the Malestream Media* (http://feministblogs.org/) focuses on issues of interest to various stripes of feminists, including many sex-related issues.

CONCLUSION

I have shown that various forces have had an impact on the pluralism that is sexuality and the Internet—and the Internet, at present, continues to reflect that diversity. It is essential that the most repressive ends of the spectrum not dictate what is available online. The diverse meanings inherent in the human sexuality complex (Noonan, 1998a, 2004b), and recent advances and debates in sexology and the social sciences as a whole, argue for maintaining that pluralism. We must take a proactive approach to ensuring sexual health for all by fostering self-empowerment, wherein the strength of the Internet lies. Sexual pleasure, personal happiness, satisfaction with life, and personal interconnectedness with others is also a strong part of that mix. Sexual diversity is the norm on the Internet, despite efforts to sanitize and homogenize it to conform to the level of psychosexual development of children. Various communities have adopted it to help inform others of their sexual realities. Among scientists, sexologists are among a broad spectrum of social science professionals utilizing the Web, for example, to promote better research and to disseminate its results to more people. In the balance, these factors can only bode well for sexology—and for our collective sexual health.

REFERENCES

An adult affair. (1997, January 4). *The Economist, 342.* [Available: http://www.elibrary.com/]

Anderson, P. B., de Mauro, D., & Noonan, R. J. (Eds.). (1996). *Does anyone still remember when sex was fun? Positive sexuality in the age of AIDS* (3rd ed.). Dubuque, IA: Kendall/Hunt Publishing Co.

Archive for Sexology. (2005). *The Magnus Hirschfeld archive for sexology at Humboldt University in Berlin.* http://www2.hu-berlin.de/sexology/

Bancroft, J., & Vukadinovic, Z. (2004, August). Sexual addiction, sexual compulsivity, sexual impulsivity, or what? Toward a theoretical model. *Journal of Sex Research, 41*(3), 225–234.

Bender, C., Dix, A. J., Rhulen, A. (Producers), Bress, E., & Gruber, J. M. (Directors). (2004). *The butterfly effect.* Infinifilm: Beyond the movie: The science and psychology of chaos theory [Feature film extras on DVD]. New Line Home Entertainment.

Blackerby, R. F. (1993). *Application of chaos theory to psychological models.* Unpublished doctoral dissertation, University of Texas at Austin. Excerpts available at (http://www.perfstrat.com/rfb/chaostoc.htm)

Bolton, R. (1995). Rethinking anthropology: The study of AIDS. In H. ten Brummelhuis & G. Herdt (Eds.), *Culture and sexual risk: Anthropological perspectives on AIDS* (pp. 285–313). Luxembourg: Gordon and Breach.

Carter, S., & Snow, C. (2004, May). Helping singles enter better marriages using predictive models of marital success. Presentation at the 16th Annual Convention of the American Psychological Society, May 2004. [Available: http://www.eharmony.com/singles/servlet/about/research]

Caslon Analytics. (2005). *Caslon Analytics note: Usenet.* (http://www.caslon.com.au/usenetnote.htm)

CBS News. (2004, September 5). Porn in the U.S.A. *60 Minutes.* http://www.cbsnews.com/stories/2003/11/21/60minutes/main585049.shtml

Centers for Disease Control and Prevention (CDC). (2003, December 19). Internet use and early syphilis infection among men who have sex with men—San Francisco, California, 1999–2003. *Morbidity and Mortality Weekly Report (MMWR), 52*(50), 1229–1232. http://www.cdc.gov/mmwr/preview/mmwrhtml/mm5250a4.htm

Centers for Disease Control and Prevention (CDC). (2004a, February 20). Using the Internet for partner notification of sexually transmitted diseases—Los Angeles County, California, 2003. *Morbidity and Mortality Weekly Report (MMWR), 53*(6), 129–131. http://www.cdc.gov/mmwr/preview/mmwrhtml/mm5306a4.htm

Centers for Disease Control and Prevention (CDC). (2004b, April 30). Notice to readers: Innovative STD prevention programs. *Morbidity and Mortality Weekly Report (MMWR), 53*(16), 346–347. http://www.cdc.gov/mmwr/preview/mmwrhtml/mm5316a5.htm

Clatts, M. C. (1995). Disembodied acts: On the perverse use of sexual categories in the study of high-risk behaviour. In H. ten Brummelhuis & G. Herdt (Eds.), *Culture and sexual risk: Anthropological perspectives on AIDS* (pp. 241–255). Luxembourg: Gordon and Breach.

Cooper, A. (Ed.). (1997a, June). Special issue: Sexuality and the Internet. *Journal of Sex Education and Therapy, 22*(1), 1–92.

Cooper, A. (Chair). (1997b, August). *Sexuality and the Internet—Surfing into the next millennium.* Symposium conducted at the 105th Annual Conference of the American Psychological Association (APA), August 18, 1997, Chicago, IL.

Cooper, A. (Ed.). (2002). *Sex and the Internet: A guidebook for clinicians.* New York: Brunner-Routledge.

Cooper, A., & Griffin-Shelley, E. (2002). Introduction. The Internet: The next sexual revolution. In A. Cooper (Ed.), *Sex and the Internet: A guidebook for clinicians.* New York: Brunner-Routledge.

Cooper, A., & Griffin-Shelley, E. (2004). Online sexual activity. In D. L. Weis & P. B. Koch/R. J. Noonan & R. T. Francoeur (Chap./Update Coords.), United States of America. In R. T. Francoeur & R. J. Noonan (Eds.), *Continuum complete international encyclopedia of sexuality* (pp. 1290–1293). New York: Continuum International Publishing Group. http://www.kinseyinstitute.org/ccies/us.php#osa

Davis, C. M., & Bauserman, R. (1993). Exposure to sexually explicit materials: An attitude change perspective. *Annual Review of Sex Research, 4,* 121–209.

Delmonico, D. L. (2003, August). Cybersex: Changing the way we relate. *Sexual and Relationship Therapy, 18*(3), 259–260.

Diamond, M., & Uchiyama, A. (1999). Pornography, rape, and sex crimes in Japan. *International Journal of Law and Psychiatry, 22*(1), 1–22. http://www.hawaii.edu/PCSS/online_artcls/pornography/prngrphy_rape_jp.html

di Mauro, D. (1995a). *Executive summary: Sexuality research in the United States: An assessment of the social and behavioral sciences.* New York: Sexuality Research Assessment Project, Social Sciences Research Council.

di Mauro, D. (1995b). *Sexuality research in the United States: An assessment of the social and behavioral sciences.* New York: Sexuality Research Assessment Project, Social Sciences Research Council.

Fienberg, H. (2000, June 3). A cyberepidemic may just be a cybermarketing strategy. Washington, DC: Statistical Assessment Service. http://www.stats.org/record.jsp?type=oped&ID=56

Fogel, A., & Lyra, M. C. D. P. (1997). Dynamics of development in relationships. In F. Masterpasqua & P. A. Perna, Eds., *The psychological meaning of chaos: Translating theory into practice* (pp. 75–94). Washington, DC: American Psychological Association.

Francoeur, A. K., & Francoeur, R. T. (1974). *Hot & cool sex: Cultures in conflict.* New York: Harcourt Brace Jovanovich.

Francoeur, R. T. (1984). *Becoming a sexual person: A brief edition.* New York: John Wiley & Sons.

Francoeur, R. T. (Ed.). (1997). *International encyclopedia of sexuality* (Vols. 1–3). New York: Continuum Publishing Co. http://www2.hu-berlin.de/sexology/IES/xmain.html

Francoeur, R. T., & Noonan, R. J. (Eds.). (2001). *International encyclopedia of sexuality* (Vol. 4). New York: Continuum International Publishing Group. http://www2.hu-berlin.de/sexology/IES/xmain.html

Francoeur, R. T., & Noonan, R. J. (Eds.). (2004). *Continuum complete international encyclopedia of sexuality.* New York and London: Continuum International Publishing Group.

Francoeur, R. T., & Noonan, R. J. (Eds.) (2006-2007). *Continuum complete international encyclopedia of sexuality.* New York and London: Continuum Publishing Group. http://www.kinseyinstitute.org/ccies/

Francoeur, R. T., & Perper, T. (1997). General character and ramifications of American religious perspectives on sexuality. In R. T. Francoeur (Ed.), *International encyclopedia of sexuality* (Vol. 3, pp. 1392–1403). New York: Continuum.

Francoeur, R. T., & Perper, T. (2004). General character and ramifications of American religious perspectives on sexuality. In D. L. Weis & P. B. Koch/R. J. Noonan & R. T. Francoeur (Chap./Update Coords.), United States of America. In R. T. Francoeur & R. J. Noonan (Eds.), *Continuum complete international encyclopedia of sexuality* (pp. 1139–1144). New York: Continuum International Publishing Group. http://www.kinseyinstitute.org/ccies/us.php#relig

Fumento, M. (1990). *The myth of heterosexual AIDS.* New York: Basic Books [A New Republic Book].

Gleick, J. (1988). *Chaos: Making a new science.* New York: Penguin Books.

Glick, I. D., Clarkin, J. F., & Kessler, D. R. (1987). *Marital and family therapy* (3rd ed.). New York: Grune & Stratton.

Goldsborough, R. (1996, June 20). The lure of cyberporn. *Personal Computing.* [Available: http://www.elibrary.com/]

Greenspan, R. (2003, September 25). Porn pages reach 260 million. ClickZ Network/Stats: Traffic Patterns. http://www.clickz.com/stats/sectors/traffic_patterns/article.php/3083001

Hamman, R. B. (1996). *Cyborgasms: Cybersex amongst multiple-selves and cyborgs in the narrow-bandwidth space of America Online chat rooms.* Master's thesis, University of Essex, Colchester, UK. http://www.socio.demon.co.uk/Cyborgasms.html

Hansen, E. (2004, December 30). XXX, on a small screen near you. *CNET News.com.* http://news.com.com/XXX,+on+a+small+screen+near+you/2100-1039_3-5502413.html

Hardy, H. E. (1993). *The history of the Net.* Master's thesis, Grand Valley State University, Allendale, MI. http://www.eff.org/Net_culture/net.history.txt

Henkin, W. A. (1991/1996). The myth of sexual addiction. In R. T. Francoeur (Ed.), *Taking sides: Clashing views on controversial issues in human sexuality* (5th ed., pp. 56–75). Guilford, CT: Dushkin.

Hirsh, L. (2002, August 23). Is porn still the hidden king of e-commerce? *E-Commerce Times.* http://www.ecommercetimes.com/story/19135.html

Katz, J. (1997, December). The Netizen: The digital citizen. *Wired, 5.12,* 68–82, 274–275.

Kirkendall, L. A. (1984). Family options, governments, and the social milieu: Viewed from the twenty-first century. In L.A. Kirkendall & A.E. Gravatt (Eds.), *Marriage and the family in the year 2020* (pp. 247–267). Buffalo, NY: Prometheus Books.

Klein, M. (1990/1992). Censorship and the fear of sexuality. In O. Pocs (Ed.), *Annual editions: Human sexuality 92/93* (17th ed., pp. 32–35). Guilford, CT: Dushkin Publishing Group. (Reprinted from *The Humanist,* July/August 1990)

Klein, M. (2000, March). The myth of sexual addiction. *Sexual Intelligence, 1.* http://www.sexed.org/newsletters/issue01.html#myth

Kohl, J. V., & Francoeur, R. T. (1995). *The scent of Eros: Mysteries of odor in human sexuality.* New York: Continuum.

Laudan, L. (1994). *The book of risks: Fascinating facts about the chances we take every day.* New York: Wiley.

Lawrence, R. J. (1989). *The poisoning of Eros: Sexual values in conflict.* New York: Augustine Moore Press.

Leach, P. (1994). *Children first: What our society must do—and is not doing—for our children today.* New York: Alfred A. Knopf.

Leun, G. van der. (1995, March 1). Behavior: Twilight zone of the id. Today online sex is as wild and far ranging as the human imagination. *Time.* [Available: http://www.elibrary.com/]

Libby, R. W., & Whitehurst, R. N. (Eds.). (1977). *Marriage and alternatives: Exploring intimate relationships.* Glenview, IL: Scott, Foresman and Co.

Lyman, J. (2005, October 21). Will iPod be eye for porn? *MacNewsWorld.* http://www.macnewsworld.com/story/46892.html

Macklin, E. D., & Rubin, R. H. (Eds.). (1983). *Contemporary families and alternative lifestyles: Handbook on research and theory.* Beverly Hills, CA: Sage Publications.

Madden, M., & Lenart, A. (2006). *Online dating* Washington, DC: Pew Internet & American Life Project. http://www.pewinternet.org/pdfs/PIP_Online_Dating.pdf

Masterpasqua, F., & Perna, P. A. (Eds.). (1997). *The psychological meaning of chaos: Translating theory into practice.* Washington, DC: American Psychological Association.

McLuhan, M. (1964). *Understanding media: The extensions of man.* New York: McGraw-Hill.

Miller, J. G. (1991). Applications of living systems theory to life in space. In A. A. Harrison, Y. A. Clearwater, & C. P. McKay (Eds.), *From Antarctica to outer space: Life in isolation and confinement* (pp. 177–197). New York: Springer-Verlag.

Miller, L. (1998, February 13). Wired love advisors help link up singles on line. *USA Today,* p. 12D. [Available: http://www.elibrary.com/]

Money, J. (1985). *The destroying angel: Sex, fitness, & food in the legacy of degeneracy theory: Graham crackers, Kellogg's corn flakes, & American health history.* Buffalo, NY: Prometheus.

Money, J. (1986a). *Lovemaps: Clinical concepts of sexual/erotic health and pathology, paraphilia, and gender transposition in childhood, adolescence, and maturity.* New York: Irvington.

Money, J. (1986b). *Venuses penuses: Sexology, sexosophy, and exigency theory.* Buffalo, NY: Prometheus.

Money, J. (1995). *Gendermaps: Social constructionism, feminism, and sexosophical history.* New York: Continuum.

Money, J., & Lamacz, M. (1989). *Vandalized lovemaps: Paraphilic outcome of seven cases in pediatric sexology.* Buffalo, NY: Prometheus Books.

Moore, M. (1994). Introducing the Internet. In Sams Publishing, *The Internet unleashed.* Indianapolis, IN: Sams Publishing/Prentice Hall Computer Publishing.

Morford, M. (2005, October 21). Harness iPod's dollar power—Porn on the go. *San Francisco Chronicle* [Datebook/SFGate.com]. http://www.sfgate.com/cgi-bin/article.cgi?f=/c/a/2005/10/21/DDGLFFB16K1.DTL

Murstein, B. I. (1974). *Love, sex, & marriage through the ages.* New York: Springer.

National Research Council, Panel on Monitoring the Social Impact of the AIDS Epidemic. (1993). *The social impact of AIDS in the United States.* Washington, DC: National Academy Press.

Noonan, R. J. (1979). *Evolving marriage: The new sexualities in perspective.* Paper presented at the IV World Congress of Sexology, December 17, 1979, Mexico City, Mexico. http://www.SexQuest.com/SexualHealth/evolvmarriage.html

Noonan, R. J. (1996a). New directions, new hope for sexuality: On the cutting edge of sane sex. In P. B. Anderson, D. de Mauro, & R. J. Noonan (Eds.), *Does anyone still remember when sex was fun? Positive sexuality in the age of AIDS* (3rd ed., pp. 144–221). Dubuque, IA: Kendall/Hunt Publishing Co.

Noonan, R. J. (1997a). The impact of AIDS on our perception of sexuality. In R. T. Francoeur (Ed.), *International Encyclopedia of Sexuality* (Vol. 3, pp. 1622–1625). New York: Continuum (http://www.kinseyinstitute.org/ccies/us.php#percept).

Noonan, R. J. (1997b, August). Realizing sexual potential through the World Wide Web. In A. Cooper (Chair), *Sexuality and the Internet—Surfing into the next millennium.* Symposium conducted at the 105th Annual Conference of the American Psychological Association (APA), August 18, 1997, Chicago, IL.

Noonan, R. J. (1998a). *A philosophical inquiry into the role of sexology in space life sciences research and human factors considerations for extended spaceflight.* Doctoral dissertation, New York University (UMI publication number 9832759; see http://www.sexquest.com/SexualHealth/rjnoonan-diss-abstract.html).

Noonan, R. J. (1998b). The impact of AIDS on our perception of sexuality. In R. T. Francoeur (Ed.), *Sexuality in America: Understanding our sexual values and behavior* (pp. 248–251). New York: Continuum.

Noonan, R. J. (1998c, November). The social construction of sexual harassment and heterophobia. In R. J. Noonan, (Chair), *Alt.sex.conference II: A follow-up symposium on controversial unaddressed issues.* Symposium conducted during the 1998 Joint Annual Meeting of the Society for the Scientific Study of Sexuality (SSSS) and the American Association of Sex Educators, Counselors, and Therapists (AASECT), November 13, 1998, Los Angeles, CA.

Noonan, R. J. (1998d). The psychology of sex: A mirror from the Internet. In J. Gackenbach, (Ed.), *Psychology and the Internet: Intrapersonal, interpersonal and transpersonal implications* (pp. 143–168). New York: Academic Press.

Noonan, R. J. (2001a, November). Web resources for sex researchers: The state of the art, now and in the future [book reviews (Web reviews)]. *Journal of Sex Research, 38*(4), 348–351.

Noonan, R. J. (2001b, December). *The JSR website review companion page.* http://www.SexQuest.com/SexualHealth/JSRwebsite-reviews.html

Noonan, R. J. (2004a). Heterophobia: The evolution of an idea. In D. L. Weis & P. B. Koch/R. J. Noonan & R. T. Francoeur (Chap./Update Coords.), United States of America. In R. T. Francoeur & R. J. Noonan (Eds.), *Continuum complete international encyclopedia of sexuality* (pp. 1167–1168). New York: Continuum International Publishing Group. http://www.kinseyinstitute.org/ccies/us.php#heterophobia

Noonan, R. J. (2004b). Outer space and Antarctica: Sexuality factors in extreme environments. In R. T. Francoeur & R. J. Noonan (Eds.), *Continuum complete international encyclopedia of sexuality* (pp. 795–812). New York: Continuum International Publishing Group. http://www.kinseyinstitute.org/ccies/aq.php

Noonan, R. J. (2004c). Sexuality and American popular culture. In D. L. Weis & P. B. Koch/R. J. Noonan & R. T. Francoeur (Chap./Update Coords.), United States of America. In R. T. Francoeur & R. J. Noonan (Eds.), *Continuum complete international encyclopedia of sexuality* (pp. 1286–1287). New York: Continuum International Publishing Group. http://www.kinseyinstitute.org/ccies/us.php#popculture

Noonan, R. J. (2004d). Sexuality and terrorism in the United States. In D. L. Weis & P. B. Koch/R. J. Noonan & R. T. Francoeur (Chap./Update Coords.), United States of America. In R. T. Francoeur & R. J. Noonan (Eds.), *Continuum complete international encyclopedia of sexuality* (pp. 1137–1139). New York: Continuum International Publishing Group. http://www.kinseyinstitute.org/ccies/us.php#terrorism

Noonan, R. J. (2005a, July). Lessons from a decade of cross-cultural sexual research in 60 countries: Summary and future directions. In R. T. Francoeur, S. G. Frayser, & R. J. Noonan (Chairs), *Lessons from a decade of cross-cultural sexual research in 60 countries.* Symposium conducted by the Society for the Scientific Study of Sexuality (SSSS) during the XVII World Congress of Sexology, July 14, 2005, Montréal, Québec, Canada.

Noonan, R. J. (2005b, November). *Ethics and issues in teaching about culturally sensitive sexual topics: Lessons from* The Continuum Complete International Encyclopedia of Sexuality. Continuing Education session presented at the 2005 Conference of the Eastern and Midcontinent Regions of the Society for the Scientific Study of Sexuality (SSSS), November 6, 2005, Atlanta, GA.

Noonan, R. J. (2006, July). *The psychology of sex: A mirror from the Internet companion page.* http://www.SexQuest.com/SexualHealth/psychsexmirror.html

Noonan, R. J., & Britton, P. O. (1996, November). *Sex in cyberspace: Trends and implications for sexology.* Roundtable presentation at the 39th Annual Meeting of the Society for the Scientific Study of Sexuality (SSSS), November 15, 1996, Houston, TX.

Norden, E. (1969, March). The Playboy Interview: Marshall McLuhan. *Playboy.* http://www.mcluhanmedia.com/mmclpb01.html

Office of the Surgeon General. (2001). *The Surgeon General's call to action to promote sexual health and responsible sexual behavior 2001.* Rockville, MD: Office of the Surgeon General.

O'Neill, N., & O'Neill, G. (1972). *Open marriage: A new life style for couples.* New York: M. Evans and Company.

Patai, D. (1996). The feminist turn against men. *Partisan Review/4, 63*(3), 580–594.

Patai, D. (1998). *Heterophobia: Sexual harassment and the future of feminism.* Lantham, MD: Rowman & Littlefield Publishers.

Patai, D., & Koertge, N. (1994). *Professing feminism: Cautionary tales from the strange world of women's studies.* New York: Basic Books (A New Republic Book).

Perna, P. A., & Masterpasqua, F. (1997). Introduction. In F. Masterpasqua & P. A. Perna, Eds., *The psychological meaning of chaos: Translating theory into practice* (pp. 1–19). Washington, DC: American Psychological Association.

Pike, M. A. (1995). How the World Wide Web works. In M. A. Pike, *Special edition: Using the Internet* (2nd ed., pp. 677–691). Indianapolis, IN: Que Corporation.

Planned Parenthood Federation of America. (2003, April). *The health benefits of sexual expression* (White paper). New York: Katherine Dexter McCormick Library, Author, in cooperation with the Society for the Scientific Study of Sexuality.

Prescott, J. W. (1977). Phylogenetic and ontogenetic aspects of human affectional development. In R. Gemme & C. C. Wheeler, *Progress in sexology: Selected papers from the Proceedings of the 1976 International Congress of Sexology* (pp. 431–457). New York: Plenum Press.

Prescott, J. W. (1983, May 4). *Developmental origins of violence: Psychobiological, cross-cultural and religious perspectives.* Invited address presented at the 136th Annual Meeting of the American Psychiatric Association, New York, NY.

Rainie, L., & Madden, M. (2006, February). *Not looking for love: The state of romance in America.* Washington, DC: Pew Internet & American Life Project. http://www.pewinternet.org/pdfs/PIP_Romance_in_America_feb06.pdf

Reiss, I. L. (1990). *An end to shame: Shaping our next sexual revolution.* Buffalo, NY: Prometheus Books.

Rind, B., Bauserman, R., & Tromovitch, P. (2000). Science versus orthodoxy: Anatomy of the congressional condemnation of a scientific article and reflections on remedies for future ideological attacks. *Applied & Preventive Psychology, 9,* 211–226.

Rind, B., Bauserman, R., & Tromovitch, P. (2001a, July/August). The condemned meta-analysis on child sexual abuse: Good science and long-overdue skepticism. *Skeptical Inquirer, 25,* 68–72.

Rind, B., & Tromovitch, P. (1997). A meta-analytic review of findings from national samples on psychological correlates of child sexual abuse. *Journal of Sex Research, 34*(3), 237–255.

Rind, B., Tromovitch, P., & Bauserman, R. (1998). A meta-analytic examination of assumed properties of child sexual abuse using college samples. *Psychological Bulletin, 124*(1), 22–53.

Rind, B., Tromovitch, P., & Bauserman, R. (2001b). The validity and appropriateness of methods, analyses, and conclusions in Rind *et al.* (1998): A rebuttal of victimological critique from Ondersma *et al.* (2001) and Dallam *et al.* (2001). *Psychological Bulletin, 127*(6), 734–758.

Rose, F. (1997, December). Sex sells. *Wired, 5.12*, 218–224, 276–284.

Ross, M. W. (2005, November). Typing, doing, and being: Sexuality and the Internet. *Journal of Sex Research, 42*(4), 342–352.

Satcher, D. (2005, July 15). *Promoting sexual health: A vision for the future.* "State-of-the-art-lecture" at the XVII World Congress of Sexology, Montréal, Canada.

Schnarch, D. M. (1991). *Constructing the sexual crucible: An integration of sexual and marital therapy.* New York: W. W. Norton & Company.

Schnarch, D. M. (1997, June). Sex, intimacy, and the Internet. *Journal of Sex Education and Therapy, 22*(1), 15–20.

Simons, J. (1996, August 19). The Web's dirty secret. *U.S. News & World Report*, pp. 51–52. [Available: http://www.elibrary.com/]

Stefanac, S. (1993, April). Sex & the new media. *NewMedia, 3*(4), 38–45.

Suler, J. R. (2005, July). *The psychology of cyberspace.* Lawrenceville, NJ: Author, Rider University. http://www.rider.edu/~suler/psycyber/psycyber.html

Taylor, B. (Producer). (2005, July–August). *Hooking up* [Television 5-part documentary]. Philadelphia: American Broadcasting Company/ABC 6. (Broadcast: July 14, 21, 28, August 4, 11, 2005). http://abcnews.go.com/Technology/HookingUp/

Tharp, P. (2005, November 4). The naked "i": New XXX is sleaze in pod: Porn firms rush to sell minismut. *New York Post*, pp. 1, 3. http://www.nypost.com/news/nationalnews/53963.htm

Thayer, N. S. T. *et al.* (1987, March). Report of the Task Force on Changing Patterns of Sexuality and Family Life. *The Voice.* Newark, NJ: Episcopal Diocese of Northern New Jersey.

Thiel, S. (2005, November 21). Everything you don't want to know about your kid's sex life: An expanded version of the 100-teen-vs.-100-parent promiscuity poll. *New York Magazine.* http://www.newyorkmetro.com/lifestyle/sex/annual/2005/15079/index.html

Tiefer, L. (1995). *Sex is not a natural act and other essays.* Boulder, CO: Westview Press.

USA Today Tech Report. (1997, August 20). "Adult" sites drive many Web innovations. *USA Today*, p. 07D. [Available: http://www.elibrary.com/]

Weber, T. E. (1997, May 20). The X files: For those who scoff at Internet commerce, here's a hot market. Raking in millions, sex sites use old-fashioned porn and cutting-edge tech: Lessons for the mainstream. *The Wall Street Journal*, p. A1.

Weis, D. L. (2004a). Demographic challenges and a sketch of diversity, change, and social conflict. In D. L. Weis & P. B. Koch/R. J. Noonan & R. T. Francoeur (Chap./Update Coords.), United States of America. In R. T. Francoeur & R. J. Noonan (Eds.), *Continuum complete international encyclopedia of sexuality* (pp. 1128–1133). New York: Continuum International Publishing Group. http://www.kinseyinstitute.org/ccies/us.php#demog

Weis, D. L. (2004b). Interpersonal heterosexual behaviors: Childhood sexuality. In D. L. Weis & P. B. Koch/R. J. Noonan & R. T. Francoeur (Chap./Update Coords.), United States of America. In R. T. Francoeur & R. J. Noonan (Eds.), *Continuum complete international encyclopedia of sexuality* (pp. 1180–1187). New York: Continuum International Publishing Group. http://www.kinseyinstitute.org/ccies/us.php#children

Wikipedia. (2005). The ARPANET and nuclear attacks. In *ARPANET.* http://en.wikipedia.org/wiki/ARPANET

Wilkins, J. (1997, September 19). Protecting our children from Internet smut: Moral duty or moral panic? *The Humanist, 57.* [Available: http://www.elibrary.com/]

Working Group on a New View of Women's Sexual Problems. (2000, November 15). A new view of women's sexual problems. *Electronic Journal of Human Sexuality, 3.* http://www.ejhs.org/volume3/newview.htm

Worthington, C. (1996, October 6). Making love in cyberspace. *Independent on Sunday.* [Available: http://www.elibrary.com/]

CHAPTER 6

Internet Addiction: Does It Really Exist? (Revisited)

Laura Widyanto and Mark Griffiths
Psychology Division
Nottingham Trent University
Nottingham, United Kingdom

It has been alleged by some academics that excessive Internet use can be pathological and addictive and that it comes under the more generic label of "technological addiction" (e.g., Griffiths, 1996a, 1998). Technological addictions are operationally defined as nonchemical (behavioral) addictions that involve human–machine interaction. They can either be passive (e.g., television) or active (e.g., computer games), and usually contain inducing and reinforcing features which may contribute to the promotion of addictive tendencies (Griffiths, 1995). Technological addictions can be viewed as a subset of behavioral addictions (Marks, 1990) and feature core components of addiction, such as, salience, mood modification, tolerance, withdrawal, conflict, and relapse (see Griffiths, 1996b). This chapter reviews the empirical literature on Internet addiction and its derivatives (e.g., Internet Addiction Disorder, Pathological Internet Use, Excessive Internet Use, Compulsive Internet Use) and assesses to what extent it exists. The terms used are broadly interchangeable but for the purposes of this chapter, the terms used by the authors will be referred to as the studies are described.

Psychology and the Internet: Intrapersonal, Interpersonal, and Transpersonal Implications

Young (1999a) claims Internet addiction is a broad term that covers a wide variety of behaviors and impulse control problems. She has categorized these behaviors into five specific subtypes:

Cybersexual addiction: Compulsive use of adult websites for cybersex and cyberporn
Cyber-relationship addiction: Overinvolvement in online relationships
Net compulsions: Obsessive online gambling, shopping or day-trading
Information overload: Compulsive web surfing or database searches
Computer addiction: Obsessive computer game-playing (*Doom, Myst, Solitaire,* etc.)

However, Griffiths (2000a) has argued that many of these excessive users are not "Internet addicts" but just use the Internet excessively as a medium to fuel other addictions. Therefore, there is a need to distinguish between addictions *to* the Internet and addictions *on* the Internet. This will be revisited later in this chapter.

As we shall see, there have been a growing number of academic papers about excessive use of the Internet. These can roughly be divided into five categories:

- Survey studies that compare excessive Internet users with nonexcessive users
- Survey studies that have examined groups that are vulnerable to excessive Internet use, most notably, students
- Studies that examine the psychometric properties of excessive Internet use
- Case studies of excessive Internet users including treatment case studies
- Correlational studies examining the relationship of excessive Internet use with other behaviors (e.g., psychiatric problems, depression, self-esteem)

Although there are increasing numbers of papers on the topic of excessive Internet use, the studies are so diverse and of such differing methodological quality that any type of meta-analysis would be difficult if not impossible. The main problems with most of the studies in the area is that sample sizes are often very small, and are carried out on very specific subpopulations (e.g., students). The major problem is the lack of consistent and/or rigorous definitions of addiction and Internet addiction, which makes data comparison almost meaningless. Therefore, each of the areas previously outlined will be briefly reviewed.

COMPARISON SURVEY STUDIES OF INTERNET ADDICTION AND EXCESSIVE INTERNET USE

The earliest empirical research study to be conducted on excessive Internet use was by Young (1996a). The study addressed the question of whether or not the Internet can be addictive, and the extent of problems associated with its misuse. The DSM-IV criteria for pathological gambling were modified to develop an 8-item questionnaire, since pathological gambling was viewed to be the closest in nature to pathological Internet use. Participants who answered "yes" to 5 or more of the 8 criteria were classified as addicted to the Internet (i.e., "dependents"). A self-selected sample of 496 people responded to the questionnaire with the vast majority (n = 396) being classed as "dependents." The majority of respondents were also female (60%).

It was found that dependents spent more time online (38.5 hours a week) compared to "nondependents" (4.9 hours a week), and mostly used the more inter-active functions of the Internet, such as chat rooms and forums. Dependents also reported that their Internet use caused moderate to severe problems in their fam-ily, social, and professional lives. Young concluded that (i) the more interactive the Internet function, the more addictive it is, and (ii) while normal users reported few negative effects of Internet use, dependents reported significant impairment in many areas of their lives, including health, occupational, social, and financial.

However, there were many limitations to the study including the (relatively) small self-selected sample. Furthermore, the dependents and nondependents had not been matched in any manner. Young also advertised for "avid Internet users" to take part in her study, which would have biased her results. There was also an assumption that excessive Internet use was akin to pathological gambling and that the criteria used to operationalize excessive Internet use were reliable and valid. Despite the methodological shortcomings of Young's study, it could be argued that she kick-started a new area of academic enquiry.

Egger and Rauterberg (1996) also conducted an online study by asking ques-tions similar to those asked by Young, although their categorization of addiction was based purely on whether the respondents themselves felt they were addicted. Using an online survey, they gathered 450 participants, 84% of whom were males. They reached conclusions similar to those reached by Young. Respondents who self-reported as "addicts" reported negative consequences of Internet use, complaints from friends and family over the amount of time spent online, feelings of anticipa-tion when going online, and feeling guilty about their Internet use. Like Young's study, the Egger and Rauterberg study suffered from similar methodological limita-tions. Furthermore, most of the participants were males from Switzerland.

Brenner (1997) devised an instrument called the Internet-Related Addictive Behavior Inventory (IRABI), consisting of 32 dichotomous (true / false) items. These items were designed to assess experiences comparable to those related to Substance Abuse in the DSM-IV. Of the 563 respondents, the majority were male (73%) and they used the Internet for (a mean average) of 19 hours a week. All 32 items seemed to measure some unique variance as they were all found to be moderately correlated with the total score. Older users tended to experience fewer problems compared to younger users, despite spending the same amount of time online. No gender differ-ences were reported. The data appeared to suggest that a number of users experi-enced more problems in role-performance because of their Internet usage. Brenner concluded that the skewed distribution was consistent with the existence of a deviant subgroup who experience more severe problems due to Internet use. He also claimed there was evidence of tolerance, withdrawal, and craving. The major limitation to the study was that it was not clear whether items in the IRABI tapped into behaviors that indicated real signs of addiction (Griffiths, 1998).

In a much bigger study—the Virtual Addiction Survey (VAS)—Greenfield (1999) conducted an online survey with 17,251 respondents. The sample was mainly Caucasian (82%), male (71%), with a mean age of 33 years. The VAS included demographic items (e.g., age, location, educational background), descriptive information items (e.g., frequency and duration of use, specific Internet usage), and clinical items (e.g., disinhibition, loss of time, behavior online). It also included ten modified items from DSM-IV criteria for pathological gambling. Approximately 6% of respondents met the criteria for addicted Internet usage patterns. Tentative post-hoc analysis proposed several variables that made the Internet attractive:

- Intense intimacy (41% total sample, 75% dependents)
- Disinhibition (43% total sample, 80% dependents)
- Loss of boundaries (39% total sample, 83% dependents)
- Timelessness (most of the sample replied "sometimes," most of the dependents replied "almost always")
- Out of control (8% total sample, 46% dependents)

One of the additional areas examined was whether Internet addiction shared the same characteristics as other forms of addiction, including substance-based addictions. Early analysis revealed numerous symptoms, which Greenfield viewed as being consistent with the concept of tolerance and withdrawal in dependents, including preoccupation with going online (58%), numerous unsuccessful attempts to cut back (68%), and feeling restless when attempting to cut back (79%). Despite the large sample size, only a very preliminary analysis was conducted. Therefore, results should be interpreted with caution.

SURVEY STUDIES OF INTERNET ADDICTION IN VULNERABLE GROUPS (I.E., STUDENTS)

A number of other studies have highlighted the danger that excessive Internet use may pose to students as a population group. This population is deemed to be vulnerable and at risk given the accessibility of the Internet and the flexibility of their schedules (Moore, 1995). For instance, Scherer (1997) studied 531 students at the University of Texas at Austin. Of these, 381 students used the Internet at least once per week and were further investigated. Based on the criteria paralleling chemical dependencies, 49 students (13%) were classified as "Internet dependent" (71% male, 29% female). "Dependent" users averaged 11 hours a week online as opposed to the average of 8 hours for "nondependents." Dependents were three times more likely to use interactive synchronous applications. The major weakness of this study appears to be that dependents only averaged 11 hours a week online (i.e., just over an hour a day). This could hardly be called excessive or addictive (Griffiths, 1998). Morahan-Martin and Schumacher (2000) conducted a similar online study. Pathological Internet Use (PIU) was measured by a 13-item questionnaire assessing problems due to Internet use (e.g., academic, work, relationship problems, tolerance symptoms, and mood-altering use of the Internet). Those who answered "yes" to 4 or more of the items were defined as pathological Internet users. The researchers recruited 277 undergraduate Internet users. Of these, 8% were classed as pathological users. Pathological Internet users were more likely to be male and to use technologically sophisticated sites. On average, they spent 8.5 hours a week online. It was also found that pathological users used the Internet to meet new people, for emotional support, to play interactive games, and were more socially disinhibited. Again, an average of 8.5 hours a week online does not appear excessive, although the authors argued that it was indicative of problems surfacing in relatively short periods of being online. Furthermore, the items used to measure dependency were similar to Brenner's IRABI items. As with Brenner's study, the results claimed to be measuring Internet addiction without substantiating its existence using bona fide addiction criteria (Griffiths, 1998).

Anderson (1999) collected data from a mixture of colleges in the United States and Europe, yielding 1,302 respondents (with an almost 50–50 gender split). On average, his participants used the Internet 100 minutes a day, and roughly 6% of the participants were considered as high-users (above 400 minutes a day). The DSM-IV substance-dependence criteria were used to classify participants into dependents and nondependents. Those endorsing more than 3 of the 7 criteria were classified as being dependent. Anderson reported a slightly higher percentage of dependent student users (9.8%), most of whom were those majoring in hard sciences. Of the 106 dependents, 93 were males. They averaged 229 minutes a day compared to nondependents who averaged 73 minutes a day. The participants in the high-users category reported more negative consequences compared to the low-users participants.

Kubey et al. (2001) surveyed 576 students in Rutgers University. Their survey included 43-multiple-choice items on Internet usage, study habits, academic performance, and personality. Internet dependency was measured with a five-point Likert-scale item, asking participants how much they agreed or disagreed with the following statement: "I think I might have become a little psychologically dependent on the Internet." Participants were categorized as "Internet dependent" if they chose "agree" or "strongly agree" to the statement. Of the 572 valid responses, 381 (66%) were females and the age ranged between 18 and 45 years of age with a mean age of 20.25 years. Fifty-three participants (9.3%) were classified as Internet dependent, and males were more prevalent in this group. Age was not found to be a factor, but first-year students (mean age not reported) were found to make up 37.7% of the dependent group. Dependents were four times more likely than nondependents to report academic impairment due to their Internet use, and they were significantly "more lonely" than other students. In terms of their Internet usage, dependents who were also academically impaired were found to be nine times as likely to use synchronous functions of the Internet (MUDs and IRC / chat programs). The authors proposed that these types of applications are an important outlet for lonely people (especially students who have just moved away to college) since they can keep in touch with family and friends, and find someone to chat with at anytime. No other medium can offer such an opportunity.

Other studies such as those by Kennedy-Souza (1998), Chou (2001), Tsai and Lin (2003), Chin-Chung and Sunny (2003), Nalwa and Anand (2003), and Kaltiala-Heino *et al.* (2004) that surveyed very small numbers of students and adolescents are simply too small and/or methodologically limited to draw any real conclusions. From the studies so far discussed (in this section and the preceding one on comparison studies), it is clear that most of these "prevalence type" studies share common weaknesses. Most use convenient, self-selected participants who volunteer to respond to the survey. It is therefore difficult to plan any kind of comparable groups. Most studies did not use any type of validated addiction criteria (such as withdrawal symptoms, salience, tolerance, or relapse), and those that did, assumed that excessive Internet use was akin to other behavioral addictions like gambling and/or used very low cutoff scores which would increase the percentage of those defined as addicted. As Griffiths (2000a) observed, (i) the instruments used have no measure of severity, (ii) the instrument questions have no temporal dimension, (iii) the studies have a tendency to overestimate the incidence of the problems, and (iv) the studies do not consider the context of Internet use (i.e., it is possible for some people to be engaged in very excessive use because it is part of their job or they are in an online relationship with someone geographically distant).

It is perhaps worth noting that in addition to direct studies of Internet addiction, there have been a number of longitudinal studies examining the relationship between general Internet use (including heavy use) and various aspects of psychosocial well-being (Kraut *et al.*, 1998l, 2002; Wästlund *et al.*, 2001; Jackson *et al.*, 2003). However, none of these studies shows consistent findings and none of these studies specifically investigated Internet addiction or attempted to measure it.

PSYCHOMETRIC STUDIES OF INTERNET ADDICTION

As can be seen from early studies, a number of differing diagnostic criteria have been used in Internet addiction studies. One of the most commonly used criteria was the one used by Young (1996a) and subsequently by others. The diagnostic questionnaire consisted of eight items modified from the DSM-IV criteria for pathological gambling (see Table I). She maintained the cutoff score of five, according

TABLE I

Young's (1996) Diagnostic Criteria for Internet Addiction

Do you feel preoccupied with the Internet (think about previous online activity or anticipation of next online session)?

Do you feel the need to use the Internet with increasing amounts of time in order to achieve satisfaction?

Have you repeatedly made unsuccessful efforts to control, cut back, or stop Internet use?

Do you feel restless, moody, depressed, or irritable when attempting to cut down or stop Internet use?

Do you stay online longer than originally intended?

Have you jeopardized or risked the loss of a significant relationship, job, educational, or career opportunity because of the Internet?

Have you lied to family members, therapist, or others to conceal the extent of involvement with the Internet?

Do you use the Internet as a way of escaping from problems or of relieving a dysphoric mood (e.g., feelings of helplessness, guilt, anxiety, depression)?

to the number of criteria used to diagnose pathological gambling, although the latter had two additional criteria. Even with the more rigorous cutoff score, it was found that almost 80% of the respondents in her study were classified as dependents.

Beard and Wolf (2001) attempted to modify Young's criteria, based on concerns with the objectivity and reliance on self-report. Some criteria can easily be reported or denied by a participant, and their judgment might be impaired, thus influencing the accuracy of the diagnosis. Second, some of the items were deemed to be too vague and some terminologies need to be clarified (e.g., what is meant by "preoccupation"?). Third, they questioned whether or not the criteria for pathological gambling are the most accurate to use as a basis for identifying Internet addiction. Beard and Wolfe therefore proposed modified criteria (see Table II). It was recommended that all of the first five criteria be required for a diagnosis, since they could be met without any impairment in the person's daily functioning. Furthermore, at least one of the last three criteria should be required for diagnosis, since these criteria impact the person's ability to cope and function.

Another attempt at formulating a set of diagnostic criteria for Internet addiction was made by Pratarelli *et al.* (1999). Factor analysis was employed in this research to examine possible constructs underlying computer / Internet addiction. There were 341 completed surveys with 163 male and 178 female participants (mean age of 22.8 years) recruited from Oklahoma State University. A questionnaire consisting of 93 items was constructed, 19 of which were categorical demographic and Internet use questions, and 74 dichotomous items. Four factors were extracted from the 93 items, two principal and two minor factors.

- Factor 1 focused on problematic computer-related behaviors in heavy users of the Internet. This factor was characterized by reports of

TABLE II

Criteria for Identifying Internet Addiction (Beard & Wolfe, 2001)

All the following (1–5) must be present:
1. Is preoccupied with the Internet (thinks about previous online activity or anticipate next online session)
2. Needs to use the Internet with increased amounts of time in order to achieve satisfaction
3. Has made unsuccessful efforts to control, cut back, or stop Internet use
4. Is restless, moody, depressed, or irritable when attempting to cut down or stop Internet use
5. Has stayed online longer than originally intended

And at least one of the following:
1. Has jeopardized or risked the loss of a significant relationship, job, educational, or career opportunity because of the Internet
2. Has lied to family members, therapist, or others to conceal the extent of involvement with the Internet
3. Uses the Internet as a way of escaping from problems or of relieving a dysphoric mood (e.g., feelings of helplessness, guilt, anxiety, depression)

loneliness, social isolation, missing appointments, and other general negative consequences of their Internet use.

- Factor 2 focused on the use and usefulness of computer technology in general and of the Internet in particular.
- Factor 3 focused on two different constructs that concerned the use of the Internet for sexual gratification and shyness / introversion.
- Factor 4 focused on the lack of problems related to Internet use coupled with mild aversion / disinterest in the technology.

The data collected in this study supported the idea that a mixture of obsessive-like characteristics was present in some individuals in terms of their Internet use and that they prefer online interactions rather than face-to-face. Although this study used a more statistically tested instrument in measuring Internet addiction, some of the factors extracted (Factors 2 and 4) did not seem to indicate components of addiction in general.

More recently, Shapira *et al.* (2003) proposed a revised classification and diagnostic criteria for problematic Internet use. Furthermore, Black *et al.* (1999) pointed out that Internet Addiction Disorder (IAD) seemed to have high comorbidity with other psychiatric disorders. Because of this, the criteria need to be unique in order to evaluate the validity of Internet abuse as a distinct disorder. Shapira *et al.* discussed the concept of Glasser's (1976) work on "positive addiction." However, the concept has been questioned, since the criteria for positive addiction do not resemble many of the components of more established addictions, such as tolerance and withdrawal (Griffiths, 1996b). Moreover, in terms of Internet dependency, negative consequences have been reported along with the amount of time spent online.

Internet dependency has most commonly been conceptualized as a behavioral addiction, which operates on a modified principle of classic addiction models, but the validity and clinical usefulness of such claims have also been questioned (Holden, 2001). Other studies have also supported the concept that problematic Internet use might be associated with features of DSM-IV impulse control disorder (Shapira *et al.*, 2000; Treuer *et al.*, 2001).

However, other researchers have questioned the existence of PIU and IAD itself. Mitchell (2000) does not believe it deserves a separate diagnosis since it is still unclear whether it develops of its own accord or if it is triggered by an underlying, comorbid psychiatric illness. It has become virtually impossible to make the distinction of which develops first, especially considering how integrated the Internet has become into people's lives. It is therefore difficult to establish a clear developmental pattern. In addition, behavioral patterns of individuals with problematic Internet use are varied and hard to identify. The only general agreement seems to be that it can be associated with material and psychological consequences. Shapira *et al.* (2003) suggested the future research should delineate problems. For example, some individuals may have problems during a manic episode only, some because of the demographics of choosing the Internet as a medium to shop or to gamble. Once these factors are extricated, the individuals who are left can be assessed of addiction and impulsivity purely in terms of their Internet use.

Based on the current (yet limited) empirical evidence, Shapira *et al.* (2003) proposed that problematic Internet use be conceptualized as an impulse control disorder. They admitted that although the category is already a heterogeneous one, over time, specific syndromes have been indicated as clinically useful. Therefore, in the style of DSM IV-TR's impulse control disorder criteria, and in addition to the proposed impulse control disorder of compulsive buying, Shapira *et al.* proposed broad diagnostic criteria for problematic Internet use (see Table III).

Three brief clinical vignettes were then described to illustrate the use of the proposed criteria and the complexities of differentiating this "disorder." All the participants were college students who were heavier users (45 hours a month across at least two months, with the average student using the Internet for 15 hours a month

TABLE III

Diagnostic Criteria for Problematic Internet Use (Shapira et al., 2003)

Maladaptive preoccupation with Internet use, as indicated by at least one of the following:
Preoccupations with use of the Internet that are experienced as irresistible
Excessive use of the Internet for periods of time longer than planned
The use of the Internet or the preoccupation with its use causes clinically significant distress or
  impairment in social, occupational, or other important areas of functioning.
The excessive Internet use does not occur exclusively during periods of hypomania or mania and is
  not better accounted by other Axis I disorders.

as tracked by Florida's North East Regional Data Centre). Of the three vignettes described, two were diagnosed as problem users based on the criteria proposed.

Similarly, Rotunda *et al.* (2003) used an instrument they simply called the Internet Use Survey. It contained three formal components that explored (a) demographic data and Internet usage, (b) the negative consequences and experience associated with Internet use, and (c) personal history and psychological characteristics of participants. Components (b) and (c) included several items from DSM-IV criteria for pathological gambling, substance use dependence, and a particular personality disorder (e.g., schizoid). Their sample consisted of 393 students, 53.6% females (n = 210) and 46.4% males (n = 182). The age range was between 18 and 81 years old, with a mean of 27.6 years. The average use was 3.3 hours a day with one hour for personal use (the other time on the Internet being spent for work-related purposes). The most common usage was e-mail, surfing the web for information and news, and chat rooms. The negative consequences included 18% of participants reporting preoccupation with the Internet, 25% sometimes feeling excited or euphoric when online, 34% admitted to going online to escape other problems to some degree, and 22.6% reported socializing online more than in person. Staying online longer than planned and losing track of time were also found to be common reports.

Factor analysis revealed four main factors. The first was labeled "absorption" (i.e., over-involvement with the Internet, time management failure), the second "negative consequences" (i.e., distress or problematic behavior such as preferring to be online than spending time with the family), the third "sleep" (i.e., sleep pattern disruption such as scheduling sleep around online time), and finally "deception" (i.e., lying to others online about identity, or amount of time spent online). Internet-related impairment was conceptualized based on user absorption and negative consequences instead of frequency of use. The authors concluded by stating that to assume frequent Internet use was excessive, pathological, or addictive was potentially misleading since it ignored contextual and dispositional factors associated with this behavior.

INTERNET ADDICTION, COMORBIDITY, AND RELATIONSHIP TO OTHER BEHAVIORS

Previous studies have found that problematic Internet use cooccurs with other psychiatric disorders (Black *et al.*, 1999; Shapira *et al.*, 2000). Griffiths (2000a) has postulated that in the majority of the cases, the Internet seems to act as a medium for other excessive behaviors, and the Internet is largely being used only to carry out these behaviors. In other words, the Internet is acting as a medium and not a causal factor (Shaffer *et al.*, 2000). Some of the factors that had been found to be associated with IAD are personality traits, self-esteem, and other psychiatric disorders.

Young and Rodgers (1998) examined the personality traits of individuals who were considered dependent on the Internet using the Sixteen Personality Factor Inventory (16 PF). Dependent users were found to rank highly in terms of self-reliance (i.e., they did not feel the sense of alienation others feel when sitting alone, possibly because of the interactive functions of the Internet), emotional sensitivity and reactivity (i.e., they are drawn to mental stimulation through endless databases and information available online), vigilance, low self-disclosure, and nonconformist characteristics. The findings of this study seem to suggest that specific personality traits may predispose individuals to develop PIU. Similar findings were obtained by Xuanhui and Gonggu (2001), examining the relationship between Internet addiction and the 16 PF.

Armstrong *et al.* (2000) investigated the extent to which sensation seeking and low self-esteem predicted heavier Internet use, using the Internet Related Problem Scale (IRPS). The IRPS is a 20-item scale, covering factors such as tolerance, craving, and negative impacts of Internet use. Results indicated that self-esteem is a better predictor of "Internet Addiction" compared to impulsivity. Individuals with low self-esteem seem to spend more time online, and had higher scores on the IRPS. Although this study yielded some interesting results, it should be interpreted with caution due to the small number of participants (n = 50). Moreover, Armstrong *et al.* maintained that the 20 items indicated nine different symptoms without any statistical evidence. It would be interesting to investigate whether the items really did measure the symptoms they claimed to. Other studies have looked at the relationship between Internet addiction and self-esteem and found similar findings (e.g., Widyanto & McMurran, 2004), but again the very low sample sizes make it hard to generalize findings.

Lavin *et al.* (1999) also tested sensation-seeking and Internet dependence in college students (n = 342). Of the total participants, 43 were defined as "dependent" and 299 "nondependents." Dependents had a lower score on the Sensation Seeking Scale, which contradicted their hypothesis. The authors explained by stating the dependents tended to be sociable in their Internet usage but not to the point of sensation seeking, as it differed from the traditional concept. The traditional form of sensation seeking involves more physical activities, such as skydiving and other thrill-inducing activities, while Internet users are less physical in their sensation seeking. It is possible that the Sensation Seeking Scale touched more on the physical sensations rather than the nonphysical sensations.

Petrie and Gunn (1998) examined the link between Internet addiction, sex, age, depression and introversion. One key question was whether participants defined themselves as Internet "addicts" or not. Of the 445 participants (roughly equal gender split), nearly half (46%) stated that they were "addicted" to the Internet. This group was the Self-Defined Addicts (SDAs) group. No gender or age differences were found between SDAs and Non-SDAs. The sixteen questions that had the highest factor analytical loadings were used to construct an Internet Use and

Attitudes Scale (IUAS). Respondents' scores on this scale ranged from 5 to 61, with high scores indicating high use of and positive attitudes toward the Internet. SDAs scored significantly higher than non-SDAs, with SDAs having a mean IUAS score of 35.6 and non-SDAs a mean IUAS score of 20.9. SDAs were also found to have higher levels of depression and they were more likely to be introverted. The main problem with the study was the fact that addiction was self-defined and not assessed formally.

Shapira *et al.* (2000) employed a face-to-face standardized psychiatric evaluation to identify behavioral characteristics, family psychiatric history, and comorbidity of individuals with problematic Internet use. The study sample consisted of 20 participants (11 men and 9 women), with an average age of 36 years. Problems associated with Internet use were significant social impairment (in 19 of the participants), marked personal distress over their behaviors (in 12 of the participants), vocational impairment (in 8 of the participants), financial impairment (in 8 participants), and legal problems (in 2 participants). It was found that every participant's problematic Internet use met DSM-IV criteria for an Impulse Control Disorder Not Otherwise Specified, while only three participants' Internet use met DSM-IV criteria for Obsessive Compulsive Disorder. All participants met criteria for at least one lifetime DSM Axis I diagnosis. The limitations to the study include the small sample size, self-reported interviews, the possible existence of experimenter's bias, lack of control group, and the possibility of overestimating certain psychiatric disorders, especially bipolar disorders.

More recently, Mathy and Cooper (2003) measured the duration and frequency of Internet use across five domains, namely; past mental health treatments, current mental health treatments, suicidal intent, as well as past and current behavioral difficulty. It was found that the frequency of Internet use was related to past mental health treatments and suicidal intent. Participants who acknowledged them spent significantly greater number of hours a week online. Duration of Internet use was related to past and current behavioral difficulties. Participants who admitted to past and current behavioral problems with alcohol, drugs, gambling, food, or sex also reported being relatively new Internet users.

Black *et al.* (1999) attempted to examine the demographic, clinical features, and psychiatric comorbidity in individuals reporting compulsive computer use (n = 21). They reported spending between 7 and 60 hours a week on nonessential computer use (mean = 27 hours a week). Nearly 50% of the participants met the criteria for current disorder, with the most common being substance use (38%), mood (33%), anxiety (19%), and psychotic disorder (14%). Nearly 25% of the sample had current depressive disorder (depression or dysthymia). Results showed that eight participants (38%) had at least one disorder, with the most common being compulsive buying (19%), gambling (10%), pyromania (10%), and compulsive sexual behaviour (10%). Three of the participants reported physical abuse and two reported sexual abuse during childhood. Other results showed that 11 participants met the criteria for at least one personality disorder, with the most frequent being borderline (24%), narcissistic (19%), and antisocial (19%) disorder. Perhaps it was due to the sensitive nature of this particular study that there were a very small number of participants. However, caution is advised when interpreting the results. Other studies have postulated relationships between Internet addiction, shyness (Chak & Leung, 2004), and attention deficit hyperactivity disorder (Yoo *et al.*, 2004).

In summary, and based on the studies outlined here, it would appear that there are a range of specific personality traits, comorbid behaviors, and other psychological characteristics that may predispose individuals to developing some kind of excessive Internet use disorder. However, given that all these studies are cross-sectional, there is no way of knowing if these factors preceded the excessive use or are as a consequence of it. Therefore, more longitudinal research is needed to examine these relationships more fully. Additionally, as with many of the studies in this area, much of the research is methodologically limited and based on relatively small sample sizes. Therefore, replication studies using much bigger cohorts are needed.

INTERNET ADDICTION CASE STUDIES

Griffiths (2000a,b) mentioned the importance of case studies in the study of Internet addiction. Griffiths' own research on Internet addiction has attempted to address three main questions: (1) What is addiction? (2) Does Internet addiction exist? (3) If it does, what are people addicted to? He adopted an operational definition of addictive behavior as any behavior (including Internet use) that included six core components of addiction, namely, salience, mood modification, tolerance, withdrawal symptoms, conflict, and relapse. Using these criteria, Griffiths asserts that Internet addiction exists in only a very small percentage of users, and most of the individuals who use the Internet excessively just use the Internet as a medium through which they can engage in a chosen behavior. He also claims that Young's (1999a) classifications of Internet addiction are not really types of Internet addiction since the majority of the behaviors involve use of the medium of the Internet to fuel other non-Internet addictions. In conclusion, Griffiths stated that most studies to date have failed to show that Internet addiction exists outside a small minority of users. He therefore suggested that case studies might help in indicating whether or not Internet addiction exists, even if these are unrepresentative.

Griffiths (2000b) outlined five case studies of excessive users that were gathered over the space of six months. Griffiths concluded that of the five case studies discussed, only two were "addicted" according to the components criteria. In short, these two case studies ("Gary" and "Jamie," both adolescent males) demonstrated that the Internet was the most important thing in their lives, that they neglected everything else in their lives to engage in the behavior, and that it compromised most areas of their lives. They also built up tolerance over time, suffered withdrawal symptoms if they were unable to engage in using the Internet, and showed signs of relapse after giving up the behavior for short periods.

In the other cases of very excessive Internet use, Griffiths claimed that the participants had used the Internet as a way to cope with, and counteract other inadequacies (e.g., lack of social support in real life, low self-esteem, physical disability). Griffiths also observed that it was interesting to note that all of the participants seemed to be using the Internet mainly for social contact and he postulated that it was because the Internet could be an alternative, text-based reality where users are able to immerse themselves by taking on another social persona and identity to make them feel better about themselves, which in itself would be highly rewarding psychologically (Griffiths, 2000b).

Young (1996b) highlighted the case of a 43-year-old homemaker who appeared to be addicted to the Internet. This particular case was chosen because it was contrary to the stereotype of a young, computer-savvy male online user as an Internet addict. The woman was not technologically oriented, had reported a contented home life, and had no prior psychiatric problems or addictions. Due to the menu-driven and user-friendly nature of the web browser provided by her service provider, she could navigate the Internet easily despite referring to herself as being "computer-phobic and illiterate." She initially spent a few hours a week in various chat rooms but within three months, she reported the need to increase her online time to up to 60 hours a week. She would plan to go online for two hours, but often stayed online longer than she intended, reaching up to 14 hours a session. She started withdrawing from her offline social involvements, stopped performing household chores in order to spend more time online, and reported feeling depressed, anxious, and irritable when she was not online.

She denied that the behavior was abnormal and she did not see it as a problem. Regardless of her husband's protests about the financial cost and her daughter's complaints that she was ignoring them, she refused to seek treatment and had no desire to reduce her online time. Within a year of getting her computer, she was estranged from her two daughters and was separated from her husband. An interview took place six months later and she admitted that the loss of her family resulted in her successfully cutting down her online time without any therapeutic intervention. However, Young stated that she could not eliminate her online use completely, nor reestablish relationship with her family without intervention. It was also suggested that this case indicated that certain risk factors, that is, the type of function used and the level of excitement experienced while being online, may be associated with the development of addictive Internet use.

Black et al. (1999) also outlined two case studies. The first was of a 47-year-old man who reported spending 12 to 18 hours a day online. He owned three personal computers and he was in debt from purchasing the associated paraphernalia. He admitted to developing several romantic relationships online, despite being married with three children. He had been arrested several times for computer hacking, he spent little time with his family, and reported feeling powerless over his usage. The second case was of a 42-year-old divorced man who admitted to wanting to spend all day online. He admitted to spending 30 hours a week online, most of which he spent in chat rooms to make new friends and meet potential partners. He had dated several women he met online, and he had made no attempt to cut back, despite his parents' complaints over his "addiction." While these may be excessive, and there were negative maladaptive consequences in the first case, they do not seem to be addicted, but use the Internet excessively for functional purposes (e.g., to engage in online relationships) and did not display some of the core addiction criteria, such as mood modification, cravings, and withdrawal symptoms.

More interestingly, Leon and Rotunda (2000) reported two contrasting case studies of individuals who used the Internet for eight hours or more a day. Both were college students and neither was seeking treatment. The first was the case of Neil, a 27-year-old white male who was described as being outgoing and sociable by his college friends. He discovered an online computer game called *Red Alert* during his third year of college. The game began to replace his social activities and he changed his sleeping patterns so he could play online with the other "good players." He also reported dropping all but two of his classes and spending up to 50 hours a week online. Friends reported that his personality changed. He became short-tempered and overly sensitive, especially when it came to the time he spent online. Eventually, he stopped all his social activities; he skipped classes, his grades deteriorated, he slept all day and played all night. He did not go out to buy food and he used his grocery money to buy a faster modem. The connection speed was extremely important to him, and he would become upset and angry if the game server went offline. Due to his excessive online time, he was also close to being evicted from his apartment and he constantly lied about the extent of his involvement with the Internet. All this happened within a year of Neil's discovering the online game.

The second case was of Wu Quon, a 25-year-old male foreign exchange student from Asia who had very few friends here in North America. He stated that it was due to cultural differences, and the lack of other Asian students in college. He bought a personal computer, and he used the Internet to make contact with people globally, read news about his home country, and listened to radio broadcasts from Asia. He also used Internet Relay Chat (IRC) to keep in touch with friends and family in China. He stated that the Internet occupied his life outside of study and college time, spending eight hours a day online. He said that being able to contact his family and friends daily relieved his depression and homesickness. He claimed that he was not addicted to the Internet—it had simply become an important part of his life and routine. He admitted feeling uncomfortable when he was offline but he said that it was due to feeling disconnected and out of touch with what was happening at home. Overall, he rated his experience on the Internet as being positive.

Leon and Rotunda concluded that only Neil seemed to be dependent on the Internet since his personal and occupational life was problematic due to the time he spent online. Moreover, it was argued that Neil met the criteria for Schizoid Personality Disorder and Circadian Rhythm Disorder. Both of these were the result of his Internet use. In contrast, Wu Quon's Internet use could be seen as a remedy for his homesickness. His online time seemed to make him a happy and functional individual, although it could also be seen as the mechanism that caused him further isolation. In summary, to orient the reader, Leon and Rotunda contended that to assume that frequent Internet use is excessive, pathological, or addictive was simplistic and ignored the contextual and dispositional factors associated with the behavior. Griffiths (2000a) would argue that Neil was a computer game addict and not an Internet addict, since the Internet was clearly being used to fuel his gaming behavior. However, gaming is increasingly moving online and the immersive nature of the Internet may facilitate excessive play, leading to increased addiction in some players. Finally, it is worth mentioning that there are other case study reports of unusual Internet use in the literature (e.g., Catalano *et al.*, 1999) but it is clear from reading these that they have little to do with excessive Internet use and / or Internet addiction.

Another indirect indicator that Internet addiction may exist from a case study perspective comes from the few reports of its treatment. Most of these have used a cognitive–behavioral approach therapy to treat IAD, although these accounts usually contain some common-sense elements (e.g., Orzack and Orzack, 1999; Young, 1999a, 1999b; Hall & Parsons, 2001; Yu & Zhao, 2004). None of these treatment accounts shows that the people treated were definitely addicts, although all those under treatment certainly felt they had a problem with their excessive Internet use. Young *et al.* (1999) also conducted a survey among therapists who had treated clients suffering from cyber-related disorders. The sample consisted of 23 female and 12 male therapists, with an average of 14 years of clinical practice experience. They reported an average caseload of nine clients that they would classify as an Internet addict treated within the past year, with a range of 2 to 50 patients. The patients were more likely to complain about direct compulsive Internet use (CIU), along with its negative consequences and prior addictions, rather than psychiatric illness. Almost all the therapists (95%) felt that the problem of CIU was more widespread than the number of cases indicated.

By examining the case study evidence as a whole, it does appear that some individuals appear to be addicted to the Internet and use the Internet excessively. In the cases previously outlined, excessive use nearly always led to some sort of maladaptive behavior. However, maladaptive behavior on its own does not necessarily indicate addiction, although some of the cases outlined by both Young and Griffiths do appear to show individuals displaying all the same signs and symptoms that are found in other more traditional addictions. Clearly, there is a need for more case studies than those already published, particularly in clinical settings that may give insights in how to overcome the negative consequences.

WHY DOES EXCESSIVE INTERNET USE OCCUR?

Most of the research that has been discussed appears to lack theoretical basis since surprisingly few researchers have attempted to propose a theory of the cause of Internet addiction, despite the number of studies conducted on the field. Davis (2001) proposed a model of the etiology of pathological Internet use (PIU) using the cognitive–behavioral approach. The main assumption of the model was that PIU resulted from problematic cognitions coupled with behaviors that intensify or maintain maladaptive response. It emphasized the individual's thoughts / cognitions as the main source of abnormal behavior. Davis stipulated that the cognitive symptoms of PIU might often precede and cause the emotional and behavioral symptoms rather than vice versa. Similar to the basic assumptions of cognitive theories of depression, it focused on maladaptive cognitions associated with PIU.

Davis described Abramson *et al.'s* (1989) concepts of *necessary, sufficient,* and *contributory* causes. A *necessary* cause is an etiological factor that must be present or must have occurred in order for symptoms to appear. A *sufficient* cause is an etiological factor whose presence / occurrence guarantees the occurrence of symptoms, and a *contributory* cause is an etiological factor that increases the likelihood of the occurrence of symptoms, but that is neither necessary nor sufficient. Abramson also distinguished between *proximal* and *distal* causes. In an etiology chain that results in a set of symptoms, some causes lie toward the end of the chain (proximal), while others in the beginning (distal). In the case of PIU, Davis claimed that distal cause was underlying psychopathology (e.g., depression, social anxiety, other dependence), while the proximal cause was maladaptive cognitions (i.e., negative evaluation of oneself and the world in general). The main goal of the paper was to introduce maladaptive cognitions as proximal sufficient cause of the set of symptoms for PIU.

Distal contributory causes of PIU were discussed. It was explained in a diathesis–stress framework, whereby an abnormal behavior was caused by a predisposition / vulnerability (diathesis) and a life event (stress). In the cognitive–behavioral model of PIU, existing underlying psychopathology was viewed as the diathesis, since many studies had shown the relationship between psychological disorders such as depression, social anxiety, and substance dependence (Kraut *et al.*, 1998). The model suggested that psychopathology was a distal necessary cause of PIU, that is, psychopathology must be present or must have occurred in order for PIU symptoms to occur. However, in itself, the underlying psychopathology would not result in PIU symptoms, but was a necessary element in its etiology.

The model assumed that although a basic psychopathology might predispose an individual to PIU, the set of associated symptoms was specific to PIU and therefore should be investigated and treated independently. The stressor in this model was the introduction of the Internet, or the discovery of a specific function of the Internet. Although it might be difficult to trace back an individual's encounter with the Internet, a more testable event would be the experience of a function found online, for example, the first time the person used an online auction or found pornographic material online.

Exposure to such functions was viewed as a distal necessary cause of PIU symptoms. In itself, this encounter did not result in the occurrence of symptoms of PIU; however, as a contributory factor, the event could be a catalyst for the developmental process of PIU. A key factor here was the reinforcement received from an event (i.e., operant conditioning, whereby positive response reinforced continuity of activity). The model proposed that stimuli such as the sound of a modem connecting or the sensation of typing could result in a conditioned response. Thus, these types of secondary reinforcers could act as situational cues that contribute to the development of PIU and the maintenance of symptoms.

Central to the cognitive–behavioral model was the presence of maladaptive cognitions that were viewed to be proximal sufficient cause of PIU. Maladaptive cognitions were broken down into two subtypes—perceptions about one's self, and about the world. Thoughts about self are guided by ruminative cognitive style. Individuals who tend to ruminate would experience a higher degree in severity and duration of PIU, as studies have supported that rumination is likely to intensify or maintain problems, partly by interfering with instrumental behavior (i.e., taking action) and problem solving. Other cognitive distortions include self-doubt, low self-efficacy and negative self-appraisal. These cognitions dictate the way in which individuals behave, and some cognitions would cause specific or generalized PIU. Specific PIU referred to the over-use and abuse of a specific Internet function. It was assumed to be the result of a pre-existing psychopathology that became associated with an online activity (e.g., compulsive gamblers might realize that they could gamble online and ultimately showed symptoms of specific PIU as the association between need and immediate reinforcement became stronger). However, it should be noted that not every compulsive gambler showed symptoms of PIU.

On the other hand, generalized PIU involved spending excessive amounts of time online with no direct purpose, or just wasting time. The social context of the individual, especially the lack of social support they received and/or social isolation, was one key factor that played a role in the causality of general PIU. Individuals with general PIU were viewed as being more problematic, since their behavior would not even exist in the absence of the Internet.

Based on Davis' model, Caplan (2003) further proposed that problematic psychosocial predispositions causes excessive and compulsive Computer-Mediated (CM) social interaction in individuals, which, in turn, increases their problems. The theory proposed by Caplan, examined empirically, has three main propositions:

- Individuals with psychosocial problems (e.g., depression and loneliness) hold more negative perceptions of their social competence compared to others.

- They prefer CM interactions rather than face-to-face ones since the former are perceived to be less threatening and these individuals perceive themselves to be more efficient in an online setting.
- This preference, in turn, leads to excessive and compulsive use of CM interactions, which then worsens their problems and creates new ones at school, work, and home.

In Caplan's (2003) study, the participants consisted of 386 undergraduates (279 females and 116 males), with the age ranging from 18 to 57 years (mean age = 20 years). This study used Caplan's (2002) Generalized Problematic Internet Use Scale (GPIUS), a self-report assessing the prevalence of cognitive and behavioral symptoms of pathological Internet use along with the degree to which negative consequences affected the individual. The GPIUS had seven subscales—mood alteration, perceived social benefits, perceived social control, withdrawal, compulsivity, excessive Internet use, and negative outcomes. Also included in this study were validated depression and loneliness scales.

It was found that depression and loneliness were significant predictors of preference for online social interaction, accounting for 19% of the variance. In turn, participants' preference for online social interaction was found to be a significant predictor of their scores on pathological Internet use and negative outcomes. The data also suggested that excessive use was one of the weakest predictors of negative outcomes whereas preference for online interaction, compulsive use, and withdrawal were among the strongest. Overall, loneliness and depression were not found to have large, independent effects on negative outcomes. The result of this study appeared to support the proposition that preference for online socialization was a key contributor to the development of problematic Internet use.

Caplan noted two unexpected results in the data. First, loneliness played a more significant role in the development of problematic Internet use compared to depression. He attempted to explain this finding by stating that loneliness was theoretically the more salient predictor, since negative perception of social competence and communication skills is more pronounced in lonely individuals. On the other hand, a wide variety of circumstances that might not be related to a person's social life could result in depression (e.g., traumatic experiences). Second, using the Internet to alter mood was found to be lacking in influence on negative outcomes. For instance, it was proposed by Caplan was that there are various circumstances in which individuals use the Internet to alter their mood, and different usages of the Internet would cause different mood alterations. For example, online game playing would be exciting and fun, while reading the news could be relaxing. Therefore, in itself, using the Internet to alter mood might not necessarily lead to the negative consequences associated with preference for online social interaction, excessive and compulsive use, and experiencing psychological withdrawal.

The limitations to this study included the need for future empirical evidence pertaining to the causality of specific CM communication characteristics that could lead to the preference for online social interaction. Also, the data were collected from a sample that did not display very high degrees of problematic Internet use (median for preference was 1.28 on a scale ranging from 1 to 5; most participants did not prefer online over face-to-face social interactions). Finally, the study did not take into account the role that an individual's actual social skill and self-reported communication preference played in the development of problematic Internet use, despite the theory's emphasis on perceived social competence.

CONCLUDING REMARKS

The labels "Internet Addiction," "Internet Addiction Disorder," "Pathological Internet Use," "Problematic Internet Use," "Excessive Internet Use," and "Compulsive Internet Use" have all been used to describe more or less the same concept, that is, that an individual could be so involved in their online use as to neglect other areas of their life. However, it would seem premature at this stage to use one label for the concept, since most of the studies conducted in the field so far have presented varying degrees of differences and conflicting results.

Griffiths (2000a) argued that most of the individuals who use the Internet excessively are not addicted to the Internet itself, but use it as a medium to fuel other addictions. Griffiths (2000a) says that there is a need to distinguish between addictions *to* the Internet and addictions *on* the Internet. He gives the example of a gambling addict who chooses to engage in online gambling, as well as a computer game addict who plays online, stressing that the Internet is just the place where they conduct their chosen (addictive) behavior. These people display addictions *on* the Internet. However, there is also the observation that some behaviors engaged in on the Internet (e.g., cybersex, cyberstalking) may be behaviors that the person would only carry out on the Internet because the medium is anonymous, not face-to-face, and disinhibiting (Griffiths, 2000c, 2001).

In contrast, it is also acknowledged that there are some case studies that seem to report an addiction to the Internet itself (e.g., Young, 1996b; Griffiths, 2000b). Most of these individuals use functions of the Internet that are not available in any other medium, such as chat rooms or various role-playing games. These people appear to be addicted *to* the Internet because they engage in activities that use the idiosyncratic features of the Internet. However, despite these differences, there seem to be some common findings, most notably, reports of the negative consequences of excessive Internet use (neglect of work and social life, relationship breakdowns, loss of control, etc.), which are comparable to those experienced with other, more established addictions. In conclusion, it appears that if Internet addiction does indeed exist, it affects only a relatively small percentage of the online population. However, exactly what it is on the Internet that they are addicted to still remains unclear. What is clear, is that further research is needed.

REFERENCES

Abramson, L.Y., Metalsky, G. I., & Alloy, L. B. (1989). Hopelessness depression: A theory-based subtype of depression. *Psychological Review, 96,* 358–372.

Anderson, K. J. (1999, August) Internet use among college students: Should we be concerned? Paper presented at the annual meeting of the American Psychological Association, Boston.

Armstrong, L., Phillips, J. G., & Saling, L. L. (2000). Potential determinants of heavier Internet usage. *International Journal of Human Computer Studies, 53,* 537–550.

Beard, K., & Wolf, E. (2001). Modification in the proposed diagnostic criteria for Internet addiction. *Cyberpsychology and Behavior, 4,* 377–383.

Black, D., Belsare, G., & Schlosser, S. (1999). Clinical features, psychiatric comorbidity, and health-related quality of life in persons reporting compulsive computer use behavior. *Journal of Clinical Psychiatry, 60,* 839–843.

Brenner, V. (1997). Psychology of Computer Use: XLVII. Parameters of Internet use, abuse, and addiction: The first 90 days of the Internet Usage Survey. *Psychological Reports, 80,* 879–882.

Caplan, S. E. (2002). Problematic Internet use and psychosocial well-being: Development of a theory-based cognitive-behavioral measurement instrument. *Computers in Human Behavior, 18,* 553–575.

Caplan, S. E. (2003). Preference for online social interaction: A theory of problematic Internet use and psychosocial well-being. *Communication Research, 30,* 625–648.

Catalano, G., Catalano, M., Embi, C., & Frankel, R. (1999). Delusions about the Internet. *Southern Medical Journal, 92,* 609–610.

Chak, K., & Leung, L. (2004). Shyness and locus of control as predictors of Internet addiction and Internet use. *CyberPsychology and Behavior, 7,* 559–570.

Chin-Chung, T., & Sunny, L. (2003). Internet addiction of adolescents in Taiwan: An interview study. *CyberPsychology and Behavior, 6,* 649–652.

Chou, C. (2001). Internet heavy use and addiction among Taiwanese college students: An online interactive study. *CyberPsychology and Behavior, 4,* 573–585.

Davis, R. (2001). A cognitive–behavioral model of Pathological Internet Use. *Computers in Human Behavior, 17,* 187–195.

Egger, O., & Rauterberg, M. (1996). Internet behavior and addiction. Retrieved October 14, 2005, from the Swiss Federal Institute of Technology, Zurich: ⟨http://www.idemployee.id.tue.nl/g.w.m.rauterberg/ibq/res.htm⟩

Glasser, W. (1976). *Positive addictions.* New York: Harper & Row.

Greenfield, D. N. (1999). Psychological characteristics of compulsive Internet use: A preliminary analysis. *CyberPsychology and Behavior, 2,* 403–412.

Griffiths, M. D. (1995). Technological addictions. *Clinical Psychology Forum, 76,* 14–19.

Griffiths, M. D. (1996a). Internet addiction: An issue for clinical psychology? *Clinical Psychology Forum, 97,* 32–36.

Griffiths, M. D. (1996b). Behavioural addictions: An issue for everybody? *Journal of Workplace Learning, 8(3),* 19–25.

Griffiths M. D. (1998). Internet addiction: Does it really exist? In J. Gackenbach (Ed.), *Psychology and the internet: Intrapersonal, interpersonal, and transpersonal applications* (pp. 61–75). New York: Academic Press.

Griffiths, M. D. (2000a). Internet addiction—Time to be taken seriously? *Addiction Research, 8,* 413–418.

Griffiths, M. D. (2000b). Does Internet and computer "addiction" exist? Some case study evidence. *Cyberpsychology and Behavior, 3*, 211–218.

Griffiths, M. D. (2000c). Excessive internet use: Implications for sexual behavior. *CyberPsychology and Behavior, 3*, 537–552.

Griffiths, M. D. (2001). Sex on the Internet: Observations and implications for sex addiction. *Journal of Sex Research, 38*, 333–342.

Hall, A. S., & Parsons, J. (2001). Internet addiction: College student case study using best practices in cognitive behavior therapy. *Journal of Mental Health Counselling, 23*, 312–327.

Holden, C. (2001). "Behavioral" addictions: Do they exist? *Science, 294*, 5544.

Jackson, L. A., Von Eye, A., Biocca, F. A., Barbatsis, G., Fitzgerald, H. E., & Zhao, Y. (2003). Personality, cognitive style, demographic characteristics, and Internet use—Findings from the HomeNetToo project. *Swiss Journal of Psychology, 62*, 79–90.

Kaltiala-Heino, R., Lintonen, T., & Rimpela, A. (2004). Internet addiction? Potentially problematic use of the Internet in a population of 12–18-year-old adolescents. *Addiction Research and Theory, 12*, 89–96.

Kennedy-Souza, B. (1998). Internet addiction disorder. *Interpersonal Computing and Technology: An Electronic Journal for the 21st Century, 6*(1–2). Retrieved December 10, 2003, from http://www.emoderators.com/ipct -j/1998/n1-2/kennedy -souza.html

Kraut, R., Patterson, M., Lundmark, V., Kiesler, S., Mukophadhyay, T., & Scherlis, W. (1998). Internet paradox: A social technology that reduces social involvement and psychological well being? *American Psychologist, 53*, 1017–1031.

Kraut, R., Kiesler, S., Boneva, B., Cummings, J., Helgeson, V., & Crawford, A. (2002). Internet paradox revisited. *Journal of Social Issues, 58*, 49–74.

Kubey, R. W., Lavin, M. J., & Barrows, J. R. (2001). Internet use and collegiate academic performance decrements: Early findings. *Journal of Communication, 51*, 366–382.

Lavin, M., Marvin, K., McLarney, A., Nola, V., & Scott, L. (1999). Sensation seeking and collegiate vulnerability to Internet dependence. *Cyberpsychology and Behavior, 2*, 425–430.

Leon, D., & Rotunda, R. (2000). Contrasting case studies of frequent Internet use: Is it pathological or adaptive? *Journal of College Student Psychotherapy, 14*, 9–17.

Marks, I. (1990). Non-chemical (behaviorial) addictions. *British Journal of Addiction, 85*, 1389–1394.

Mathy, R., & Cooper, A. (2003). The duration and frequency of Internet use in a nonclinical sample: Suicidality, behavioral problems, and treatment histories. *Psychotherapy: Theory, Research, Practice, Training, 40*, 125–135.

Mitchell, P. (2000). Internet addiction: Genuine diagnosis or not? *Lancet, 355*, 632.

Moore, D. (1995). *The Emperor's virtual clothes: The naked truth about the Internet culture*. Chapel Hill, NC: Algonquin.

Morahan-Martin, J., & Schumacher, P. (2000). Incidents and correlates of pathological Internet use among college students. *Computers in Human Behavior, 16*, 13–29.

Nalwa, K., & Anand, A. P. (2003). Internet addiction in students: A cause of concern. *CyberPsychology and Behavior, 6*, 653–656.

Orzack, H., & Orzack, D. (1999). Treatment of computer addicts with complex co-morbid psychiatric disorders. *Cyberpsychology and Behavior, 2*, 465–473.

Petrie, H., & Gunn, D. (1998, December). Internet "addiction": The effects of sex, age, depression, and introversion. Paper presented at the British Psychological Society London Conference, London.

Pratarelli, M., Browne, B., & Johnson, K. (1999). The bits and bytes of computer/Internet addiction: A factor analytic approach. *Behavior Research Methods, Instruments and Computers, 31*, 305–314.

Rotunda, R. J., Kass, S. J., Sutton, M. A., & Leon, D. T. (2003). Internet use and misuse: Preliminary findings from a new assessment instrument. *Behavior Modification, 27*, 484–504.

Scherer, K. (1997). College life on-line: Healthy and unhealthy Internet use. *Journal of College Student Development, 38*, 655–665.

Shaffer, H., Hall, M., & Vander Bilt, J. (2000). "Computer addiction": A critical consideration. *American Journal of Orthopsychiatry, 70*, 162–168.

Shapira, N., Goldsmith, T., Keck Jr., P., Khosla. D., & McElroy, S. (2000). Psychiatric features of individuals with problematic Internet use. *Journal of Affective Disorders, 57*, 267–272.

Shapira, N., Lessig, M., Goldsmith, T., Szabo, S., Lazoritz, M., Gold, M., & Stein, D. (2003). Problematic Internet use: Proposed classification and diagnostic criteria. *Depression and Anxiety, 17*, 207–216.

Tsai, C-C., & Lin, S. S. J. (2003). Internet addiction of adolescents in Taiwan: An interview study. *CyberPsychology and Behavior, 6*, 649–652.

Wästlund, E., Norlander, T., & Archer, T. (2001). Internet blues revisited: Replication and extension for an Internet paradox study. *Cyberpsychology and Behavior, 4*, 385–391.

Widyanto, L., & McMurran, M. (2004). The psychometric properties of the Internet addiction test. *CyberPsychology and Behavior, 7*, 443–450.

Xuanhui, L., & Gonggu, Y. (2001). Internet addiction disorder, online behavior, and personality. *Chinese Mental Health Journal, 15*, 281–283.

Yoo, H. J., Cho, S. C., Ha, J., Yune, S. K., Kim, S. J., Hwang, J. *et al.* (2004). Attention deficit hyperactivity symptoms and Internet addiction. *Psychiatry & Clinical Neurosciences, 58*, 487–494.

Young, K. (1996a). Internet addiction: The emergence of a new clinical disorder. *CyberPsychology and Behavior, 3*, 237–244.

Young, K. (1996b). Psychology of computer use: XL. Addictive use of the Internet: A case that breaks the stereotype. *Psychological Reports, 79*, 899–902.

Young, K. (1999a). The research and controversy surrounding Internet addiction. *Cyberpsychology and Behavior, 2*, 381–383.

Young, K. (1999b). Internet addiction: symptoms, evaluation, and treatment. In L. VandeCreek & T. Jackson (Eds.), *Innovations in Clinical Practice: A Source Book* (Vol. 17, pp. 19–31). Sarasota, FL: Professional Resource Press.

Young, K., Pistner, M., O'Mara, J., & Buchanan, J. (1999). Cyber disorders: The mental health concern for the new millennium. *Cyberpsychology and Behavior, 2*, 475–479.

Young, K., & Rodgers, R. (1998, August). *Internet addiction: Personality traits associated with its development.* Paper presented at the 69th annual meeting of the Eastern Psychological Association.

Yu, Z. F., & Zhao, Z. (2004). A report on treating Internet addiction disorder with cognitive behavior therapy. *International Journal of Psychology, 39*, 407.

PART II

Interpersonal

CHAPTER 7

Revisiting Computer-Mediated Communication for Work, Community, and Learning

Caroline Haythornthwaite and Anna L. Nielsen
Graduate School of Library and Information Science
University of Illinois at Urbana-Champaign
Champaign, Illinois

> Introduction
> Revisiting CMC and Internet Debates
> Unbundling Users and Their Online Activities
> Online and Offline Integration
> Wrapping Up
> References

INTRODUCTION

The debates about the usefulness and appropriateness of computer-mediated communication (CMC) are well known. Arguments against CMC highlight the way the reduced cues of the environment make it ill-suited for building trust, close friendships, and complex relationships. At the same time, arguments for CMC celebrate the liberation from cues associated with offline bodies, personae, status, and gender (e.g., Turkle, 1995; for reviews of debates about CMC, see Culnan & Markus, 1987; Haythornthwaite *et al.*, 1998; Herring, 2002). More recently, debate has moved to the societal level, but still centers on the same dichotomy. One side argues that time online is time taken from real relationships, while the other extols the benefits of online relationships and communities (e.g., Nie, 2001; Kraut *et al.*, 1998; for reviews of debates about the Internet, see Boase & Wellman, 2005; DiMaggio *et al.*, 2001; Haythornthwaite & Wellman, 2002; Wellman *et al.*, 1996).

As a number of scholars have noted, CMC and the Internet are relentlessly marching into use in everyday life (Wellman & Haythornthwaite, 2002; Bakardjieva & Smith, 2001), taking their place regardless of perceived or actual outcomes, settling in as an essential, ubiquitous, and invisible part of our communication infrastructures. They are becoming embedded (Howard & Jones, 2003), indispensable (Hoffman *et al.*, 2004), even ordinary (Herring, 2004) and banal (Graham, 2004). The

Psychology and the Internet: Intrapersonal, Interpersonal, and Transpersonal Implications

technologies are disappearing as novelties (Bruce & Hogan, 1998), and achieving a social translucence (Erickson *et al.,* 2002). However, it is this very ubiquity, the boringness, the domesticity which is now a compelling reason for studying them. Star's "call to study boring things" (1999, p. 377), although referring to the study of technological infrastructures, is as important for the daily use of such now-boring media as e-mail as it is for the presence of the Internet in daily life (see also Silverstone, 1999).

With more than two decades of CMC use, it is time to take stock, revisit empirical and theoretical work, and consider its increasingly taken-for-granted use. CMC is also now so interconnected with the Internet that you cannot discuss one without the other. This chapter refers to them both separately and together, but with the understanding that neither can be teased apart from the other at this stage. Since valuable and comprehensive reviews and collections exist (including those previously noted), the following does not provide an exhaustive summary of previous work. Instead, debates about CMC and the Internet[1] are reviewed, looking at ways to reconcile conflicting results, and concluding with some new questions to ask in light of the new ubiquity of CMC.

REVISITING CMC AND INTERNET DEBATES

As noted, the lines demarking the two sides of the debate about the impact of computer media and the Internet on social interaction are well drawn (see Table I). Arguments both for and against CMC focus on the "reduced cues" of the environment (Culnan & Markus, 1987; Short *et al.,* 1976), i.e., the way communication is reduced to text-only exchanges, without the additional cues of voice, facial expression, body position, and personal appearance. On the downside, the lack of cues makes CMC ill-suited for conveying confirmatory communication cues—for example, a smile to go with an ironic comment. Online communication hampers the ability to convey messages unambiguously and to verify meaning through other communication cues. On the negative side, this can lead to a lack of trust in the exchange and in the relationship with the other person. Individuals have to work harder to make themselves clear, conventions of communication have to be created and adopted between communicators and among online group members (Clark & Brennan, 1991; DeSanctis & Poole, 1994). This process can take more time (Walther, 1995) and more effort (Haythornthwaite *et al.,* 2000) for online than

---

[1] Debates about computer-mediated communication (CMC) began before the presence of the Internet. Arguments that were first made about the alienating effects of text-based CMC, for example, the way the relative anonymity of e-mail led to behaviors such as "flaming," have been picked up again regarding the Internet and applied to all aspects of online activity, from online chat rooms to surfing the Web. Because these are not synonymous (CMC is only one aspect of the Internet), and because discussion of the Internet follows that of CMC by quite a few years, the distinction is made here between CMC and the Internet.

TABLE I

Arguments Against and For Computer Mediated Communication (CMC)

ARGUMENTS AGAINST CMC	ARGUMENTS FOR CMC
Lean communication	Rich communication
Text-based, reduced cues, impoverished communication environment (Daft & Lengel, 1986)	Emoticons and acronyms (McLaughlin *et al.*, 1995), language cues (Herring, 2002)
Ill-suited to emotional, expressive, complex communications (Daft & Lengel, 1986)	Group-defined genres and rules of conduct (Bregman & Haythornthwaite, 2003; DeSanctis & Poole, 1994; Orlikowski & Yates, 1994; McLaughlin, *et al.*, 1995)
Takes longer to build relationships (Walther, 1995)	Interpersonal self-disclosure, emotional support; shared history; online communities (e.g., Baym 2000; Haythornthwaite *et al.*, 2000; Hearne & Nielsen, 2004)
DISINTEGRATIVE OUTCOMES	INTEGRATIVE OUTCOMES
Antisocial flaming (Lea *et al.*, 1992), Irresponsible individual actions (e.g., Dibbell, 1996)	Connects disparate others: Brings in peripheral players, spanning time and space (Sproull & Kiesler, 1991)
Decreased social involvement (Nie, 2001); Abandonment of local relationships (Kraut *et al.*, 1998)	Maintains connections even when distributed (LaRose *et al.*, 2001; Hampton & Wellman, 2002)

for face-to-face communications. This set of criticisms essentially argues that CMC is deficient in providing a communication environment that allows the kinds of communication exchanges necessary for strong, close ties (the argument here refers primarily to work and friendship ties where interaction and contact are sustaining features of the tie, rather than kin ties where expectations of interaction can be quite different). Whether starting a new relationship or continuing one, CMC has been perceived as inadequate to build and sustain strong, close ties, that is, those requiring trust, self-disclosure, mutual and shared understanding, and resulting in close work and friendship relationships.

Some communicators take advantage of the lack of cues, and the lack of exposure of themselves in online communications. This leads some to engage in flaming (abusive language), and others to act as "trolls" online (deliberately disrupting online communities). Disruptive and antisocial behavior is easier to engage in online when you don't have to face the people you are annoying, but so is revealing personal details of yourself and engaging in fantasy behaviors. Arguments for CMC acknowledge the reduced cues of the environment, but find this to be a positive aspect. The reduced cues can increase participation and egalitarian treatment because of the lack of face-to-face interaction; individuals are able to be judged online only by their text-based communication, freed of the binding status associations inherent in face-to-face situations. Asynchronous CMC allows people to reflect before posting, giving them time to build an argument or answer to a question, and to think twice before posting a potentially flaming response. Anonymous CMC provides a barrier between the self online and the self offline, providing the possibility of presenting a new or different persona online.

Those who found positive outcomes for cue-reduced, anonymous CMC may be disappointed at the way social cues have been rediscovered, for example, in language that marks us by gender (Herring, 1996, 1999, 2002), and reintroduced into online communications, such as in emoticons, acronyms, and domains of e-mail addresses (McLaughlin *et al.*, 1995). CMC is not (and perhaps never was) as cue-less as thought, and thus as unable to maintain interpersonal ties. Many studies show that members of online communities develop and feel strong personal ties to others in their CMC environment (Haythornthwaite *et al.*, 2000; Baym, 2002) and are able to recreate aspects of offline community, such as introducing roles and rituals, policing rules of behavior (e.g., Baym, 2000; McLaughlin *et al.*, 1995), and creating a communal history (Hearne & Nielsen, 2004).

The arguments against CMC have been taken up anew in discussions of the Internet; CMC is not rich enough to support close interpersonal relations, and therefore those who spend time on the Internet are losing out on the benefits of such ties. Geographically based communities suffer when individuals spend time online with strangers and people in other geographic regions. Their time online withdraws support and time spent in the geo-communities in which they live, leading to a loss of social capital in local communities and nations of people "bowling alone" (Putnam, 2000). Studies find support for the disintegrative effects of time online, with reduced interactions with local others, and particularly those in the home (Kraut *et al.*, 1998; Nie, 2001).

Arguments for CMC and the Internet point out that local relationships may not be possible, and that a home-based view ignores the very real ties that exist across distance and give benefit to individuals. Early CMC studies pointed out how organizations could involve peripheral workers by using e-mail to communicate between central and remote offices (Sproull & Kiesler, 1991). Scholarly networks online have become a mainstay of international contact and information exchange among like-minded academics (Walsh & Bayma, 1996; Walsh *et al.*, 2000; Nissenbaum & Price, 2004). Other benefits accrue in conjunction with community ties. Recent studies find that students away at college were able to benefit from e-mail contact with home (LaRose *et al.*, 2001); those who have moved from one neighborhood to another were able to maintain contact with former neighbors (Hampton & Wellman, 2002); and farmers isolated on their farms during the UK foot-and-mouth disease crisis were able to stay in touch with others in the region and around the world while unable to travel to towns, markets, and neighboring farms (Hagar & Haythornthwaite, 2005).

People do not so much bowl alone as bowl with those in their personal networks, which may extend geographically, supported by travel and CMC (Wellman *et al.*, 1996). Geographical communities now often turn to information and communication technologies as ways to enable communities, not as competition to their existence. This movement was captured early in the notion of *freenets*, now more commonly called *community networking initiatives*, and discussed by researchers in the area of *community informatics* (e.g., see the *Journal of Community Informatics*, http://ci-journal.net/index.php).

One reason the arguments are so polarized is that too often the forms, users, and uses of CMC have been treated as a singular entity. What is found in one situation, with one set of people, is felt to be true for everyone. This is more true for popular press and utopian/dystopian discussions than for contemporary research on CMC, but is still found in views that speak of "the Internet" as if it were one monolithic object, and as if people interacted with "the Internet" and with others through the Internet in one and only one way. Monolithic views ignore differences in who is using the Internet, for what purpose, at what times and places, to and from what cultural contexts, with whom, and for what kinds of tasks, interactions, and outcomes.

Two trends are evident in CMC research. First, a number of recent studies unbundle users and uses, articulating differences among online users rather than between those online and those not online. These studies distinguish among online activities of communication, information seeking, relationship maintenance, work, learning, and entertainment, and examine the social relations and worlds maintained through and by means of online communication.

The second major trend treats online and offline as two parts of a whole, looking for where online and offline serve a joint purpose, such as contacting friends and family or keeping a (geo-)community informed and connected. In contrast to studies that seek to deconstruct the Internet into its component parts—for example, categories of users or types of media—this approach looks at how CMC and Internet activity have penetrated into all aspects of life, making it integral to every constituency, disappearing into the background as an invisible infrastructure and a taken-for-granted aspect of life (Bruce & Hogan, 1998; Star, 1999).

The sections that follow explore research that exemplifies these two major trends in CMC and Internet research, and the way Internet access and use integrates—or infiltrates—as a standard at work and home.

UNBUNDLING USERS AND THEIR ONLINE ACTIVITIES

As CMC and the Internet have extended beyond work-based communication, so has research on what differences may be found among users and the contexts in which they use CMC. Studies of computer use, CMC, and the Internet started by counting how many people owned a computer, used applications such as e-mail, or had access to the Internet. Differences across socioeconomic demographics were evident, with early users characteristically young, white, male, of high socio-economic status, and located in developed countries. While the profile of who has access is now more inclusive, recent studies show that more than just access matters in looking at Internet use. Thus, as will be discussed, while differences in access across socioeconomic level are decreasing, aspects of use such as the amount of time spent online or the nature of online activities still distinguish users. Other aspects of users are also now being considered, such as how differences in the number of years of being online affects use, as well as how individual psychology and adopter characteristics play a role in use and outcomes of Internet use.

As more and more resources go online, and so much commerce, education, and information is posted and conducted online, some ask why use continues to differ across demographics. A number of researchers find the answer relates to online content and whether that content is of interest and meaningful in individuals' lives. Thus, attention turns from *who* is using the Internet to *what* is online for them to use. A corollary to this is *who else* is online and thus what communication partners are available for CMC and Internet users to engage with online. Once uses between and among people are considered, then the dynamics of interpersonal relations, group interaction, and social networks come into play, providing further insight into CMC and Internet use, as will be described further.

The following sections describe first the way current studies are unbundling users and their online activities, in terms of individual characteristics, and usefulness of online content. This is followed by consideration of group and network perspectives on Internet use, and a social network tie-based view of media use that helps to reconcile contradictory results about the impact of new media.

USERS OF CMC AND THE INTERNET

Until recently, it has been taken for granted that those who started using CMC and the Internet in the early days were the model for later users. However, this ignored how the first waves of users fit the profile of early adopters of innovation: they were more cosmopolitan, more socially active, and had higher income and education levels (Nie *et al.*, 2002; Rogers, 1995). Early users were also largely young, white, affluent, and male. This has lead to cautions that social impacts of the Internet may reflect attributes of the users rather than of the Internet (Nie, 2001; Howard *et al.*, 2002; Kavanaugh & Patterson, 2002). Nie (2001) has observed that connectivity is found for the already well-connected, that is, the affluent and socially active who can afford computers and Internet access, and who have others in their social circle similarly connected and therefore available for interaction (see also Kavanaugh & Patterson, 2002). Better connectivity is also found for extroverts than introverts (Kraut *et al.*, 2002), and for those in close work or friendship ties (Haythornthwaite & Wellman, 1998; Haythornthwaite, 2001, 2002), other characteristics that predict individuals and pairs to already be well-connected. What happens next with CMC and the Internet may be considerably different when late adopters and those from new and different demographics increase their numbers online, but it is probable that it will still be the well-connected who make the most of the opportunities these technologies offer.

Users now increasingly represent people of every color and stripe, and studies are giving attention to distinguishing the pros and cons for each group and what members do online. Studies have mainly concentrated on how traditional measures of demographics affect use, for example, gender, race, and socioeconomic status, with a concern for addressing the now named "digital divide" (NTIA, 2000, 2002). Results in the United States show that those online are now approximately evenly divided among men and women, but what men and women do online differs. Men do more work, searching for sports, political, financial information and news, shopping online, stock trading, online auctions, visiting government websites, and downloading music. Women look more for health and religious information, research new jobs, and play games (Howard, 2002). Women also do more communicating with family and help set up family members with Internet connections (Boneva & Kraut, 2002; Kazmer & Haythornthwaite, 2001).

While American whites still show more access than minorities, use is increasing among African-Americans and Hispanics. Yet, the latter two groups spend less time online (Howard *et al.*, 2002) and, along with senior citizens, are reported as the least likely to go online (Madden & Rainie, 2003). Howard *et al.* (2002) find, in the U. S., that while overall numbers of people online were beginning to suggest that differences by gender and race were disappearing, differences were still evident in how much time was spent online, with minorities online less often and for less time than whites. Such differences may be the result of perceived usefulness, as has been noted, but may also be a continuing expression of general levels of societal interconnection. As noted previously, early awareness of innovations occurs among those with high socioeconomic status who are better connected to hear about new things and affluent enough to adopt them. Moreover, when these people connect online, they are more likely to find a critical mass (Markus, 1990) of others like them and resources of interest to them.

Many others studies are being undertaken to examine CMC and the Internet in new ways and with new concerns. Following is a brief list of the focus areas of various studies: English and non-English speakers (e.g., Warshauer, 2000); racial, ethnic, and cultural backgrounds (Kolko *et al.*, 2000); rural and urban participants (Hagar & Haythornthwaite, 2005); children and teens (Livingstone, 2002; Livingstone & Bober, 2005); working age adults and retirees (Anderson & Tracey, 2002; Nie & Erbring, 2000; UCLA CCP, 2000); time online and activities online by user group (Nie & Erbring, 2000; UCLA CCP, 2000; Wellman & Haythornthwaite, 2002); years of experience online (Howard *et al.*, 2002; LaRose *et al.*, 2001); age and lifestage (Anderson & Tracey, 2002; Livingstone, 2002; Livingstone & Bober, 2005); and genres and language use (Bregman & Haythornthwaite, 2003; Cherny, 1999; Crystal, 2001; Herring, 1999; Kolko *et al.*, 2000; Orlikowski & Yates, 1994).

ONLINE CONTENT AND USEFULNESS

Newer research gives attention to the context in which technology, CMC, and the Internet are introduced, and particularly the relevance of online content and connections to various potential and actual users of CMC and the Internet. Katz and Rice (2002b), for example, found that while differences in use persist across gender, age, household income, education, and race, they disappear after controlling for awareness of the Internet, suggesting the issue is not access per se, but perceived usefulness. As they note,

> access barriers to the Internet are not primarily technical or financial, though those are real and difficult. Rather, the barriers seem to lie heavily in the realm of cultural perceptions about what is possible with the Internet and the nature of Internet activities. (Katz & Rice, 2002b, p. 99)

For the Internet to draw people there must be a meaningful introduction of the technology into people's lives, and content that is useful and salient to them, such as online resources in your own linguistic or cultural language (Warschauer, 2000, 2003). Examination of content in relation to users can help contribute to understanding successful or unsuccessful use, and may provide explanations of why use differs across groups and locations.

GROUPS, NETWORKS, AND COMMUNITIES

Spears et al. (2001), Warschauer (2003), and DeSanctis and Poole (1994) direct our attention to the importance of group context with respect to use of CMC. DeSanctis and Poole's concept of *adaptive structuration* emphasizes how groups set their own norms, with communication standards created and reinforced through actual use, and attention given to media features that others talk about. Spears et al. (2001) point out that differences in what groups attend to—what is *salient* to the group members—affects the norms that are adopted. Both sets of authors point out that because of differences across groups, communication behaviors that emerge in one group need not necessarily appear in another.

Use of CMC can also be distinguished by the associations between communicators. Differences in uses and impact of CMC have been considered in terms of who is talking to whom (e.g., strangers, family, friends, coworkers) and the social networks of communicators. A number of studies have explored this for populations of researchers (Haythornthwaite & Wellman, 1998; Koku et al., 2001) and students (Haythornthwaite, 2001, 2002; LaRose et al., 2001). Studies also look at larger aggregates, such as use by online groups and organizations (e.g., Kling, 1996; Spears et al., 2001; Orlikowski et al., 1995), geographic communities supported by information and communication technologies (e.g., Gurstein, 2000; Keeble & Loader, 2001;

Cohill & Kavanaugh, 2000; Turow & Kavanaugh, 2003), virtual communities (e.g., Baym, 2000; Cherny, 1999; Haythornthwaite *et al.*, 2000; Haythornthwaite, in press; Jankowski, 2002; Kendall, 2002; Reid, 1995), and online learning communities (e.g., Haythornthwaite & Kazmer, 2004; Renninger & Shumar, 2002).

SOCIAL NETWORKS

Social network studies look at CMC use in terms of who is communicating with whom (Garton *et al.*, 1997). This view cuts across notions of similar users to address directly what people are doing with each other online, and via different media. Networks of interconnectedness rather than aggregates of groups or users are examined. These studies take into consideration context, group activities, and structures, as well as media use (e.g., Haythornthwaite, 2002; Haythornthwaite *et al.*, 1998; Wellman *et al.*, 1996).

Some results from social network studies of media use suggest that the conflicting results found for the use of CMC and of the Internet may be reconciled by looking more closely at the kinds of ties various media support (Haythornthwaite, 2002, 2005). Network studies have found that media use differs according to the strength of the tie between communicating pairs. However, the difference is not in *what* media are used, but *how many*; those with stronger ties use more of the available media to communicate than do those who maintain weaker ties (Haythornthwaite & Wellman, 1998; Haythornthwaite, 2001, 2002; Koku *et al.*, 2001). Moreover, it appears that pairs add media to their repertoire in the same way. Those who are weakly tied, and use only one or two media to communicate, use the same one or two media. Strongly tied pairs also use these media, but add on more private and asynchronous means of communication (Haythornthwaite, 2002, 2005).

While there have been CMC debates about what kinds of *messages* could be sent via the lean medium of e-mail versus the rich medium of face-to-face meetings, and Internet debates about what kinds of *relationships* can be maintained online versus those that need the rich contexts of home or office, both have failed to acknowledge that we use *both* online and offline for a *variety* of messages and relationships. We maintain some strong ties, talking about all sorts of things through any and all means available, and we maintain many weak ties, with interaction about only a few things, maintained through one generally available means of communication. Network views take us beyond the aggregate views that until now gave all-or-nothing statistics about use of a medium, failing to capture the variability in use across the many kinds of ties we maintain.

While there are advances in understanding the role of CMC and online interaction in relation to offline activities, there are still few studies that examine the use of multiple media. As each new CMC application is introduced, it takes its place in individuals' communication repertoires alongside existing media. Yet, many studies still continue to examine one medium, for example, e-mail or blogs or instant messaging. Looking at the use of multiple means of communication is an essential step for understanding the place of each medium in the communication behaviors of individuals, groups, and communities. General notions of multiple media use suggest a complementarity among media, in keeping with media richness perspectives. In this case, one means of communication is considered appropriate for immediate, emotionally charged communications (usually considered to be face-to-face communication) and another for more instrumental informational exchanges, such as setting up a meeting (e.g., e-mail). Early writings attempted to place media along a richness scale from rich to poor in terms of immediacy of feedback, ability to carry cues, etc., and to consider and examine what communications should be channeled through each means (Daft & Lengel, 1986; Trevino *et al.*, 1990; Rice, 1992; Rice & Shook, 1990). More recent research has taken a different view of multiple media use and has examined use by individual pairs rather than across organizations or organizational groups (e.g., managers). This work shows that the closer the tie, the more media pairs use to communicate: that is, rather than *substitute* one medium for another for different kinds of communications, pairs *add* media. This has been shown to hold among co-located researchers (Haythornthwaite & Wellman, 1998), online learners (Haythornthwaite, 2001), and distributed scientists (Koku *et al.*, 2001).

Tie-Based View of Media Use

An interpersonal, tie-based view of media helps to reconcile earlier disparate results. If we recast the arguments for and against CMC in terms of network ties, the arguments against CMC, notably, the inability to convey emotion or complex thought, can be seen as an argument that CMC is unable to convey cues sufficient to sustain strong work or friendship ties. The argument that CMC can be a rich means of communication is also an argument about the ability to maintain strong ties. Richness has appeared in CMC communications by the continuous bootstrapping of communicators, that is, by those busy building stronger interpersonal and community-wide ties that include introducing and adopting subtleties of online language (including symbols such as emoticons and acronyms, and also local social norms for language use and conversation content). In keeping with DeSanctis and Poole's (1994) adaptive structuration, this richness in communication is seen as arising from interactions among participants, with norms and conventions growing and appearing over time. Those who communicate often, and who want to create and/or maintain a relationship, are likely to work at ways of getting their message across, either through inventive adaptations of language or through use of multiple channels. Thus, use and usage build on each other to support pair ties, and eventually whole networks of ties.

At the other end of the spectrum, we find that the wide connectivity associated with CMC and the Internet provides good support for weak ties, bringing access to those outside our immediate social circle, letting us get advice from strangers, and keep in touch with central activities (Constant *et al.*, 1996). Yet, as communication moves online, or indeed moves from any one medium to another, such weak tie connections are most at risk of dissolution because this is their only means of contact. Thus, weak ties are most at risk with any change, and here we may find some answer to why CMC and Internet use can be disintegrative. (For more on this subject, see Haythornthwaite, 2002, 2005.)

ONLINE AND OFFLINE INTEGRATION

The second major trend in research explores the synergies between online and offline communication and relationships. This research is driven, in part, by recognition of the way CMC and the Internet have become routine parts of daily life, rather than occupying a separate realm of existence. Phenomena that were separate from daily life, such as cyberspace, cyberworlds, and online communities, have been appropriated into everyday life. Instant messaging has moved from teen chat to business tool (Cho *et al.*, 2005; Quan-Haase *et al.*, 2005), online communities from programmer domains to business communities of practice, e-mail from business tool to interpersonal communication. Comprehensive studies show that when we look at what is really happening, we see that while it sometimes creates surprising outcomes (such as the vitality of online communities, marriages between people who met and courted online), more often CMC and the Internet support daily routines (Katz & Rice, 2002a).

TOGGLING

Recently, a number of writers have specifically addressed the intersection between worlds of communication, including a major study by the Pew Foundation (Fallows, 2004) which examined the way people "toggle between the offline and online worlds for activities" (p. iii). In addition to the work of Katz and Rice (2002a, 2002b) and Warschauer (2003) discussed previously, a number of other writers also name and address the integrative approach.

Haythornthwaite and Wellman (2002) discuss how the use of the Internet is no longer the "dazzling light" shining down from above. Instead, "[w]e are moving from a world of Internet wizards to a world of ordinary people routinely using the Internet as an embedded part of their lives. It has become clear that the Internet is a very important thing, but not a special thing." (p. 4). Other CMC researchers follow a similar theme, for example, Herring's (2004) piece titled "Slouching toward the Ordinary." Howard and Jones (2003) draw our attention to "how new communication tools are embedded in our lives and how our lives are embedded in new media"

(p. 2), with new media "rapidly and deeply embedded in our organizations and institutions" (p. 2), and conclude by considering "network" as a new metaphor for understanding the context of the internet (small "i") which shifts analysis away from the separate monolith of the Internet (capital "I") to where connections are made.

Similar to Jones' appeal to the network metaphor and connectivity, Kazmer and Haythornthwaite (2001; Kazmer, 2002) and Haythornthwaite and Hagar (2004) appeal to Strauss' (1978) concept of *social worlds* rather than on- and offline worlds. Social worlds consist of the people who share activities, space, and technology, and who communicate with one another. This view focuses our attention on shared activities, looking for meaningful combinations of actors and activities, rather than considering only pieces of that activity as enacted through single means of communication.

DOMESTICATION

As CMC and the Internet have moved out of the office and the classroom, they have also found new embedding contexts. Studies now look at trends in the domestication of the Internet, examining computer adoption and use in the household as well as how the Internet is used at home (e.g., Cummings & Kraut, 2002; Kraut *et al.*, 2002; Kraut, Kiesler *et al.*, 1998; Kraut *et al.*, 1998; Kiesler *et al.*, 2000; Silverstone & Haddon, 1996; Lally, 2002). Others look at the overlap with home activity. For example, Salaff (2002) examined how work is managed at home when teleworkers bring the office into the domestic space; and Haythornthwaite and Kazmer (2002) looked at how learners fit their online education into their offline home and work spaces and responsibilities. Kazmer (in press) has gone further to suggest that online learning may be particularly successful for those who are embedded in compatible work environments, such as library science students already working in nonprofessional positions in local libraries.

LIMITS TO GROWTH

As use of CMC and the Internet grows, some newer trends suggest other ways in which these technologies are affecting daily life. As has been noted, one major change is the number of hours spent online. The question is, where are the 16 + hours a week that experienced users spend online coming from (Nie, 2001)? At present, we do not have a clear answer, but as the time online increases—if it continues to—it may lead to noticeable changes in how we allocate our attention. It has already been noted that the "24/7" concept of the day is breaking down divisions between at-work and off-work hours. Ubiquitous access means ubiquitous accessibility, and managing this may be one of the next great challenges for high-access users.

New trends in online scams and spam are impinging on the ability to function online, particularly through e-mail. The Pew Internet and American Life Project reported that 25% of e-mail users found spam to have reduced their use of e-mail; "60 percent of that group says spam has reduced their e-mail use in a big way, 52 percent of e-mail users say spam has made them less trusting of e-mail in general, and 70 percent of e-mail users say spam has made being online unpleasant or annoying" (Fallows, 2004). Intervention from government and regulators may be the only way to deal with this onslaught, although little is happening at present to ameliorate this problem (at least in the United States). Most solutions currently in place are technological rather than regulatory.

Regulation and control are seen in other aspects of online communication, largely directed at public access to the Internet. Fears of use for antisocial and criminal behavior have led, in the U. S., to laws about use of public access sites. The U. S. Children's Internet Protection Act requires Internet filters to be placed on library computer terminals as a condition of federal funding (whether or not libraries agree with the concept of filtering), and the U. S. Patriot Act allows federal agents access to records of library use and histories of use on public terminals and in businesses (Doyle, 2002).

WRAPPING UP

This review of studies of CMC and the Internet reveals that there is still a strong concern with the way online interaction changes communication behavior and the way we maintain relationships. As in early CMC debates, the Internet has extended both the use of online connections and concerns about its impact on local family and communal relations. As such, they tap into a longstanding debate about the loss of community with every new wave of migration, urbanization, and technological change. Change is definitely happening in the way we spend our time (16 + hours online for experienced users), where technology is located (increasingly in the home), where we can be reached (anywhere by mobile phones and wireless computing), and when (as global connectivity crosses time zones, and as at-home and mobile computing extends the work day). Our challenges for the future are in managing and balancing the demands of the 24/7 access with priorities in our lives, including family, community (both local and online), work, and education.

While earlier research tended to treat CMC and the Internet as monolithic concepts, the penetration of these technologies into so many aspects of everyday life, to so many people and for so many purposes, has created a need for more nuanced work. In studies conducted so far, this is achieved through two major research trends: (1) research that unbundles users, their activities and contexts, exploring use by each and every constituency and highlighting differences across user communities; and (2) research that examines of the integration of CMC and the Internet into everyday life. These views complement each other. While the everyday life approach forces us to see the overlap between online and offline interactions, the unbundling approach reminds us that differences exist in who is and is not online, and what they do there. It is not sufficient yet to take the Internet as so ordinary that it is invisible. A taken-for-granted view gives license to move resources and interaction online, failing to consider who and what may be left behind. Thus, it is important that research continue to address both of these areas.

Both views point to important new questions about CMC and Internet use. To conclude, we suggest that instead of continuing to ask what can or cannot be done online, the next generation of researchers should ask:

- How will we integrate the CMC and the Internet into everyday life?
- Where will resources move online, disappearing from other forms, creating a mediated world of information?
- What will be the impact and demands on institutions and organizations as online interaction becomes mandatory? How will work be measured when conducted anywhere, anytime?
- How will various cultures appropriate the Internet? Or will Internet culture appropriate them?
- How will the upcoming, born-with-digital generation drive uses, norms, and expectations about accessibility and use?

REFERENCES

Anderson, B., & Tracey, K. (2002). Digital living: The impact (or otherwise) of the Internet in everyday British life. In B. Wellman & C. Haythornthwaite (Eds.), *The Internet in everyday life* (pp. 139–163). Oxford, UK: Blackwell.

Bakardjieva, M., & Smith, R. (2001). The Internet in everyday life: Computer networking from the standpoint of the domestic user. *New Media and Society, 3*(1), 67–83.

Baym, N. K. (2000). *Tune in, log on: Soaps, fandom, and online community.* Thousand Oaks, CA: Sage.

Baym, N. K. (2002). Interpersonal life online. In L. A. Lievrouw & S. Livingstone (Eds.), *The handbook of new media* (pp. 62–76). Thousand Oaks, CA: Sage.

Boase, J., & Wellman, B. (2005). Personal relationships: On and off the Internet. In D. Perlman & A.L.Vangelisti (Eds.), *Handbook of personal relations* (pp. 709–723). Oxford, UK: Blackwell.

Boneva, B., & Kraut, R. (2002). Email, gender and personal relationships. In B. Wellman & C. Haythornthwaite (Eds.), *The Internet in everyday life* (pp. 372–403). Oxford, UK: Blackwell.

Bregman, A., & Haythornthwaite, C. (2003). Radicals of presentation: Visibility, relation, and co-presence in persistent conversation. *New Media and Society, 5*(1), 117–140.

Bruce, B. C., & Hogan, M. P. (1998). The disappearance of technology: Toward an ecological model of literacy. In D. Reinking, M. McKenna, L. Labbo, & R. Kieffer (Eds.), *Handbook of literacy and technology: Transformations in a post-typographic world* (pp. 269–281). Hillsdale, NJ: Erlbaum.

Cherny, L. (1999). *Conversation and community: Chat in a virtual world.* Stanford, CA: CSLI Publications.

Cho, H-K, Trier, M., & Kim, E. (2005). Evaluating instant messaging in developing working relationships. *Journal of Computer Mediated Communication.* Retrieved September, 17, 2005, from (http://jcmc.indiana.edu/vol10/issue4/cho.html)

Clark, H. H., & Brennan, S. E. (1991). Grounding in communication. In L. B. Resnick, J. M. Levine, & S. D. Teasley (Eds.), *Perspectives on socially shared cognition* (pp. 127–149). Washington, DC: American Psychological Association.

Cohill, A. M., & Kavanaugh, A. L. (2000). *Community networks: Lessons from Blacksburg, Virginia* (2nd ed). Boston, MA: Artech House.

Constant, D., Kiesler, S. B., & Sproull, L. S. (1996). The kindness of strangers: The usefulness of electronic weak ties for technical advice. *Organization Science, 7(2)*, 119–135

Crystal, D. (2001). *Language and the Internet.* Cambridge, UK: Cambridge University Press.

Culnan, M. J., & Markus, M. L. (1987). Information technologies. In F. M. Jablin, L. L. Putnam, K. H. Roberts, & L. W. Porter (Eds.), *Handbook of organizational communication: An interdisciplinary perspective* (pp. 420–443). Newbury Park, CA: Sage.

Cummings, J., & Kraut, R. (2002). Domesticating computers and the Internet. *The Information Society, 18(3)*, 221–232.

Daft, R. L., & Lengel, R. H. (1986). Organizational information requirements, media richness, and structural design. *Management Science, 32(5)*, 554–571.

DeSanctis, G., and Poole, M. S. (1994). Capturing the complexity in advanced technology use: Adaptive structuration theory. *Organization Science, 5(2)*, 121–147.

Dibbell, J. (1996). Taboo, consensus, and the challenge of democracy in an electronic forum. In R. Kling (Ed.), *Computerization and Controversy* (pp. 553–568). San Diego, CA: Academic Press.

DiMaggio, P., Hargittai, E., Neuman, W. R., & Robinson, J. P. (2001). Social implications of the Internet. *Annual Review of Sociology, 27*, 307–336.

Doyle, C. (2002). The USA Patriot Act: A sketch. CRS Report for Congress. Congressional Research Service: The Library of Congress. Retrieved September 17, 2005, from (http://www.fas.org/irp/crs/RS21203.pdf)

Erickson, T., Halverson, C., Kellogg, W. A., Laff, M., & Wolf, T. (2002). Social translucence: Designing social infrastructures that make collective activity visible. *Communications of the ACM, 45(4)*. 40–44.

Fallows, D. (2004). *The Internet and daily life.* Pew Internet and American Life Project. Retrieved September 17, 2005, from (http://www.pewinternet.org/PPF/r/131/report_display.asp)

Fallows, D. (2003). Spam: How It Is Hurting Email and Degrading Life on the Internet. Pew Internet and American Life Project. From http://www.pewinternet.org/pdfs/PIP_Spam_Report.pdf.

Garton, L., Haythornthwaite, C., & Wellman, B. (1997). Studying online social networks. *Journal of Computer-Mediated Communication, 3(1).* Retrieved September 17, 2005, from (http://www.ascusc.org/jcmc/vol3/issue1/garton.html)

Graham, S. (2004). Beyond the "dazzling light": From dreams of transcendence to the "remediation" of urban life—A research manifesto. *New Media & Society, 6(1)*, 16–25.

Gurstein, M. (2000). *Community informatics: Enabling communities with information and communications technologies.* Hershey, PA: Idea Group Publishing.

Hagar, C., & Haythornthwaite, C. (2005). Crisis, farming, & community. *Journal of Community Informatics, 1(3).* Retrieved September 17, 2005, from (http://ci-journal.net/viewarticle.php?id=89&layout=html)

Hampton, K., & Wellman, B. (2002). The not so global village of Netville. In B. Wellman & C. Haythornthwaite (Eds.), *The Internet in everyday life* (pp. 345–371). Oxford, UK: Blackwell.

Haythornthwaite, C. (2001). Exploring multiplexity: Social network structures in a computer-supported distance learning class. *The Information Society, 17(3)*, 211–226.

Haythornthwaite, C. (2002). Strong, weak and latent ties and the impact of new media. *The Information Society, 18(5)*, 385–401

Haythornthwaite, C. (2005). Social networks and Internet connectivity effects. *Information, Communication, and Society, 8(2)*, 125–147.

Haythornthwaite, C. (in press). Social networks and online community. In A. Joinson, K. McKenna, U. Reips, & T. Postmes (Eds.), *Oxford handbook of Internet psychology*. Oxford, UK: Oxford University Press.

Haythornthwaite, C., & Hagar, C. (2004). The social worlds of the web. *Annual Review of Information Science and Technology, 39*, 311–346.

Haythornthwaite, C., & Kazmer, M. M. (2002). Bringing the Internet home: Adult distance learners and their Internet, home, and work worlds. In B. Wellman & C. Haythornthwaite (Eds.), *The Internet in everyday life* (pp. 431–463). Oxford, UK: Blackwell.

Haythornthwaite, C., & Kazmer, M. M. (Eds.) (2004). *Learning, culture, and community in online education: Research and practice*. New York: Peter Lang.

Haythornthwaite, C., Kazmer, M. M., Robins, J., & Shoemaker, S. (2000). Community development among distance learners: Temporal and technological dimensions. *Journal of Computer-Mediated Communication, 6*(1). (http://www.ascusc.org/jcmc/vol6/issue1/haythornthwaite.html)

Haythornthwaite, C., & Wellman, B. (1998). Work, friendship, and media use for information exchange in a networked organization. *Journal of the American Society for Information Science, 49*(12), 1101–1114.

Haythornthwaite, C., & Wellman, B. (2002). The Internet in everyday life: An introduction. In B. Wellman & C. Haythornthwaite (Eds.), *The Internet in everyday life* (pp. 3–41). Oxford, UK: Blackwell.

Haythornthwaite, C., Wellman, B., & Garton, L. (1998). Work and community via computer-mediated communication. In J. Gackenbach (Ed.) *Psychology and the Internet* (pp. 199–226). San Diego, CA: Academic Press.

Hearne, B., & Nielsen, A. (2004). Catch a cyber by the tale: Online orality and the lore of a distributed learning community. In C. Haythornthwaite & M. M. Kazmer (Eds.), *Learning, culture and community in online education: Research and practice* (pp. 59–87). New York: Peter Lang.

Herring S. C. (1996). Gender and democracy in computer-mediated communication. In R. Kling (Ed.), *Computerization and controversy*. (2nd Ed.) (pp. 476–489). San Diego, CA: Academic Press.

Herring, S. C. (1999). The rhetorical dynamics of gender harassment on-line. *The Information Society, 15*(3), 151–167.

Herring, S. C. (2002). Computer-mediated communication on the Internet. *Annual Review of Information Science and Technology, 36*, 109–168.

Herring, S. C. (2004). Slouching toward the ordinary: Current trends in computer-mediated communication. *New Media & Society, 6*(1) 26–36.

Hoffman, D. L., Novak, T. P., & Venkatesh, A. (July, 2004). Has the Internet become indispensable? *Communications of the ACM. 47*(7): 37–42.

Howard, P., & Jones, S. (Eds.) (2003). *Society online*. London: Sage.

Howard, P., Rainie, L., & Jones, S. (2002). Days and nights on the Internet. In B. Wellman & C. Haythornthwaite (Eds.), *The Internet in everyday life* (pp. 45–73). Oxford, UK: Blackwell.

Jankowski, N. W. (2002). Creating communities with media: Histories, theories, and scientific investigations. In L. A. Lievrouw & S. Livingstone (Eds.), *The handbook of new media* (pp. 34–49). Thousand Oaks, CA: Sage.

Katz, J. E., & Rice, R. (2002a). Syntopia: Access, civic involvement, and social interaction on the net. In B. Wellman & C. Haythornthwaite (Eds.), *The Internet in everyday life* (pp. 114–138). Oxford, UK: Blackwell.

Katz, J. E., & Rice, R. E. (2002b). *Social consequences of Internet use: Access, involvement, and expression*. Cambridge, MA: MIT Press.

Kavanaugh, A., & Patterson, S. (2002). The impact of computer networks on social capital and community involvement in Blacksburg. In B. Wellman & C. Haythornthwaite (Eds.), *The Internet in everyday life* (pp. 325–344). Oxford, UK: Blackwell.

Kazmer, M. M. (2002). *Disengagement from intrinsically transient social worlds: The case of a distance learning community*. Unpublished doctoral dissertation. University of Illinois at Urbana Champaign.

Kazmer, M. M. (in press). Beyond C U L8R: Disengaging from online social worlds. *New Media and Society.*

Kazmer, M. M., & Haythornthwaite, C. (2001). Juggling multiple social worlds: Distance students on and offline. *American Behavioral Scientist, 45*(3), 510–529.

Keeble, L., & Loader, B. D. (Eds.) (2001). *Community informatics: Shaping computer-mediated social relations.* New York: Routledge.

Kendall, L. (2002). *Hanging out in the virtual pub: Masculinities and relationships online.* Berkeley, CA: University of California Press.

Kiesler, S., Lundmark, V., Zdaniuk, B., & Kraut, R. E. (2000). Troubles with the Internet: The dynamics of help at home. *Human Computer Interaction, 15*, 323–351.

Kling, R. (Ed.). (1996). *Computerization and controversy: Value conflicts and social choices,* (2nd edition.) San Diego, CA: Academic Press.

Koku, E., Nazer, N., & Wellman, B. (2001) Netting scholars: Online and offline. *American Behavioral Scientist, 44*(10), 1752–1774.

Kolko, B. E., Nakamura, L., & Rodman, G. B. (Eds.). (2000). *Race in cyberspace.* New York: Routledge.

Kraut, R., Kiesler, S., Boneva, B., Cummings, J., Helgeson, V., & Crawford, A. (2002). Internet paradox revisited. *Journal of Social Issues, 58*(1), 49–74.

Kraut, R., Kiesler, S., Mukhopadhyay, T., Scherilis, W., & Patterson, V. L. (1998). Social impact of the Internet. *Communications of the ACM, 41*(12), 21–22.

Kraut, R., Patterson, V. L., Kiesler, S., Mukhopadhyay, T., & Scherilis, W. (1998). Internet paradox: A social technology that reduces social involvement and psychological well-being? *American Psychologist, 53*(9), 1017–1031.

Lally, E. (2002). *At home with computers.* Oxford, UK: Berg.

LaRose, R., Eastin, M. S., & Gregg, J. (2001). Reformulating the Internet paradox: Social cognitive explanations of Internet use and depression. *Journal of Online Behavior, 1*(2). Retrieved June 17, 2005, from (http://www.behavior.net/JOB/v1n2/paradox.html)

Lea, M., O'Shea, T., Fung, P. & Spears, R. (1992). 'Flaming' in computer-mediated communication: Observations, explanations, implications. In M. Lea (Ed.) *Contexts of Computer-Mediated Communication* (pp. 89-112). New York: Harvester Wheatsheaf.

Livingstone, S. (2002). *Young people and new media: Childhood and the changing media environment.* Thousand Oaks, CA: Sage.

Livingstone, S., & Bober, M. (2005). *UK children go online: Final report of key project findings.* UK: Economic and Social Research Council. Retrieved May 31, 2006, from (http://news.bbc.co.uk/1/shared/bsp/hi/pdfs/28_04_05childrenonline.pdf)

Madden, M., & Rainie, L. (2003). America's online pursuits: The changing picture of who's online and what they do. Pew Internet and American Life Project. Retrieved June 17, 2005, from (http://www.pewinternet.org/pdfs/PIP_Online_Pursuits_Final.PDF)

Markus, M. L. (1990). Toward a "critical mass" theory of interactive media. In J. Fulk & C. W. Steinfield (Eds.), *Organizations and communication technology* (pp. 194–218). Newbury Park, CA: Sage.

McLaughlin, M. L., Osborne, K. K., & Smith, C. B. (1995). Standards of conduct on Usenet. In S. G. Jones (Ed.), *CyberSociety: Computer-mediated communication and community* (pp. 90–111). Thousand Oaks, CA: Sage.

NTIA (2002). *A nation online.* National Telecommunications and Information Agency, U. S Commerce Department. Retrieved September 17, 2005, from (http://www.ntia.doc.gov/ntiahome/dn/index.html)

NTIA (2000). *Falling through the net: Toward digital inclusion.* National Telecommunications and Information Administration, U. S. Commerce Department. Retrieved September 17, 2005, from (http://www.ntia.doc.gov/ntiahome/digitaldivide/)

Nie, N. H. (2001). Sociability, interpersonal relations, and the Internet: Reconciling conflicting findings. *American Behavioral Scientist, 45*(3), 420–435.

Nie, N. H., & Erbring, L. (February 17, 2000). *Internet and society: A preliminary report*. Stanford Institute for the Quantitative Study of Society (SIQSS), Stanford University, and InterSurvey. Retrieved September 17, 2005, from (http://www.stanford.edu/group/siqss/)

Nie, N. H, Hillygus, D. S., & Erbring, L. (2002). Internet use, interpersonal relations, and sociability: A time diary study. In B. Wellman & C. Haythornthwaite (Eds.), *The Internet in everyday life* (pp. 215–243). Oxford, UK: Blackwell.

Nissenbaum, H., & Price, M. E. (2004). *Academy and the Internet*. New York: Peter Lang.

Orlikowski, W. J., & Yates, J. (1994). Genre repertoire: The structuring of communicative practices in organizations. *Administrative Science Quarterly, 39*, 541–574.

Orlikowski, W. J., Yates, J., Okamura, K., & Fujimoto, M. (1995). Shaping electronic communication: The metastructuring of technology in the context of use. *Organization Science, 6*(4), 423–444.

Putnam, R. D. (2000). *Bowling alone: The collapse and revival of American community*. New York: Simon & Schuster.

Quan-Haase, A., Cothrel, J., & Wellman, B. (2005). Instant messaging for collaboration: A case study of a high-tech firm. *Journal of Computer Mediated Communication*. Retrieved September 17, 2005, from (http://jcmc.indiana.edu/vol10/issue4/quan-haase.html)

Reid, E. (1995). Virtual worlds: Culture and imagination. In S. G. Jones (Ed.), *CyberSociety: Computer-mediated communication and community* (pp.164–183). Thousand Oaks, CA: Sage.

Renninger, A., & Shumar, W. (Eds.) (2002). *Building virtual communities: Learning and change in cyberspace*. Cambridge, UK: Cambridge University Press.

Rheingold, H. (2003). *Smart mobs: The next social revolution*. New York: Perseus Books.

Rice, R. E. (1992). Task analyzability, use of new media, and effectiveness: A multi-site exploration of media richness. *Organization Science, 3(4),* 475–500.

Rice, R. E., & Shook, D. E. (1990). Relationships of job categories and organizational levels to use of communication channels, including electronic mail: A meta-analysis and extension. *Journal of Management Studies, 27(2)*, 195–229.

Rogers, E. M (1995). *Diffusion of innovations* (4th Ed.). New York: The Free Press.

Salaff, J. (2002). Where home is the office: The new form of flexible work. In B. Wellman & C. Haythornthwaite (Eds.), *The Internet in everyday life* (pp. 464–495). Oxford, UK: Blackwell.

Short, J., Williams, E., & Christie, B. (1976). *The social psychology of telecommunications*. London: John Wiley & Sons.

Silverstone, R. (1999). *Why study the media?* London: Sage.

Silverstone, R., & Haddon, L. (1996). Design and the domestication of information and communication technologies: Technical change and everyday life. In R. Mansell & R. Silverstone (Eds.), *Communication by design: The politics of information and communication technologies* (pp. 44–74). Oxford: Oxford University Press,

Spears, R., Lea, M., & Postmes, T. (2001). Social psychological theories of computer-mediated communication: Social pain or social gain? In W. P. Robinson & H. Giles (Eds.), *New handbook of language and social psychology* (pp. 601–623). Chichester: Wiley.

Sproull, L. & Kiesler, S. (1991). *Connections: New Ways of Working in the Networked Organization*. Cambridge, MA: MIT Press.

Star, S. L. (1999). The ethnography of infrastructure. *American Behavioral Scientist, 43*(3), 377–391.

Strauss, A. L. (1978). A social world perspective. *Studies in Symbolic Interactions, 1*, 119–128.

Trevino, L. K., Daft, R. L., & Lengel, R. H. (1990). Understanding managers' media choice: A symbolic interactionist perspective. In J. Fulk & C. W. Steinfield (Eds.), *Organizations and communication technology* (pp. 71–94). Newbury Park, CA: Sage.

Turkle, S. (1995). *Life on the screen: Identity in the age of the Internet*. New York: Simon & Schuster.

Turow, J., & Kavanaugh, A. L. (2003). *The wired homestead: An MIT sourcebook on the Internet and the family*. Cambridge, MA: MIT Press.

UCLA Center for Communication Policy (2000). *The UCLA Internet report: Surveying the digital future.* Retrieved May 31, 2006, from (http://digitalcenter.org/pdf/InternetReportYear One.)

Walsh, J., & Bayma, T. (1996) Computer networks and scientific work. *Social Studies of Science, 26,* 661–703.

Walsh, J. P., Kucker, S., Maloney, N. G., and Gabbay, S. (2000). Connecting minds: Computer-mediated communication and scientific work. *Journal of the American Society for Information Science* 52(14), 1295–1305.

Walther, J. B. (1995). Relational aspects of computer-mediated communication: Experimental observations over time. *Organization Science, 6*(2), 186–203.

Warschauer, M. (2000). Language, identity, and the Internet. In B. E. Kolko, L. Nakamura, & G. B. Rodman (Eds.), *Race in cyberspace* (pp. 151–170). New York: Routledge.

Warschauer, M. (2003). *Technology and social inclusion.* Cambridge, MA: MIT Press.

Wellman, B., & Haythornthwaite, C. (Eds.). (2002). *The Internet in everyday life.* Oxford, UK: Blackwell.

Wellman, B., Salaff, J., Dimitrova, D., Garton, L., Gulia, M., & Haythornthwaite, C. (1996). Computer networks as social networks: Collaborative work, telework, and virtual community. *Annual Review of Sociology, 22,* 213–238.

The Virtual Society: Its Driving Forces, Arrangements, Practices, and Implications

Conrad Shayo
Information and Decision Sciences Department
California State University, San Bernardino
San Bernandino, California
Lorne Olfman, Alicia Iriberri, and Magid Igbaria
School of Information Systems and Technology
Claremont Graduate University
Claremont, California

INTRODUCTION

During the last decade, the adjective "virtual" has become a commonplace descriptor of social forms where people do not have to live, meet, or work face to face in order to create goods and services or maintain significant social relationships. There are specialized literatures about these new social forms, such as virtual corporations, virtual organizations, virtual communities, virtual libraries, and virtual classrooms, as well as related practices such as e-commerce, e-business, telecommuting, computer-supported cooperative work (CSCW), tele-education, teleconferencing, telemedicine, telemarketing, and teledemocracy. There is general agreement in the

Psychology and the Internet: Intrapersonal, Interpersonal, and Transpersonal Implications

literature that the profound impact of information technology (IT)[1] and its rapid adoption by individuals, groups, organizations, and communities has given rise to the proliferation of "virtual societies." While computer networks figure frequently as enablers and shapers of virtual societies, other kinds of information and communication technologies, including paper mail, telephone, and fax, also play roles in linking and establishing relationships between people and groups (Woolgar, 2002). Although some of the literature celebrates the flexibility and enhanced possibilities of these new forms of "virtual social life," there are also important critical empirical studies of specific virtual social forms that examine the possible losses.

In this chapter, we examine the driving forces behind the growth of virtual societies and discuss existing arrangements and practices at the individual, group, organization, and community levels. We also examine the implications of how people will live and work in societies where these arrangements and practices are widespread and mixed with face-to-face relationships. Our discussion follows the model of virtual society presented in Fig. 1.

Figure 1 describes an evolutionary model conceptualizing an entire hierarchy for studying the virtual society and summarizes both the driving forces and arrangements that are critical components of this proposed framework. Specifically,

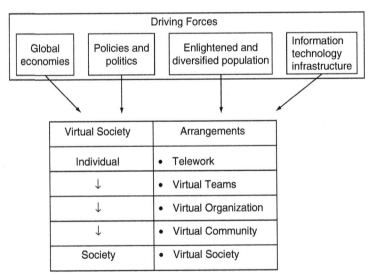

Figure 1 A Framework for the Virtual Society.

---

[1] Information technology comprises computer software and hardware of all types, workstations, computer networks, robotics, and smart chips.

this chapter is organized as follows: We first discuss the driving forces which include global economics, policies, and politics, enlightened population, and information technology infrastructure; second, we describe existing arrangements and practices at the individual, group, organization, and community levels. Finally, we examine the dilemmas and implications of the virtual society on peoples' lives and work.

DRIVING FORCES

The virtual society transcends cities, states, nations, and continents, and represents an evolutionary as opposed to a revolutionary movement. Although information technology (IT) is the main enabling force of the virtual society, other components are also at work, namely, economic, political, cultural, and social forces (Agres *et al.*, 1998). This section discusses these macro forces at a more finite level—identifying the forces that are moving us to a virtual society. As shown in the framework presented in Fig. 1, the finite level forces include global economies, policies, and politics, enlightened and diversified population, as well as the information technology infrastructure. These forces continue to create the necessary conditions for the eventual realization of the virtual society. Current virtual workplace arrangements and practices of "virtuality" include telework (at the individual level), virtual teams (at the group level), virtual corporations (at the organizational level), and virtual communities (at the community level). Other arrangements and practices continue to evolve. Once a critical mass of these virtual activities and practices permeates all levels of society, the outcome will be the virtual society. Following Beniger's (1986) thesis that we are currently in the information society,[2] we argue that the seeds of the virtual society already exist in the womb of the information society and we are already seeing some of the results. The economic, social, political, and technological forces unleashed by the information society are inevitably leading us to the virtual society.

GLOBAL ECONOMIES

During the last five decades, the world has witnessed an unprecedented expansion of business into global markets (World Bank, 2003, 2004, 2005). These gains build upon the economic spiral set forth by the agricultural and industrial revolutions (Beniger, 1986). Although some developing countries moved directly from agriculture-based to IT-based economies (e.g., Jordan and Panama), most have

---

[2] In the U. S., the information society emerged in the mid-1950s, when more than 50% of the workforce was engaged in information and service-related activities. The information society is also known, among other terms, as the post-industrial society (Bell, 1973), knowledge economy (Drucker, 1969), wired society (Martin, 1978), or the credential society (Collins, 1979).

followed the traditional growth path in the creation of national income, that is, from agriculture to manufacturing, and then from manufacturing to services (World Bank, 2003). The world domestic product (GDP) was estimated at $52 trillion in 2003—an increase of more than 140% since the end of the Second World War.

The ascendance of economic liberalism in the last decade, characterized by deregulation, the end of the Cold War, privatization, free markets, outsourcing, lower tariffs, and the move toward more democratic and egalitarian systems in industrializing nations, has opened new opportunities for trade and investment. Taxes on international trade declined between 1995 and 2005. Trade in low- and middle-income economies continued to register unprecedented growth. Within this period, East and South Asian countries registered an average economic growth of more than 7.5% per year, with China and India leading the way. At the same time, high and upper middle-income economies grow at the modest rates of between 2.0% and 3.5% (World Bank, 2005).

According to David (1997), the trend toward reduction of income inequalities among nations has increased effective demand for goods and services and made it beneficial for transnational and multinational corporations to increase direct private foreign investment in developing and industrializing countries. Most of this money was invested in telecommunications, insurance, finance, energy, computers, and travel services. Indeed, whereas direct investment inflows among developing countries declined by 14% in 2004 relative to 2003, the global flow of direct investment to developing countries surged by 40% to $233 billion (UNCTAD, 2005). At the same time, the global trade and investment in low- and middle-income nations increased from 33.4% to 51.8% of their GDP, as opposed to only a 5.3% increase in high-income countries. There are signs that developing countries are gradually eroding the dominance of the developed countries in real income per capita (Krugman, 2000). According to World Bank projections, the world's GDP could grow to more than 65 trillion in the next 20 years (World Bank, 2004).

Outsourcing business activities on a global scale has become an important emerging trend for businesses and governments. Some firms have a significant amount of their value creation activities throughout the world. Firms are appreciating the need to think globally as they move to tap markets beyond their domestic boundaries. Local and global competition is forcing firms to identify opportunities for growth and increased market share for their products and services. The cliché is now "Think globally, but act locally!" Firms routinely move an important piece of work, such as a proposal or design idea, across time zones and countries so they can work on them literally around the clock. Others are outsourcing the functions of complete business units offshore. Borders are becoming transparent for work and trade as global money becomes more of a reality, and regional trading blocs such as North American Free Trade Agreement (NAFTA), the European Union (E.U.) and the Association of South East Asian Nations (ASEAN) move forward.

Moreover, new investment in IT infrastructure by national governments and multinational corporations has enabled businesses with diverse business models and forms of organizational control to operate in multiple countries seamlessly. For example, reliable and robust IT infrastructures within the NAFTA, ASEAN, and E.U. trading blocs have reduced coordination and transportation costs dramatically. Most countries are working on improving their IT infrastructures as well. Global businesses can now link directly to their customers, suppliers, and partners around the world more cost effectively than ever before. For example, Nike Inc. has distributed most of its other business value-creating activities to a network of suppliers and business partners all over the world, while focusing in the United States on product design, marketing, and sales service. Product designers in the U. S. are linked with contractors in Asia and elsewhere through sophisticated IT networks and Computer Integrated Manufacturing (CIM) systems. Computerized control and coordination systems monitor each value-creating activity. This capability makes it possible to set prices, balance supply and demand, and control the physical distribution of sneakers through designated retail outlets all over the world. Other organizations, such as General Motors, Toyota, and Kodak, have similar global arrangements.

The Industrial Development Corporation (IDC) estimates that the average spending for online buyers will be $800 per person by 2008 (IDC, 2004–2008 Report). In the U. S. alone, Internet total retail purchases, that is, Business to Customer (B2C) sales, will be well over $130 billion. On the Business to Business (B2B) side, Gartner Consulting estimates that B2B purchases via Internet EDI, e-marketplaces, extranets, and other sell-side initiatives, will increase from $919 billion in 2001 to more than $8.5 trillion in 2005 (Gartner Consulting, Press Release, 2001).

The global efforts to standardize economic operations by enhancing free trade policies, creating robust telecommunications infrastructures, changing the nature of payment and money, upgrading global monetary standards and policies, and adopting a common language for conducting business, are moving us to the virtual workplace and, eventually, a virtual society.

POLICIES AND POLITICS

The world's trading partners have differing views of governments' role in IT implementation (Fagerberg *et al.*, 2004). Governments, businesses, and users have concerns about ownership, access, and distribution of information. Governments play a major role in emphasizing the importance of telecommunications to national and business infrastructures by building and maintaining national backbones and helping to provide gateways to other nations. While a few governments still treat IT policy as part of the national science policy, most governments have realized the need to treat science policy and IT policy as two separate entities (Metcalfe, 1995).

In the early 1980s, the Singapore government initiated and established the first formal IT policy in 1980. It was expanded in 1986 to include communication infrastructure as a key element of the new national IT strategy. The National

Computer Board in Singapore in 1992 announced the IT2000 Plan, resulting in the creation in 1998 of SingaporeOne, the world's first nationwide broadband network. Today, this network covers 99% of the island and has direct connectivity to all the key cities in Asia Pacific.

In September 1993, the United States government introduced the National Information Infrastructure Initiative (NIII), the main thrust of which was to link businesses, governments, researchers, educators, and the general public with telecommunications networks that will provide access to huge information resource databases from anywhere, anytime. Individuals and organizations will have access to educational resources, healthcare data, and government information. They will also have the ability to conduct e-commerce transactions. Whereas the Office of Science and Technology Policy continued to coordinate overall research and development activities in the country, responsibility for the implementation of the NIII was distributed among the various government departments, such as the department of energy and the department of commerce. Each department subsequently developed its own information policy under the NIII (IT21, 1999). For example, through the Internet Two Initiative, the Department of Education wants every school in the United States to have access to the Internet. Internet penetration as a percentage of the population in the United States increased from 54% in 2001 to 68% in 2005. By 2007, it is estimated that more than 70% of all U. S. workers will have Internet access.

Inspired by the NIII effort in the U. S., the E.U. launched the European Information Society project in the same year. The Bangemann Report detailed the overall IT vision for the E. U. The main objective was to narrow the digital divide between Europe and the U. S., and to maintain global competitiveness of European enterprises. (Anttiroiko, 2001). Each member of the E. U. has embarked on initiatives that clearly demonstrate commitment toward creating a global marketplace. For example, the Danish government is aggressively pushing the country toward a virtual workplace. It developed a technical blueprint for achieving this goal, including a plan to have 75% of households equipped with personal computers and modems by the year 2000. Estimates indicate that by 2005, almost 20% of Denmark's work force will comprise teleworkers (Jensen, 2000).

Although the general thrust by governments toward creating a virtual national community is not yet commonplace worldwide, some countries' political commitment to building virtual communities is noteworthy because it is the government that is taking the responsibility to create the foundation for change.

ENLIGHTENED AND DIVERSIFIED POPULATION

According to projections of the Bureau of Labor Statistics (Fullerton & Toossi, 2001), the United States workforce is becoming increasingly diverse. Fullerton and Toossi (2001) project that by the year 2010, 48% of the workforce will be women, African Americans will compose 13% of the U. S. workforce, Asians 6%, and Hispanics 13%. It is also projected that by the year 2050, one-half of the U. S. population will consist of African Americans, Asians, Hispanic, and Native Americans (Fernandez, 1991). Further, the nature of jobs will also change, with professional, technological, and sales jobs becoming the fastest growing sectors (Horrigan, 2004).

On the global level, 29% of the GDP of the world is produced by the U. S. Sixty-four percent of the world's GDP is concentrated in North America, Japan, and Western Europe. This means 14% of the world population produces and consumes 64% of the world's wealth. However, it is projected that in the next 20 years, global income inequalities will be reduced dramatically and emergent developing and industrializing nations will create and consume more than 50% of the world's wealth (David, 1997). At the heart of this development is the ability of the various populations of the world to engage in global production and operations that employ information, communication, and transportation technologies. Increased availability of information that provides diverse viewpoints on local and international issues will hopefully make people more enlightened and allow them to become fully informed participants in the global and local civil society.

Use of these technologies requires individual computer and information literacy skills. Computer skills include knowledge of what computers can and cannot do, an understanding of computer jargon and buzzwords, as well as programming and typing skills. Information literacy includes knowledge of what information is needed to make specific decisions, when and who needs what information, when computers should or should not be used to get information, sources for various types of needed information, and how to validate and secure information. Countries whose people are computer and information literate will have a temporary edge in performing virtual work. However, this edge will disappear as other nations increase the computer and information literacy of their citizens.

People need exposure to IT at a young age to be able to build effectively on their learning and adapt to change. School curricula are starting to offer computer classes in the elementary grades to expose children during their formative years to the ways they can use information to enrich their futures. Moreover, there is a general effort by the education and training industry to incorporate computer-based learning games and simulations in their instructional designs in order to leverage the interest and experience that young people already have with playing computer games. Some of the learning games and simulations being developed are individual-based, while others are team-based to build team skills. A new generation of computer and information literates will have the requisite skills to interact in a virtual workplace.

The evolution of a virtual society is dependent on having people understand, accept, and implement the consequences of the new virtual society culture. Some studies show that having access to a networked PC is necessary but not sufficient condition for Internet use. It is important to woo new users by providing them with relevant demonstrations and exemplars of how other people are benefiting from Internet use (Liff *et al.*, 2002).

Moreover, the growth of the virtual society will help both dual-career parents and single-parent families to balance childcare needs and family responsibilities and commitments. Work can frequently be completed from home, under specific conditions, for a designated number of days during normal business hours. Specifically, working parents will find it easier to balance their professional aspirations with their desire to spend quality time raising their children. Additionally, more people are now taking their college training and certification programs online at a distant location without regard to physical location (Simonson *et al.*, 2002).

As shown in Table I, the Internet usage growth rate has increased significantly in the last five years (2000–2005). The top five areas with the highest growth rates include the Middle East, Latin America/Caribbean, Africa, Asia, and Europe. During these five years, Internet usage grew by 160% worldwide. The highest penetration is still in the developed world: North America (68%), Europe (36.8%), and Oceania/Australia (49.2%).

There is therefore a need to increase the computer competency and information literacy of all potential players in the global virtual society. This should be the responsibility of national governments, global businesses, and individuals. All stakeholders should also accept an altered social norm. This new social form is biased toward people who have good computer skills, are information literate, are willing to accept changes in work processes, and are able to address and reconcile social and physiological impacts. Workers will also have to accept the idea that the job security offered by corporations is a thing of the past

INFORMATION TECHNOLOGY INFRASTRUCTURE

The interest and growth in the virtual society has been further spurred by advances in IT and subsequent investments in IT infrastructure. Increased demand for goods and services on a national and global scale has increased the need for faster and reliable information processing and telecommunication technologies. As noted by Beniger (1986),

> [information] technology appears autonomously to beget [information] technology and,
> … innovations in matter and energy processing create the need for further innovation in
> information processing and communication. (p. 434).

Advances in telecommunication and network technology and the reduction in hardware and software costs have been equal to the challenge. Interorganizational information systems (IOS) allow computer networks to process data and share information across organizational boundaries (Applegate *et al.*, 2002). IOSs are

TABLE I

World Internet Usage and Population Statistics as of July 23rd 2005 (IWS, 2005)

World Regions	Population (2005 Est.)	Population % of World	Internet Usage, Latest Data	Usage Growth 2000–2005	% Population (Penetration)	World Users %
Africa	896,721,874	14.0 %	16,174,600	258.3 %	1.8 %	1.7 %
Asia	3,622,994,130	56.4 %	323,756,956	183.2 %	8.9 %	34.5 %
Europe	731,018,523	11.4 %	269,036,096	161.0 %	36.8 %	28.7 %
Middle East	260,814,179	4.1 %	21,770,700	311.9 %	8.3 %	2.3 %
North America	328,387,059	5.1 %	223,392,807	106.7 %	68.0 %	23.8 %
Latin America/Caribbean	546,723,509	8.5 %	68,130,804	277.1 %	12.5 %	7.3 %
Oceania/Australia	33,443,448	0.5 %	16,448,966	115.9 %	49.2 %	1.8 %
World Total	6,420,102,722	100.0 %	938,710,929	160.0 %	14.6 %	100.0 %

being used to expand organizational relationships by decoupling value chain activities while maintaining a controlled and coordinated environment. The Nike Inc. example, cited earlier, is a case in point. IT allows each organization linked by an IOS to concentrate on its core competence. (Many transnational and multinational organizations, however, now have a multitude of core competencies, for example, GE). Nike Inc. decided to concentrate on product design, sales and marketing, and service as its core competence. The outcome is a virtual organization that has the global advantages of economies of scale and scope but the responsiveness of a small local company.

Technology by itself does not ensure the coming of the virtual society. Rather, it is an enabler and shaper. Digital technology has made it possible to convert characters, sounds, pictures, and motions into a computer language. Codification of data, including text and numbers as well as multimedia digitalization, allows us to be less time- and location-dependent. The emergence of multimedia standards, and the shift to distributed computing and inter-networking, are providing the raw power for digital convergence. A cornucopia of supporting technologies have emerged, including the Inter/Intra/Extranet, elaborate a bit on these electronic mail, groupware, video-conferencing, workflow, data management, data warehousing, and improved networking capabilities.

In the 1990s, the Internet moved from supporting only science and research to becoming an integral tool for commerce. The Internet is at the forefront of the global growth of these enablers. The growth of the Internet has been astounding. The growth rate in the number of Internet hosts is exponential. For example, in 1995, 148 of 185 (86%) United Nations members had Internet service, compared to 46% in 1991 (Chon, 1996). By 2004, almost all countries of the world (209) had Internet service (ITU, 2003), and over 29 million businesses worldwide had domain addresses (Verisign, 2004).

Interactive communications are required if business is to be conducted virtually on the Internet (or its successors). Electronic mail is the foundation for such communication and is available at relatively modest cost, but the simple sending of text messages is not enough. Multimedia applications are coming to increase the gains of groupware, video-conferencing, data management, and data warehousing in the virtual world. Improved networking infrastructures will underlie the higher bandwidth, security, and reliability that enable this technology.

Internet electronic commerce is replacing traditional electronic commerce, which relied on value-added and private messaging networks—both of which were relatively expensive and provided limited connectivity. Traditional electronic commerce tools, such as electronic data interchange (EDI), fax, symbol technology, barcoding, inter-enterprise e-mailing, and file transfer technologies, are being augmented, and, in some cases, replaced by the Internet (Pyle, 1996). Internet technologies (networks, computers, software, etc.) continue to increase in capability and functionality. The new technology holds many possibilities for virtual societies. It enables individuals, groups, communities, organizations, and societies, among others, to exchange information, do business, participate in newsgroup discussion, and publish information electronically. The new technology enables innovative ways of communicating and doing business. It is an important element of creating the virtual society.

The new advances in IT are also shaping the evolution of the virtual society. The current manifestations of the virtual society, which include telework, virtual teams, virtual corporations, virtual libraries, virtual museums, telemedicine, and e-government, are possible because the potential benefits seem to outweigh the costs. As these current practices become entrenched, they will be accepted as standard practice—and, hence, shape the future of the virtual society. Future advances in distributed networks, distributed databases, bandwidth, storage, and network security will continue to influence the evolution of the virtual society.

EXISTING ARRANGEMENTS AND PRACTICES

In this section, we cover four different arrangements and practices in the virtual society: telework, virtual teams, virtual organizations, and virtual communities.

TELEWORK

A global telework survey conducted by AT&T in July 2003 found that about 80% of companies worldwide expect to have employees who telework in the next two years, an increase of 54%. The companies surveyed also expected to increase their material and financial support for telework by 32% (Hodson, 2005). The survey also identified the main drivers for the increase in telework on a global scale as (a) better network access to remote locations, (b) better communication facilities, and (c) the globalization of business operations. It is expected that by 2008 about 100 million people will telework at least one day per month, with the highest proportion of these living in the U. S.

The International Telework Association and Council released survey results indicating that more than 24 million Americans (about 20% of the workforce) performed telework at home, a 100% increase from those who performed telework at home in 1997 (ITAC, 2004). The average teleworker was 40.2 years old and earned an average annual income of USD $51,000. Sixty (60%) were married and 46% had children at home. According to the U. S. Department of Transport, the number of teleworkers in the United States is expected to reach 50 million by 2020.

Telework was based on the idea that work could be moved to the workers, rather than moving the workers to the work. Twenty years ago, this meant individuals could telework from their homes rather than traveling to their workplaces. But with recent advances in information and communication technologies, it is possible for people to work in other remote locations such as local centers, hotel rooms, and Internet cafes. They could also work while in trains or client premises. So, the general definition of telework encompasses any type of working remotely from the office, using information and telecommunication technologies (DTI, 2003).

Teleworking has grown due to the demands of three constituencies: employees, organizations, and society. First, substantial changes to the family structure have made employees demand more flexible work arrangements. For example, traditional families with a working husband and a stay-at-home wife are down to 10% of American families (Schepp, 1990). The growth of dual-career families, that is, those with pre-school age children, those with older children, and those with a dependent spouse or parent, may increase the work–family conflict resulting from trying to perform multiple roles as worker, spouse, and parent. Telecommuting provides a flexible work arrangement by allowing employees to eliminate time-consuming and unproductive tasks, such as commuting to the workplace. Telecommuting also provides more flexibility on when and where work is completed.

Attitudinal changes have also contributed to the demand for more flexible work options. The selfishness and materialism that characterized the 1980s and 1990s have given way to greater concern for personal and family time (Wright, 1993; Eckersley, 2004). Employees seek to live in pleasant surroundings, participate in leisure activities, and have time for family. They are more concerned about the quality of life, and they seek work arrangements that allow them to fulfill their desires. Thus, the telework arrangements may make it easier for individuals to achieve a better balance between their work and personal lives.

Second, due to demographic changes, organizations need to make accommodations to attract and retain employees. The next generation of workers will be much smaller than the current workforce. As older workers, who are experienced and trained, retire, the smaller pool of younger workers will cause a shortage of needed employees. Flexible work options will be required to recruit and retain quality employees.

Pressures toward cost reduction and productivity improvement are also pushing organizations to adopt teleworking programs (Vega, 2003). Teleworkers are more productive and have better home lives once they start working, at least part-time, from home. Further, the fixed costs of teleworking are lower than the costs associated with conventional offices.

Societal demands for environmental awareness are the third factor contributing to the demand for flexible work. In the United States, teleworking helps organizations deal with the regulatory requirements of the Clean Air Act (1977) and the Americans With Disabilities Act (1990). The Clean Air Act requires large companies to reduce the number of automobiles commuting to work on a daily basis. Allowing employees to work at home helps organizations to comply with this legislation. The Americans With Disabilities Act requires organizations to make reasonable accommodations for disabled employees to perform their jobs. Allowing physically challenged individuals to telework allows organizations to comply with this legislation as well. Flexible work also provides an organization with a contingency plan to cope with disasters. Recent weather problems and other disasters which paralyzed the U. S. east coast required employers to consider alternate work arrangements. Scientists have projected that if we do not reduce global warming pollution, the average global temperatures could increase by 2 to 8° F over the next century—potentially causing coastal flooding, heat-related deaths, and lung-related ailments (Houghton, 2004).

As public concern for the environment continues to increase, both individuals and organizations are attempting to make more environmentally conscious decisions. Teleworking reduces the number of people commuting to work, thereby contributing to lower traffic congestion and less air pollution (Choo *et al.*, 2002). This, in turn, contributes to improved health due to reduced incidences of lung diseases, cardiovascular morbidity, neurological diseases, and occupational diseases (Yoganathan & Rom, 2001).

On balance, companies appear to use productivity improvements and cost reductions for justifying telecommuting more than they use regulations or disaster-prevention as a rationale. Companies also cite that new advances in computer technology are making IT managers able to remotely support the teleworker and troubleshoot computers and other technology at the teleworker's home office (Vega, 2003). Greater productivity is obtained by the employer though zero tardiness, less time taken due to illness or family crisis, improved recruiting due to larger labor pool, lower attrition rates, and lower subsidies provided to cover transport, parking, or catering. The employee benefits through fewer work interruptions, avoidance of travel difficulties, increased personal safety, ability to cope with family matters, and reduced child and/or elder care. The society or community pays less taxes and gains better health through reduced vehicle service costs for roads, reduced road maintenance and gas emissions, and less need to build and maintain alternative modes of transport (Vega, 2003). Overall, all the benefits translate to reduced transaction and coordination costs needed to manage the company in order to ensure long-term growth and profitability.

VIRTUAL TEAMS

Virtual teams are defined as specialized groups that operate without the physical limitations of distance, time, or organizational boundaries, and use electronic collaboration technologies and other techniques to lower travel and facility costs, reduce project schedules, and improve decision-making time and communication (Mittleman & Briggs (1998). Seven basic types of virtual teams have been identified (Mittleman & Briggs, 1998):

Networked teams: Individuals who collaborate to achieve a common goal or purpose.

Parallel teams: Individuals who carry out special assignments, tasks, or functions that the regular organization does not want or is not equipped to perform.

Project or product-development teams: Groups that conduct projects for users or customers for a defined, but typically extended, period of time.

Work or production teams: Teams that perform regular and ongoing work. Such teams usually exist in one function, such as accounting, finance, training, or research and development.

Service teams: Teams created onshore or offshore to provide certain specialized services, such as customer support services or help desk services.

Management teams: Managers brought together either to deliberate and decide on an emergent organizational problem or operate as specialized steering committees.

Action teams: Individuals collaborating to offer immediate responses, often to emergency situations.

Two factors appear to guide organizations to adopt virtual teams. First, the change in organization structure away from traditional hierarchies toward distributed operations creates the need to bring together cross-functional expertise to solve problems. Moreover, organizations recognize that they can acquire specific kinds of expertise, which is too costly to maintain locally, by going outside the organizational boundaries. Second, advances in networking, computer, and communications technologies have lead to the development of methods that can support meetings across time and space (see technology discussion under Driving Forces section).

A team is also known as a *work group*. In terms of socio-technical systems terminology, groups can be seen as having both technical and social systems components. The technical system defines the work process and task accomplishment goals that derive from that process. The social system defines the group process and the quality of work and life goals that are required to make the group function effectively. In order to achieve all of these goals, groups/teams have certain requirements. Table II, derived from Mandviwalla and Olfman (1994), outlines these requirements in terms of their technical and social system components.

Teams carry out multiple subtasks in order to accomplish their overall goal, and they perform these subtasks using a variety of work methods. The subtasks are typically embedded in many layers of complexity but, for illustrative purposes, we look at a high level set of subtasks that lead to the final goal of a team. For example, take a team charged with developing a new product. It must do market research, create design alternatives, do market testing, and so forth. Each of these high level subtasks requires different work methods, including survey design, data collection and analysis, and engineering.

TABLE II

Group/Team Requirements

Technical System	Social System
Multiple group tasks	Development of the group
Multiple work methods	Interchangeable interaction methods
	Permeable group boundaries
	Adjustable group context
	Multiple behavioral characteristics

Throughout the work process, teams must maintain their social functions. They develop over time as members learn to work together. This requires that teams be able to communicate in a variety of ways. They must be able to share documents, as well as to use written, spoken, and visual approaches to communication. Throughout the team's life, various members may join or leave due to needs for specific expertise or other behavioral factors (e.g., someone decides to take a new job). Moreover, team members must be supported so that they can easily fit into the group tasks, and the group must be able to manage its process, given the needs of the various members plus the goals set for the team.

The complexity of group work as outlined in these requirements is further complicated by the concept of virtuality. Varying the time and space dimensions of the team process adds additional levels of complexity to the concept of the group or team.

CONCEPTS OF TIME AND PLACE

Johansen (1988), borrowing from the work of DeSanctis and Gallupe (1987), outlines two dimensions for considering time and place. *Time* refers to the synchronicity of a meeting and can be either synchronous (takes place at the same time for all participants) or asynchronous (takes place independent of time). *Place* refers to the physical location of the meeting and can be either in the same place (everyone in one room) or in different places (team members spread across two or more rooms). Different places can be along one hallway, on different floors of the same buildings, in different buildings in the same metropolis, or in different spaces across the global landscape (e.g., in a car, on an airplane, in another country).

Synchronous/colocated meetings are the most traditional for groups, and are usually referred to as face-to-face meetings. Everyone must be in the same room during the same time period in order to carry out the team meeting. Alternatively, by relaxing one or both of the "same" constraints, a variety of other possibilities present themselves.

Synchronous/separated meetings include participants who are located in more than one setting (typically in different venues). All participants' actions and/ or words are seen and/or heard as they occur. Of course, if the meeting locations are in different time zones, participants are not meeting at the same clock times.

Asynchronous/colocated meetings imply that the participants work in one venue, but they contribute to a common task and associated group process by using a single repository that is physically restricted from "outside" access. Asynchronous/ separated meetings extend the concept to allow communications to be made at any time, and to and from a variety of locations.

Most likely, a virtual team will use some or all of these methods to conduct their business. They may begin with a synchronous meeting (possibly face to face). Later, the focus may be on asynchronous communications as subtasks are being accomplished. At certain milestones, synchronous communications may be utilized to ensure the highest level of exchanges among participants.

VIRTUAL TEAM TECHNOLOGIES

Virtual teams began to be a reality with the advent of teleconferencing, which enabled groups to communicate synchronously in separate locations via audio. However, these groups had to have copies of mutual paper documents available at the outset of a meeting (or had to depend on fax to transfer documents across locations "on the fly"), and there was a reduction in potential information via the voice-only medium, which was further muffled through a speakerphone arrangement. Video-conferencing potentially added another level of richness to such meetings, but the high costs and poor quality of transmissions reduced the demand for this technology. As with all technology, time has improved transmission quality, but costs are still relatively high.

By the late 1970s, the idea that groups could meet through the computer was being realized (Hiltz & Turoff, 1978). Computer conferences aimed to exploit the potential for asynchronous/separated meetings by providing a structured forum through which to exchange messages. In essence, this structure remains one of the key methods for facilitating asynchronous group interactions, although it is now manifested in the form of Internet tools such as email, chat rooms, bulletin boards, and listservs. These technologies tend to serve distance education and virtual communities rather than virtual teams in organizations.

The 1980s saw the development of more sophisticated forms of computer-based technology that exploited each of the combinations of time and place. Ventana's Group Systems was designed to create an electronic meeting room to enhance support for face-to-face meetings. It provides features such as anonymous communications and support for various group process activities, such as idea generation and voting. Later it was extended to support other types of meetings, especially those that are synchronous but separated. Another software package that has probably had the biggest impact, in terms of numbers of users, on team work and virtual teams is Lotus Notes. It provides sophisticated asynchronous meeting support through "databases" that can store multimedia communications.

The idea that teams can utilize computer technology to enhance their work and group processes is often termed "computer-supported cooperative work" (CSCW). The products that support these activities are typically termed *groupware*. Groupware not only enables a full range of meeting types, but also supports the flow of documents across work tasks, and builds an organizational memory that can be used to support future tasks (Coleman, 1997; Khoshafian & Buckwitz, 1995).

Synchronous groupware includes (a) desktop and real time data conferencing, (b) electronic meeting systems, (c) electronic display, (d) video-conferencing, and (e) audio conferencing (Coleman, 1997):

> *Desktop and real-time data conferencing.* This includes interaction via individual computer workstations, interchange and storage of common documents, plus additional facilities such as electronic chat, whiteboard, and desktop audio and video links.
>
> *Internet chat/instant messenger.* Allows team members to have typed conversations.
>
> *Whiteboard.* Allows team members to view a shared document, to diagram ideas on their computers, and to see the notations and comments of other participants.
>
> *Multipoint–multimedia technology.* Includes full-motion video in addition to the chat, whiteboard, and audio links. Allows team members to see and hear one another and to create and edit still-frame documents or images.
>
> *Electronic meeting systems (EMS).* Used in face-to-face settings to increase the productivity of group deliberation and decision making. EMS range in complexity from simple voting or polling systems, with wireless data-entry keypads that each participant uses to cast a ballot (and a projection system to process and display the results), to computer-aided systems in which each participant uses a laptop computer to provide input to a central display screen.
>
> *Electronic display.* Computer-based whiteboards allow team members to display the shared whiteboard on their computer monitors.
>
> *Video-conferencing.* Includes a combination of three technologies: desktop video, specialized video facilities, and video walls. *Desktop video* allows audio and video communication and frequently includes document-sharing capabilities. *Video facilities* employs video equipment and high bandwidth networks that transmit full-motion video. *Video walls* are shared audio and video spaces that are open all the time. People in the halls, conference rooms, and offices of one location are continually able to see and hear team members in other locations walking through halls, working in conference rooms, and sitting at their desks.

Audio conferencing. Where individuals communicate with each other using the traditional telecommunications infrastructure, the H.323 video-conferencing protocol, or the Voice over Internet Protocol (VoIP), for example, a bridge-mediated conference call involving three or more participants.

Asynchronous groupware. Includes (a) e-mail, (b) group calendars and schedules, (c) bulletin boards and Web pages, (c) non-real-time database sharing and conferencing, and (d) workflow applications.

E-mail. A written message, that can have a computer file attached, is sent over a network from one computer to another.

Group calendars and schedules. Calendaring involves the manipulation of information on an individual's calendar; scheduling involves the communication and negotiation of information, meetings, and other items that need to be coordinated among individual calendars.

Bulletin boards and Web pages. These are shared work spaces for the posting of messages and ideas, the display and editing of documents, and for non-real-time discussions about questions that do not require immediate answers. Bulletin boards or Web sites are accessible to all team members and selected stakeholders.

Non-real-time database sharing and conferencing. Shared database systems usually accept a wide range of data, including multimedia information. Information frequently is distributed on servers throughout the organization, and individual team members have extensive freedom to search the database and to transfer the information to personalized databases.

Collaborative notebooks allow the authoring and editorial access to a common notebook and facilitate and manage collaborative authoring, document sharing, and editorial review by multiple users.

Workflow applications. Allow the design and operation of repetitive business processes that involve sequential steps. Useful for teams that are engaged in assembly-line work, service, or production and those engaged in operational or reengineering tasks.

With the increasing bandwidth of the Internet, the full complement of document-based, audio, and video support will be readily available on every worker's desktop and in their mobile computers. This can only increase the number of virtual teams that will be operating in organizations all across the globe.

VIRTUAL ORGANIZATIONS

The purpose of organizations is to enable groups of people to effectively and efficiently coordinate efforts and resources at their disposal in order to achieve stated organizational goals or objectives. Organizations rely on a structure to achieve their goals or objectives. The structure of an organization can be defined as the sum total of the different ways in which it divides its labor (people) and other resources (technology, capital equipment, databases, etc.) into distinct tasks (processes) and then achieves coordination among them (Mintzberg, 1979). Traditionally, organizational managers have used a hierarchical structure with well-defined lines of command, control, and communication to coordinate the optimal assignment of people and other resources to processes. However, dynamic competitive forces in industry, including global competition, strategic alliances, re-engineering, popular management techniques, such as total quality management, and rightsizing and downsizing, all mandate a more dynamic assignment of available scarce resources to processes. The ability of IT to collapse distance and time provides a wider range of resources from which to draw.

The problem can be formulated as follows: Demand for goods and services (information, travel, automobile) from an organization (Internet service provider, travel agency, car manufacturer) must be satisfied through the assignment and coordination of available resources (computer networks, databases, skilled personnel, IT, raw materials, capital equipment) (Mowshowitz, 1997). Assume for a moment that the Internet service provider is a multinational organization with headquarters in British Columbia, Canada, but has operations all over the world. Whereas a centralized command, control, and communication structure may be suitable for the Internet service provider to assign and coordinate its resources to meet a service request in western Canada, a decentralized command, control, and communication structure may be suitable to provide the same service in South Africa or Australia. The same could be said of the travel agency or the car manufacturing company. A virtual organization structure can provide an optimal dynamic allocation of resources to meet the demand requirements as long as there is a logical separation of customer demand, resources needed to satisfy that demand, and the decision makers who allocate the resources (Mowshowitz, 1997). A virtual organization structure will provide the Internet service provider with the agility and flexibility required to meet consumer demand anywhere anytime in the world. It can be said that in the virtual society, organizational structure follows demand and performance requirements.

Organizations competing in volatile technological and business environments must be agile, flexible, responsive, and boundaryless (Eichinger & Ulrich, 1995), which is possible under a virtual organization model. The organizational theory literature labels agile, flexible, responsive or dynamic organizational forms as "fuzzy" models that are organic as opposed to crisp or mechanistic structures. Fuzzy structures are appropriate for organizations that need to cope with conditions of uncertainty (Buchanan & Boddy, 1992). The dynamic nature of the technological and business environment in a virtual society favors fuzzy organizational structures. The virtual organizational structures qualify as a fuzzy structure (Donaldson & Preston, 1995).

According to Mowshowitz, the optimal assignment of resources to processes required in virtual organizations influences managerial decision making and management relations with its employees, external organizations, suppliers, and the community. Flexible assignment of resources "favors temporary relationships based on explicit rather than implicit agreements" (Mowshowitz, 1997, p. 37). Propensity toward temporary relationships means that a virtual organization will be characterized by high levels of trust, shorter-term contracts with its employees, a greater use of teleworkers, outsourcing to external organizational activities that fall outside the organization's core competencies, and ability to switch from one supplier to another in order to obtain cost-effectiveness.

These characteristics would cause the local community in which the organization operates to have negative perceptions of the actions of the virtual organization management. However, such feelings and perceptions would abate as we achieve a critical mass of virtual organizations and move toward a virtual society.

VIRTUAL COMMUNITIES

Virtual communities have emerged from a surprising intersection of human needs and technology. When the ubiquity of the telecommunications network is combined with the information-structuring and storing capabilities of computers, a new communication medium becomes possible. Virtual community is a term commonly used to describe various forms of computer-mediated communication, particularly long-term, textually mediated conversations among large groups. It is a group of people who may or may not meet one another face-to-face, and who exchange words and ideas through the mediation of computer networks and bulletin boards. As we are observing among the weblog or "love connection" communities, the range of activities is immense. People chat. They argue. They exchange property, ideas, and gossip. They plan, make friends, even fall in love. They do everything people do when they get together face-to-face but, by using computers, they do it separated in space and time. Electronic interactions in which people don't know others make new kinds of communities possible.

This section discusses three arrangements and practices of virtual communities, namely, teledemocracy, virtual museums, and weblogs. Teledemocracy deals with how voters can further their interests and participate in the politics and governance of their community. Virtual museums deal with the use of home-based PCs to link into vast collections of paintings, sculptures, drawings, prints, architecture, photography, film, and video without regard to distance or time. Weblogs (or blogs) are personal online journals that contain individual opinions about products, people, companies, or any hot issues of the day. Other arrangements, such as virtual gaming, virtual auctions, virtual tourism, virtual classrooms, or virtual sex, are not covered in this chapter.

TELEDEMOCRACY

The rapid evolution of information and the new potentials for communication, particularly the unprecedented global telecommunications and information networks explosion, and the trend toward a global social society will have profound impacts on various phenomena such as work, social life, entertainment, education, and democracy (Becker & Slaton, 2000).

Teledemocracy is a generic term that combines the understanding of the way citizens are empowered with the enabling technologies of computer networking, and associated hardware, software, services, and techniques (Keskinen, 1995). The major change that teledemocracy has brought to societies is to ensure that political decisions be made in accordance with people's attitudes and desires. Teledemocracy has the potential of facilitating personal and community evolution by enabling them to build social value structures and to make their own future (Koumirov, 1994).

Teledemocracy has grown due to the demands of three constituencies: (a) citizens (or voters), (b) elected leaders, and (c) societal demands for voicing public opinion and communicating with potential leaders vying for political office. First, increased citizens' or voters' participation in the information revolution has caused substantial changes to their perception of the role of government. In modern societies, citizens want to shift from being "the governed" into "self-government." They want to be actively involved in the political work instead of being mere subordinates. They want to have more power, authority, and control over their own lives. Ordinary citizens can play a major role in helping to decide what kind of society they want to live in. They can take an active role in sociopolitical decision making in order to make their lives better and to manage their own affairs. They can participate in agenda setting, planning, and policy-making. They ask for the power to be handed back to them. Technology, now, can easily empower them. It promotes a new form of direct citizen participation and direct democracy—teledemocracy.

Citizens can use IT to share information about issues and priorities vital to their future, and be informed about the critical trends and choices facing communities, nations, and the planetary society. IT can provide documentaries and investigative reports that will give citizens an in-depth understanding of the challenges they face. A vibrant civil and democratic society flourishes on a well-informed citizenry (Elgin, 1994). The increased number of informed citizens might increase the need for a more conscious direct democracy.

Additionally, citizens also need to know what others think and feel about different issues and priorities. When a population understands what others think about key issues, they can mobilize into a collective interest group with singleness of purpose and action.

Elected leaders are the second constituency contributing to the demand for teledemocracy. Due to availability of electronic means of communication and social changes and demands, elected leaders need to realize critical political transformations that may redistribute their political power. They should know that the next generation of citizens is more informed, more knowledgeable, and more enthusiastic. They should understand that citizens can and should take an active role in sociopolitical decision making. Elected leaders need to use IT to communicate with citizens, colleagues, and government agencies. In so doing, they can explicitly persuade, negotiate, listen, and answer questions to meet their stakeholders' desires. One example is the last two U. S. presidential elections in which the presidential candidates established virtual community spaces to solicit financial support as well as recruit and engage supporters.

The successes of online fund raising by John McCain ($6.4 million) and Bill Bradley ($1 million) in the 2000 U. S. presidential elections showed that the Internet is potentially a powerful instrument for organizing grassroots' activists, raising money, and getting out the vote. In the 2004 presidential campaign, the presidential contestants used the Internet with varying degrees of success. Howard Dean led the way by effectively using the Internet to make fundraising appeals, organize local net meetings, blogging, and allowing grassroot activists to make decisions as they saw fit (Cornfield, 2004). By September 2003, Howard Dean, with $25.4 million, was number one in total money raised among the candidates. Although Dean lost to Senator John Kerry in the primaries, political analysts agree that Dean revolutionarized online campaigning (ibid.). Senator Kerry went on to adopt some of the Dean's fundraising strategies and was able to raise $26 million through the Internet, compared to President George Bush's $4 million. The various campaign strategies adopted by the candidates during the 2004 presidential campaign are too numerous to cover here. For more literature on the potential power of the Internet to bring political renewal to civil society, see the work of Shane (2004).

Citizens' wishes can push elected leaders to adopt teledemocracy. Teledemocracy can also improve the relationship between citizens and policymakers and decrease the gap between the governors and the governed. Citizens can interact electronically with their elected leaders and hold weekly or monthly electronic meetings. These meetings can establish some accountability between the public and their elected leaders. Citizens can also give timely feedback to elected leaders by providing inputs to those who govern. Holding electronic town meetings may provide a forum for citizens to build a working consensus on major issues and priorities (Elgin, 1994). Here, elected leaders meet with groups of citizens to explain and/or defend their agendas and policies. These may assure that citizens feel engaged, involved, and invested in decision making and responsible for society and its future.

Societal demands for voicing public opinion and communicating with potential leaders vying for political office is the third factor contributing to the demand for teledemocracy. Governments may need to increase their funding for telecommunication infrastructures to generate the level and quality of communication needed to support teledemocracy in order to choose a more inclusive sustainable future. Faster, cheaper, more diverse, and more interactive communication has the potential to increase citizen participation and involvement in the democratic process in terms of voicing their opinions and electing the "right" leaders. Local information networks should be designed to promote civic participation by offering government information and communication at little or no cost. This may increase citizen interest in other community activities, thus tightening communal ties and increasing participation in community governance. However, this may necessitate changes in the role of government as we know it today (Shane, 2004).

Perhaps a more dramatic change for the future will be a shift in governmental processes. Traditionally, a representative government is used so that people are able to elect those they believe will uphold governmental rules effectively and represent their interests. In this setting, elected representatives are agents of those who elect them. In a virtual society, however, these agents may no longer be necessary because people could perform governmental functions virtually (i.e., virtual voting on issues). While we foresee an increase in electronic meetings for global commerce, we expect an even greater impact will be made by simplified distribution in the government and political arenas.

Teledemocracy allows citizens who wish to make informed choices concerning candidates, government policy, or regulation to retrieve information from government databases (Koumirov, 1994; Shane, 2004). Citizens can engage in more thorough and substantive discussions rather than merely listening to a brief advertisement or sound-byte. They can also vote electronically for candidates and issues. Of course, this assumes freedom of press and speech, something for which many countries are still striving.

However, there are some issues that need to be addressed: (1) *Access to the Internet:* A broad-based access to the Internet must be ensured. As shown in Table I, there is a large section of the global society that does not have access to the Internet. It is imperative that everyone have computer Internet access either from home or from a community location. At a minimum, one should have a wireless device, such as a cellular phone, that has Internet access. (2) *Security and privacy:* Unsecured transmission is often a main deterrent for rapid growth of tele-democracy. Here, security includes authentication, integrity, accuracy, and confidentiality. We need to verify the identity of the participants so that the authenticity of the information being transmitted can be ensured. Citizens need also to ensure that the information is confidential and only the participants know the content. Individuals also need to have protected "anonymity." (3) *Mechanism for coordination:* The system should ensure that different viewpoints are presented, with impartial refereeing of messages and automated negotiation.

Several projects have been initiated to examine tele-democracy in several countries. In November 1996, the Dutch province of North Brabant conducted an experiment to test the applicability of an Internet-based software for public debate. They invited 100 residents and organizations to discuss aspects of land use for the region under the banner. They debated the issue using an Internet-based application, which allowed moderated discussion, periodic polling of participants, and voting (Jankowski *et al.*, 1997). Norway's Telenor Research and Development developed a communication system to support local politicians. The system allowed elected leaders to make calls, set up telephone conferences, use e-mail, and exchange documents among them and other government offices (Ytterstad *et al.*, 1996).

Virtual Museums

A virtual museum allows users to use their PCs to walk through and explore digital representations of various artifacts in virtual 3-dimensional space on the Internet. The user can use a mouse or joystick to move around. The aim is to make the museum exhibits more accessible and visitor friendly. The index home page provides an introduction to the collection highlights. Visitors who need more detailed information can dig deeper by choosing the specific detailed items they wish to explore. Virtual museums contain interactive databases which have many collections focusing on different subjects such as art, science, history, zoology, music, archeology, and biology. Virtual museums provide a new way for people to access vast collections of paintings, sculptures, drawings, prints, architecture, photography, film, and video without regard to distance or time. The Virtual Library of Museums (VLMP, 2005) includes a list of links to museum sites throughout the world. The site has links to more than 400 museums in North America alone.

For example, if you visit the website of the Metropolitan Museum of Art in New York, the index webpage provides you with an overview of works currently on display in the museum's various galleries. When you select a specific collection, you can also choose the floor you want to visit. A floor plan is then provided for you to select the images you want to see. The site also offers you an online gift and bookshop, various educational resources, and a calendar of special exhibitions and other planned museum activities. For some of the collections, sound samples are available in RealAudio, WAV, and AU formats. Other collections provide QuickTime clips of selected information.

The French Ministry of Culture has helped create a virtual museum that contains more than 130,000 paintings from the great art museums of France. The original project was started 25 years ago and was text based. In 1994, webpages were added to allow visitors to see the pictures and virtually navigate through the different collections. People are allowed to make digital or hard copies of the museum work to build their own private collections or use in the classroom but are prohibited to make or distribute them for profit or commercial advantage. Visitors can view the museum collections in French or English. According to Mannoni (1997), in real life, legal limitations or poor physical condition of the paintings and sculptures would have made it impossible to put all the paintings in the same place. The Boston Computer Museum allows you to walk through the museum in real time (O'Rourke, 1996). The index home page requires you to fill in a quick survey that establishes you as a visitor. This allows you to communicate with other visitors in the museum through the "Who is Out There" feature. You virtually talk with others and almost get a sense of being there. You can learn virtually how a desktop computer is put together or design your own robot. The ability to dance on the keyboard, dive into a microprocessor, or control a robot over the Net is the next best thing to being there (O'Rourke, 1996).

However, there are limitations. Current technology does not yet provide an complete aesthetic experience. The information provided about the collections may not be detailed enough for serious scholarly work. Scholars needing more detail will have to wait—only the layman benefits from the current technology. This means a lot of images need to be digitally scanned to meet scholars' needs. Laws regarding intellectual property rights create further complications, and there are frequently bandwidth problems with large visual and audio files. This means that the true value for the museum materials is yet to be established.

WEBLOGS

Weblogs (or *blogs*) are the fastest growing area of Internet users. They are a great illustration of virtual society. Blogs have moved beyond personal diaries to serious political and cultural debates, scientific opinions, and social commentary.

"Bloggers," as the authors call themselves, create personal online journals that contain information about themselves, opinions about products, people, companies, politics, or any hot issues. They then share their online journals with other bloggers. For example, during the 2004 U. S. presidential campaign, it was the Internet bloggers' community that pointed out the forgery in the documents related to President George Bush's military service in the National Guard during the Vietnam War period (BGD, 2004).

According to a survey conducted by the Pew Internet and American Life Project in January 2005, 27% of Internet users reported that they read blogs—a 58% jump from results shown in a 2004 survey. The study also found that the Internet has more than 8 million blogs, and more blogs are appearing at the rate of about 35,000 new ones each day. Blogging has also taken a global dimension, with Internet users from all over the world sharing their opinions and experiences.

The bloggers' community has come to be taken seriously by politicians and companies alike. Ignoring negative ideas or opinions shared by bloggers about a particular political candidate or a specific consumer product can be very damaging, especially when the comments are not responded to immediately. A politician may lose an election as a result, and a company may lose customers or suppliers, through the expanding power of these blogs.

Companies such as General Motors and Microsoft have established their own corporate blogs. A media analysis and business intelligence company, the "General Motors FastLane" blog that is run by Bob Lutz, one of GM's corporate executives, averages about 4,500 visits per day with more than 60 comments per posting (BICR1, 2005) The GM blog provides information about company products and new designs, and responds to negative comments provided by other bloggers. Microsoft Corporation also created a company blog called "Channel 9" to mitigate the negative opinions being provided by other members of the bloggers' community and provide information about new products, designs, future strategies, and trends. Other companies such as Macromedia, IBM, CISCO, and FORD Motor Company have established their own blogs (Abram, 2005).

DILEMMAS AND IMPLICATIONS OF THE VIRTUAL SOCIETY

Coincidental to the driving forces just explored, the onset of the virtual society has far-reaching implications for governments, researchers, educators, businesses, individuals, and for society in general.

GLOBAL POLICY AND ECONOMICS

It is generally agreed that one of the major activities driving the virtual society is Internet electronic commerce. The Internet upholds an open culture where information is freely exchanged and no accounting for transactions is required. This environment has been in existence since the introduction of the Internet, but increased commercialization and globalization makes this openness inefficient, and policies to balance openness and market efficiency are difficult to formulate (Greenstein, 2000).

POLITICS AND POLICY

Access rights, primarily censorship and intellectual property, are becoming an increasingly important policy issue for global businesses. Security and privacy and the creation of methods for rendering monetary tender for transactions are also coming under scrutiny by countries, businesses, and users of global services.

Although a number of countries have adopted national policies that support globalization, issues related to access rights, specifically censorship and intellectual property, need addressing on an international basis. For example, copyright laws in the

United States are twenty years old and some say they are not appropriate for inter-preting fair use issues that arise in an electronic world (Ficsor, 2002). Inappropriate or unfair use court rulings may hinder electronic commerce. Individual countries may resolve problems of access within their borders—but resolutions need to cross global boundaries. World governments need to enact international laws and policies that foster electronic distribution and dissemination of data, yet protect the creators of the data. They also need to address the problem of transborder data flows.

Internet security and privacy remain elusive. The Internet was initially designed by researchers to share information electronically after a nuclear disaster, and security was not a design constraint. Expansion of the Internet revealed seri-ous security flaws as evidenced by Internet-based intrusions, such as the rampant theft of passwords from service providers and banks, theft of funds from banks, and identity theft (Lininger & Wines, 2005).

Bhimani (1996) states that an adequate security and privacy solution needs to uphold five fundamental requirements: (1) maintain confidentiality of the par-ties involved in the transaction, (2) authenticate the parties involved in the com-munication, (3) provide data integrity, (4) provide for future non-repudiation by parties involved in the transaction, and (5) include, if necessary, the selection of parts of a transaction which should be hidden from viewing by a party or parties. Confidentiality is typically provided through data encryption. Authentication, data integrity, and non-repudiation are enabled through digital signatures and public-key certificates. Although various governments and businesses have established their own data encryption standards and privacy laws, there is a need to address these issues at a global level. The International Telecommunication Union (ITU) should be given the responsibility of bringing together national governments and industry to adopt international protocols that support Internet security and privacy.

There is also a need for a global policy governing monetary exchange methods. The status of electronic payments is still ill-defined and fraught with tech-nological and institutional problems (Panurach, 1996). Insecurity, primarily ano-nymity, is the primary technical issue. A few of the institutional constraints include:

(1) government regulations that could easily bring the downfall of elec-tronic payments,
(2) resistance from financial institutions, which face a reduction in invest-ment funds by adopting these new payment technologies, and,
(3) resistance from consumers who must accept the new methods.

ENLIGHTENED AND DIVERSIFIED POPULATION

It is true that the world population is becoming more computer and infor-mation literate. However, people won't use a technology unless they are sure their transactions are secure and private. Issues related to employee monitoring (currently, in the United States, any communication done on company property, such as a laptop or cell phone, is literally owned by that company), the right to obtain and correct information, and the right to authorize the use of one's information continue to occupy individuals, businesses, and governments. Although universal laws that protect individual rights to privacy are not envisaged in the near future, this is an issue to be addressed by the virtual society.

Moreover, people tend to resist technologies that impact their behavior negatively. Virtuality means less physical interaction. Social and psychological ramifications of virtual societies are therefore eminent. Since we spend about one-third of our productive life at work, the consequences of workplace redesign related to virtual organizational structures should be examined. For example, a few years ago, it was a status symbol to carry a pager. A pager signified that one had critical knowledge or skills or was wired in to important people. Today, most workers view a pager as a leash that may be used by their bosses to check on then anytime and anyplace. The same can be said of a company-provided cellular phone. Researchers need to examine the effects on people when an 8 a.m. to 5 p.m. workday is no longer the norm or when a telework contract can require someone to work awkward hours.

The role of human behavior as a driving force toward a virtual society cannot be overemphasized. Most people are social beings and derive satisfaction in their lives through interactions with other people. Researchers need to study the effects of these altered social designs, that is, temporary work contracts, dehumanization, minimal face-to-face interactions, and information overload, as well as how people resist the forces that will propel us into a virtual society.

The process of education has changed very little since the advent of computer technologies underlying the virtual society (Alavi *et al.*, 1995). New methods of education may change the way people learn but current research has not yet fully explored the effect of technology on the outcomes of education taking into consideration the models of learning and the methods of teaching (Leidner & Jarvenpaa, 1995). The current effort to create a learning objects economy is a step in the right direction (Shayo & Olfman, 2006); however, future research should concentrate on issues of educational delivery by applying existing learning theory to understand the effect of technology on learning. There is also a need to evaluate whether education should be the sole responsibility of the individual or whether there is an effective mix of organizational and individual education.

Ideally, a virtual organization should be able to consummate temporal contracts with skilled workers who have proven track records anywhere in the world. Such contracts would be meritorious and should not consider country of national origin, race, religion, or sex. Whereas this presents great opportunities for organizations and information technology-literate workers, it also has implications for wealth distribution between the technological haves and have-nots. It is up to national governments to establish policies that will protect wealth distribution within their national borders and implement affirmative measures that provide equal opportunity for all citizens (Rosecrance, 2000).

INFORMATION TECHNOLOGY AND IT INFRASTRUCTURE

While IT provides faster transmission of information, it affords the logical separation of work from work processes and the resources required to perform the work processes. This gives managers the flexibility to focus on effective accomplishment of the work requirements objectively. As noted previously, the flexible allocation of resources (e.g., labor, time, hardware, software) to work processes, favors a virtual organizational structure. The virtual organizational structure, in turn, favors ephemeral labor contracts, telework, short-term supplier contracts, and outsourcing. Given the long-term nature of existing organizational arrangements, it is natural for there to be resentment from employees, suppliers, and the labor community. For example, one of the grievances in a recent labor strike between General Motors and the United Auto Workers labor union (June, 1998) centered on the outsourcing issue. There is a dearth of research on the impact of such resentment on emergent virtual organizations.

Another challenge for the virtual organization is how to reduce switching and contract costs and how to handle temporal alliances and partnerships in order to protect company secrets such as special formulas or marketing strategies. These two problems are formidable since few or no studies exist from which companies can learn. However, as we move into the virtual society, virtual organizations will have to find solutions to such problems. Organizations may institute strict and draconian nondisclosure agreements that may be impractical to enforce.

At the microlevel, individuals should have the ability to become perpetual learners and apply their knowledge to new situations. As technology changes, so too will the need to master and use the new technology (Scharmer, 2001). The rate at which individuals and organizations are able to learn and apply new knowledge to new situations may become the only sustainable competitive advantage in the virtual society (Teece, 2001). As advocated by Nonaka and Teece (2001), multidisciplinary studies will be needed to evaluate the psychological and social impacts of increased burdens on people to be knowledgeable about various technologies and to learn continuously.

SUMMARY AND CONCLUSION

This chapter provides important insights into the forces, dilemmas, and implications of the oncoming virtual society. We identified and discussed the main forces and exposed the issues and complexities involved. Additional research is needed to examine the relevance of such forces and issues in a virtual societal context. The framework provided in Fig. 1 was aimed at organizing our knowledge from prior literature and identifying the boundaries of the "virtual society" phenomenon. The arrangements covered select areas seen as specific instances of the virtual society. We hope that this chapter highlighted the issues and complexities involved as we move into a more virtual world and that it will stimulate research in field settings on the driving forces, issues, dilemmas, and prospects facing the virtual society.

REFERENCES

Abram, C. (2005). Big list of corporate blogs. Retrieved from the Web November 5, 2005. (http://www. chrisabraham.com/2005/06/big_list_of_cor.html)

Agres, C., Edberg, D., & Igbaria, M. (1998). Transformation to virtual society: Forces and issues. *The Information Society, 14*(2), 71–82.

Alavi, M., Wheeler, B. C., & Valacich, J. S. (1995). Using IT to reengineer business education: An exploratory investigation of collaborative telelearning. *MIS Quarterly, 19*(3), 293–312.

Anttiroiko, A.-V. (2001). Toward the European Information Society. *Communications of the ACM, 44*(1), 31–35.

Applegate, L. M., Austin, R. D., & McFarlan, F. W. (2002). *Corporate information systems management: Texts and cases*, 6th Ed. Boston: McGraw-Hill.

Becker, T. D. (1997). *True tele-democracy. [TAN+N and You]*. Retrieved from the Web August 2, 2005. (https://fp.auburn.edu/tann/tann2/editor.html)

Becker, T. D., & Slaton, C. D. (2000). The future of teledemocracy: Visions and theories—action experiments—global practices. Westport, CT: Praeger Publishers.

Becker, T. D., & Slaton, C. D. (2000). *The future of democracy*. Westport, CT: Praeger Publishers.

Bell, D. (1973). *The coming of post-industrial society: A venture in social forecasting*. New York: Basic Colophon.

Beniger, J. (1986). *The control revolution: Technological and economic origins of the information society*. Cambridge, MA: Harvard University Press.

BGD (2004). Bush Guard Documents Forged. Retrieved from the Web November 5, 2005. (http://www.littlegreenfootballs.com/weblog/?entry=12526_Bush_Guard_Documents-_Forged)

Bhimani, A. (1996). Securing the commercial Internet. *Communications of the ACM, 39*(6), 29, 35.

BICR1, 2005. Blogging and Its Impact on Corporate Reputation. Retrieved from the Web November 5, 2005. (http://www.cymfony.com/files/pdf/res_blogging.pdf)

Buchanan, D., & Boddy, D. (1992). *The expertise of the change agent, public performance, and backstage activity*. New York: Prentice Hall.

Campbell, S. (1997). Market memo: Will tele-medicine become as common as the stethoscope? *Health Care Strategic Management, 15*(4), 1, 20.

Chon, K. (1996). Internet inroads. *Communications of the ACM, 39*(6), 59–60.

Choo, S., Mokhtarian, P. L., & Salomon, I. (2002). *Does telecommuting reduce vehicle-miles traveled? An aggregate time series analysis for the U.S.* Retrieved from the Web August 2, 2005. (http://www.its.berkeley.edu/publications/ITSReviewonline/spring2003/trb2003/choo-telecomuting.pdf)

Coleman, D. (1997). Groupware: The changing environment. In D. Coleman (Ed.), *GroupWare: Collaborative strategies for LANs and Intranets*. Upper Saddle River, NJ: Prentice Hall.

Collins, R. (1979). *The credential society: An historical sociology of education and stratification*. New York: Academic Press.

Cornfield, M. (2004). The Internet and Campaign 2004: A Look Back at the Campaigners. Retrieved from the Web November 5, 2005. (http://www.pewinternet.org/pdfs/Cornfield_commentary.pdf)

David, G. (1997). *Technological change, globalization, and productivity.* Speech delivered to C-SPAN on December 26. George David, CEO for United Technologies Corporation.

DeSanctis, G., & Gallupe, R. B. (1987). A foundation for the study of group decision support systems. *Management Science,* 33(5), 589–609.

Donaldson, T., & Preston, L. E. (1995). The stakeholder theory of the corporation: Concepts, evidence, and implications. *Academy of Management Review,* 20(1): 65–91.

Drucker, P. (1969) *The age of discontinuity.* New York: Harper and Row.

DTI (2003). Department of Trade and Industry (DTI) Telework guidance. (September 2003), Retrieved from the Web November 5, 2005. (http://www.dti.gov.uk/er/individual/telework.pdf)

Eckersley, R. (2004). *A new world view struggles to emerge. The Futurist* 38(5), 20

Eichinger, R., & Ulrich, D. (1995). Are you future agile? *Human Resource Planning, 18*(4), 30–41.

Elgin, D. (1994). *The awakening earth: Global communications and the social brain.* Morrow, New York. Retrieved from the Web August 2, 2005. (https://fp.auburn.edu/tann/tann2/elgin.html)

Fagerberg, J., Mowery, D. C., & Nelson, R. R. (Eds.). (2004). *The Oxford handbook of innovation.* New York: Oxford University Press.

Fernandez, J. P (1991). *Managing a diverse work force.* Lexington, MA: Lexington Books.

Ficsor, M. (2002). The Law of Copyright and the Internet: The 1996 Wipo Treaties, Their Interpretation, and Implementation. New York: Oxford University Press.

Fullerton, H. N., & Toossi, M. (2001). *Labor force projections to 2012: The graying of the U. S. workforce. Monthly Labor Review,* 127(2), Bureau of Labor Statistics, The U. S. Department of Labor.

Gartner Consulting (2001). *Worldwide business-to-business internet commerce to reach $8.5 trillion in 2005.* Retrieved from the Web August 2, 2005. (http://www.gartner.com/5_about/press_room/pr20010313a.html)

Greenstein, S. (2000). Commercialization of the Internet: The Interaction of Public Policy and Private Choices or Why Introducing the Market Worked so Well. Working Paper #0010, The Center for the Study of Industrial Organization, Northwestern University. Retrieved from the Web November 5, 2005. (http://www.csio.econ.northwestern.edu/Papers/2000/CSIO-WP-0010.pdf)

Hiltz, S. R., & Turoff, M. (1978). *The network nation: Human communication via computer.* Reading, MA: Addison-Wesley.

Hodson, N. (2005). Statistics; Telework Statistics Jul-05 and Information Society Statistics. Retrieved from the Web November 5, 2005. (http://www.noelhodson.com/index_files/teleworkstatistics.htm#_Toc90872859)

Horrigan, M. (2004, February). Employment projections to 2012: Concepts and context. *Monthly Labor Review, 127*(2), Bureau of Labor Statistics, The U. S. Department of Labor.

Houghton, J. (2004). *Global warming: The complete briefing.* New York, NY: Cambridge University Press.

ITAC Press Release (2004, September 2). *Work at home grows in past year by 7.5% in U.S.; Use of broadband for work at home grows by 84%.* Retrieved from the Web August 2, 2005. (http://www.workingfromanywhere.org/news/pr090204.htm)

IT21 (1999). Information Technology for the Twenty-First Century: A Bold Investment into America's Future. Retrieved from the Web November 5, 2005. (http://www.nitrd.gov/pitac/it2/initiative.pdf)

ITU World Telecommunications Development Report 2003: Access Indicators for the Information Society. World Summit of the Information Society, Geneva 2002. Retrieved from the Web November 5, 2005. (http://www.itu.int/ITU-D/ict/publications/wtdr_03/material/WTDR2003Sum_e.pdf)

Jankowski, N., Leeuwis, C., Martin, P., Noordhof, M., & van Rossum, J. (1997). *Tele-democracy in the province: An experiment with Internet-based software and public debate.* Paper prepared for Euricom Colloquium June 19–21. Retrieved from the Web November 5, 2005. (http://www.socsci.kun.nl/maw/cw/publications/tdinprov.html)

Jankowski, N., Leeuwis, C., Martin, P., Noordhof, M., & van Rossum, J. (1997). *Tele-democracy in the province: An experiment with Internet-based software and public debate.* Paper prepared for Euricom

Colloquium June 19–21. Retrieved from the Web November 5, 2005. (http://www.socsci.kun. nl/maw/cw/publications/tdinprov.html)

Johansen, R. (1988). *Groupware: Computer support for business teams.* New York: Free Press.

Jensen, T.F. (2000). Electronic commerce and telework trends: Conditions for the development of new ways of working and electronic commerce in Denmark. Retrieved from the Web November 5, 2005. (http://www.ecatt.com/country/denmark/natreport.pdf)

Keskinen, A. (1995). Introduction to Tele-democracy and Information Networks. In A. Keskinen (Ed.), *Tele-democracy—On societal impacts of information networks.* Helsinki, Finland: Painatuskaskus. Retrieved from the Web August 2, 2005. (https://fp.auburn.edu/tann/tann2/auli.html)

Khoshafian, S., & Buckwitz, M. (1995). *Introduction to groupware, workflow, and workgroup computing.* New York: Wiley & Sons.

Koumirov, V. (1994). Teledemocracy. Retrieved from the Web November 5, 2005. (http://www.tml.tkk. fi/Opinnot/Tik-110.501/1996/seminars/works/koumirov/netsec.html)

Krugman, P. (2000). Can America stay on top? *Journal of Economic Perspectives, 14*(1), 169–175.

Leidner, D. E., & Jarvenpaa, S. L.(1995). The use of information technology to enhance management school education: A theoretical view. *MIS Quarterly, 19*(3), 265–291.

Lininger, R., & Wines, R. D. (2005). *Phishing: Cutting the identity theft line.* Indianapolis, Indiana: John Wiley & Sons

Liff, S., Steward, F. & Watts, P. 2002. "New public places for internet access: Networks for practice–based learning and social inclusion," In: Steve Woolgar (Ed.). Virtual Society? Thechnology, Cyberbole, Reality. Oxford: Oxford Universtiy Press, pp. 78–98.

Mandviwalla, M., & Olfman, L. (1994). What do groups need? A proposed set of generic groupware requirements. *ACM Transactions on Computer-Human Interaction, 1*(3), 245–268.

Mannoni, B. (1997). A virtual museum. *Communications of the ACM, 40*(9), 61–62

Martin, J. (1978). *The wired society.* Englewood Cliffs, NJ: Prentice-Hall.

Metcalfe, S. (1995). The economic foundations of technology policy: Equilibrium and evolutionary perspectives. In P. Stoneman (Ed.), *Handbook of the economics of innovation and technological change* (pp. 409–512). Oxford, UK: Blackwell.

Mintzberg, H. (1979). *The structuring of organizations.* Englewood Cliffs, NJ: Prentice-Hall.

Mittleman, D. D., & Briggs, B. O. (1998). Communication technology for teams: Electronic collaboration. In E. Sunderstrom and Associates (Eds.), *Supporting work team effectiveness: Best practices for fostering high-performance* (pp. 246–270). San Francisco, CA: Jossey-Bass.

Minton, S. Opitz, E. Orozco, J., Chang, F.,Frantzen, S. J., Koch, G., Coughlin, M., Copeland, T. G., and Toncheva, A. (2004). Worldwide IT Spending 2004-2008 Forecast: The Worldwide Black Book, IDC Report #32321.

Mowshowitz, A. (1997). Virtual organization. *Communications of the ACM, 40*(9), 30–37

Nonaka, I., & Teece, D. J.(2001). Research directions for knowledge management. In I. Nonaka & D. Teece (Eds.). *Managing industrial knowledge: Creation, transfer and utilization* (pp. 330–335). Thousand Oaks, CA: Sage Publications,.

O'Rourke, J. (1996). Virtual museum: Computers on computer. *Rural Telecommunications, 15*(5), 10.

Panurach, P. (1996) Money in electronic commerce: Digital cash, electronic fund transfer, and e-cash. *Communications of the ACM, 39*(6), 45.

Pyle, R. (1996). Commerce and the Internet. *Communications of the ACM, 39*(6), 23.

Rosecrance, R. N. (2000). *The rise of the virtual state: Wealth and power in the coming century.* New York: Basic Books.

Scharmer, C. O. (2001). Self-transcending knowledge organizing around emerging realities. In I. Nonaka & D.Teece (Eds.), *Managing industrial knowledge: Creation, transfer and utilization* (pp. 68–90). Thousand Oaks, CA: Sage Publications.

Shane, P.M. (2004). *Democracy online: The prospects for political renewal through the Internet.* New York: Routledge.

Shayo, C., & Olfman, L. (2006). The learning objects economy: What remains to be done? In D. Galletta & P. Zhang (Eds.). *Human-computer interaction and management information systems—Applications.* Advances in Management Information Systems, Volume 5. Armonk, NY: M. E. Sharpe, Inc.

Simonson, M., Smaldino, S. E., Albright, M. J., & Zvacek, S. (2002). *Teaching and learning at a distance: Foundations of distance education.* 2nd Ed. New York: Prentice Hall.

Schepp, B. (1990). *The telecommuter's handbook: How to work for a salary without ever leaving the house.* New York: Pharos Books

Teece, D.J. (2001). Strategies for managing knowledge assets: The role of firm structure and context. In I. Nonaka & D. Teece (Eds.), *Managing industrial knowledge: Creation, transfer and utilization* (pp. 125–144). Thousand Oaks, CA: Sage Publications

UNCTAD World Investment Report 2005 (WIR 05): Transnational Corporations and the Internationalization of R&D. United Nations New York and Geneva. Retrieved from the Web November 5, 2005. (http://www.unctad.org/en/docs/wir2005_en.pdf)

Vega, G. (2003). *Managing teleworkers and telecommuting strategies.* Westport, CT: Praeger Publishers.

Verisign, Inc. (2004). *The domain name industry brief.* 2(3). Retrieved from the Web November 5, 2005. (http://www.verisign.com/stellent/groups/public/documents/newsletter/031399.pdf)

VLMP (2005). Virtual Library Museum Pages. Retrieved from the Web November 5, 2005. (http://vlmp.icom.museum/)

Woolgar, S. (2002). Five rules of virtuality. In S. Woolgar (Ed.), *Virtual society? Technology, cyberbole, reality.* New York, NY: Oxford University Press.

World Bank (2003). World Development Indicators 2003. Retrieved from the Web November 5, 2005. (http://www.worldbank.org/data/wdi2003/index.htm)

World Bank (2004). World Development Indicators 2004. Retrieved from the Web October 19, 2005. (http://www.worldbank.org/data/wdi2005/)

World Bank (2005). World Development Indicators 2005. Retrieved from the Web November 5, 2005. (http://www.worldbank.org/data/wdi2005/)

Wright, P. C. (1993). Telecommuting and employee effectiveness: Career and managerial issues. *International Journal of Career Management, 5,* 4–9.

Yoganathan, D., & Rom, W. N. (2001). Medical aspects of global warming. *American Journal of Industrial Medicine, 40*(2), 199–210.

Ytterstad, P., Akselsen, S., Svendsen, G., & Watson, R. T. (1996). Tele-democracy: Using information technology to enhance political work. Retrieved from the Web November 5, 2005. (http://www.misq.org/discovery/articles96/article1/)

CHAPTER 9

Internet Self-Help and Support Groups: The Pros and Cons of Text-Based Mutual Aid*

Storm A. King
East Longmeadow, Massachusetts
Danielle Moreggi
PIR Psychology Department
University of New Haven
New Haven, Connecticut

Introduction
The Psychology of Text-Based Relationships
Self-Help as Mutual Aid
Text-Based Mutual Aid
Results of a Replication Survey
Pros and Cons of Internet Self-Help Groups
Internet Support Groups and Text-Based Group
    Therapy
Ethical Considerations in Researching Text-
    Based Mutual Aid
Conclusion
References

INTRODUCTION

The Internet is anarchy. No one owns it, no one controls it, and no government can exert political authority over it. There are no precedents for the types of social changes that the Internet is bringing. In just the last decade, the Internet has gone from being the domain of academics, the tech-savvy, and mostly male-dominated, to being an essential part of most individual life and all businesses in the United States. The significant difference between the Internet and all previous communication technologies is that the Internet is an unregulated "from many to many" broadcasting paradigm.

* Much of the material for this chapter was first reported in the lead author's dissertation, titled "The therapeutic value of virtual self-help groups." He thanks Dr. Jean Millay for her editorial contribution, and Dr. William Froming for his guidance during the (long) dissertation process.

Psychology and the Internet: Intrapersonal, Interpersonal, and Transpersonal Implications

Several organizations are engaged in comprehensive research into the social dynamics of Internet use and the psychological characteristics of the text-based relationships that form online. The Pew Internet and American Life Project (PEW) publishes the results of its widely varied Internet research on its website, and the Association of Internet Researchers hosts an annual international convention where researchers investigating all aspects of online behavior present their results. There are many social science research efforts currently in progress that are making clearer the unique ethical dilemmas that face researchers in this field.

The Internet is increasingly becoming an essential part of people's lives. A recent Harris Poll announced the percentage of all U. S. adults who have access to the Internet has increased from almost 40% in 1998 to almost 75% by June of 2005. Three-quarters of all online adults said they had used the Internet to search for health-related information (Harris Interactive, 2005).

Internet-connected people send e-mail at least as often as they use the phone. They send significantly more e-mail than regular postal mail (now referred to as "snail mail") (Pew, 2002). They socialize with strangers in text-only virtual communities, and the relationships that emerge in these forums face unique and subtle challenges. The normal cues used to make social judgments of others are not present in a text-based environment. The asynchronous nature of most text-based relationships can be an advantage, and also an obstruction to the creation of personal, therapeutic relationships. And yet, four years ago, 28% reported using the Internet to access, visit, or participate in an online self-help group (Pew, 2001). Today, that figure is even higher. Millions and millions of people are seeking and finding a form of text-only peer support that came into existence and matured in just the past 10 to 15 years.

Self-organized self-help groups appeal to vast numbers of people who want to learn from and share with others who are coping with the same predicaments they confront. The Internet has enabled the formation of many thousands of e-mail and Web-based text-only self-help discussions. Many of these are devoted to topics for which there are not enough potential members in any one geographic area to make a "real life" self-help group possible. Self-help Internet groups are defined by the members' expectations that they will read about the experiences of others with whom they have a common disorder or condition, and that they will have an opportunity to share their experiences if they choose to.

These online forums contain an increasing number of clients who are in therapy with a professional mental health clinician. Internet self-help group members participate in a form of emotional support in which the interpersonal dynamics are different from traditional support networks. Mental health professionals will continue to have more and more clients using Internet self-help therapy. Therapists must obtain an accurate understanding of the hazards of text-based interpersonal dynamics, and of the unique potential therapeutic value available, to be able to more completely help their clients who are engaged in text-only self-help efforts.

THE PSYCHOLOGY OF TEXT-BASED RELATIONSHIPS

Computer mediated communication (CMC) is a field of research that dates back to the first use of computers as communication devices, well before the current proliferation of home personal computers (PCs). Early work in this field centered on the study of small work groups of people who communicated by computer, in the process of working together to design and/or produce a commercial product (Kiesler *et al.*, 1984). In the past decade the price of a no-frills desktop PC that can connect to the Internet has fallen from over $2,000 to around $500 today. The increase in Internet use has been fast and broad, and the language used to describe it is still evolving. New words, such as "cyberspace" and "virtual communities" have been added to the common lexicon, and it is common to refer to the use of the Internet as being "online." *Online* is used here to describe the entire range of CMC activity, from asynchronous e-mail transmissions, browsing the World Wide Web (WWW) to synchronous chat room participation. Current research in the CMC field includes studies designed to make explicit the psychological and social factors involved in text-only relationships.

Internet research findings need to be interpreted with the understanding that there is no such thing as "the Internet." The term "using the Internet" includes a wide range of possible activities, within a wide assortment of text-based and graphical Web-based environments. What someone reports as their experience online depends on what their intentions are, and the particular Internet text-based environment in which they participate. A chat room for "single 20s" is a far different social and psychological environment than a moderated e-mail list devoted to recovery from cancer. Real-time chat rooms that function as Internet self-help groups also exist, especially on provider networks such as America Online (AOL). Due to the constraint of having to schedule one's time online to participate in such groups, though, they are far less populated than the asynchronous e-mail lists. Note, however, that the psychology of real-time and asynchronous text relationships are not the same. Due to the scarcity of research results from synchronous text-based self-help groups, this chapter focuses mostly on the pros and cons of asynchronous text-only Internet self-help groups.

When discussions of the pros and cons of Internet self-help arise, it is important to acknowledge that any aspect of the Internet can function as either a positive or a negative influence, depending on the motives of the individual user and the overall context of their participation. Some factors, such as anonymity, are both a major pro and a big con. Typing to text-only public forums from one's private space frequently enhances the online experience, and also creates some challenges.

Text that is conversational in nature is a relatively new phenomenon. During a lifetime of exposure to text in books and print media, people develop the firm impression that these written messages always represent the well-thought-out and carefully edited views of the writer. Text-only social interactions through CMC, however, are frequently the product of someone "typing off the top of his or her head." Text-based communications often appear colder and more impersonal than the author intended, and humor and sarcasm are particularly difficult to convey in text-only environments. Without tone of voice or body language to give it the correct context, typed sarcasm may come across as anger and aggression.

People access virtual communities to find others with similar interests (Madara et al., 1988). People who are traditionally socially ostracized due to having a stigmatized disorder or condition are becoming empowered as they find and connect with each other online, in a manner not possible face-to-face (f2f). Internet virtual communities are fulfilling people's need for affiliation, information, and support, and allowing diverse groups a greater political voice (McKenna & Bargh, 1998).

There is a diminished sense of social presence in text-based communications (Sproull & Kiesler, 1984). The lack of tactile sensory feedback and the privacy of being in one's own home contribute to a different sense of being connected socially. It is easier to communicate to strangers, at least partly because there is less interpersonal risk and little logistic or social cost involved (Sproull & Faraj, 1995; Wellman, 1996). The kind of social situational feedback that one normally uses to regulate one's behavior is missing (Kiesler et al., 1984). People experience an enhanced opportunity to feel at ease with others, and, conversely, to be challenging toward others. Conditions of age difference, ethnic group membership, and gender have much less influence over online interactions than they do f2f.

In text-based environments, the differences between people that would otherwise inhibit the formation of a personal relationship are hidden. This promotes a sense of group membership that is dependent solely on the limited perceptions of the individual available through CMC. When individual differences are less conspicuous, group membership becomes more prominent (Postmes et al., 2002).

Virtual community participation is "an imaginative rather than a sensory experience" (Reid, 1994). Control over impression formation is enhanced in text-only mediums, because people have more command over the timing and content of their self-disclosures (Walther, 1996). People judge one another online based on perceived group similarity or difference. They engage in an over-attribution process (Lea & Spears, 1992) and assume things about others based on their own unconscious projections. In their mind's eye, they fill in a picture of others online with whatever cues they have, never fully aware that a large part of that picture is based on their own assumptions and misattributions.

"If all computer-mediated communication systems can be said to have one single unifying effect upon human behavior, it is that usage tends to cause the user to become less inhibited." (Reid, 1994). This tendency toward uninhibited behavior has been noted since the earliest studies of text-only communications (Sproull & Kiesler, 1984). This disinhibition increases self-disclosure and allows people to meet in a more profound manner than they would f2f (Donn & Sherman, 2002).

The emotional content of the interaction is more controllable than a f2f encounter (Noonan, 1998). People tend to self-disclose more, and sooner in the relationship, than they would if they had met f2f (Joinson, 1998).

Becoming less inhibited can have negative consequences. The improbability of any local, real life repercussions for online social behavior has produced a new psychological phenomenon; people can feel free to express themselves in a manner that is much more unrestrained compared to the way they would act f2f. Communication occurs without the normal pressures that are imposed by the need to maintain social order (Huang & Alessi, 1996). Interactions in text-only environments occur without the f2f group norms normally used to regulate behavior (Finn & Banach, 2000). Identified factors of text-based environments that contribute to the potential for disinhibition are anonymity, lack of visual cues, asynchronous communications, unwarranted projections about others, opportunities to present alternative identities, and minimization of authority (Suler, 2004).

It is easy and common for misunderstandings to occur in text-only communication. The only context one has available to interpret the communication is any prior communications from that source. The only cues to guide understanding conversational text are any "emoticons" added to the message. *Emoticons* are extra text added to indicate the state of mind of the writer, such as humor :-) or sadness :-(. Judgments of others made without the normal sensory clues can consist of distorted, emotionally laden projections (King, 1995). "The tendency to project stereotypical attributes on others occurs precisely because of the lack of individuating information communicated by the medium, and is promoted by the deindividuating conditions of CMC, such as the physical isolation" (Walther, 1997, p. 364). The cognitive process of stereotyping takes place more easily in text-only environments. Emotional content is the hardest to correctly place in context. One group of researchers told of a misunderstood Internet self-help group member as follows: "The original message sender complained that group members were 'overreacting' to a previous message's level of despair, taking the message out of its context, or misinterpreting a previous comment as a personal attack, rather than simply an observation" (Waldron *et al.*, 2000).

The lack of sensual clues and relative anonymity in text-based relationships creates a level playing field for online social interactions. The normal situational and visual clues that tell someone about the status and position of another are absent (Kiesler *et al.*, 1984). In contrast to f2f communications, text-based interactions do not automatically include information about social status, such as age or how expensive one's clothing is. Indications about race, body language, and facial expressions that might normally inhibit inappropriate responses are not available online (Finn & Banach, 2000).

There is a mood congruent effect to text-based relationships (King, 1995). The frame of mind one is in at the time they read a particular message is a much larger part of the context in which the message is interpreted than it would be if one had f2f sensual clues available. To demonstrate this effect, suppose a group member is responded to with a message such as "I disagree with what you said." There is range of interpretations to that statement, depending on the overall context. When tone of voice is absent, all messages seem somewhat ambiguous; people unconsciously decide what contextual information to use to guide their understanding of interpersonal communications, using cues from what is salient to them at the time. If someone has had a good day, and is feeling confident, calm, and composed, they will understand "disagree with you" as an opportunity to elaborate their point. If the same person had a bad day and is primed to become angry, they will interpret the same message as a personal attack on their integrity. From that state of mind, they may reply with a derogatory comment about the sender, deviating from the topic of the group. This is how a "flame war" gets started, that is, an online discussion that has degenerated into a series of personal attacks (Goode & Johnson, 1991). During a flame war, a moderately active virtual community will suddenly become very active, producing many times the normal volume of daily messages. Flame wars do not occur at the same rate in all regions of online text-based communication. Just as you would expect more arguments to occur in a bar than a church, more flame wars occur in open political and religious discussions groups than in Internet self-help groups. Of all the different types of text-based groups, flame wars (as measured by the rate of hostile communications posted to the group) actually occur least often in Internet groups that have the highest frequency of emotionally supportive messages, such as Internet self-help groups (Preece & Ghozati, 2001).

SELF-HELP AS MUTUAL AID

Self-help group participation is more common now than ever. Addiction-oriented 12-step groups, such as Alcoholics Anonymous, account for the vast majority of the f2f groups attended. In fact, over 6,000,000 adults a year have contact with an addiction self-help group (Humphreys *et al.*, 2004). Members share their experiences and strengths in order that they may better cope with their common problem. It is this self-referenced, rather than authoritarian, instruction, support, and guidance that is the defining feature of all self-help, mutual aid groups.

One of the main therapeutic factors of self-helps groups is their ability to normalize a stigmatizing condition, to take the embarrassment away from having an undesirable disorder (Madara, 1999; McKenna & Bargh, 1998). "Generally speaking, membership in a self-help group provides important new roles for a person otherwise disqualified from being normal" (Levine & Perkins, 1987, p. 248). Kaufmann (1996) talks about the ability of self-help groups to be therapeutic in a focused, specific manner. She calls this therapeutic effect "an antidote to stigmatization." She reports that people who join self-help groups "do so only because they are accepted as members sharing a common predicament of mental distress. This is ostracism in reverse; only those with the stigmata may join the group." (Kaufmann, 1996, p. 12).

The term self-help is misleading, though, since it implies that people are involved in an effort to help only themselves. In fact, a defining feature of self-help groups is that people help one another. A *mutual-aid group* is the term preferred by researchers, because it better represents the therapeutic process actually occurring. The term *mutual aid* also captures another important element of these groups—helper therapy. Helper therapy is that part of the therapeutic value of these groups that is available because each person can be both a receiver of help and a helper. Humphreys and Rappaport (1994) suggested that the terms *self-help* and *mutual-aid groups* be used interchangeably in the professional research literature, though, because the term self-help is the preferred term among self-help members. The recommended term for groups that are organized and led by a professional mental health worker is *support groups.*

The goals of participation vary greatly from group to group, and as a result, it is not possible to compare outcomes across self-help groups in general. Humphreys and Rappaport (1994) suggest that it may be more beneficial for researchers to pay greater attention to the nonclinical (and harder to quantify) changes brought about by participation in self-help groups. From the point of view of the self-help group member, an increase in the number of one's friendships or a change in one's worldview may have more practical significance and greater personal value than a decrease in depression or an increase in self-esteem. The authors raise an important question that is relevant to Internet mutual-aid groups, though: Does group membership ever harm people? This is an underaddressed issue for both f2f and Internet self-help groups.

Jacobs and Goodman (1989) defined self-help groups as member-governed organizations in which members share a "common predicament, problem, or concern; a reciprocal process of help–intended activity and minimal fees aimed at maintenance rather than profit." The authors point out that there is a wide range of formats for, and sizes of, self-help groups. What different groups have in common is "self-governance, homogeneity of concern, a democratic ideology, and nonprofit status" (Jacobs & Goodman, 1989, p. 583). The therapeutic value of these groups derives from the way they function to normalize the experiences of the members.

The new member, who frequently has felt stigmatized and criticized (or, at the very least, isolated and not understood), frequently finds immediate acceptance as a member of the group. That sometimes stunning experience seems to be a vital step toward making the cognitive, emotional, and behavioral changes necessary for more effective functioning and improved quality of life (Jacobs & Goodman, 1989, p. 538).

Helper therapy is the therapeutic value these groups provide when a member becomes a helper as well as someone receiving help. When functioning as a helper, the group member's self-worth is enhanced and he/she is empowered in a therapeutic manner. Helping others, especially newer members, validates the member as an important part of his or her self-help community. When someone shares what they have learned, it makes that knowledge more permanent, and thus more valuable, to the giver of it.

The growth in the number of self-help groups is due to their special ability to meet people's needs for peer support and practical information (Madara, 1997). Dissatisfaction with traditional medical models for solving emotional disorders, and the general destigmatization of seeking peer support, has fueled this growth. Humphreys (1997) expressed the value members receive as follows:

> At a time when membership in mainline religions is declining, some Americans seem to be finding spiritual renewal in small groups. Even mutual aid self-help groups that do not address spirituality as directly as do 12-step groups may benefit members' spiritual lives. The experience (distinct from the intellectual realization) of learning that we need not suffer life's burdens alone, that we have a place in the human community, and that we have something both to offer and to receive from other beings is too profound to be captured by such terms as "improved mental health" or "better coping." (Humphreys, 1997 p. 15).

TEXT-BASED MUTUAL AID

Thousands of email and Web-based self-help groups exist on the Internet. There is one devoted to every imaginable condition or disorder. Some are very active, generating 50 or more messages a day. Many generate about 50 messages a month. A large but unknown number of these lists are no longer active at all. Such groups often function as communities, developing their own culture and norms (Rhinegold, 1993; Walther, 1996; Wellman, 1996).

Participants in online communities often carve out roles for themselves just as they do in physical communities. For example, there are protagonists, experts, people who befriend others, people who always try to respond, witty people, sarcastic people, and lurkers who watch silently. (Preece & Maloney-Krichmar, 2003).

Social support, practical information, shared experiences, positive role models, helper therapy, empowerment, professional support, and advocacy efforts are all therapeutic factors that Internet self-help groups share with face-to-face groups (Madara, 1999). The asynchronous nature of e-mail online support groups provides the additional advantages of 24-hour availability, selective participation in responding to messages, anonymity and privacy, immediate and/or delayed responding, and recording of transmissions (Sparks, 1992). Members can save notes for later study. They also have a much higher ability to decide which topic to respond to, or to start a new topic at any time, in Internet self-help groups compared to f2f ones.

In an article titled *Who Talks? The Social Psychology of Illness Support Groups,* Davison *et al.* (2000) researched self-help group participation by people diagnosed with the twenty most prevalent and deadly physical and mental disorders. They examined Internet self-help groups and f2f groups in four major U. S. metropolitan areas. They counted the number of the f2f self-help groups that exist for the target disorders in each of the four large metropolitan areas. They contacted each group to get the frequency with which the group met and the average attendance size of the group. They counted contributions to online bulletin board forums (on AOL and the Internet) devoted to the same twenty disease categories used in the f2f survey. The results of the f2f group survey confirmed that Alcoholics Anonymous (AA) is by far the largest and most well-attended f2f self-help organization in the U. S. "Of the 12,596 total groups identified for all of the conditions studied, across all cities sampled, AA groups constituted 10,966, or 87%, of the group counts" (p. 209). Based on the number of groups (and group size), the disorders that have the highest rates of f2f self-help group memberships are, in order, alcoholism, AIDS, breast cancer, and anorexia. Attendance was lowest for heart disease, hypertension, migraine, ulcer, and chronic pain. Diseases viewed as the most embarrassing and stigmatizing had the highest rates of self-help group participation.

The results of this study of online self-help groups showed that chronic fatigue syndrome had the highest activity level of the Internet groups, and multiple sclerosis had the highest activity on AOL. Combining both the Internet and AOL activity of the online groups, the top four disorders, listed in order of participation are multiple sclerosis, chronic fatigue syndrome, breast cancer, and anorexia. The authors explain these results by stating that "virtual support can be very attractive to those whose disability impairs mobility." It is particularly useful for people with rare conditions, who cannot get together physically. Alcoholism was ranked the eleventh most prevalent type of group online. The authors postulate that the large availability of f2f AA groups makes the online AA seem "a poor substitute for the group experience." The research revealed that "having an illness that is embarrassing, socially stigmatizing, or disfiguring leads people to seek the support of others with similar conditions (p. 213)." The most frequently attended self-help groups, both f2f and online, were the groups devoted to disorders that were rated as "embarrassing to talk about" (Davison *et al.*, 2000).

One of the first published reports of an online self-help group was in 1984, in an article in the *Exchange Network*, the newsletter of the National Volunteer Center. Ed Madara, then the director of the New Jersey Self-Help Clearinghouse, wrote about a weekly online text-based conference taking place on CompuServe. The members were all disabled. They used the computer conference to offer each other emotional support and practical information. The organizer of this group was deaf and blind. He used a Braille keyboard to enter his messages, and an early version of a text-to-audio software program to hear replies from other members of the group. This may have been the first online self-help group. Madara wrote at that time what turned out to be a very prophetic statement about the experience; "embarrassing to talk about" (Madara, 1984).

An analysis of 500 messages posted to an online self-help group devoted to people with a knee injury found that almost 45% of the messages were of a supportive nature. People posted their personal stories, presumably containing what happened to them and what they had to go through to deal with the injury. Almost one-third of the messages were of this type. The rest were mostly factual information, given in response to questions asked of the group. No hostile responses or postings were part of that sample (Preece, 1999).

Observations of an online self-help group for people with an eating disorder pointed out the advantage the online anonymity provides to this group in particular: Not being present with each other f2f meant that no one had to worry about judgments related to his/her physical appearance. This gave an extra level of safety to people who are often overly concerned with such judgments. The author made the strong statement that "the urgency of grasping the therapeutic benefit of online support groups can be seen in the astronomical costs (and often ineffective) results of traditional health care" (Walstrom, 2000 p. 762). Using a "microlevel" discourse analysis qualitative methodology, the author was able to document, in its naturalistic setting, the effective coping strategies that members shared. The authors conclude that the virtual nature of online self-help groups decreases the evaluation anxiety that is present when people with an eating disorder meet in a f2f group. As a result, the reduced accountability and decreased evaluation anxiety enhance participation in the online self-help group, increasing the therapeutic value members receive (Walstrom, 2000).

A randomized research study reported about the value of text-based self-help for teenagers who suffered from cystic fibrosis (CF), and who were being treated by the Johns Hopkins CF clinic (Johnson et al., 2001). Teens with this disorder can not be as physically active as they would otherwise and often are kept at home by their families. CF in teens is the kind of rare disorder for which geographic separation prevents most children from meeting for peer support f2f. The researchers created a "highly interactive Web-based support service" that included an area for the subjects to post text messages to each other. The goal of this study was to explore how such a group might impact teens' perceptions of (1) their disease, (2) their available peer support, and (3) their assessment of the usefulness of the virtual support group. At the start of the study, all participants were surveyed to assess their knowledge about CF and their perceptions about the type of support they received from both peers and the staff of the Johns Hopkins clinic. Their opinion about the potential value of the Internet as a support environment was also recorded. Half of the teenagers in the study group were assigned to use the online resource at the start of the year-long study. They were given the this survey again at the five-month point. A comparison cohort group was made to wait until five months into the study before using the Web resource. Both cohorts were surveyed again at the end of the one-year study. The forum that allowed the subjects to interact socially with each other was the most frequently used part of the site. The results showed a significant increase in the subjects' perceptions of their support from peers. "The most significant event that this project catalyzed was an opportunity for the participants to bond and to discuss both typical adolescent issues and those specific to CF" (Johnson *et al.*, 2001).

The appeal of Internet text-based communications to someone with hearing loss is self-evident. A random sample survey of an online self-help group for deaf people found two factors that predicted active participation in the group. One was a lack of real world social support. Members with fewer friends or family they were emotionally close to were the most active participants. They were able to find the support they had been missing from their online self-help group. They were also the members most likely to remain part of the group for the longest time. The predictive factor was members' coping ability prior to joining the group. People less severely disabled, who were already coping well and using real-world professional help as well as other online resources, were more active in the group than were other members. For this cohort, the online support represented a useful opportunity to give support to others, engendering the therapeutic benefit of helper therapy. Members who had family and f2f friends that participated with them as active members of their online group reported the highest level of emotional benefits from their participation. The authors believe that having friends and family join in as fellow Internet self-help group members is easy to do and very therapeutic in a unique manner (Cummings *et al.*, 2002).

Walther and Boyd (2002) published an extensive analysis of Usenet self-help groups. They gathered data from 340 subjects who responded to a survey. The results were revealing not only for what the participants found to be of value in their online groups, but also for what participants reported to be the disadvantages of f2f self-help groups. Members endorsed items on the survey related to the potential for embarrassment if offline friends and family were to know about the details of the problems they were sharing with their online group. This study found that members felt that their online peers judged them to a lesser degree than their real-life acquaintances did. Online self-help groups have a unique therapeutic advantage in that members experience decreased concern about the potential for embarrassment when they self-disclose in text-based relationships (Walther & Boyd, 2002).

An analysis of two weeks of notes to an Internet Usenet self-help group for depression revealed, "Comments intended to convey support, acceptance, and positive feelings (i.e., emotional support, agreement, and humor) were observed over seven times more frequently than comments that conveyed negative sentiments (i.e., disagreement / negative)" (Salem *et al.*, 1997, p. 198). About half the notes contained a message intended to help another member. Compared to similar f2f groups, the online group had a much higher rate of self-disclosure but a less formal structure and group process. There was a surprising lack of gender difference in the amount of, and type of, messages posted, with men participating and self-disclosing at nearly the same rate as women. In the two weeks that this group was studied, some members felt it had grown too big, and started their own smaller and more private group. The ease with which text-only Internet groups can be formed makes this kind of splinter group formation much more common online than f2f, and less disruptive. As with other studies that employed naturalistic observation, the researchers noted the need to take extra precautions in the manner in which they reported the contents of the notes. Members had posted very personal information, not thinking that their message might end up published in an academic journal (Salem *et al.*, 1997).

One group of researchers reported that Internet self-help groups remove access barriers caused by time constraints, geographic distance to the group, disability of the member, limitations in the ability of the member to communicate, scheduling problems, rarity of a disease that would limit the availability of membership, and fear of f2f participation. Online self-help provides a much broader and different mixture of social support, and an enhanced sense of universality and diversity (Braithwaite *et al.*, 1999).

One survey of Internet self-help groups reported what members perceived to be the unique value of their online group. Highly rated responses included increased opportunity to share experiences with others, the convenience of the service, and the convenience of being in your own home. Nearly half the respondents cited "the variety of the participants" as being one of the most beneficial factors. "By taking away the barriers of social status, location, physical attributes, and emotional inhibitions, Internet groups provide people with a communication tool designed to help them address specific problems." (Dubin *et al.*, 1997). An important and reliable finding is that members who rate online self-help groups as valuable are frequently using the online self-help group to supplement f2f self-help or professional therapy (King, 1994; Stein, 1997; Dubin *et al.*, 1997).

One gains status in f2f relationships by offering support that others regard as valuable and advice that others consider correct. Online, the question of legitimacy and authority is not nearly as clearly established. Galegher *et al.* (1998) researched how online self-help group members establish legitimacy and authority. They compared three Usenet support groups to three Usenet hobby groups over a three-week period. Messages on the online self-help groups more often contained a reference to the length of time the originator had been a member of that group. Members were deliberately and overtly establishing themselves as an authority in, at least, the workings of that group, and by inference, in associated recovery or with coping strategies. Newcomers established themselves by asking pertinent, important questions. The questions that were posted "out of the blue," with no mention of how long the member had been part of the group or any information that legitimized the poster, were the ones that most often went unanswered. In the hobby groups, this was not the case, and the addition of information to legitimize the member did not seem important to other members and did not have the same consequences that it did in the support groups. The researchers found that the length of the average message was longer in the support groups, and there was more self disclosure of intimate details (Galegher *et al.*, 1998).

There are unique disadvantages to text-based self-help groups. Members negatively affected tend to drop out of the group. Only the "sturdy" group members, those not overly put off by the occasional flame war or by messages disruptive to the group process, are left to answer any research questions. This self-selection process positively biases the outcome of self-help research studies. In the online environment, it is particularly difficult to determine how many people have tried text-based self-help and did not find it helpful.

An article that illuminates the negative potential of online self-help groups focused on the experiences of women seeking help from online groups and from online therapy. Finn and Banach (2000) reviewed the literature and reported about the benefits as well as the hazards of therapeutic text-only relationships. The list of the unique potential hazards include "inaccurate information, online harassment, loss of privacy, and cyberstalking" (p. 794). The authors note that "socialization for survival in cyberspace has not yet become part of the normal growing-up experience of women" (p. 792) and conclude that the risks and dangers of these online resources were not yet common knowledge.

There have been documented cases of groups that had to disband due to the high levels of disruption they experienced. Waldron et al. (2000) reported of an online group for sexual abuse survivors that received so many sexually explicit advertising messages that the groups choose to disperse rather than continue in that environment. These researchers documented the ease with which an online self-help member can have his/her privacy violated by another member who, not being intentionally harmful, did not understand the nuances of online self-help participation. This occurred when a member's real-life address was mistakenly made public to the group. The sender had intended the e-mail to go only to one other member (Waldron et al., 2000). Other researchers have warned about the potential for what they observed during a flame war. The Internet self-help email list became "a breeding ground for inappropriate venting, where endless venting with no resolution and no self-reflection was, at best, a wasteful exercise" (Worotynec, 2000, p. 808).

Some aspects of text-only self-help groups function both as an advantage and a disadvantage at the same time. For example, the number of participants can be much larger than what most community meeting spaces could accommodate. Any member may type to the group at anytime. While this makes for beneficial communications with a much more diverse membership than is possible f2f, it also exposes the member to the potential for information overload. Many online self-help group members join very active groups with high hopes, only to find themselves swamped by the large volume of e-mail. In any new social endeavor, if the rules about what is acceptable behavior are unknown, people unconsciously try to apply the guidelines that they know work in f2f interactions. For example, in f2f situations, it is normally not acceptable to ignore a fellow member of one's social support group. When involved in a very busy e-mail list, however, most people have to ignore some percentage of the messages in order to limit their commitment to the group to the amount of time that is feasible for them. Some people will be able to adjust their expectations and feel free to read only messages they have time to digest or respond only when they have something of significance to say. Other members will choose the simpler, less (perceived) risky path of dropping out completely.

The asynchronous nature of the communications is also both an advantage and a disadvantage. On the one hand, it makes possible ease of scheduling and the ability to participate in more than one self-help group during the same period of time. On the other hand, it is the source of much of the frustration and misunderstanding that arise from not having corrective feedback immediately available to guide one's interpretation of text-only communications.

RESULTS OF A REPLICATION SURVEY

Much of the data so far discussed has been given further validity through a replication survey. Questions related to online self-help initially asked by King in 1994 were again asked by Walther and Boyd (the survey was done in 1995, the results published in 2002), again in 1997 by Salem et al., and finally by King again in 2001. The compared results of the studies showed high consistency in many answers.

The opportunity to share experiences and the convenience of Internet self-help groups were very important to respondents in all the surveys, as was the availability of groups on the Internet that did not exist in face-to-face context, for a variety of reasons. There was also high congruence across the studies in the high proportion of people who appreciated the ability to think carefully about their words before they are sent, in a way not possible in face-to-face situations, and the ability to express themselves about potentially uncomfortable topics, the way they could not with friends and family.

Almost half (46%) stated that they had, at one point, dropped out of an Internet self-help group, but by far the most common reason was that there were simply too many messages. Most respondents said that there were few or no negative messages being posted in their groups.

Interestingly, this survey also offered a glimpse into "lurkers," those who read the messages of self-help groups, but do not post messages themselves. Lurkers are a small percentage of group members (fewer than 10%), and there are no differences in the length of time that they have been involved in the group, compared to those who actively post. In contrast, however, lurkers perceive the proportion of supportive messages posted to be much lower and are less likely to feel emotionally connected to the group. They rate privacy to be much more important to them, and a sense of community to be less important.

Respondents acknowledged that misunderstandings happen easily, and that it is important to be careful about expressing emotions online. Almost 75% stated that the feelings surrounding heir Internet group were very different from the feeling of support gained in a face-to-face group. Clearly, Internet support groups are a unique form of support, but for many rare conditions, there are no face-to-face equivalents.

PROS AND CONS OF INTERNET SELF-HELP GROUPS

The therapeutic value of Internet self-help groups is evident from the consistent reports from members who have benefited from their online participation. The text-based groups are the only form of peer support available to the majority of respondents. Motivation for participating in online self-help is congruent with what has been previously reported about the value of f2f self-help groups. One consistent finding from f2f studies of mutual aid is that members rate highest the value of access to others with similar concerns. This is also true for online groups. In both the replication study and the ones it duplicated, respondents reported "access to others" to be the highest ranked valuable and therapeutic factor. Despite the hazards involved in text-only communications, millions of people log on every day and type about their experiences, strengths, and hopes to each other. A summary of the pros and cons of Internet text-based mutual aid is provided here in list form.

ADVANTAGES THAT ONLINE SELF-HELP GROUPS SHARE WITH F2F GROUPS

- Groups help normalize the behavior or condition in question. The conditions, which have been marginalized and stigmatized, become acceptable by association with others for whom this condition or behavior is a common condition.
- The members become empowered by exposure to the experiences and positive coping strategies of others. This empowerment initially manifests as hope, which is an important factor in effecting cognitive or behavioral change.
- Groups provide exposure to role models along with expanded opportunities for social interaction.
- The group tends to focus on the inner strengths of the individual, rather than on the person's pathology (Riessman, 1997).

ADVANTAGES UNIQUE TO ONLINE SELF-HELP GROUPS

- Convenience of access. The asynchronous online self-help groups are available to members any time of day and any day of the week.
- Increased access to diverse members. The nature of text-based relationships removes most of the influence of status, age, and even gender.
- People in rural or other remote areas (there is the same lack of access in small towns) now have access to a wide range of self-help support that was previously unavailable to them.
- Access to peers who are experiencing disorders and conditions that do not have f2f groups.
- There is no need for oral fluency or public speaking abilities. People who would be too embarrassed to speak in public easily engage in public typing.
- Portability. Members do not have to leave the group if they move to a new region (Finn and Lavitt, 1994; King, 1994). "Exchanges can be interrupted by other tasks without affecting the quality of communication" (Kurtz, 1997).
- In the online self-help groups, relationships can form by "backchannel" communications—private e-mail sent between two people who met in the group forum.

DISADVANTAGES THAT ONLINE SELF-HELP GROUPS SHARE WITH F2F GROUPS

- It is difficult to assess the therapeutic value or to predict which of the members are being helped. Online groups are similar to f2f groups in that there is a strong self-selected positive bias; the group is composed of people who found value in their membership.
- There is a potential exposure to misinformation, along with the possibility of raising false hopes. There is little data regarding the downside of f2f self-help groups, but the potential for the dissemination of false information is mentioned by several of the research articles reviewed here (Madara, 1997; Humphreys, 1997).

DISADVANTAGES UNIQUE TO THE ONLINE SELF-HELP GROUPS

- Technology issues. Membership in online communities is limited to people with access to computers and the ability to type. Learning how to

access and participate in a desired online group may be far more complicated than showing up for a f2f meeting.
- Misunderstandings due to the nature of text-based relationships. There is
  a propensity for disinhibition, projection, and transference, when there are
  no visual or auditory inputs that can place the text in its proper context
  or assist the correct interpretation of that text.
- High signal-to-noise ratio. There are few controls in online self-help
  groups to prevent people from posting erroneous information or messages that are off the topic.
- Individual and group privacy is not fully guaranteed on the Internet.
  Search engines can access the archived text records of most public online
  self-help groups.
- Absence of group rules and guidelines. The sharing of wrong information
  among members and the inability to dispute it in a timely manner can be
  troublesome (Finn, 1999).
- Online groups are subject to the problems of all e-mail users. Individuals
  may become the target of verbal harassment, junk e-mail, or observation
  without their knowledge (Madara, 1997).

INTERNET SUPPORT GROUPS AND TEXT-BASED
GROUP THERAPY

Hundreds of mental health professionals worldwide are now offering to
establish a therapeutic relationship over the Internet by use of e-mail exchanges and/or
real-time chat rooms, most often for a fee. A survey of 136 websites offering some
form of Internet therapy, usually for a fee, revealed that fully one-third of the
sites were hosted by someone who had no mental health-related degree or license
(Heinline *et al.*, 2003). There is no governing body that can monitor the quality of
care provided online or the competency of the professionals providing treatment.
"A poorly informed consumer in crisis who has a history of mental health difficulties will be an easy target for incompetent or fraudulent Internet counseling service
providers" (Sampson *et al.*, 1997).

Internet support groups can be thought of as professionally assisted text-
based mutual aid. Facilitated group therapy online is very rare, compared to the
number of people that use the open, unmoderated Internet self-help groups. These
text-only support group environments represent an underused resource that can be
potentially very therapeutic to appropriate clients. In a small, closed, and moderated online support group, the therapeutic advantages of text-based relationships
outweigh the disadvantages. These online groups can be organized and moderated
by mental health professionals as an adjunct to f2f therapy with clients, and as a

method of last resort for someone in need who is unwilling or unable to present for f2f treatment.

There are unique legal and moral obligations a therapist has to clients that he/she treats in an Internet support group. Part of that obligation can be accommodated by extensive initial screening for the appropriateness of the client to this type of intervention. It is very important to solicit fully informed consent prior to treatment. There is an obligation to inform potential clients about the advantages as well as the disadvantages of text-only relationships. Other ethical, legal, and moral imperatives remain but are less defined; for example, it is not clear how a licensed mental health worker can provide online services to people from other states and other countries, when their license to practice is most often restricted to one state.

The occurrence of this type of text-based group therapy, and its obvious advantages to some, is spurring regulatory bodies to attempt to accommodate the new communication technologies. Until more empirical data on Internet group therapy is available, therapists need to proceed slowly and assist one another in evaluating their groups to ensure that clients are receiving quality care. The use of e-mail by therapists to consult with each other, and other mental health professionals, is a growing practice. Research results from studies of the value of Internet therapy can guide professionals involved in creating and leading text-based mutual-aid support groups.

Several organizations have developed guidelines for Internet therapy. Many of these guidelines apply to the situation faced by a professional leading an Internet support group. The National Board for Certified Counselors, Inc. (NBCC) has developed a set of standards for the ethical practice of what they call WebCounseling. The standards include this one: "WebCounselors need to mention on their websites those problems they believe to be inappropriate for WebCounseling. While no conclusive research has been conducted to date, those topics might include sexual abuse as a primary issue, violent relationships, eating disorders, and psychiatric disorders that involve distortions of reality."

The International Society for Mental Health Online was formed in 1997 to promote the understanding, use, and development of online information and technology for the international mental health community. One of the goals of this organization is to explore and develop the use of computer-assisted communication in the work of mental health. The ISMHO website provides an excellent set of ethical guidelines for working with clients in text-based environments. One guideline that applies to Internet support groups read as follows:

Another issue specific to online mental health services is that the counselor can be a great distance from the client. This may limit the counselor's ability to respond to an emergency. The counselor should therefore in these cases obtain the name and telephone number of a qualified local (mental) health care provider (who preferably already knows the client, such as his or her primary care physician).

One of the advantages of text-based relationships is the ease and convenience of access. By providing a text-based therapeutic environment on an e-mail discussion list, both the clients and the therapist have the ability to schedule their participation at their optimal time. One factor that limits interpersonal closeness on the large, open self-help online groups is the lack of boundaries. Such open forms are loosely organized and members frequently come and go without notice to others involved. An online support group has boundaries set in advance, in terms of the number of members and the time commitment required to participate. The moderation of the group prevents the kind of argumentative flame wars that can disrupt open online self-help groups. When the therapist has the ability as a moderator to approve every message before it is posted to the group, they can ask members to reconsider a potentially disruptive message. This is a capacity not possible with f2f groups.

There is also nothing preventing group members from sending each other private e-mail. Members could be encouraged to bring such "backchannel" relationships to the group process. There is no equivalent to this capacity in f2f groups. It would be similar to two group members whispering to each other, a disruptive event in a f2f group. In the online group, any member can send private messages to any other member. The ability of the facilitator to also have concurrent private conversations with individual members is a unique advantage of Internet support groups.

There is an alternative to both Internet self-help groups and Internet support groups. An open unmoderated "self-help" group that is hosted by a trained mental health professional has many of the advantages of Internet mutual-aid groups with fewer of the disadvantages. The host can act as an administrator and as a supportive influence in the group discussions. A group of this type was hosted by Dr. Hsiung, who published a report with the explanatory title *The best of both worlds: An online self-help group hosted by a mental health professional* (Hsiung, 2000). Rather than leading the group as in the f2f model of group therapy, the host focused on how to "empower the helpers in the group" (p. 947). The group is not moderated, but the host did at least scan every message as it was posted. The host reserved the right to prevent someone from further posting if they ignored the rule to "Please be civil, even when provoked" (p. 943).

ETHICAL CONSIDERATIONS IN RESEARCHING TEXT-BASED MUTUAL AID

The ease of public access of Internet-based groups, though it brings the advantages of broad participation and increases the likelihood of a person's finding the support they need, also brings the possibility of exploitation. Researchers have discovered the wealth of data in personal postings to public Internet spaces, which brings up an ethical dilemma: People frequently put very personal information online, with the intent of only communicating with a specific group and not with a researcher looking for data. Having personal information appear in a journal can make the person feel exploited, even violated, especially with postings to groups dealing with sensitive subjects, such as sexual abuse or AIDS.

Unlike a researcher taking notes at a face-to-face support meeting, no one knows whether anyone is reading their online postings unless you tell them. Waskul and Douglass (1996) highlight this concern. They claim that Internet text-based social interaction is never completely public or private, but is always a mixture of both. It is public in terms of accessibility, but often private in content. It requires that researchers respect the private nature of the group's existence, expectations, and its text content, regardless of the public nature of its format. This is especially so since the media is often very quick to pick up any topic about the Internet which is negative or controversial, and any data used by a researcher may end up being splashed across a newspaper or magazine read by millions of people.

CONCLUSION

Many of the findings regarding the value of Internet self-help groups agree with results from studies of real-life self-help groups. Access to others with similar concerns, exposure to others' self-disclosures and the opportunity to help others all operate in online self-help groups as elements of their therapeutic value. Existing research survey data, combined with anecdotal observations and case reports, indicate that members of online self-help groups receive benefits that go beyond what f2f groups can offer. A vast number of such groups exist only online, devoted to topics for which there is no f2f self-help. There is a higher level of self-disclosure online than in comparable f2f groups. Text-based social support relationships formed in virtual communities are very real and valuable to the people involved. They often result in an effort to meet f2f.

For people who live in rural settings, people with disabilities that inhibit their movement, and for others who are emotionally unable or unwilling to seek f2f support, online self-help forums are their only opportunity to experience the benefits of peer support. Madara (1999) mentions a group devoted to survivors of traumatic car accidents and one for victims of stalkers. People confined to hospital beds, people with rare disorders, people without transportation, or someone who is caretaking for a disabled person and can not leave their side to attend a f2f group can now connect to the world, find others like themselves, and share their experiences and strengths and coping strategies (Madara & White, 1997).

One study reported that there are 1.7 million people who are homebound in the U. S. because of a disability. In addition to their actual disability, they often have to cope with depression, loneliness, and lack of social interaction (Finn, 1999). Even for people who have family and friends who are supportive, as well as f2f social support readily available, an unwillingness to burden others or a belief that only fellow sufferers can understand them keeps many from using the available support (Joinson, 2003). Shift workers often have a hard time attending f2f self-help groups because they are at work at the time the meetings are held. Text-based mutual aid is the only kind readily available to people in such circumstances.

Text-only therapeutic relationships are certainly not a panacea. The unique disadvantages of text-based communication may not be evident, especially to a newcomer. It is hard to tell much about who someone is and what their motives are when all you see is the text they write. People do not have relationships with a blank page. People fill in the missing pieces in their picture of others they meet online, never fully aware that the picture they are forming is based in large part on their own unconscious desires regarding who they want that person to be and how they want them to act. This occurs at the same time the person is taking advantage of the anonymity inherent in text-only communications to present their best possible face. A feedback loop can arise, as these selective presentations are responded to in kind, creating a "hyperpersonal aspect" to Internet communications (Walther, 1996). "Hyperpersonal interaction is not inherently harmful, but its effects on support-group members, particularly those who are psychologically vulnerable, should be the subject of scrutiny by human service professionals and researchers" (Waldron et al., 2000).

For the person who is motivated to participate in a text-based social support network, the Internet offers a tremendous variety of "invite yourself in, open to anyone" mutual-aid communities. When others in that forum quote one's messages or acknowledge one's contribution, it generates a very real sense of having achieved status in that group. Frequent posting of short, helpful, and/or self-disclosing messages seems to be the way to raise one's social status in text-based groups. Status and power in such virtual communities is gained or lost in a different manner from that in "real life," but the exact mechanism is one of many questions for future research to elucidate.

A fundamental therapeutic element of Internet self-help groups is the way they function as normative communities. This is the process by which members become less stigmatized. The experience of mutual aid transforms them from being abnormal in general society to normal within the group. This empowers the individual member in a unique and powerful manner. This normalization can not be duplicated by professional counseling. It is implemented primarily through the process of reciprocal self-disclosure. It is amazing how powerfully therapeutic it is for a new member when they are first exposed to the implicit knowledge and factual evidence that other people have coped with the same obstacles and challenges, with the assistance of the group, with which the new member had been struggling alone.

Internet self-help groups are one of the means that people in need can use to make a therapeutic connection with others, but for every advantage that is known to exist about these text-based therapeutic forums, there is at least one disadvantage. We have made great strides in coming to understand this medium, and how we interact with it and through it, but many interesting research questions are yet to be resolved. For example, Internet groups are much easier to join than f2f ones. What are the consequences of their being much easier to leave as well? Not having a f2f social presence reduces anxiety about sharing. What is the effect of not experiencing the hugs and handshakes and other personal contact that comes with f2f groups? Future research will elaborate on what is known from current results. Many of the variables of text-based mutual-aid interpersonal interactivity remain to be more fully investigated.

REFERENCES

Braithwaite, D., Waldron, V., & Finn, J. (1999). Communication of social support in computer mediated self help groups. *Health Communication, 11,* 123–151.

Cummings, J. N., Sproull, L., & Kiesler, S. B. (2002). Beyond hearing: Where real world and online support meet. *Group Dynamics: Theory, Research and Practice, 6*(1), 78–88.

Davison K. P., Pennebaker J. W., & Dickerson S. S. (2000). Who talks? The social psychology of illness support groups. *American Psychologist, 55*(2), 205–217.

Donn, J. E., & Sherman, R. C. (2002). Attitudes and practices regarding the formation of romantic relationships on the Internet. *CyberPsychology & Behavior, 5*(2), 107–123.

Dubin, J., Simon, V., & Orem, J. (1997). *Analysis of survey results.* Presented as a paper for New York University School of Social Work, NY.

Finn, J. (1999). An exploration of helping processes in an online self-help group focusing on issues of disability. *Health and Social Work, 24*(3), 220–231.

Finn, J., & Banach, M. (2000). Victimization online: The downside of seeking human services for women on the Internet. *CyberPsychology & Behavior, 3*(5), 785–796.

Finn, J., & Lavitt, M. (1994). Computer-based self-help groups for sexual abuse survivors. *Social Work With Groups, 17,* 21–46.

Galegher, J., Sproull, L., & Kiesler, S. (1998). Legitimacy, authority, and community in electronic support groups. *Written Communications, 15,* 439–530.

Goode, J., & Johnson, M. (1991). Putting out the flames: The etiquette and law of email. *Online,* 61–65.

Harris Interactive Inc. (2005). Number of "Cyberchondriacs"—U. S. Adults Who Go Online for Health Information Increases to Estimated 117 Million. The Harris Poll #54, July 15, 2005. Retrieved May 20, 2005 from http://www.harrisinteractive.com/harris_poll/index.asp?PID=584

Heinline, K., Welfel E., Richmond, E., & Rak, C. (2003). The scope of WebCounseling: A survey of services and compliance with NBCC Standards for the Ethical Practice of WebCounseling. *Journal of Counseling and Development, 81,* 61–69.

Hsiung, R. (2000). The best of both worlds: An online self-help group hosted by a mental health professional. *CyberPsychology and Behavior, 3*(6), 935–950.

Huang, M., & Alessi, N. E. (1996). The Internet and the future of psychiatry. *American Journal of Psychiatry, 153*(7), 861–869.

Humphreys, K. (1997). Individual and social benefits of mutual aid/self-help groups. *Social Policy, 27*(3), 12–20.

Humphreys, K., & Rappaport, J. (1994). Researching self-help/mutual aid groups and organizations: Many roads, one journey. *Applied and Preventive Psychology, 3,* 217–231.

Humphreys K., Wing, S., McCarty D., Chappel J., Gallant, L., Haberle, B. *et al.* (2004). Self-help organizations for alcohol and drug problems: Towards evidence-based practice and policy. *Journal of Substance Abuse Treatment, 26*(3), 151–158.

Jacobs, K., & Goodman, G. (1989). Psychology and self-help groups: Predictions on a partnership. *American Psychologist, 44*(3), 536–545.

Johnson, K., Ravert, R., & Everton, A. (2001). Hopkins teen central: Assessment of an Internet-based support system for children with cystic fibrosis. *Pediatrics, 107*(2), 396.

Joinson, A. (1998). Causes and implications of disinhibited behavior on the Internet. In J. Gackenbach (Ed.), *Psychology and the Internet: Intrapersonal, interpersonal and transpersonal implications* (pp. 43–60). San Diego, CA: Academic Press.

Joinson, A. (2003). *Understanding the psychology of Internet Behavior.* New York: Palgrave MacMillan.

Lea, M., & Spears, R. (1992). Paralanguage and social perception in computer-mediated communication. *Journal of Organizational Computing, 2*, 321–341.

Kaufmann C. L. (1996). The lions den: Social identities and self help groups. *The Community Psychologist, 29*, 11–13.

Kiesler, S., Siegel, J., & McGuire, T. W. (1984). Social psychological aspects of computer-mediated communication. *American Psychologist, 39*(10), 1123–1134.

King, S. A. (1994). Analysis of electronic support groups for recovering addicts. *Interpersonal Computing and Technology: An Electronic Journal for the 21st Century 2*(3), 47–56. Retrieved May 20, 2005, from http://www.helsinki.fi/science/optek/1994/n3/king.txt

King, S. A. (1995). Effects of mood states on social judgments in cyberspace: Self focused sad people as the source of flame wars. Retrieved May 20, 2005, from http://webpages.charter.net/stormking/mood.html

Kurtz, L. F. (1997). *Self-help and support groups: A handbook for practitioners.* Thousand Oaks, CA: Sage Publications.

Levine, M., & Perkins, D.V. (1987). Self help groups. In M. Levine, D.V. Perkins, and D. M. Perkins, (Eds.), *Principles of community psychology: Perspectives and applications.* New York: Oxford University Press.

Madara, E. J. (1984). MASH in its newest and most futuristic form—The computer networks. *Exchange Networks,* Summer 1984, 7–8.

Madara, E. J. (1997). The mutual-aid self-help online revolution. *Social Policy, 27*(3), 20–26.

Madara, E. J. (1999). From church basements to world wide web sites: The growth of self-help support groups online. *International Journal of Self Help & Self Care, 1*(1), 37–48.

Madara, E. J., Kalafat, J., & Miller, B. N. (1988). The computerized self-help clearinghouse: Using "high tech" to promote "high touch" support networks. *Computers in Human Services, 3*(3/4), 39–53.

Madara, E. J., & White, B. J. (1997). On-line mutual support: The experience of a self-help clearinghouse. *Information & Referral, 19*, 91–108.

Mann, C., & Stewart, F. (2000). *Internet communication and qualitative research: A handbook for researching online.* Thousand Oaks, CA: Sage Publications.

McKenna, K. Y. A., & Bargh, J. A. (1998). Coming out in the age of the Internet: Identity "demarginalization" from virtual group participation. *Journal of Personality and Social Psychology, 75,* 681–694.

Noonan, R. J. (1998). The psychology of sex: A mirror from the Internet. In J. Gackenbach (Ed.), *Psychology and the Internet: Intrapersonal, interpersonal and transpersonal implications* (pp. 143–168). San Diego, CA: Academic Press

Pew. (2001). *Online communities: Networks that nurture long-distance relationships and local ties.* Pew Internet and American Life Project Survey, October 31, 2001. Retrieved July 30. 2005, from http://www.pewinternet.org/reports/toc.asp?Report=47

Pew. (2002). *Counting on the Internet.* Pew Internet and American Life Project Survey, December 29, 2002. Retrieved July 30, 2005 from http://www.pewinternet.org/reports/toc.asp?Report=80

Postmes, T., Spears, R., & Lea, M. (2002). Inter-group differentiation in computer-mediated communication: Effects of depersonalization. *Group Dynamics, 6*, 3–16.

Preece, J. (1999). Empathic communities: Balancing emotional and factual communication. *Interacting with Computers: The Interdisciplinary Journal of Human–Computer Interaction, 12*, 63–77.

Preece, J., & Ghozati, K. (2001). Observations and explorations of empathy online. In R. R. Rice & J. E. Katz (Eds.), *The Internet and health communication: Experience and expectations* (pp. 237–260). Thousand Oaks, CA: Sage Publications

Preece, J., & Maloney-Krichmar, D. (2003) Online communities. In J. Jacko & Sears, A. (Eds.) *Handbook of human–computer interaction* (pp. 596–620). Mahwah, NJ: Lawrence Erlbaum Associates

Reid, E. M. (1994). Cultural formations in text-based virtual realities. M. A. Thesis, University of Melbourne. Retrieved May 20, 2005 from http://www.ludd.luth.se/mud/aber/articles/cult-form.thesis.html

Riessman, F. (1997). Ten self-help principles. *Social Policy, 27*(3), 6–11.

Rheingold, H. (1993). *The virtual community: Homesteading on the electronic frontier.* New York: Harper Collins.

Salem, D. A., Bogat, G. A., & Reid, C. (1997). Mutual help goes on-line. *Journal of Community Psychology, 25*(2), 198–207.

Sampson, J., Kolodinsky, R. W., & Greeno, B. P. (1997). Counseling on the information highway: Future possibilities and potential problems. *Journal of Counseling and Development, 75*, 203–211.

Sparks, S. (1992). Exploring electronic social support groups. *American Journal of Nursing, Dec*, 62–65.

Sproull, L., & Kiesler, S. (1984). Encountering an alien culture. *Journal of Social Issues, 40*(3), 31–48

Sproull, L., & Faraj, S. (1995). Atheism, sex, and databases: The Net as a social technology. In B. Kahin & J. Keller (Eds.) *Public access to the Internet.* Cambridge: MIT Press.

Stein, D. J. (1997). Psychiatry on the Internet: Survey of an OCD mailing list. *Psychiatric Bulletin, 21*, 95–98.

Suler, J. (2004). The online disinhibition effect. *CyberPsychology and Behavior, 7*(3), 321–326.

Waldron, V. R., Lavitt, M., & Kelley, D. (2000). The nature and prevention of harm in technology-mediated self-help settings: Three exemplars. In J. Finn & G. Holden (Eds.), *Human services online: A new arena for service delivery* (pp. 267–393). New York: Haworth.

Walther, J. B. (1996). Computer-mediated communication: Impersonal, interpersonal, and hyperpersonal interaction. *Communication Research, 23*(1), 3–43

Walther, J. B. (1997). Group and interpersonal effects in international computer-mediated collaboration. *Human Communication Research, 23*(3), 342–369.

Walther, J. B., & Boyd, S. (2002). Attraction to computer-mediated social support. In C. A. Lin & D. Atkin (Eds.), *Communication technology and society: Audience adoption and uses* (pp. 153–188). Cresskill, NJ: Hampton Press.

Walstrom, M. K. (2000). "You know, who's the thinnest?": Combating surveillance and creating safety in coping with eating disorders online. *CyberPsychology & Behavior, 3*(5), 761–781.

Waskul, D., & Douglass, M. (1996). Considering the electronic participant: Some potential observations on the ethics of online research. *The Information Society, 12*(2), 129–140.

Wellman, B. (1996). An electronic group is virtually a social network. In S. Kiesler (Ed.), *Culture of the Internet.* (pp. 179–205). Mahwah, NJ: Lawrence Erlbaum.

Worotynec, Z. S. (2000). The good, the bad, and the ugly: Listserv as support. *CyberPsychology & Behavior, 3*(5), 797–810.

CHAPTER 10

Cyber Shrinks: Expanding the Paradigm

Joanie Farley Gillispie
Department of Behavioral and Biological Sciences
University of California, Berkeley Extension
Mill Valley, California

INTRODUCTION

The mental health profession is unprepared that within a few years there may be as many people seeking professional counseling over the Internet as there are looking for it face-to-face (Alleman, 2002, p. 199).

Many things are happening in cyberspace that affect the practice of mental health. Some professionals now conduct therapy entirely online. Others are beginning to include some aspects of electronic communication in their clinical practices. Patients want to know if online therapy is effective, or they come to us wanting to understand worrisome cyber behaviors. Some seasoned clinicians are adamant that conducting therapy electronically is impossible, while others believe that Internet-driven mental health services will eventually become a viable part of health care (Fisher & Fried, 2003; Grohol, 2005; Morahan-Martin, 2004). What's a professional to do?

How much is the Internet impacting the profession and practice of mental health? A lot. One third of the 700 professionals attending a risk-management workshop in California raised their hands when asked if they were seeing patients with Internet-related problems (D. Nickelson, personal communication, Feb. 4, 2005). The responses of these clinicians reinforce the public's perception that many of us are engaging in unhealthy cyber behaviors. But are we? Estimates are that 68% of American adults are online daily (Rainie, 2005). This figure jumps to nine out of ten young people who spend 2–10 hours per day multitasking online (Roberts

Psychology and the Internet: Intrapersonal, Interpersonal, and Transpersonal Implications

et al., 2005). With so many communicating in cyberspace, it is no wonder that clinicians estimate about 30% of their practice concerns either professional issues online (D. Nickelson, personal communication, Nov. 14, 2005) or the problematic Internet use of patients (Gillispie and Gackenbach, in press).

Written for mental health clinicians, this chapter offers an overview of professional issues arising from widespread Internet use. Several topics of interest to clinicians are discussed concerning how the Internet is changing their work and their patients. First, as with any new subfield of psychology, a review of the research about Internet use is important before professionals consider practicing online *or* treating patients with cyber problems. This review sets the stage for reframing risk management in cyberspace. Next, examples of clinical practice online are considered with the goal of expanding the paradigm so that mental health clinicians ill feel more comfortable and competent treating cyber problems online and offline.

PROFESSIONAL ISSUES ONLINE

EXPANDING THE PARADIGM (WIIFM? PX!)

(What's in it for me? Please explain!)

The profession of mental health is online: conducting research, testing, communicating with and counseling patients, supervising, teaching, consulting, and conducting the business of psychology. Is this a good thing? We now have 10 years of data, lots of discussion, many questions, but few answers. The Internet has not only amplified the way we communicate but changed who we are online. To quote Turkle (2005), "in cyberspace your words are your deeds, your words are your body. And you feel these word-deeds and this word-body quite viscerally" (p. 1). Before venturing into the digital age professionally, we need to be able to interpret the exchange of "word-deeds and word-bodies" as they manifest at light-speed in cyberspace discourse. How do we feel about communicating this way? How does it change our patients and us?

For clinicians, the first steps into a new arena are usually ethical and legal ones. At this point in time, terra firma legal and ethical guidelines for mental health professionals can be cautiously applied to cyberspace (see the California Psychological Association's "Tips for Telepsychology," 2005), and the fit is not perfect. Problems exist when applying psychological theories, jurisprudence, and assumptions about behavior to the vastness of cyberspace communication. Further, the Internet encourages a multiplicity of ways of being that challenge theories and systems of psychology. For example, offline models of psychotherapy lean heavily on an accurate assessment of a person's stage of development, identity, affiliations, and soundness of reality testing in order to craft interventions. Online, however, these constructs are mutable and highly sensitive to technological interference or interaction effects, perhaps due to the archtexture of the Internet itself, they are even resistant to classification entirely. Haraway (1991) believes that the Internet has upset social hierarchy and political power, especially the status of gender, race, sexuality, and class. She urges us to analyze the human-computer, the cyborg,

> a hybrid of machine and organism, a creature of social reality and fiction...a condensed image of both imagination and material reality ... transgressed boundaries, potent fusions, and dangerous possibilities which progressive people might explore as one part of needed political work (pp. 149–151).

Everything online is mediated by the cyborg. It is not human-to-human discourse but human-machine-human, and the machine keeps changing its stripes. Online is not like face-to-face. There are heightened similarities and exponential differences. First, everyone has a voice. Second, no one is in charge (Voice Over Internet Protocol, 2005). We have cyberqueer theory, which now applies to all of us. The Internet allows projections of alternative sexualities and makes it easy for the straight to bend a little (Plant, 2001). In concert with who we are on ground, cyberqueer theory applies to all of us because we can now be *out* in any way we want to be, Dicey or poignant admixtures of fantasy and realism are the norm. Everyone can lie or express their true identities online. This freedom makes it even more difficult for clinicians to understand the cyborg and navigate their psyches (and ours) in cyberspace.

One cannot simply upload psychology (or anything else, for that matter) to cyberspace without a radical shift in perspective (British Association for Counseling Practitioners, 2005; Grohol, 1998; Jones, 2000; 1998; Turkle, 2005). Radicalism begins with the status quo, questions that challenge existing epistemologies and power:

1. Who's in control online?
2. How technologically competent should clinicians be?
3. What is good and bad "netiquette"?
4. Where does *e*therapy take place?
5. How does privacy, confidentiality, and anonymity online compare to offline?
6. How do the following manifest online: diversity, culture, identity, relationship, sexuality, discourse, power, body, emotion, competency, efficacy, harm, and contraindications?
7. How do we know what we know about practicing in cyberspace?

OVERVIEW OF THE RESEARCH

FROM RESEARCH TO PROFESSIONAL PRACTICE

The route from radicalism to practice often depends on voices that back the system and won't be silenced. With the Internet, both the vocies and the system itself are radicalized. The heuristic in Psychology that evidence-based practice, derived of course from rigorous research, promotes positive therapeutic outcomes (Zane, 2005) is foundational. However, data from studies investigating professional issues online have not yet been digested by the average clinician (Alleman, 2002; Ritterband *et al.*, 2003). Further, the research available is limited by methodological problems, lack of generalizability (Alleman, 2002; Kraut *et al.*, 2004; Skinner & Zack, 2004), and the radical nature of cyborg interactions. Fortunately, evidence about the efficacy of online treatment and professional practices are starting to appear in the psychological literature and in continuing educational workshops. This information should help clinicians expand their skills by increasing knowledge of cyber culture, the cyborg, as well as psychology online (Barnett & Sheetz, 2003; Glueckauf *et al.*, 2003; Ragusa & VandeCreek, 2003).

There are several concerns that clinicians should keep in mind when review-ing the research. Online research, testing, and Internet-based experimenting have clear advantages (Allman, 2002; Lukoff, 2005). On the plus side is increased access to participants, especially special populations such as the disabled, the elderly, or other groups that may not participate in research because of stigma (e.g., drug deal-ers or sexual offenders). Also, more can be accomplished in less time and with lower overall expenditures.

But there is a downside. Negative effects of Internet-based research include the inability to debrief subjects immediately, over-reliance on computer technol-ogy, lack of generalizability, and inaccuracies in integrating offline data with online outcomes with offline treatment. Typically, there is more variance with online data, which may result in inaccurate, but still published, data and studies. Further, test security is a significant problem online, as any experiment in the public domain can be pirated (Naglieri *et al.*, 2004).

However, experimenting and testing using the Internet is fast becoming a standard method of research (Reips, 2000). For example, online clinical trials inves-tigating the effectiveness of Web-based cognitive behavioral interventions for panic disorder (Farvolden *et al.*, 2004) and self-help skills for depression (Clark *et al.*, 2004) have shown promising results for patients in reducing symptom severity and increasing treatment compliance.

In addition to cyber-based research in professional journals, there are many personal and public cyber stories that provide fodder for the analyst and angst for a public that looks to us to help solve these human problems. The Internet allows our children get to know and understand people from all corners of the world but they are also engaging in cyber sexual behaviors that are making front-page news. But they are not doing anything adults aren't doing: online compulsions, cyber affairs, E-Bay shop-a-holics, Internet porn, live cam sexual exploitation of infants, and online gaming are front page news. Parents are shocked, kids are connected more to their online lives than to their communities, and Judges want to know how the Internet shapes anti-social acts of convicted individuals who have used the Internet as an accessory to their offenses (e.g., terrorist threats online, cyber stalking, youth sex offenders who are consumers of online porn, and pedophiles who file-share child pornography,). It's not only mental health clinicians who are concerned about how to help their patients, either on- or offline, but social scientists and policy makers are paying attention. They want to begin informing the public about trends emerging from Internet use, especially the positive and negative psychosocial correlates, rather than wait the 30 years it took to disseminate information about the social and behavioral effects of television viewing (Roberts et al., 2005).

Just what do the data suggest and what do clinicians need to get from this research to help their patients? Ten years ago experts were concerned that the Internet would corrupt our youth, destroy families, suck up all our time, and turn us into automatons. As a result, a new disorder called Internet Addiction emerged (Young, 2005, 1998, 1996). Early estimates of how much time online was too much ranged from 4 to 10 hours per week (Young, 1998). Now, 2 to 10 hours *per day* does not necessarily appear to lead to problems (Rainie, 2005). Youth aged 8 to 18 who were classified as heavy Internet users by the Kaiser Internet Survey (Roberts *et al.*, 2005) reported spending more time with friends and family, more time for recreation and part-time jobs, and good report cards, than less frequent users (p. 51). The investigators concluded that these results "raise a red flag against too easily concluding that time spent with media is synonymous with time taken from other activities" (Rainie & Horrigan, 2005). One of the earliest studies examining the psychological and social correlates of Internet use found that 10% to 15% of college students were more likely to experience depression, social isolation, adjustment difficulties, and drop-out of school as a result of excessive Internet use (Kraut *et al.*, 1998). However, eight years later, these findings were disconfirmed (Kraut *et al.*, 2002; Morahan-Martin & Schumacher, 2003; Nichols & Nicki, 2004; Rainie & Horrigan, 2005; Seaman, 2005).

THE ONLINE–OFFLINE CONNECTION

The Internet is not a panacea. Divergent opinions abound concerning whether online habits are a cause or effect of offline psychological distress. There is also disagreement about whether cyber problems and mental disorders can be treated successfully online. Nevertheless, cyber research about our online habits suggests that some online behaviors do have deleterious offline consequences. The three As of cyberpsychology communication (access, anonymity, autonomy) (Suler, 2004, 2005) appear to facilitate the emergence of certain problems offline. Psychologist D. Jacobs, Professor Emeritus at Loma Linda University in Redlands, California, and leading authority on gambling and compulsive behaviors, believes that certain premorbid experiences, especially trauma, may tip the scales toward pathological Internet use. Jacobs views any repetitive behavior, either offline or online, as an anxiety-reduction, stress-management strategy. He finds that the accessibility and privacy of certain online activities, such as shopping, gambling, and cyber porn, may increase one's addiction potential. But Jacob cautions that this "transference" is likely to occur only in predisposed individuals (D. Jacobs, personal communication, Oct. 17, 2005).

Other investigators propose that Internet-driven pathology per se does not exist. Denegri-Knott and Taylor (2005) believe that offline pathology is just acted out online. Preexisting conditions, such as other addictions, impulse control disorders, and anxiety or mood disorders, make it appear that the Internet is the cause of the problem rather than the effect. Yet, others disagree and propose that factors such as isolation, male gender, and personality types such as introversion, predict problematic Internet behaviors more robustly than one's offline psychological state (Koch & Pratarelli, 2004).

The interactivity of Internet technology increases every year. It is itself a disinhibitory process, potentially creating more of the necessary preconditions for Jacob's theories about compulsivity and impulse control problems online leading to pathological Internet use. Widyanto and Griffith's review, *Internet Addiction: Does It Really Exist?*, explains that the addiction potential of the Internet arises from the unique constructs of Internet technology (see Chapter 6, this issue). Never before has so much been available so quickly, so easily, and with so much realism.

Internet use taps our glut potential (Greenfield, 2004). We stay online longer as a result and do more, increasing the potential for offline effects (Martin & Petry, 2005; Thornburgh & Lin, 2002). Internet activities feel good. We get into a zone online. It's actually a mental state akin to lucid dreaming (J. Gackenbach, personal communication, June 7, 2006). This is one of the reasons we often find ourselves online more than we had planned to be. Online communications engender arousal, disinhibition, intimacy, and autonomy (Morahan-Martin and Shumacher, 2000; Suler, 2004) which can either inhibit or facilitate positive behaviors offline. For example a shy person can learn how to communicate with others online and then transfer these new skills to face to face encounters. Or, someone who regularly flames others in email may be reinforcing negative patterns of communication which spill into his or her communications offline.

Beard (2005) and others (Grohol, 2005; Kaltiala-Heino *et al.*, 2004; Shaw & Gant, 2002) concur that determining whether pathological Internet behaviors exist is complex, depending as much on contextual factors as psychological ones. Beard asks mental health professionals to be more proactive,

> rather than waiting for a crisis to occur and then picking up the pieces. Introducing new technologies and simultaneously using psychology to counteract negative effects may lessen the onset of difficulties and the development of crises ... regardless of whether or not internet addiction is a true "addiction," there are people developing a harmful dependence on the internet (2005, p. 13).

CYBER SEX AND THE POTENTIAL FOR HARM

Sexuality online is by far the biggest Internet-driven concern of parents, adults who work with kids, and couple's therapists. Clinicians will eventually encounter a cybersex issue that pushes the limits of their current knowledge. The effects of cyber sex and sexuality online are just beginning to be discussed in the literature. This discourse tends to minimize the negative social constructions of sexuality offline and focus primarily on the cyber issue.

Mental health practitioners need to be conversant with the culture of sexuality rather than assume that all cyber sexual activities are problematic. However, the data suggests that three cyber sexual activities: cyber affairs, compulsive cybersexual behaviors, and consuming cyber child pornography online, have increased potential to acted out offline (Quayle & Taylor, 2003). Adults who engaged in compulsive cybersex activities were found to have weaker social affiliations and were more likely to engage in a deviant lifestyle offline, but it is not clear which came first (Stack *et al.*, 2004). Initially, more men viewed cybersex online and were more likely to engage in a cyber affair, but now gender differences are disappearing. However, there are differences in the kinds of cyber sex activities males and females choose to experience. Men tend to explore sexual activities online for arousal, while women engage in emotionally intimate cyber chat first before progressing to sexual intimacy (Boies *et al.*, 2004; Subrahmanyam *et al.*, 2004). Several investigators have determined that the cyber psychology constructs (Suller, 2005) of anonymity and disinhibition fuel cybersexual behaviors, including cyberstalking and online infidelity. Approximately 30% of these online sexual behaviors migrate offline (Begner, 2005; Bell, 2001; Cooper, 2002; Cooper *et al.*, 2002).

Because the Internet has become the primary vehicle for both the production and worldwide transmission of child pornography (Bowker & Gray, 2004), file sharing and downloading these materials was found to contribute to an increased risk of offline sexual offending for adults with a sexual interest in children (Begner, 2005; Freeman-Longo, 2000; Quayle & Taylor, 2003; Thornberg & Lin, 2002). In addition, Internet technology itself increases the harm because it enables offenders to groom multiple victims. Massive distribution of sexually explicit materials depicting children appears to trigger, maintain, and reinforce sexual arousal, which contributes to offline offending (Nichols & Nicki, 2004). As many as 30% of sexual offenders at a California corrections reception center have the Internet as a component of their offense (M.R., personal communication, June 2006).

Mental health professionals today much expand their knowledge beyond harmful sexual activities online and realize how media use in general shapes sexuality, identity, affiliation, and behavior, especially with young people, before they help their patients with online issues (Lloyd, 2002). Adult cyber sexual issues are challenging online and offline but mental health professional are especially chanllenged when it comes to adolescent sexuality. While we do have some data regarding the cyber sexual behaviors of adults, there is very little we understand about adolescent sexual behaviors either offline or online (Moser *et al.*, 2004). In this country, there are political and attitudinal barriers to asking youngsters enough questions about their sexual habits. This makes it hard to assess how cyber sex activities may affect a young person's offline development. Unfortunately, few will describe the full range of their sexual behaviors unless specifically asked by clinicians (Bridges *et al.*, 2003).

Today's youth is saturated by surround-sound media sexuality. It has become so much a part of their discourse and culture, so embedded in everyday habits that online sex merges seamlessly into offline sex. Few adults really get this and clearly are not engaging in enough discourse with kids about sexuality. Byt kids are. They love to talk about sex, just not with most adults. Hooking up online, on cell phones, and on their iPods have made formerly private (and often secret) sexual acts public, shocking educators and parents. Covert (and subliminal) sexual and social messages, thousands of times more available online, appear to be shaping young people's attitudes and changing some of their sexual behaviors even more than explicit sex sites online (Subrahmanyam *et al.*, 2004).

While there is a dearth of information about adolescent sexuality in this country (Moser *et al.*, 2004), there *is* data emerging from other parts of the world that can help clinicians understand the effects of cybersexual habits on young peoples' offline behaviors. Swedish teens, ages 15–18, reported that they initiated more kinds of varied sexual behaviors offline as a result of cyber sex sites. Investigators also found that youth who consumed online pornography tended to use condoms during vaginal sexual intercourse only to prevent pregnancy. Unfortunately, these teens also reported a higher likelihood of engaging in unprotected anal sex as a result of viewing explicit anal sexual contact online because these scenarios did not emphasize safer sex practices in terms of prevention of sexually transmitted diseases (Haggstron-Nordin *et al.*, 2005).

Hopefully, more studies concerning Internet sexual activities will include adolescents (Gross, 2004) and investigate both positive and pro-active online habits as well as the sensationalism that surrounds cyber sex. For example one of the most positive uses of the Internet for sexual purposes is for Sex Ed (Morahan-Martin, 2004). Clearinghouses like the Sexuality Information and Education Council of the United States (SEICUS,org) and radio sex guru Dr. Drew (drdrew.com) allow kids to ask questions and get answers about sex and their sexuality. At this point, it is tempting to generalize findings from online sexuality research and assume that most Internet sex is harmful. However, investigators suggest that in the absence of compulsive, violent, or exploitative cyber habits, most Internet-driven behaviors, including sexual- and youth oriented ones, represent positive connections with others (Cooper & Griffin-Shelley, 2002; Noonan, 1998).

RISK MANAGEMENT IN CYBERSPACE

Legal and Ethical Concerns

Both cyber-shrink and cyber-patient liability issues have no precedent. The potential benefits-to-risk ratio of practicing psychology online leaves many of us confused and concerned about doing the right thing. Clearly, there are laws and ethical guidelines, confidentiality and privacy issues, professional development requirements, and maintaining comprehensive liability coverage are necessary for cyberspace practice. David Nicholson, APA's Practice Directorate expert, and Jeffery Thomas, California's Board of Psychology's Interim Chair, acknowledge that there is no case law at this point that drives standard of care in cyberspace (D. Nickelson, personal communication, November 14, 2005; J. Thomas, personal communication, October 20, 2005). Nickelson states that no professional licensing bodies have consensus regarding inclusive or exclusive criteria for practicing online.

What are we talking about anyway? Even the terminology lacks consistency and parameters distinguishing it from on ground practice. Is it telehealth, telemedicine, online counseling, etherapy, online therapy, ehealth, or a hybrid system? Now these descriptors are used interchangeably, often leaving us with comparing apples and oranges in the research. In addition to few directions and specific online professional guidelines for mental health professionals, recent advances in Voice Over Internet Protocols (VOIP) allow Internet users to operate outside the jurisdiction of the Federal Communications Commission's (FCC) state and federal regulations. The FCC does not regulate the Internet and has no way to safeguard the public interest online for *any activity* much less therapeutic ones (*Voice Over Internet Protocol,* 2005). According to Jeffery Thomas, Interim Executive Director California Board of Psychology, no one has yet been sued for practicing outside one's scope of practice by inadvertently, ignorantly, or intentionally causing harm to a patient with online therapeutic communications. But in a litigious and digital world it is a matter of when not if. Lessig (2005), assumes that legal and ethical issues concerning confidentiality or privacy on the Internet for all of us will require much more input from research institutions and the government than is currently the case (J. Thomas, personal communication, Oct. 20, 2005).

The lack of guidelines and standards in cyberspace is sobering to many clinicians who already communicate with their patients and colleagues online. Some may continue to conduct therapy online or utilize hybrid systems, while others avoid cyber practice entirely because they are sure that cyber psychological interventions are not effective and may even be anti-therapeutic. Alleman (2002) summarizes the jurisprudence issues of psychology online as placing clinicians in a double bind:

[there is] a crazy quilt of state and local laws with no protective guidelines established for internet services… If a professional believes that the risks are too great to allow the practice of ethical psychotherapy online, he or she should not attempt to provide it. This does not change the fact however that other professionals have already arrived at a different conclusion. Nor does it in the least influence the fact that potential clients will continue searching for counseling online. …If the ethical counselor is not online, who is? Going forward, the greatest ethical risk we may face is that we will write the rules or enforce the laws in such a way that competent, principled professionals are forced to exclude themselves from online availability. It cannot possibly be ethical to create such a trap for potential clients who are merely seeking help through technology that is available to them (p. 204).

PROFESSIONAL LIABILITY

How do clinicians protect themselves online? Major professional organizations, such as the American Psychology Association's Insurance Trust (APAIT), do not specifically include or exclude online therapy and have no plans to do so in the future. Stuart Benas, APAIT Supervisor of Field Underwriting, explains that the goal of a good insurance policy is to "cover the practice of psychology and if your practice is online, it should be covered." Benas adds that whether you are insured for online professional services or not is different from whether you may get sued (S. Benas, personal communication, Oct. 17, 2005).

How do clinicians make sure they use the Internet wisely without clear professional standards and when the digital method of delivery changes often? It's already hard to keep up with basic hardware and software upgrades. Old technologies expire and some new technologies age out of the market in a few years. Don Tapscott (2005) writes in the *Wall Street Journal* that the next 5 years will bring more "bundled" Internet services that orchestrate and link hundreds of devices we use every day through high-quality digital technology. As we become more dependent on these bundled services, both the clinician and consumer will become more technologically expert. Thus, it will not be incumbent upon the clinician alone to insure that a patient understands online communication technology.

A recent article in the California Psychological Association's (CPA) *Briefings* newsletter illustrated the liability of being unable to protect patients' and psychologists' privacy in a digital world. From a risk management perspective, this is a clinician's nightmare because cyberspace cannot be controlled. The CPA article discusses ways to protect personal information by using the "latest" web tool, Zaba Search, which supposedly can be used to protect your online information. However, by the time the article went to press, Zaba Search was no longer operative. In the online world, just when you think you understand how to use the system more wisely, new services, websites, and information disappear (Privacy? What privacy? 2005).

Societal concerns about privacy and freedom of expression continue to be played out in cyberspace as the government struggles with protection of the public versus individual rights online. In 2004, the Supreme Court overturned the 1998 Child Online Protection Act, ruling that Congress could not devise a plan to protect children from explicit sex sites that would not "trample the First Amendment" ("A law too far," 2004. p. B8). Identity theft could become a legal quandary for clinicians who maintain a presence online. Whittaker (2004) calls the phenomenon of stealing a web domain or online identity "cybersquatting" (p. 2). When websites expire, nothing prevents others from usurping the domain name and redirecting the innocent Web surfer to another site entirely. There are steps one can take to protect online communications. Encryption software and firewalls are recommended but are often difficult to install and expensive. Although the cyberspace issues in professional practice may seem more like science fiction than science, Skinner and Zack (2004) propose that all of these online risk management issues are no more insurmountable than those in the traditional office.

COMPETENCY AND SCOPE OF PRACTICE

In addition to technological and liability concerns online, an important dilemma that therapists face is how to practice within their scope of training in a field that is too new to have outcome-based criteria for training. At this point, most professional organizations lean on the law as it now stands in determining a clinician's duty and standard of care in the electronic delivery of mental health services. Clearly, the Internet, either as an adjunct to office practice or as a stand-alone cyber-experience, has great potential to provide mental health interventions. Most professionals erroneously assume that they can transfer existing skills to the Internet rather than first becoming familiar with Internet communication constructs, the culture of cyberspace, and cyber psychology (Glueckauf et al., 2003).

Koocher and Morray (2000) surveyed state attorneys general, asking how different jurisdictions regulated telepsychology. Their findings have been adapted by the California Board of Psychology in their January 2005 newsletter. Before engaging in the remote delivery of mental health services via electronic means, the California Board of Psychology's *Tips for Telepsychology* encourages practitioners to:

1. Carefully assess their cyber competence and consider the limitations in cyberspace.
2. Consult with one's professional liability insurance carrier and obtain a written confirmation of expanded coverage that includes Internet modalities.
3. Obtain consultation from colleagues and provide all patients with clear written guidelines for online treatment.

4. Document consultation and written plan in event of adverse incident.
5. Craft limits of confidentiality inclusive of electronic communication modalities.
6. Inform patients about special limitations of electronic services.
7. Assure clarity in third-party billing distinguishing *in vivo* versus virtual modalities ("Tips for Telepsychology," 2005, pp. 3–5).

As the history of communications media illustrates, even if there were discrete criteria for Internet practice, technological advances would soon change the online interaction enough so that the criteria may no longer apply. Talk about double bind! For example, research from two years ago examined text-only communications but now Internet technology has moved us beyond the written word, allowing interactive audio and graphics to add substantially to text. Soon immersible screens will enable users to insert themselves into the graphic, and haptic technology will bring the experience of touch. Multimedia and increased sensory effects with undoubtedly impact the way we communicate with each other online and thus shape professional competency guidelines. Soon, if we want to practice in cyber space, it will not be enough to have expertise in clinical issues but we will also need training in technology and computer science.

Specific guidelines for online practice have been established by some professional organizations. The British Association for Counseling Practitioners offers mental health clinicians guidance for online counseling, covering important topics such as scope of practice, assessing client suitability, legal and ethical mandates, confidentiality, online supervision, and data protection and storage issues (British Association for Counseling Practitioners, 2005). The American Counseling Association is another organization that has developed ethical guidelines for what they call "Technological Applications" of the counseling relationships which include informed consent, online security, emergency procedures, and maintaining a web domain (The American Counseling Association, 2005).

However, specific guidelines, separate from existing professional literature, are not yet incorporated into U.S. and Canadian professional organizations. Psychologist and attorney David Nickelson, the American Psychological Association's (APA) Director of Technology Special Projects, states that few constraints exist for either the practitioner or the consumer who is online. Nickelson acknowledges that telemedicine physicians now regularly use Internet technology for diagnostic purposes, but that online therapy exists at this point without enough expertise or mainstream acceptance. According to Nickelson and others (Maheu *et al.*, 2001; Mallen, 2004) due to the dot com bust, etherapy has not gained the market share that was originally anticipated (D. Nickelson, personal communication, Nov. 14, 2005). As a result, professionals need a good reason to allocate time and resources to invest in new treatment modalities, even online ones. Currently, few economic or professional incentives exist to convince clinicians that emental health services are viable. However, with more research about the effectiveness of online therapy "comprehensive, personalized, engaging, and empirically validated treatments could be quickly and easily distributed over the Internet" (Ritterband *et al.*, 2003, p. 528). Skinner and Zack (2004) raise an additional point about third-party payers. Insurers currently have no reason to reimburse for, or encourage, cyber therapy. But as soon as online treatment models show outcomes that are both cost- and therapeutically effective, insurance companies will likely become instant converts.

Just as insurers are invested in controlling the escalation of healthcare costs through gate-keeping mechanisms, professional licensing boards also limit who can practice. Skinner and Zack (2004) believe that state licensing organizations realize that online therapy models could eventually be counter to their own existence because "it is an easy next step to eliminating a regional licensing system in cyberspace altogether and consequently invalidating their existence" (p. 438). The authors point out that therapists from most other countries do not have restrictive national, jurisdictional, or clinical licensing requirements. European, South American, African, and Asian countries have much less exclusive regulations for providing services to patients who live elsewhere. For example, online connections with a therapist in Zimbabwe, a Jungian analyst in London, or a Milan Family Systems clinician may be easier than getting to an office appointment in one's own community.

Just *where* does online therapy take place? Conceptually on online professional practice jurisprudence has no precedent. The boundaries between cyberspace and geography are permeable and changeable. Experts disagree even about the most basic logistics of where is the therapist, where is the patient, and where is the jurisprudence? The American Psychological Association's stance is that there are two perspectives at play here (APA, 2004). The clinician would benefit if the jurisprudence was determined by the licensing state agency or board. If etherapy treatment is considered to occur in their state of licensure, then on ground risk management parameters will protect the professional relationship. On the other hand the consumers want the freedom to connect with a provider regardless of where one is licensed. Consumers want it both ways though: they want the freedom to access any treatment provider and they want protection from professional boards in the state where they reside should there be a breach from the standard of care (D. Nickelson, personal communication, November 14, 2005).

Derrig-Palumbo and Zeine (2005) propose that protection of the client is best accomplished when the etherapy is considered to take place in the state of licensure,

Therapists have the following options and considerations: (1) Proceed and defend as necessary that the therapy takes place where the therapist practices. (2) Only see clients in the state in which you are licensed. (3) Provide other services, such as life coaching, to clients in states other than the state in which you are licensed (2005, pp. 208–209).

However, Thomas disagrees and interprets the states' licensing regulations to mean that therapists must conduct in-person therapy only in that state where they are licensed, with patients that reside also in that state. Thus these parameters should also apply to online therapy. Can you forsee a jumble to state to state boundaries issues, especially for clinicians who work in neighboring states or who fly around the country to testify or vacation but still have the occasional contact with patients?

Most clinicians do not know their own state's regulations concerning geographical boundaries and amount of time allowed to practice outside of those. For example, there is a provision in California that allows clinicians to work outside state boundaries for 30 days per year, either consecutively or in total. Other states like New York have different configurations of days allowed in total. Thomas proposes that online therapy with patients in other states could be considered "outside state's boundaries of the licensed clinician". He suggests that clinicians living in communities bordered by other states should obtain licenses for those states as well (J. Thomas, personal communication, October 20, 2005) which may not go over very well with clinicians who would then find themselves spending more time and money renewing and complying with more practice requirements.

Finally, Kraut (2004) suggests that future jurisdictional issues could be solved by state license reciprocity, but this seems unlikely when some states require different cutoff exam scores and different training requirements than do others in order to obtain license to practice in their jurisdictions. In summary, we are not sure where professional services using the Internet take place or exactly how we should label and define therapy online. Most importantly, should licensing agencies and professional organizations adopt a proactive, obstructionist, or wait-and-see stance toward online therapy? As the interactivity of text, voice, and touch online sync with other media to enhance the online experience, we can be sure that online and offline issues will continue to challenge our thinking and our methods.

EMERGING CLINICAL ISSUES

THEORY IN CYBERSPACE

As has been discussed, the primary concerns regarding online therapy appear to be legal and ethical ones, not clinical ones, but it is the clinical issues in cyberspace that intrigue clinicians, and hopefully, will result in more professional competency online, as well as more equitable access to mental health services for consumers. Current risk management topics do not address whether or not clinicians' knowledge about cyber psychology and Internet communication is adequate to provide treatment online. Most just assume that if you are a competent clinician in the office, you are competent online (Mallen, 2004). Questions such as How can I best help my patients use the Internet for health purposes? How do I conceptualize and treat a patient's problematic cyber habit? or How do culture, diversity, and identity manifest online? generate little discourse. At the most reductionist level, do we treat cyber problems online, offline, or both?

Diversity and difference define cyberspace communications making generalizations and interpretations difficult. What is available online makes us laugh and resonate with others. But there is also the other side. Deviance and "the norm" are just a click away from each other. The Internet facilitates global terrorism and live web cam footage of the sexual exploitation of infants as well as other dehumanizing and compulsive behaviors. Who we are online may or may not be representative of our offline identities. Much of society, especially our youth, is so inured to media effects that fantasy and fact are synonymous with their perceptions of reality. While mental health providers are required to stay abreast of diversity issues offline, no requirements exist for exposing mental health professionals to the growing body of literature about the way we represent ourselves online. Clinicians are often unable to interpret media culture or how this affects on ground behaviors, especially of youth (Taffel, 2005) Some authors propose that clinicians should document self-study in the area of Internet psychology and not practice in cyberspace until there is consensus about what clinicians need to understand about cyber behaviors and cyber treatment. Glueckauf et al. (2003) consider Internet-driven health services a viable option already, especially for the disenfranchised, despite the lack of professional guidelines and practice models. They predict that more clinicians will work online because it provides greater access to underserved populations, increases efficiency of health delivery, is cost effective, and is driven by a clear grass-roots demand for services.

John Suler, psychologist and author from Rider University, offers a comprehensive Continuing Education course online entitled *Psychotherapy and Clinical Work in Cyberspace.* He begins this course with a joke: How many psychologists does it take to do computer-mediated psychotherapy? None, the computer can do it all by itself! (2005, n.p.). Suler (2005) believes that clinicians unfamiliar with online issues are anxious about the future of therapy the old-fashioned way and tend to discount the efficacy of online therapy. He offers courses on important topics such as analyzing cyberspace as a psychological space, comparing the offline and online disinhibition effect, and how to evaluate text as a barometer of mental status, information processing, and interpersonal style.

Derrig-Palumbo and Zeine are also proponents of the online modality. They propose that "many of the cognitive–behavioral theories work best with online therapy" (2005, p. 5). They assert that many approaches such as Imago therapy, Cognitive–Behavioral Therapy (CBT), or Rational Emotive Behavior Therapy "can be easily modified to be conducted online. This concept can ease many therapists' concerns about preserving their modality and professional identity online" (2005, p. 31). The authors interviewed CBT experts Albert Ellis,

Donald Meichenbaum, Aaron Beck, and others, asking them how they would conduct therapy online. Ellis discussed the ABC's of Rational Emotive Therapy online with individuals, couples, and adolescents. Ellis believes that online is the "same as face-to face." Derrig-Palumbo and Zeine's interview with Meichenbaum provided helpful ideas about using the Web for psycho-educational purposes with depressed or anxious patients, but no discussion ensued about how to help patients screen sites to make sure that the educational information is accurate. Further, the transference dynamic between the clinician and the patient online was explained by Derrig-Palumbo and Zeine as follows:

> When sitting in front of a monitor instead of the client, therapists need to be very cautious not to allow their reactions to surface. They may think "I don't have to hide my feelings because she isn't watching, nor is she sitting in front of me." It is important to be fully aware that the same transference and countertransference issues that therapists encounter when face-to-face with their clients may also occur during online therapy (2005, p. 932).

However, others disagree and do not view the online dynamic as the same as face-to-face. Cyber psychology and Internet technology influence communication (Lloyd, 2002), identity (Subrahmanyam *et al.*, 2004), disclosure (Suler, 2004), and the therapeutic relationship online (McKenna *et al.*, 2002) in profoundly unique ways. Nickovich *et al.* (2005) propose that transference issues online are much more complex than a two-way exchange face-to-face because the exchange is continually mediated by the computer. This dynamic is shaped (e.g., channeled, co-constructed, changed, recreated) by the Internet, somewhat akin to the intersubjective experience articulated by Stolorow *et al.* (1994). In addition, macro- and microlevels of analysis proposed in Heisenberg's uncertainty principal are also a useful way to conceptualize understanding the dynamic in cyberspace, that is to say, the act of looking at and measuring something changes its form and function.

At the most basic level, when clinicians want to know how to work with patients, psychological theory becomes a heuristic means of transforming what patients say into clinical data that then organize therapeutic intervention strategies (McWilliams, 1994, 2004). Mallen (2004) believes that Internet communication has definitely reached critical mass, at least enough so that we need to begin to apply the heuristic of psychological theories to its discourse, but suggests that assuming existing theories are adequate or even an accurate way to interpret in cyberspace is misleading and leaves clinicians with "a mixed bag" of therapeutic skills (p. 74). Depending on which research is cited, some investigators are convinced that patients' face-to-face disclosures are more honest than online ones (Mallen *et al.*, 2003) and thus cannot be clinically interpreted effectively online. Suler, however, proposes just the opposite—that computer-mediated communication is often more uninhibited and contains more honest disclosures of personal information than do face-to-face encounters (Suler, 2004). Does online technology facilitate interpretation in cyberspace more readily way because we are more aware and disinhibited and thus willing to share personal information that is not constrained by the subtleties of in person judgments and rules of social hierarchy? The point here is that clinicians must be ready to test their hypotheses about patients online too, just like they do in the office, and not assume etherapy is either good or bad. Unlike face-to-face interactions, text has one clear advantage. It certainly provides a record of conversations however, one where the clinician and the patient can revisit, clarify, and reframe as needed. The cyber problems that affect our patients require practitioners to expand and reframe their knowledge. When the interaction is online, clinical skills do not just morph into digital ones.

EFFICACY OF ONLINE TREATMENT

How do clinicians become familiar with best practices online? For the past 5 years, researchers have investigated Internet-based mental health services, but most providers do not know how to utilize the data (Day & Schneider, 2002; Fisher & Fried, 2003; Gillispie & Gackenbach, 2006; Grohol, 1998; Mallen, Bay, & Green., 2003). While there are criteria for evaluating the accuracy and professionalism of online mental health sites, much of what passes for etherapy or patient education is questionable. The stakes are high for consumers with urgent mental health needs because they often do not know how to determine whether a site is legitimate or not. Patients often want their therapists to review this information that they found on the Internet (Morahan-Martin, 2004).

The International Society for Mental Health Online (ISMHO) is one of the earliest professional resources specifically designed to help consumers and professionals survey the most scientifically vigorous mental health sites online. It offers good resources and search tools for the clinician and consumer. The ISMHO, a nonprofit organization, was formed in 1997 to promote the understanding, use, and development of online communication, information, and technology for the international mental health community. It currently has over 200 members from as many countries. The Society helps clinicians become expert in cyber-psychological issues, offline and online. Opportunities for research, training, case consultation, and cyber-practice guidelines are disseminated to members. The ISMHO provides discussion forums where clinicians can consult about Internet-related professional issues or benefit from the case conferences of other professionals. It also educates the consumer about online therapy. Online therapy sites that belong to this organization must comply with the ISMHO mission and criteria for Internet psychology.

Another strategy to help professionals connect with legitimate health sites is to look for the equivalent of an online seal of approval. The Health on the Internet Foundation Code of Conduct (HONcode, 2005) is an online consumer service that reviews health websites for professionalism and accuracy. HONcode was established in 1995 as the first international society dedicated to helping consumers find health information from the most reliable and up-to-date sources. Currently, the HONcode website offers information in 29 languages. It lists all known hospital health information websites as part of an online resource to consumers from anywhere in the world. In addition, HONcode specializes in what they call "cross-border talk" health and research conferences, and case consultation for health professionals and consumers in 72 countries. Any Internet health-based organization or private practitioner that wants to offer services online and wishes to belong to HONcode must adhere to the Web standards devised by their Board of Directors, health professionals from 17 countries. However, there is no system that is able to monitor or ensure members' compliance. The HONcode seal signals to readers that this particular website complies with the following legal and ethical guidelines:

1. Authority: Differentiates between medical fact and opinion.
2. Compatibility: Works to support face-to-face relationships with other health providers.
3. Confidentiality: Websites exceed legal jurisdictional health information privacy.
4. Attribution: Clear references, accurate links, and updates of clinical information displayed at the bottom of page.
5. Justifiability: Claims regarding treatments are supported by evidence.
6. Authorship: Webmaster displays e-mail address clearly.
7. Sponsorship: Support for website clearly identified, including identities of all commercial and noncommercial organizations.
8. Honesty in Advertising: If advertising is a source of funding, it will be clearly stated and presented to viewers in a manner that differentiates it from the original material created by the organization operating the site.

There is one problem, however. As legitimate as the HONcode's reputation is, little is known about how the average person interprets such seals of approval. Most consumers either do not know about these online consumer protection organizations or do not use them. Unfortunately, researchers have identified a major problem in the way online health information websites are accredited; evidently, these trusted seals often "promise more than deliver" (Burkell, 2004, n.p).

E-Health, Telehealth, and Telemedicine (2001) by Marlene Maheu, Pamela Whitten, and Ace Allen, was written for clinicians considering online therapy. The authors predicted that advancements in telecommunications technology would "reshape the standard of health care and revolutionize the way patients consumed therapy" (pp. 2–4), but so far, this has not happened from a professional standpoint. In addition, troubleshooting potential clinical problems online referred exclusively to medical models of tele-health and text-only communication for therapists. Their advice for risk management to mental health clinicians is that therapists comply with tele-health laws. But, here's another double bind for clinicians, state Boards of Psychology have determined does *not* include Internet-based psychological practice at this time (Barnett & Sheetz, 2003; American Psychological Association, 2004).

Riva's (2005) review of virtual reality (VR) explores the efficacy of online therapy. He found 371 articles written in the past 3 years showing VR is an effective behavioral and psychotherapeutic treatment modality for those who suffer from specific phobias, depression, obesity, male erectile disorders, and cognitive disorders. Riva explains that the immersion of VR assists with the process of change for the patient on sensory, visual, emotional, and cognitive levels. VR therapy is a reinforcing experience that serves as a catalyst for new learning, cognitive restructuring, and behavior change.

Perhaps the best news about online psychology concerns traditionally disenfranchised peoples. Recent studies suggest that effectiveness of online therapy may be greatest for those who are either reluctant to participate in treatment for fear of stigma or negative career effects, or for those who are unable to meet in person. Online treatment appears to also be effective for trauma and stress-based conditions; however, more research is needed (Andersson *et al.*, 2005). Online group and individual therapy also show positive results with the following behavioral health problems: smoking cessation, weight loss, eating disorders, headaches, panic attacks, maintaining physical exercise goals, tinnitus, diabetes, bedwetting, and post-cancer and heart attack recovery treatments (Ritterband *et al.*, 2003). Ritterband and his colleagues reviewed Web-based, behavioral treatment models for patients who preferred receiving help from their own homes. They received a combination of psycho-educational and interactive CBT interventions online. Interestingly, while all the groups studied showed symptom improvement, significant gains as a result of online therapy were reported for even traditionally difficult problems: the weight loss and trauma patient groups.

Finally, Ritterband and colleagues do acknowledge that developing Internet interventions "is an arduous, sometimes tedious, and always time-intensive process" (p. 530). It necessitates an interdisciplinary approach but once completed, the protocol can be utilized for many patients. In addition, once the disorder is identified as appropriate for the Internet, interventions are operationalized, that is, broken down into measurable components, and evaluation mechanisms built into the program so revisions can occur based on users' treatment success. For patients who suffer from debilitating problems such as panic, posttraumatic stress disorder, diabetes, or other health-risk behaviors, the multimedia aspect of online treatment coalesces the power of multimodal learning strategies simultaneously. Internet therapies are highly structured, personalized, self guided, and engaging, thus increasing meaning and efficacy for the patient. These states create continual feedback loops that encourage self monitoring and more patient involvement in tracking treatment gains (p. 531).

EXPANDING THE CLINICAL PARADIGM [:-C, :-W, (:: () ::)]

[: -C just totally unbelievable; :-W speaking in forked tongue; (:: ( ) ::) offering support]

At this point, becoming expert with online therapy may happen by default. As more of us work online to address traditional barriers to treatment skill in analyzing the interaction among machine, technology, and the human will certainly evolve. Patients who live in rural communities, who have certain phobias, who feel stigma about their condition, or who experience mobility limitations have real difficulty initiating face-to-face treatment. In addition, finding local clinicians or specialists who are approved by insurance providers is especially difficult, but now connecting with practitioners online is easy, either for online or offline treatment. Often, insurers are receptive to approving a course of treatment for a difficult problem when a clinician's credentials are easy to access online.

An example of a psychologist who helps mental health providers reach those who would not be able to benefit from treatment is David Lukoff, professor at the Saybrook Institute in San Francisco, California. Lukoff provides training in the online delivery of mental health services to counselors who work with Native peoples in rural Alaska. According to Lukoff, health care providers in Alaska have always recognized the utility of the distance modality because of geographic, financial, and cultural barriers (D. Lukoff, personal communication, Nov. 16, 2005). Lukoff's sample treatment website (see Table I) includes direct links to assessment protocols, collateral providers for medication management, educational materials, indigenous support from a university in Connecticut 3,000 miles away, and access to a 12-step program (Lukoff, 2005)

TABLE I

Mental Health Internet

Lesson 2.1 A Fisherman in Alaska with a Dual Diagnosis

Treatment Issues
The three cases in Lesson 2 cover a wide range of conditions, including depression, PTSD, substance abuse, medical illnesses, and sleep disorders. They are presented with links to illustrate the range of Internet resources available on clinical topics. This first case concerns rural mental health delivery. It is based on my experience teaching a workshop on the Internet to mental health workers on the Aleutian Islands of Alaska. Many were village-based counselors who had only 36 hours of training and no college education, and yet they provide multiple mental health services ranging from hospice care to detox. Many are now embracing the Internet to fill in their gaps in training and information on assessment and therapy.

Case

John is a 29-year-old man living in the rural Alaskan town of King Cove. He works seasonally on the fishing boats, but when not fishing, he abuses alcohol. Recently, he has begun using amphetamine as well. He is a dually diagnosed patient. For the past 2 years, he has been taking Zoloft for treatment of Major Depression. He has been referred to the mental health clinic because he has an enlarged liver, presumed to be related to his abuse of alcohol. He states that he doesn't see the connection between his liver problem and drinking, and doubts that he's an alcoholic since he doesn't drink when he's working on the fishing boat. He is part Aleutian Indian and has expressed interest in learning more about his Native American background.

Treatment Issues

Denial

The first therapeutic objective is to convince John that he *does* have a serious problem related to alcohol and that his health is being affected by it. An online interactive test would demonstrate to John that he does meet criteria for alcohol dependence.

Internet Resources

EXERCISE: Take the *Alcohol Screening Test* as John, making up responses to fit someone who has an alcohol problem (www.health.org)

These are links to pictures from the University of Utah Medical School pathology mini-tutorial on the effects of alcohol on the liver that can be shown to John.
Normal Liver Micronodular cirrhosis of liver, gross.
This is a brochure on substance abuse from the National Clearinghouse for Alcohol and Drug Information that can be printed out and given to John.
Alcohol: What You Don't Know Can Harm You

Alcoholics Anonymous

John agrees to get involved with a 12-step program. However, there is no AA meeting currently being held in the small Alaskan village where he lives. However John lives one block from the clinic and is quite willing to come in to use the computer to read the Big Book of Alcoholics Anonymous and to join an online AA group when he is on shore.

Internet Resources
Big Book of Alcoholics Anonymous

Below are links to online AA groups
About.com > AA Online Meetings > LampLighters
A large e-mail AA Group with over 10,000 members.

Aleutian Roots

John's recovery could be aided by expanding his social support network for sobriety, including reconnecting with his indigenous roots. In addition to finding local resources, an Internet search on the Aleutian Indian Tribe turned up these sites.

Internet Resources
University of Connecticut Arctic Circle Web Site

This site contains information on the Aleutian Indians.
Four Worlds Institute for Human and Community Development
The Four Worlds Institute is an organization whose principles are based on the traditional teachings of North American tribal peoples.

TABLE I (*Continued*)

Clinical Education
Internet Resources

Information on Zoloft is available on several sites, as you'll learn in lesson 4. Here is the information from the Internet Mental Health Site: *Zoloft (Sertraline)*

Dual Diagnosis patients present unique treatment challenges. Visit Kathleen Sciacca's *Dual Diagnosis Website: Mental Illness, Drug Addiction and Alcoholism.*

RESOURCE KEY:
Audio
Website
Document
Quiz

As comprehensive and clinically appropriate as the example given is, clinicians still express concern about adequacy of the online modality to motivate patients to participate fully in treatment. A recent study of online therapy found that the electronic form of therapeutic communication resulted in higher levels of participation than did traditional offline methods of therapy. Day and Schneider (2002) conducted an experiment comparing distance versus face–to-face therapy. Their findings suggest that patients tried harder and participated more because of the distance model. The authors surmised that the text-based, time-delayed technology required more effort in transposing thought to text. In addition, the privacy and anonymity online appeared to encourage high levels of disclosure with this group of patients. The data to date tells us that online treatment appears to increase patient motivation and treatment compliance, which may in turn change the fact that one-third of new patients offline drop out within the first three sessions (Lober & Satow, 1975).

Informal case consultation may also begin to change the clinical landscape as clinicians begin to treat more and more patients who present with a cyber issue and they themselves begin to use the Internet as a communication tool in their practices. They ask questions like do you practice online? Or what's the Standard of Care in cyber space? They want to know when the Internet is appropriate for patient services? For example, as education is such an essential part of therapy, patients may come to expect referrals to web-based National, International, or major research organizations for information about diagnosis, medication, or adjunct treatment. Further, patients need to know the empirical data if it is germane to their health issue. There are now established and effective online treatment protocols for many mental health disorders (panic disorder and cancer support among others) that could have great benefit to patients either as an adjunct to face-to-face therapy or as collateral treatment.

The vignettes below are examples of realistic clinical scenarios that any mental health practitioner may encounter in his or her office but for which there are no treatment protocols. Discussing the online and offline legal, ethical, and treatment considerations with colleagues begins the process of increasing our facility with online clinical and professional issues. How would you eframing the following psychological interventions?

- What kinds of patients would you consider using a hybrid (online/ offline) model of treatment?
- Would you feel competent providing therapy for a couple because one partner is having a cyber affair?
- A colleague wants you to review her website for clarity and professionalism. You are uncomfortable with the marketing strategies used and the direct links to purchasing her books and tapes. Is this unethical, unprofessional, or a legitimate way to grow your practice?
- Should you refer a patient to an online 12-step program?
- What do you say when a 14 year-old patient tells you that she receives hate mail from classmates via Instant Messaging.
- What would you say to a colleague calls you for a consultation regarding an adult patient who regularly chats with teenagers on MySpace to give them "a supportive ear."
- How would you conceptualize the treatment for a patient who admits to being addicted to cyber porn?
- Do you continue therapy with a patient who has moved to another state via email and telephone?
- How would you advise a colleague who conducts therapy using an online and offline system of treatment despite the fact that their liability insurer has attached a rider to their policy excluding Internet-based practice because there are no professional standards or laws enforceable in cyber space?

Thinking deeply about our patients is what we do. When there is a cyber component it is incumbent upon us to conceptualize treatment in new ways. Online practice issues provide us with an opportunity to challenge our on ground mind-sets. Cyber problems that patients bring to us like affairs, harassment, and compulsions are certainly treatable but may be especially difficult to contain within cyberspace. Problems may have offline or online components, or both which may require different case formulations and thus different interventions. For example, a cyber affair may be an adaptive way to explore a different sexual identity or begin to acknowledge what is missing in one's current relationship. In contrast, a cyber affair may be a part of a cycle of impulsivity that will escalate and be eventually acted out offline.

Because interactions in cyberspace are less inhibited in both positive and negative ways, clinicians must decide if problem cyber behaviors are even treatable using their existing repertoires of knowledge and skills. Can a patient's Internet behavior be analyzed or diagnosed as healthy fantasy projected into the collective unconscious of cyber space and thus provide both figure and ground? Are doing things on line that you would not do offline cathartic, a release of socially constrained angst, a safe and creative form of expression, meaning, and personal growth? Or, are one's cyber habits, if repeated often enough, eventually going to leak offline, especially as Internet technologies involve our physiological responses (Haptics) as well as portable, imbedded, and 3-D screens allow us to feel inserted into the screen? Time will tell. As behavioral and mental health clinicians we are in a good position to assist our profession, the public and our patients in understanding communication, identity, and relational issues in the digital age what healthy online behavior looks like but only if we do not merely upload theory and practice to cyber space. What's a practitioner to do? We wonder which should be treated first—the online issues or the offline effects of cyber problems? The rubric for treating a harmful cyber behavior could be abstinence, immersion, in vivo exposure, or involve harm reduction strategies or a combination of all of these. In other words, professionals who work in cyberspace or who treat cyber problems will still need to assess, consult, try different treatment strategies, and continually analyze the dynamic of cyborg. Clearly online is not the same as offline. The horizontal power structure and multiple selves that define cyber culture and cyber psychology move us beyond transference and counter transference into an intersubjective double helix of possibilities. Even if we are not online ourselves professionally, more and more of our patients will have an online issue that needs our help It is only a matter of time that the digital age will require that we are much more informed about cyber culture than is currently the case.

The Internet has given us an opportunity as health communicators to examine the limitations of our personal and professional assumptions. Fortunately, this paradigm shift forces us and our profession to be more effective in the ways we have needed to be all along: making psychology more accessible to those who need it and creating more meaningful discourse around the topics of diversity.

If we choose to work online or not, we still live offline. Let's hope that the thrill, the realities, and unknowns of cyberspace interactions will transform the systems of psychology that needed a good overhaul while at the same time preserving, extending, and enhancing the value that our profession brings to our connections with each other.

Haraway's Cyborg Manifesto is a philosophy that can be applied to expanding the paradigm for clinicians.

> Now we are all hybrids of machine and organism [there is] pleasure in the confusion of boundaries…urging us towards a greater unity…holding incompatible things together because both or all are necessary and true …

> Embracing the skillful task for reconstructing the boundaries of daily life, in partial connection with others, in communication with all of our parts … Cyborg imagery can suggest a way out of the maze of dualisms in which we have explained our bodies and our tools to ourselves. It means both building and destroying machines, identities, categories, relationships, space stories. Though both are bound in the spiral dance, I would rather be a cyborg than a goddess (1991, pp. 30–31).

Let's analyze the spiral dance of the cyborg together and move towards more respectful, joyful, authentic, and sustainable ways to live in harmony. (411^_^), :-)? Translation: Japanese emoticon and net lingo acronym for Got the information on that?) ("Smileys and Emoticons for E-mail and IM," 2005).

REFERENCES

A law too far. (2004, June 30). *San Francisco Chronicle*, p. B 8.

Alleman, J. R. (2002). Online counseling: The Internet and mental health treatment. *Psychotherapy: Theory / Research / Practice / Training, 39*(2), 199–209.

American Counseling Association (2005). *American Counseling Association code of ethics*. Alexandria, VA.: American Counseling Association.

American Psychological Association (APA). (2004). *APA statement on services by telephone, teleconferences, and Internet.* Retrieved October 26, 2004, from ⟨http://www.apa.org/ethics⟩

Andersson, G., Bergstrom, J., Carlbring, P., & Lindefors, N. (2005). The use of the Internet in the treatment of anxiety disorders. *Current Opinion in Psychiatry, 18*, 73–77.

Barnett, J. E., & Scheetz, K. (2003). Technological advances and telehealth: Ethics, law, and the practice of psychotherapy. *Psychotherapy: Theory, Research, Practice, Training, 40*(1/2), 86–93.

Beard, K. (2005). Internet addiction: A review of current assessment techniques and potential assessment questions. *CyberPsychology & Behavior, 8*, No.1, 7–14.

Begner, D. (2005, January 31). The making of a molester. *The New York Times Magazine*, pp. 26, 61.

Bell, D. (2001). Cybersexual. In D. Bell & B. Kennedy (Eds.), *The cybercultures reader* (pp. 392–395). New York: Routledge.

Boies, S., Cooper, A., & Osborne, C. (2004). Variations in Internet-related problems and psychosocial functioning in online sexual activities: Implications for social and sexual development of young adults. *Cyber Psychology and Behavior, 7*(2), 207–230.

Bowker, A., & Gray, M. (2004). *An introduction to the supervision of the cybersex offender.* Federal Probation, *68*, Iss. 3, 3–6.

Bridges, A., Bergner, R., & Hesson-McInnis, M. (2003). Romantic partners' use of pornography: Its significance for women. *Journal of Sex and Marital Therapy, 29*, 1–14.

British Association for Counseling Practitioners. (2005). FYI: Updated best practice inline THS, WIIFM?PX! *Counseling and Psychotherapy Journal, 16*(4), 44.

Burkell, J. (2004). Health information seals of approval: What do they signify? *Information, Communication & Society, 7*(4), 491–509.

Clark, G., Eubanks, D., Reid, E., Kelleher, C., O'Conner, E., & DeBar, L. (2004). Overcoming depression in the Internet (ODIN) (2): A randomized trial of a self-help depression skills program with reminders. *Journal of Medical Internet Research, 7*(1), Article e16. Retrieved November 12, 2005, from ⟨http://www.jmir.org/2005/1/e16/⟩

Cooper, A. (Ed.). (2002). *Sex and the Internet: A guidebook for clinicians.* New York: Brunner-Rutledge.

Cooper, A., Delmonico, D., & Berg, R. (2002). Cybersex users, abusers, and compulsives: New findings and implications. *Sexual Addiction and Compulsivity: Journal of Treatment and Prevention, 7*(1–2), 5–30.

Cooper, A., & Griffin-Shelley, E. (2002). *Online sexual activity: Continuum complete international encyclopedia of sexuality,* pp. 1290–1386. New York: Continuum International Publishing Group.

Cooper, J., & Weaver, K. (2003). *Gender and computers: Understanding the digital divide.* New York: Lawrence Erlbaum.

Day, S., & Schneider, P. (2002). Psychotherapy using distance technology: A comparison of face-to-face, video, and audio treatment. *Journal of Consulting Psychology. 49*(4), 499–503.

Denegri-Knott, J., & & Taylor, J. (2005). The labeling game: A conceptual exploration of deviance on the Internet. *Social Science and Computer Review, 23*(4), 39–47.

Farvolden, P., Denisoff, E., Selby, P., Bagby, M., & Rudy, L. (2004). Usage and longitudinal effectiveness of a web-based self-help cognitive behavioral therapy program for panic disorder. *Journal of Medical Internet Research, 7*(1), Article e7. Retrieved November 12, 2005, from http://www.jmir.org/2005/1/e7/

Fisher, C. B., & Fried, A. L. (2003). Internet-mediated psychological services and the American Psychological Association ethics code. *Psychotherapy: Theory, Research, Practice, Training, 40*(1/2), 103–111.

Freeman-Longo, R. (2000). Children, teens, and sex on the Internet. *Sexual Addiction and Compulsivity, 7*, 75–90.

Gillispie, J. F. (2006). Got therapy? Professional issues online. In J. Gillispie & J. Gackenbach. *Cyber.rules: Negotiating healthy Internet use: A guide for clinicians, educators, and parents.* New York: W.W. Norton. (in press).

Gillispie, J. F., & Gackenbach, J. (in press). *Cyber.rules: Negotiating healthy Internet use, A guide for clinicians, educators, and parents.* New York: W. W. Norton.

Glueckauf, R., Pickett, T., Ketterson, T., Loomis, J., & Rozensky, R. (2003). Preparation for the delivery of telehealth services: A self-study framework for expansion of practice. *Professional Psychology, Research, and Practice, 34*(2), 159–163.

Greenfield, P. (2004). Developmental considerations for determining appropriate Internet use guidelines for children and adolescents. *Applied Developmental Psychology, 25*, 751–762.

Grohol, J. (2005). *Dr. John Grohol's psych central.* Retrieved November 16, 2005, from http://www.psychcentral.com/

Gross, E. (2004). Adolescent Internet use: What we expect, what teens report. *Journal of Applied Developmental Psychology, 25*(6), 633–649.

Haggstron-Nordin, E., Hanson, U., & Tyden, T. (2005). Associations between pornography consumption and sexual practices among adolescents in Sweden. *International Journal of STD & AIDS, 16,* (2), 102–108.

Haraway, D. (1991). A cyborg manifesto: Science, technology, and socialist–feminism in the late twentieth century. Donna Haraway (Ed.). *Simians, cyborgs and women: The reinvention of nature* (pp. 149–181). New York: Routledge.

HONcode. (2005, April 11, 2005). *HON code of conduct (HONcode) for medical and health web sites.* Retrieved April 11, 2005, from http://www.hon.ch/HONcode/conduct.html

International Society for Mental Health Online [ISMHO]. (2000, January 9). *Suggested principles for the online provision of mental health services online, Version 3.11.* Retrieved October 10, 2005, from http://www.ismho.org/suggestions.htm

International Society for Mental Health Online [ISMHO]. (2005). *Mission statement of ISMHO.* Retrieved May 13, 2005, from http://www.ismho.org/mission.htm

Jones, S. G. (1998). *Cybersociety: Revisiting computer-mediated communication and community* (pp. 185–205). Thousand Oaks, CA: Sage Publications.

Jones, S. G. (2000), *Virtual culture: Identity and communication in cyber society.* S. Jones (Ed.). Cybersociety 2.0 (pp. 185–205). Thousand Oaks, CA: Sage Publications.

Kaltiala-Heino, R., Lintonen, T., & Rimpela, A. (2004). Internet addiction? Potentially problematic use of the Internet in a population of 12–18-year-old adolescents. *Addiction Research and Theory, 12*(1), 89–96.

Koch, W., & Pratarelli, M. (2004). Effects of intro/extraversion and sex on social Internet use. *North American Journal of Psychology, 6*(3), 371–382.

Koocher, G., & Morray, E. (2000). Regulation of telepsychology: A survey of State Attorneys General. *Professional Psychology Research and Practice, 31*(5), 503–508.

Kraut, R. (2004). Ethical and legal considerations for providers of mental health services online. In R. Kraut, J. Zack, & G. Strickler (Eds.), *Online counseling: A handbook for mental health professionals* (pp. 123–144). San Francisco: Elsevier.

Kraut, R., Zack, J. & Strickler, G. (Eds.). (2004). *Online counseling: A handbook for mental health professionals.* San Francisco CA: Elsevier.

Kraut, R., Olson, J., Banaji, M., Bruckman, A., Cohen, J., & Couper, M. (2004). Psychological research online: Report of board of scientific affairs' advisory group on the conduct of research on the Internet. *American Psychologist, 59*(2), 105–117.

Kraut, R., Kiesler, S., & Boneva, B. (2002). Internet paradox revisited. *Journal of Social Issues, 58*(1), 49–74.

Kraut, R., Lundmark, V., Patterson, M., Kiesler, S., Mukopadhyay, T., & Scherlis, W. (1998). Internet paradox: A social technology that reduces social involvement and psychological well-being. *American Psychologist, 5,* 1017–1031.

Lessig, L. (2005, May). *The second conference on online deliberation: Design, research, and practice.* Paper presented at the annual meeting of Stanford University Center for Internet and Society, Stanford, CA.

Lloyd, B. T. (2002). A conceptual framework for examining adolescent identity, media influence, and social development. *Review of General Psychology, 6*(1), 73–91.

Lorber, J., & Satow, R. (1975, July). Dropout rates in mental health centers. *Social Work, 20*(4), 308–312.

Lukoff, D. (2005). *Navigating the mental health internet, lesson 2.1.* Retrieved November 16, 2005, from http://www.spiritualcompetency.com/nmhi/course_nmhi.asp

Maheu, M., Whitten, P., & Allen, A. (2001). *E-health, telehealth, and telemedicine: A guide to start-up and success.* New York: Jossey-Bass.

Mallen, M. (2004). Online counseling research. In R. Kraut, J. Zack, & G. Strickler (Eds.) *Online counseling: A handbook for mental health professionals* (pp. 69–89) San Francisco: Elsevier.

Mallen, M., Day, S., & Green, M. (2003). Online versus face-to-face conversations: An examination of relational and discourse variables. *Psychotherapy: Theory, Research, Practice, Training, 40*(1/2), 155–163.

Martin, P., & Petry, N. (2005). Are non-substance-related addictions really addictions? *American Journal on Addictions, 14*(1), 1 & 3.

McKenna, K. Y. A., Green, A. S., & Gleason, M. E. J. (2002). Relationship formation on the Internet: What's the big attraction? *Journal of Social Issues, 58*(1), 9–31.

McWilliams, N. (1994). *Psychoanalytic diagnosis.* New York: Guilford Press.

McWilliams, N. (2004). *Psychoanalytic psychotherapy.* New York: Guilford Press.

Morahan-Martin, J. (2004). How Internet users find, evaluate, and use online health information: A cross-cultural review. *CyberPsychology & Behavior, 7*(5), 497–510.

Morahan-Martin, J., & Schumacher, P. (2000). Incidence and correlates of pathological Internet use among college students. *Computers in Human Behavior, 16,* 13–29.

Morahan-Martin, J., & Schumacher, P. (2003). Loneliness and social uses of the Internet. *Computers in Human Behavior, 19*(6), 659–671.

Moser, C., Kleinplatz, P., Zuccarini, D., & Reiner, W. (2004). Situating unusual child and adolescent sexual behavior in context. *Institute for Advanced Study of Human Sexuality, 13,* No.3, 569–589.

Naglieri, J., Drasgow, F., Schmidt, M., Handler, L., Prifitera, L., Margolis, A., & Velasquez, R. (2004). Psychological testing on the Internet: New problems, old issues. *American Psychologist, 59*(3), 150–162.

Nichols, L., & Nicki, R. (2004). Development of a psychometrically sound Internet addiction scale: A preliminary step. *Psychology of Addictive Behaviors, 18*(4), 381–384.

Nicovich, S. G., Boller, G. W., & Cornwell, T. B. (2005). Experienced presence within computer-mediated communications: Initial explorations on the effects of gender with respect to empathy and immersion. *Journal of Computer-Mediated Communications, 10*(2). Retrieved October 12, 2005, from http://jcmc.indiana.edu/vol10/issue2/nicovich.html

Noonan, R. (1998). The psychology of sex: A mirror of the Internet. In J. Gackenbach (Ed.), *Psychology and the Internet* (pp. 143–166). San Diego, CA: Academic Press.

Plant, S. (2001). Coming across the future. In D. Bell & B. Kennedy (Eds.), *The cybercultures reader* (pp. 225–336). New York: Routledge.

Privacy? What privacy? (2005, August/September). *Briefings*, No. 000. Sacramento: California Psychological Association.

Quayle, E., & Taylor, M. (2003). Model of problematic Internet use in people with a sexual interest in children. *Cyberpsychology and Behavior, 6*(1), 93–106.

Ragusa, A., & VandeCreek, L. (2003). Suggestions for the ethical practice of online psychotherapy. *Psychotherapy, Research and Practice, 40*(1/2), 94–102.

Rainie, L. (2005, November 3). *Privacy online: How Americans feel and why they are changing their Internet behaviors*. Retrieved November 7, 2005, from http://www.pewinternet.org/ppt/2005%20-%2011.4.05%20Privacy%20-%20Cong%20Internet%20Caucus.pdf

Rainie, L., & Horrigan, J. (2005, January 25). *A decade of adoption: How the Internet has woven itself into American life*. Pew Internet and American Life Project. Retrieved from http://www.pewinternet.org/PPF/r/148/report_display.asp

Reips, U. (2000). The web experiment method: Advantages, disadvantages, and solutions. In M. H. Birnbaum (Ed.), *Psychological experiments on the Internet* (pp. 89–114). San Diego, CA: Academic Press.

Ritterband, L., Gonder-Frederick, L., Cox, D., Clifton, A., West, R., & Borowitz, S. (2003). Internet interventions: In review, in use, and into the future. *Professional Psychology, Research and Practice, 34*(5), 527–534.

Riva, G. (2005). Virtual reality in psychotherapy: A review. *CyberPsychology & Behavior, 8*, No. 3, 220–230.

Roberts, D., Foehr, U., & Rideout, V. (2005, March). *Generation M: Media in the lives of 8–18-year-olds*. Menlo Park, CA: Kaiser Family Foundation Study.

Seaman, B. (2005). *Binge: What your college student won't tell you*. Hoboken, NJ: John Wiley.

Shaw, L., & Gant, L. (2002). In defense of the Internet: The relationship between Internet communication and depression, loneliness, self-esteem, and perceived social support. *Cyber Psychology and Behavior, 5*(2), 157–171.

Skinner, A., & Zack, J. (2004). Counseling and the Internet. *American Behavioral Scientist, 48*(4), 434–446.

"Smileys and Emoticons for Email and IM" (2005). Retrieved November 21, 2005 from http://www.netlingo.com/lumenu2.cfm?category=Chat+Acronym

Stack, S., Waserman, I., & Kern, R. (2004). Adult social bonds, and the use of Internet pornography. *Social Science Quarterly, 85*(1), 75–89.

Stolorow, R., Atwood, G., & Brandchaft, B. (1994). *The intersubjective perspective*. New York: Jason Aronson.

Subrahmanyam, K., Greenfield, P., & Tynes, B. (2004). Constructing sexuality and identity in an online teen chat room. *Applied Developmental Psychology, 2*, 651–666.

Suler, J. (2004). The online disinhibition effect. *Cyberpsychology and Behavior, 7*, 321–326.

Suler, J. (2005). *The psychology of cyberspace*. Retrieved November 16, 2005, from http://www.rider.edu/~suler/psycyber/psycyber.html

Taffel, R. (2005). *Breaking through to teens*. New York: The Guildford Press.

Tapscott, D. (2005, February). The Telephonosaurus. *The Wall Street Journal*, February 22. Retrieved from http://online.wsj.com/articles/O.SB110902664738560249.html

Thornburgh, D., & Lin, H. (2002). *Youth, pornography, and the Internet*. Washington, DC: National Academy Press.

Tips for telepsychology. (2005, January). *Board of Psychology Update, 12*, 2.

Turkle, S. (2005). *Digerati: The cyberanalyst.* Retrieved February 4, 2005, from http://www.edge.org/digerati/turkle/

Voice over Internet protocol. (2005). Federal Communications Commission, Consumer and Governmental Affairs Bureau. Retrieved on November 14, 2005, from http://www.fcc.gov/voip/

Whittaker, J. (2004). *The cyberspace handbook.* New York: Routledge.

Widyanto, L., & Griffiths, M. (2006). *Internet addiction: Does it really exist? (Revisited).* Jayne Gackenbach (Ed.). *Psychology and the Internet: Intrapersonal, Interpersonal, and Transpersonal Implications.* 2nd. Ed.. New York: Academic Press.

Young, K. (1996, August). *Internet addiction: The emergence of a new clinical disorder.* Paper presented at the 104th annual meeting of the American Psychological Association, Toronto, Canada.

Young, K, (1998). *Caught in the Net: How to recognize the signs of Internet addiction and a winning strategy for recovery.* New York: John Wiley.

Young, K. (2005). *A therapist's guide to assess and treat Internet addiction: An exclusive guide for practitioners.* Retrieved July 25, 2005, from http://secure4.mysecureorder.netadditction/other/therapist_guide.htm

Zane, N. (2005, November). Evidenced-based practice in psychology: Challenges for effectively serving ethnic minority populations. *The California Psychologist, 38*(6). 15–16.

PART III

Transpersonal

CHAPTER 11

From Mediated Environments to the Development of Consciousness II

Joan M. Preston
Department of Psychology
Brock University
St. Catharines, Ontario, Canada

Introduction
Ecological Perception
Media as Ecological Environment
Orientation and Space
Space and Consciousness
References

"So she sat on, with eyes closed, and half believed herself in Wonderland, though she knew she had but to open them again, and all would change to dull reality"

Lewis Carroll
Alice's Adventures in Wonderland

"…the perceptual qualities of shape and motion are present in the very acts of thinking….and are in fact the medium in which the thinking itself takes place…"

Rudolph Arnheim
Visual Thinking

INTRODUCTION

New media have developed rapidly with advancements in technology and software, and the way we conceptualize media continues to change. The notion of television as a "magic window" is outdated. Films, video games, and virtual reality installations manipulate and simulate creatures, actions, and places in what we typically refer to as "mediated environments." To understand how a flat screen can be seen as a place, theorists and researchers have turned to Gibson's (1979) ecological theory of perception. Gibson asked how an aware, mobile organism

Psychology and the Internet: Intrapersonal, Interpersonal, and Transpersonal Implications

functions in its environment. He explains how we perceive not only natural environments, but static and moving visuals as well. As we will see, our environment provides visual and spatial information essential to the development of awareness. If we accept the view that thought is based in abstract visual–spatial imagery, then media may play a role in the development of consciousness. Can mediated environments be created that take us beyond self-referential awareness to transcendence?

Sensation-based theories of perception present many problems that Gibson resolved in his explanation of visual perception. (For a detailed discussion, see Reed, 1988.) Gibson argued that visual information resides in the optical array and perception is based on detecting information. Thus, perception itself is both direct and motivating. For Gibson, there is a perceptual flow of information whenever we move. Each gradient of optical information is available only from a particular point, with gradients changing as we move. Therefore, optical information specifies not only objects and events in the environment but also the location of the self; the self is always present in the environment. Because it focuses on the navigational and other behavioral affordances of the optical display as well as the dynamic interaction of perceiver and environment, Gibson's ecological theory of perception was adopted widely by virtual reality (VR) designers and video game (VG) developers. Of particular interest are issues of presence and flow and veridicality.

PRESENCE

Gibson's concepts of presence and perceptual flow are relevant both to media (especially virtual reality) and to consciousness. In media research and theory, the concept of presence has proven especially important because individuals report involvement, immersion, or absorption in media. Presence, and how to define it, has been the focus of considerable research and theoretical attention across several academic disciplines.

Presence is central in the consciousness literature. Hunt (1995) distinguishes the role of immediate awareness in two fundamental forms of symbolic cognition: referential and presentational symbolism. As he explains, consciousness enters representational thought primarily as felt meanings in order to choose and direct our thought and not as its substance. In presentational symbolism, "meaning emerges as a result of an experiential immersion in the expressive patterns of the symbolic medium. It appears as spontaneous, preemptory imagery and is fully developed in the expressive media of the arts" (p. 42). A receptive, observing attitude allows such meaning to emerge. Hunt notes that representational and presentational forms of symbolism are necessarily intertwined. For example, intonation, gesture, and emphasis are presentational aspects of referential language use. The arts contain referential intentionality and shared codes in the form of styles, but "meaning emerges more intuitively and spontaneously from an ongoing absorption in the expressive medium itself as the 'surface' of conscious awareness" (p. 42). Hunt also describes a rare and special sense of felt reality and clarity, with a concomitant sense of exhilaration, freedom, and release. This vital presence, he says, is very close to Maslow's (1962) "peak experience" and Csikszentmihalyi's (1990) "flow experience." For Hunt, then, there are two forms of self-referential awareness: one that is subordinated to the instrumental 'set' in which the individual is responsive to representational information available in the environment. The other is manifested in "spontaneous presentational states" that are more intuitive and linked to the individual's personal meanings. Our tendency to experience engagement in external versus internal events has been identified as a dimension of individual differences or personality (Ashton *et al.*, 2004; McCrae & Costa, 1997; Roche & McConkey, 1990; Tellegen & Atkinson, 1974). This dimension is usually referred to as "absorption" or "openness to experience."

Hunt states that presence–openness is the basic organization of perception itself. Positive transpersonal experiences have been found to be related to high levels of spatial analytic ability and balance (Hunt *et al.*, 1992; Spadafora & Hunt, 1990), to scores for tests of spatial orientation and balance (Gackenbach & Bosveld, 1989; Swartz & Seginer, 1981), and spatial intelligence (Cranson *et al.*, 1991). Hunt (1989) suggests that spatial abilities, then, would be a framework needed for the full development of presentational states that are based on the reuse and rearrangement of basic spatial and perceptual structures.

With development, our abstract self-referential capacity resolves into spatial metaphors detached from the array. For Lakoff (1987), these metaphors include, among others: center/periphery, high/low, inside/outside, container, paths, and forces. For Lakoff (1987) and Hunt (1995), not just representation but the existence of feeling states require these abstract spatial metaphors. So enhanced self-reference allows the experience of "Being as Presence—a realized state, not a concept" (Hunt, 1995). That is, our experience of Self is ultimately based in ecological information, and existence or presence is "real."

If media are going to be able to facilitate the development of consciousness, we will have to understand the spatial and perceptual aspects of the mediated environment. As well, it is clear that, in addition to individual differences among media participants, mediated events differ in the degree to which they evoke referential versus presentational symbolic cognitions. We need to understand which visual information and styles of presentation facilitate presence as well as vital presence or flow.

In unmediated perception, presence is taken for granted. In mediated perception, it is argued that two separate environments are simultaneously available—the natural one in which the participant is actually present and the one displayed by the medium (although the need to establish and maintain one's orientation presumably precludes simultaneous presence). However, there is little agreement about the definition of mediated presence.[1] In their review of the topic, Lombard and Ditton (1997) describe six conceptualizations of presence, including the sense of nonmediation in mediated environments. Typically, in the field of communications, presence is said to occur when the participant's feelings of being present in the mediated environment take precedence over the immediate physical environment (for example, see Heeter, 1992; Sheridan, 1992; Slater et al., 1994; Steuer, 1995). Research has been directed to issues of measurement and factors that determine presence. Ever since the term "telepresence" was coined (e.g., Minsky, 1980), the feeling of "being there" has been central to the development of teleoperation (e.g., remote manipulation, such as the Canadarm) and virtual reality (VR). However, degree of "feeling present" is typically operationalized in research as the participant's evaluation or rating of an event on investigator-selected Likert-type scales, giving little information about what presence refers to for individual participants.

Many factors have been shown to contribute to presence, including the representational richness of a mediated environment (number of senses/amount of information, etc.), display features (such as screen size, field of view (FOV)), attention, perception, and other mental processes linking incoming data with current concerns and past experiences, including individual differences in absorption. In VR and VG, a concept similar to absorption is engagement (e.g., Laurel, 1991)—a primarily emotional state with cognitive components that engenders a first-person feeling in the participant.

Information and interactivity have been linked since the early designers of media interface devices (e.g., Bush, 1945), and greater interactivity is generally believed to increase the participant's sense of immersion (Vorderer, 2000). However, availability of interaction does not guarantee immersion. Grodal (2000) has pointed out that, in VGs, interactivity is relative to players' skills. According to both Csikszentmihalyi (1990) and Turkle (1984), media need to involve the participant's optimal mental level and motor capacity in order to elicit a higher experience of involvement, immersion, or flow. Zahorik and Jenison (1998) argue for a view of presence, based on Heidegger and Gibson, that is tied to the individual's successfully supported action in the environment (natural or virtual). They accept Gibson's (1979) proposal that perceptions are veridical to the extent that they support successful action in the environment and note that this moves the locus of determination of veridicality away from the perceiver's mental states. That is, when "at least one action of the self" is "successfully supported in a given environment, then perception of self-existence must be veridical" (Zahorik & Jenison, 1998, p. 87).

---

[1] Mediated presence information is available on the website for the International Society for Presence Research. URL is (http://ispr.info/)

VERIDICALITY

Veridical visual perception is grounded in information specific to the environment. Veridicality does not reside in the individual's mental states, as suggested by other views, but is determined by the information available in the perceiver's environment. Thus, a mediated environment may be highly veridical, depending on its available perceptual information. Gibson (1979) says that we detect ecological information directly in the optical array and perceptual veridicality exists when we use this information to successfully act or behave in the environment. Veridicality and presence seem to go hand in hand.

Motion-produced information specifies more than the surface features of an object. It also specifies structural properties such as mass, rigidity, and center of motion. When we look at actual objects, we can "see" these properties as we or the objects move. Under the conditions prevailing during the development of the visual system, motion-produced information was veridical—optical structures were produced only by the corresponding real-life events.

Veridicality is no longer guaranteed because we can produce optical arrays with a variety of devices. However, the laws of optics may assure that perception in mediated environments also gives rise to these motion-based information structures. Therefore, the understanding of presence has involved studies of the effects of the fidelity of perceptual information, the range or number of channels of information presented to viewers of mediated environments, and other factors affecting the nature of the array, including screen size (e.g., see Preston, 1998; Witmer & Singer, 1998).

Skilled media creation puts the participant into a mediated environment with its available affordances. Some media, such as first-person VGs and VR, make apparent navigation available. As a participant seems to move within the mediated environment, the optical flow specifies self-location (the ecological self) and the changing gradients provide a path of view. Thus, some media provide an action space having similarities (as well as differences) with the natural environment.

CONTINUITY

In the physical environment, perceptual information has (except at a few singular points) both a spatially continuous structure and a temporally continuous structure. In mediated environments, such spatial and temporal continuity is typically limited, except in certain high-quality virtual environments. Display features of mediated environments may alter or disrupt perceptual flow and may affect the co-perception of the self and environment and the experience of presence. For example, all immersive VR and some other mediated environments are first-person point-of-view (POV). The POV self-motion (POV-SM) technique most closely portrays what we would see if we were present and moving about in the mediated environment. It most closely resembles our real-life direct perception. It preserves spatial and temporal continuity. POV-SM should and does effectively elicit presence. But many non-POV environments also elicit presence. What must be preserved to elicit presence?

In his research, Kraft showed, to adult viewers, simple visual stories where two aspects of event structure that maintain spatial coherence (establishing shots and directional continuity) were manipulated to yield four visual narratives (Kraft *et al.*, 1991). When establishing shots are absent, directional continuity was sufficient to specify the layout and the directionality of actions. However, when directional continuity was violated, establishing shots, even though they provided important information about the layout, were not useful for the viewer to remember the flow of action. Kraft argues that violations of directional continuity prevented viewers from drawing the necessary inferences for representing the underlying actions of the characters. An example from popular media is Quentin Tarantino's nonlinear film, *Pulp Fiction*, which intentionally altered directional continuity.

Viewers are able to comprehend edited sequences, as long as those sequences adhere both to perceptually based rules that prevent unintended apparent movement, and to continuity based rules that preserve coherence and consistency. This demonstrates that continuity may be achieved in visual narratives without requiring uninterrupted visual flow. That is, just as we are able to track objects that become occluded while we move around a real-life location, we are able to use perspective structure information when scenes are edited *as long as* the editing maintains a coherent sense of space and time. Consistent with Gibson, Kraft concludes that the psychological effects of cinematic structure may be derived, not from arbitrary film conventions, but from our experience with the natural visual world. Because Gibson's direct perception is based on navigation, we need to be concerned with properties of the forms of movement-produced visual information in mediated environments. It is these properties that seem to influence the experience of mediated presence.

ECOLOGICAL PERCEPTION

In his approach to space perception, Gibson distinguished the optic array (the array of stimuli) from both the layout of the environment and the perceiving individual. As Reed (1988) notes, this led Gibson to completely rethink the nature of the process of obtaining stimulation, including rejecting the concept of stimulus altogether, and instead offering the concept of ecological information residing in the optical array. For Gibson, awareness is not subjectively constructed (Reed, 1988, p. 303), but is based on detectable environmental information. Gibson's ecological optics provided a framework for understanding both the natural and the mediated environment. He identified similarities and differences between them and explained that screen images do not replicate moving objects, but optical information available in the media does specify object motion. Like the natural environment, the media are optical arrays or environments that make ecological information available to perceivers.

GIBSON'S THEORY

Gibson's theory of perception is based on information. As Reed (1988) notes, this is in contrast to sensation theories with their thorny psychological and epistemological problems. Perception is "direct" since ecological information specifies its source. Gibson (1966) viewed visual information as optical, residing in the naturally arising structure of the optical array. In other words, perception is not internal, not based on "having sensations" but on directly "detecting information" available in the ambient light.

What we perceive are "affordances," the functional properties of objects, spaces, and events. We perceive affordances of things for behavior, offerings that can be detected and used by observers. These affordances are not abstract physical properties, but functional, ecologically relevant properties, such as texture or manipulability. Affordances are offerings, not requirements (for example, we can remain standing when an object affords sitting). A specific object may have many affordances and these are detected by the perceiver who becomes directly aware of external optical ecological information. Each perceived affordance has its own meaning and use for the individual who, thus, learns to differentiate the meaning of an object in terms of its relevance to one's activities and needs. Affordances are not possibilities, but real and external facts. Nor are they subjective. A particular object may yield different affordances to different individuals precisely because affordances are functional, that is, related to both the person and the environment.

Because we perceive affordances of things for behavior, affordances for action, perception is always simultaneously of the self and of the environment. In other words, we each perceive ourselves in the natural world. As Reed (1988, p. 280) explains, the purpose of perception is to keep observers in contact with their surroundings, where the organized environment is replete with information capable of supporting perception and where observers either succeed or fail to adequately perceive this information.

Instead of distinguishing between space and time, Gibson uses the concepts of persistence and change as reciprocals. The layout of a particular place is typically permanent in that some features, such as the ground, sky, and other substantial surfaces, persist for the longer term. For Gibson, changes in the qualities of substantial surfaces, (shape, position, composition, texture, color, etc.) count as ecological events. As Reed (1988, p. 286) points out, an object is a group of substantial surfaces forming a topologically discrete entity that persists for a minimal time and undergoes its own characteristic change. Although places and objects are persistent, information changes as the individual moves through the environment. Movement produces a perceptual flow of optical information. Each gradient is visible only from a specific point of observation. As we navigate, then, we have a "path of view" of our environment where information about objects and events persists or changes. As we move, some hidden objects become visible while others are occluded.

Every observer has a path of view and, although individual paths of view are changing, the set of all possible paths of view persists. As Reed (1988) summarizes, the environment is public and persistent. That is, "the transition between what is visible from here now (a single observation point) and what is visible in ambulatory perception (the observable habitat)—which amounts to the connectedness of the layout of the environment of all animals—is itself visible" (p. 289). As Gibson proposed, because experience is based on awareness over time, we can explore and share our environment. We perceive ourselves inhabiting the environment due to invariant and perspective structures. From a given point of view, we see a unique optic array, with some parts occluded and with particular perspectives of the visible parts. As we move, the occlusion relationships and the perspective forms change. These changes are the perspective structure of the array, a kind of optical flow specifying the path of locomotion. The invariant optical structure is whatever persists despite changes in the perspective structure. Perspective structures specify where we are going and invariant structures specify what is ahead.

Instead of cognitive maps for navigation, Gibson viewed locomotion as perceptual control of action, that is, movement through cluttered semi-enclosures involving perception of objects and their affordances. Individuals orient to the persisting features of the layout and perceive that they can reach a place if the nested places through which they must pass are sufficiently open and provide surfaces that are continuously supported.

As we move along a path, objects that we pass disappear from sight behind us, while new vistas open up in front when previously hidden objects become visible. Each vista is what is seen from "here," but *here* is an extended region, not a point. Vistas are serially connected in that the end of one opens up to another, and this connectivity persists. Hidden aspects of a particular vista are not necessarily invisible, but to find the occluded, we need to detect the continuity between the visible and the hidden. Gibson pointed out that cluttered environments offer a choice of vistas and, to find a hidden place, we need to see which vista must be opened next, which occluding edge hides the goal.

Shared awareness occurs because we all perceive the persisting environment specified by the invariant structure of the optical array and, as we move, we perceive our own changing points of view specifying the environment's perspective structure. Representations evolved in this context of shared awareness as social mediators. Representations are the results of processes of information selection and display by the creator/speaker that make others aware of something. Representations permit affordance meaning to be perceived indirectly, and humans have developed various means for marking surfaces (writing, drawing; painting, electronic media) and communicating with voice, gesture, sound-making devices, etc.

Gibson stated that we perceive the self inhabiting the environment, not just our own path of view but those of all observers. Having a point of view/ path of view is an ecological fact rather than a physical (or mental) fact. A specific point of view produces a unique optic array. Motion perspective specifies the path of locomotion, thus perspective structure is a kind of optic flow, in contrast with traditional perspective that specifies a point of view. Each person's locomotion changes the perspective structure of the optical array (i.e., changes occlusion relationships) for that individual. In spite of the changes of perspective structure, some aspects of the optical pattern persist and these are the invariant structure. Gibson argues that the invariant structure in an array specifies what any observer on any path would see. It is the invariant structure that specifies the environment independently of the self.

Gibson's theory of perception explains shared awareness using perspective structure and invariant structure. The perspective structure specifies the changing environment, the changing points of view, as the observer moves. The persisting environment is specified identically to all observers by the invariant structure of the optical array. Thus, we can share awareness while simultaneously having our own point of view. Perception is both informational and social. Our shared awareness provides the context for the evolution of representations, including pictures, symbols, signals, and so forth. We are all able to display information to make it available to others. However, Gibson distinguished between information-based vision and derived information, or representation-based information that is dependent on cultural conventions. When information specifying affordance meanings is available in the environment, they can be perceived directly. Information in representations is perceived indirectly. Pictures, language, film, and other media are meaningful in a way that is part ecological, but also partially cultural and narrative. Reed (1988) has pointed out that Gibson clearly indicated that "mediated apprehension gets combined and used with direct apprehension." For humans, direct and indirect perception, individual and social awareness, are always mixed, although direct perception is primary.

ECOLOGICAL SELF

Neisser (1991) argues that there are many sources of self-knowledge, giving rise to different aspects of self. He proposes that there are at least five aspects of self. Two perceptually given aspects of self are the *ecological self* and the *social self*. Both are directly specified in infancy by co-perception of the environment and self that occurs with activity in the environment. People are clearly different from other "objects" in the environment, capable of mutual gaze, contingent gestures, reciprocal vocalizations, etc. The information specifying interpersonal interactions includes reciprocity, the contingency of each participant's actions on those of the partner. Neisser states that interpersonal perception is probably functional from birth. It is clearly important in our choice of media; the most popular media, historically, whether books, television, or film, are drama. In newer media, such as VGs, we have seen the rapid development of both creator-imposed complex narrative and games permitting complex participant-led narrative, for example, "live-action team-play" VGs.

For Gibson, the ecological self is the self that inhabits the environment. In 1966, Gibson argued that organisms actively obtain information, not only about the environment, but about the self, through awareness of their own movements and actions. Because Gibson views it as inseparable from movement through one's surrounding array, perception is functional rather than static. For Gibson, each position/path of a moving individual creates a specific cone-shaped visual field which expands in the direction one is moving and contracts in the direction from which one has come, thus locating the individual within the environment. This is called *perceptual flow* or *streaming perspective*.

Whenever movement occurs, of the individual or an object in the environment, corresponding changes occur in the array. Movement produces changes in the gradients of flow, surface, and texture, and we use this information to coordinate our behavior. What we perceive directly is the "immediate ecological situation"—an ambient array which includes not only the environment but the self—our own position and our own actions. Gibson insisted (1979, p. 126) that all direct perception is *co-perception* of the environment and the self. That is, all perception of an ambient array is simultaneously and intrinsically a self-perception of the specific position of oneself in that array. Hunt (2004b) points out that, for Gibson, there is no outward "there" without "here." The surrounding array *gives back*—like a shadow—the exact position of the ecological self from which a creature of specific shape and speed would experience *that* array, that is, open horizon ahead and flow past of surrounding feedback implies a "hole" filled by the embodied ecological self.

Motion perspective not only carries information about distances to objects, but also information about the direction in which the individual is moving. As optical information flows with the perceiver's movement, it simultaneously provides information about objects and events as well as the self so that we always know where we are in the environment. For Gibson, self perception is "the perception of the active aware self encountering the environment" (Reed 1988, p. 233).

The ecological self, the self that inhabits its environment, brings together directly and indirectly apprehended information. Therefore, experiences in one's real-life environment and in one's simulated environment are expected to affect one another. For example, a VG player can use appropriate real-life skills, knowledge, and strategies to solve or resolve game situations, while VR training (e.g., pilot training, reduction of fear of flying) is expected to transfer to real-life events. The ecological self, whether in virtual space or the natural environment, has available both direct and mediated apprehension.

NATURAL VERSUS MEDIATED ENVIRONMENT

Gibson's theory provided a framework for understanding media, explaining how we perceive still and moving media, and how they relate to the natural environment. Gibson clearly separated environmental information from the creation of media which, for visuals, involves the structuring of light by individuals who select and display optical information. Affordance meanings are perceived directly in the natural environment. They can also be perceived indirectly in representations and artists have an ability to select and display information in a way that facilitates our perception of affordance meanings.

Gibson notes that the display of invariant structure in "moving" media is more important than the availability of perspective structure. For example, film editing is done to preserve invariant information across sequences. We do learn to deal with editing techniques, including cuts, dissolves, flashbacks and flashforwards in time, interwoven subplots, and the like, but programs for young children wisely employ fewer and simpler types of edits.

Mediated environments, some of which make available apparent navigation, have similarities with and differences from natural environments. Theorists have identified different spatial zones, some of which have considerable relevance to POV motion illusions. Cutting and Vishton (1995) have described three zones—personal space, action space, and vista space—and identified the dominant sources of perceptual information within each. For example, some pictorial sources of information (occlusion, relative size, and relative density) are invariant with distance. Within action space, the circular region immediately beyond personal space where we can move and act quickly, the effective sources of perceptual information are two of the pictorial sources—occlusion and relative size, plus motion perspective, height in the visual field, and binocular disparity. In simulations, motion perspective can be created by POV camera. Action space is typically the ecological environment of action VGs.

Because motion perspective dissipates with distance, Cutting and Vishton state that vista perception by a pedestrian is "generally unperturbed by the motions of the observer." This occurs because only monocular and static sources of vista information are available in large quantity to the pedestrian. Four pictorial cues are important: occlusion, relative size, height in the visual field, and aerial perspective. They note that *vista space* is the region in which very large paintings are most effective in either revealing layout or deceiving the eye so that extended layout is seen (e.g., Pozzo ceiling). However, some media vistas, for example, flight simulator VGs, permit apparent speed of movement, making motion perspective relevant as an important source of information to the participant.

Previc (1998) describes four perceptual zones. Two areas are linked to (1) grasping and manipulating within arm's reach and (2) reading, other complex form perception and visually mediated social interactions involving facial perception. His action extrapersonal zone (AcE) is a 360° surround, where pictorial depth cues (e.g., linear perspective, relative size) tend to predominate. Previc states that the major spatial function of AcE is to orient and navigate in relation to objects and places in topographically defined external space. His ambient extrapersonal zone (AmE) is concerned with spatial orientation and "its mode of processing is designed to interpret self-motion within a stable world by preconscious mechanisms." In contrast to the theories of Cutting and Vishton, its apparent stability does not mean that important motion processing does not occur.

The major visual cues of AmE are those important to maintaining spatial orientation and postural control: horizontal cues, linear perspective, and motion flow. Such wide field-of-view information signals self-motion. In media simulations, Previc notes that the effectiveness of motion flow is evidenced in vection and postural changes produced by wide-FOV moving surrounds. Ambient visual processing provides critical input that complements the outputs of AmE corporeal senses (vestibular and somatosensory–proprioceptive) to achieve effective postural control, spatial orientation, and image stabilization. Stimulation of each of these senses is capable of inducing postural alterations and spatial orientation illusions in flight and in the simulation of cycloconvergence. Previc points out that motion information in AmE includes all 3 types of angular motion (yaw, pitch, roll) and predominantly one type of linear motion (centrifugal expanding flow, associated with forward locomotion). The vestibular system is the most important body-orientation system for AmE, because it usually provides the most reliable and valid inertial information concerning the direction of the head relative to gravity and it may be critical in establishing the left–right coordinate frame because of its fundamental asymmetry. Previc emphasizes the importance of the AmE system because its overall body-in-space coordinates serve as the bedrock for all perceptual systems. For Previc, as well as for Gibson, the basic orienting system is essential for perception and for action. It is simulation of the AmE environment where media creators may be able to influence the development of consciousness.

MEDIA AS ECOLOGICAL ENVIRONMENT

Depictions of objects and spaces triggered debates about reality, perspective and how these depictions are related to theories of perception. Plato was concerned that illusionary representations were immoral because the use of perspective distorted the proportions of reality (e.g., a distant tree might be drawn half as tall as a near tree of the same size). Fortunately, Plato's view now has little effect on art and perspective is a ruling principle for most image making. Some believe that mimesis is the ideal and the goal is to make an image so technically perfect that the viewer of the illusion confuses image and reality. Others disagree, for example, artist René Magritte painted a picture of a pipe and wrote below it (in French), "This is not a pipe." Before the age of virtual reality, it is difficult to think of instances of mimesis. Except perhaps briefly (with examples like holograph and trompe l'oeil), we are unlikely to accept an image as real, although Star Trek's Holodeck offered a vision for the future and, today, many museums and art or science centers offer virtual reality installations.

Assumption of realism has moved to a debate about what is portrayed, a debate that encompasses many fields including philosophy, art, psychology, and computer science. Panofsky (1988) states that perspective is a symbolic form for conveying intellectual content. He says that perspective does not represent vision but one of the possible representations of seeing. As such, perspective is a figurative principle. Gombrich (1993) notes that perhaps the world may never look like an image, but an image may be made to look like the world; thus perspective is a representational technique for creating the mimetic ideal.

Avant-garde art may use perspective but have no interest in mimesis. As Swiss-born artist, Paul Klee (1973) states, "images do not reproduce what is visible; images render something visible." Modern theorists understand that the artist/photographer/filmmaker/game designer makes choices that affect the creation. Representing physical reality may not be a goal, but the representation of emotion or other types of content, as, for example, Kandinsky's Composition VIII (Guggenheim, NY).

Turner painted the same scene under different conditions of light. The evidence seems rather clear that artists choose aspects of their compositions. The same is true of photographs, and this is no longer debated in an era of software for digital photo manipulations and the creation of digital film graphics. Even when photos are not digitally altered, photographers make choices consistent with their own goals.

Visuals are not the only perceptual information available in media. Many presentations also make available information for auditory and other perceptual systems. Visual imagery, music, and other production features, such as lighting and mise en scene, all elicit emotion and can affect the visual focus of attention. Chion (1990) claims that what we see is always altered by what we hear because sound engages the very structuring of vision by framing it. Several investigators of film music have shown that characteristics of music can influence direct as well as indirect judgments of the film (Bolivar *et al.*, 1994; Bullerjahn & Güldenring, 1994; Lipscomb & Kendall, 1994; Marshall & Cohen, 1988; Thayer & Levinson, 1983; Vitouch, 2001). Aspects of music, such as rhythm, tempo, and temporary synchrony, alter temporal congruence (of sounds and visuals) and may determine the visual focus of attention (Cohen, 2000). Cohen (1999, 2000, 2005; Cohen &

MacMillan, 2004) has also demonstrated that music can alter mood and increase viewer absorption. These influences of music are greater when there is more visual ambiguity. Media creators usually select music that is congruent with the visuals. Smith (1999) argues that such congruence heightens or intensifies the affective qualities of the image, that is, viewers feel emotion more strongly than they would with the music or image alone.

Any medium permits a range of options to the creator. The role of artistic talent cannot be ignored; otherwise, we could all paint like Rembrandt or Van Gogh, capture people like Imogen Cunningham or Annie Leibovitz do in their photographs, and so forth. Most media are representational and intentionally so. Viewers are often willing to adopt an instrumental set while the director-controlled images cue the audience to the director-intended message. Media creators can alter the impact of structure to elicit inferencing, and a simple demonstration illustrates the role of style or form. I show my students several pictures of "cat" which yield a variety of meanings (a black-and-white line drawing of a cat with heart-shaped spots, a colorful cartoon cat, a photo, and paintings of a realistic-looking cat and a colorful abstract version of a cat). However, media do not consist of form alone. Klee (1973) emphasized that content is essential; it is the impetus for form, but content is impossible without the appropriate form to hold it. For Klee, design emphasizes process in analysis and synthesis, and whether it is called intuition, unconscious processes, or inspiration, creative forces must be balanced with conscious processes. Kandinsky (see Knight, 2001) described content as the emotion in the artist's soul, while form serves to embody it. He argued that intuition was critical whenever a media creation called for viewer input or choice because intuition was needed to evaluate and choose among available design solutions. As he explained, media creators begin with content but complete harmony exists only when the content creates the form.

PICTURES

Because Gibson defines information independently of receiver and object, we can ask what information is present in naturally occurring environments that is the same or different from mediated representations. With pictures, Gibson points out that they are flat, ordinarily reduced in size compared to environmental objects, and subject to other differences and limitations. However, differences should not be viewed as discrepancies between picture and scene predicted by a projective model. In fact, Gibson's research demonstrated that, when viewed from a wide variety of positions and distances, pictures do provide adequate information for viewers to perform visual–spatial tasks nearly as well as when they are viewing the actual scenes.

In 1971, Gibson specified that a picture "is a surface so treated that a delimited optical array to a point of observation is made available that contains the same kind of information that is found on the ambient optic arrays of an ordinary environment" (p.277). As Reed (1988) notes, we do not look at a picture's surface, but at what is depicted by means of markings. He continues that the way in which a picture makes information available may be conventionalized and culturally specific; however, the information itself is not conventional, it is ecological.

When perspective is displayed in a static scene, it helps the observer to see a realistic spatial display of a section of a scene. Perspective pictures provide spatial awareness to viewers for a captured segment of an optical array. Sense of realism arises because the sector of the optical array captured by the picture contains some of the same structure as the scene. Of course, the information displayed by the picture surface is incomplete relative to the real scene.

Because information displayed by pictures can be the same kind of information displayed by physical reality, viewers can experience "media reality." Thus, the picture cannot be a physical or natural environment. As well, a picture contains information about its own surface (e.g., texture and brush strokes of paint, graininess of photographs). Although the artist determined what is displayed in the frame, viewers of pictures may look at a pictured scene from several angles and distances, and may also choose to look at the picture surface (for example, to see how paint is layered or juxtaposed, the pattern of paintbrush strokes, the texture of the surface on which the scene is displayed). At an art gallery, viewers may take advantage of the full array of information available, not just the scene, but the type of material to which paint has been applied, type of paint or other artist's media, how the paint was applied (layers, types of brushes, types of brush strokes). Even nonspecialists are readily able to distinguish Van Gogh's thick paint strokes from Renoir's little brush strokes. A gallery may present a piece to facilitate an effect. The Albright-Knox Art Gallery in Buffalo, NY, chose to hang a huge Jackson Pollock on a wall at the end of a long hallway. As the viewer walks closer to the painting, it fills one's field of view (FOV), creating the illusion of walking into the painting.

A static medium collapses perspective and invariant structure. We can see only the particular point of view chosen by the artist, photographer, etc. For Gibson, perspective structure of a static medium is a special case of flow, seeing from a point, not a path. If the perspective of a scene is displayed in a picture, it does not induce an illusion of reality, according to Gibson (1979, p. 282–284), but rather induces an awareness of being in the mediated world, which he emphasizes "is no illusion." Picture perspective (seeing from a point of observation) is not ordinary seeing (from a path). We need movement in a medium to provide information for seeing from a path.

MEDIA AND MOVEMENT

In pictorial representations, viewers readily recognize objects or events. Even simple line drawings contain some spatial information, and perspective drawings include some 3-dimensional spatial information. That is, pictures are ecological spaces. With the advent of film, mediated environments provided much more spatial information as an object or individual moved within a scene. Early movie cameras were heavy and stationary. Early filmmakers like the Lumière brothers made "actualities," short films about real life. For example, to make "Arrivée d'un train" (1895), they carried their camera to a Paris train station, placed it beside the track, and filmed the locomotive as it approached the station, stopped, and passengers disembarked.

As camera technology and camera techniques advanced, filmmakers incorporated more spatial navigation into scenes. Cameras permitted directors to pan, dolly, and zoom, and cinematographers presented movement from third-person and first-person perspectives. In first-person POV (point-of-view), the camera showed what the viewer would see if present in the scene. POV self-motion (POV-SM), widely used in film, video games, and virtual reality, shows what the viewer would see if present in and moving about the mediated environment.

Movement in real and virtual action space elicits both emotions and visceral responses. The perception–emotion link was investigated by Lang (1995), who found that subjectively judged valence and arousal of pictures elicit reliable psychophysiological responses. Researchers have observed emotional responses to moving pictures where viewers reported "simulation symptoms" and showed post-test decrements on a variety of tasks (e.g., Biocca & Rolland, 1998; Cheung et al., 1995; Kellogg & Gillingham, 1986; Kennedy et al., 1993, 1997; Kennedy & Stanney, 1996; Lombard et al., 1995; Reeves & Nass, 1996; Regan & Price, 1994). Some theoretical models assume a direct link between emotion during viewing and the occurrence of negative effects, including motion sickness symptoms and post-test decrements, and some investigators (e.g., Kennedy et al., 1993) further assume that symptoms yield poor performance.

Recently, research attention has been directed to media entertainment and its primary function of enjoyment (Bryant & Vorderer, 2006; Zillmann & Vorderer, 2000). The popularity of participant motion in virtual space in video games and VR entertainment points to positive outcomes and psychological appeal. Participants' interpretations of "symptoms" when viewing apparent-motion displays may differ as a function of the way these individuals process similar ecological information in the natural environment (Hann et al., 2005; Preston, 2005). That is, skills and abilities of the ecological self affect reactions to mediated as well as natural information. Participants who readily orient to motion experiences in the natural environment should also readily orient to apparent motion in mediated environments and show few post-participation deficits when they exit the medium.

ORIENTATION AND SPACE

ORIENTATION

The ecological or perceptual self pays attention to spatial and perceptual information in the environment. This allows us to maintain our orientation in natural and mediated environments as well as to orient ourselves when we enter a mediated environment and to reorient when we return to the natural environment. Gibson focuses on the importance of orientation as necessary for adequate perception of the environment. With motion, whether self-motion or movement of something in the environment, the individual adjusts to changing stimulation. Information input into the active exploratory system changes with motion, thus generating further information. Reed (1988) notes that Gibson is pointing out the fact that "there could be neither perception, nor action, without a functional basic orientation system" (p. 227).

For Gibson, self-perception or proprioception is a component of the functioning of all perceptual systems. Thus, we can become aware of our own behavior through all the senses—vision, audition, kinesthesia, etc. Functional proprioception emphasizes both the "awareness of the results of changes in the observer's relation to the environment" and "each perceptual system's intricate capacities for adjustment to changing stimuli" (Reed, 1988, p. 227). We have a "basic orienting system" that incorporates all the perceptual and action systems and enables us to maintain our orientation to all the forces and surfaces around us. Movement requires several types of orientation including orienting the body (e.g., gravity and other forces), maintaining equilibrium, and proprioception of posture.

Lack of orientation disrupts perceptual exploration and action. This is true for both natural and mediated environments, since performance decrements on spatial and navigational tests following simulations are commonly observed in both. Explanations typically point to the types of stimuli and motion symptoms. However, the availability of direct apprehensions to the participant in virtual action space points as well to real-life factors influencing post-simulation performance. Therefore, we need to determine whether relevant real-life factors, including participation in sports, especially sports involving 3-D space, nausea, ocular difficulties, disorientation, and enjoyment of 3-D entertainment, influence simulation emotion, symptoms, and performance outcomes. Researchers have already begun such investigations. A literature search shows a plethora of new studies of orientation (including spatial frames of reference, spatial information updating, and reorientation) and disorientation (including causes, consequences, and prevention).

We can become disoriented when we spin ourselves around or when we watch certain mediated events. Siegel (1979–80) has noted that stimuli which produce dizziness, a symptom elicited in both simulations and the natural environment, can rarely be separated into distinctly positive versus negative. He continues that play is one method for producing dizziness, with the motivation being creative and autonomous exploration of the internal or external environment. He points out that when dizziness has negative effects (e.g., autonomic arousal), those effects tend to overshadow positive effects (e.g., cortical arousal). When stimuli involve motion in virtual action space, symptoms (each of which reflects disruption of spatial orientation to some degree) need not be interpreted as negative. They may be viewed as enjoyable if the participant views the medium as play, has high spatial and perceptual abilities that facilitate orientation, and/or if the participant enjoys similar real-life events. These individuals may interpret symptoms as a natural and expected part of a motion experience. To the extent that the participant has difficulties with similar real-life events, motion stimuli may produce autonomic arousal and the individual will feel uncomfortable and disoriented and have poorer post-viewing performance.

POV AND PERCEPTUAL FLOW

Gibson used film to study self-motion (as part of a research program on pilot training) and identified motion perspective as a relevant perceptual variable. Gibson (1954, p. 321) states that the analysis of motion perspective for a large portion of the visual field "suggests that the impression of *forward* movement of the observer can be produced optically without any contribution from the vestibular or muscle sense." He reports that observers of a moving picture of "a landing field ahead of an airplane" reported an experience of locomotion along a glide path toward a visible spot on the ground, and even more compelling experiences of locomotion can be induced using the panoramic motion picture. We can experience such locomotion in flight simulators used for pilot training and testing, in first-person flight simulation video games and some films, as well as other VR and VG applications. The 1968 film *2001: A Space Odyssey*[2] pioneered technical effects used to create the "Star Gate," streaming, whirling lights representing space travel.

Technological and cinematic advances allow us to better imitate the perceptual experience of the natural environment. The subjective or point-of-view (POV) camera increases interface transparency because it simulates the spatial component of direct perception specifying where the viewer is within a spatial array, and POV Self-Motion (POV-SM), common in VR simulations, VGs, and some films, provides the navigational component, the perceptual flow of locomotion (Preston, 1998). With its increased navigational realism, simulating a path of view, POV-SM is associated with the experience of immersion or presence in mediated environments.

---

[2] The 1968 film *2001: A Space Odyssey* (screenplay by Stanley Kubrick & Arthur C. Clarke, who also wrote the book). More information is available at the Internet Movie Data Base (http://www.imdb.com/)

Gibson argues that affordance meanings can be perceived indirectly, via meaningful still and moving pictures, in a way that is part historical (i.e., experience) and part cultural as well as ecological. Our social and individual processes of cognition and awareness are thoroughly mixed; mediated apprehension gets combined and fused with direct apprehension (Gibson, 1976, unpublished, cited by Reed, 1988, p. 307). The ecological self, the self that inhabits its environment, brings together directly and indirectly-apprehended information. Therefore, experiences in one's real-life environment and in one's simulated environment are expected to affect one another. In a study focusing on virtual action space (Preston, 2005), participants experienced simulated environments from the "subjective point-of-view," that is, the viewer saw what would be seen if present in and moving about the space (POV-SM). Therefore, it was expected that factors relevant to real-life action space as well as those occurring in virtual action space would affect participant interpretation and responses.

Eighty-six university students (45 men, 41 women, mean age 20 years) volunteered to view, on a large screen (7.5 feet wide), 10 short POV-SM clips (race car, railroad, sky diver, airplane, luge/sled, dune buggy, wind surfing, stunt plane, fighter plane, and roller coaster). After each clip, participants indicated their emotional responses and degree of motion symptoms. Participants also completed a questionnaire and pre- and post-viewing tests measuring balance and perceptual and spatial abilities. The questionnaire yielded scores about real-life variables including enjoyment of rides, type and amount of sports participation, and typical real-life symptoms (nausea, vision difficulty, balance difficulty). Greater sports participation was associated with more enjoyment of the clips and better post-test balance. It was also related to higher post-test spatial scores. Participants having real-life nausea rated the clips as more arousing and dominant and reported stronger symptoms during viewing. Participants having real-life difficulty with balance reported higher emotional ratings and did more poorly on the perceptual and spatial post-tests. Participants reporting real-life nausea, as well as vision and balance difficulties, performed poorly on the spatial post-test.

The indices of sports participation, real-life symptoms (difficulties with nausea, vision, and balance), and enjoyment of rides taken together provided information about participants' ability to establish and maintain basic orientation to events in the natural environment, while the post-tests indexed ability to reorient following viewing POV-SM media. Participants who are better able to maintain basic orientation in the natural environment may interpret motion symptoms during viewing as a normal and expected part of the experience of motion. They enjoyed the viewing experience more and also performed better on the post-tests, indicating that they were better able to orient to the virtual event and to reorient to real-life.

For Gibson, the perceptual systems are functional, actively obtaining information about both the self and the environment. We continuously adjust to changing stimulation. To function in the natural environment, to perceive and to act, the individual must establish and maintain orientation to the environment. Lack of orientation interferes with direct perceptual exploration. We not only actively maintain orientation when experiencing changing optical information, but we reorient as we move to and from natural and mediated environments. Mou *et al.* (2004) conducted a study of spatial updating by participants in augmented reality (AR) environments. These are systems that blend computer-generated virtual objects or environments with real environments. Participants performed tasks in mobile AR systems having either an environment-stabilized (ESF) or a body-stabilized (BSF) frame of reference. In the ESF condition (objects remained in place when the person moved, as is typical in the natural environment), participants were able to update the location of objects to perform a spatial task when they rotated their body. The findings also indicated that spatial memory is orientation dependent. In the BSF condition, objects maintained their position relative to the participant's body (e.g., an object directly in front of the person remained directly in front when the person rotated 90°). Naive users initially used an environment-stabilized frame to perform the spatial task, but after just 2 minutes of exposure, their representation changed to body-stabilized frame. Our "basic orienting system" incorporates all the perceptual and action systems and enables us to maintain our orientation to all the forces and surfaces around us. This study demonstrates how readily we can do this in virtual space.

Reed (1988) states that wherever our eyes look, the world ordinarily does not tilt, swing, or distort; rather, we see an upright world where we are moving or tilting. When moving, we use the wide-angle visual field to help us navigate through a terrain because horizontal cues, linear perspective, and motion flow provide visual cues important to maintaining spatial orientation and posture control (Gibson, 1966, 1979; Previc, 1998). We continuously detect environmental information and changes in that information to update our spatial awareness. Reed (1988) argues that the goal of perception is to obtain clear information out of a sea of potential stimulation, thus perceptual activity is one of selection. In an unfamiliar space, we perceptually explore to identify relevant information to support our actions. In both natural and mediated environments, maintaining our basic orientation (using continuous spatial updating) facilitates good information selection, on which adequate or successful perception depends.

SPACE AND CONSCIOUSNESS

Debate over the underlying nature of thought takes essentially two positions: (1) thought as propositional logic (e.g., Pylyshyn, 1984) versus (2) thought based in abstract visual–spatial imagery (e.g., Arnheim, 1969; Hunt, 1995; Lakoff, 1987; Johnson, 1987; Shepard, 1978). Hunt (1995) explains how Gibson's theory of ecological perception, especially his notions about self-in-the-world and perceptual flow, is linked to the development of consciousness. Gibson locates a unitary space–time in the here–there, whither–whence flow of the perceptual array itself. He also views awareness as a direct resonance with the flow of the world. Hunt notes that Gibson's direct perception specifies where we are in relation to the navigational affordances of a display and navigation produces changes in the gradients of flow, surface, and texture. He continues that it is difficult to imagine a creature oriented in an array in which it does not recognize selected patterns as especially relevant. Therefore, Hunt argues that, "If self-reflective symbolic cognition is, as Neisser (1976) and Bartlett (1932) have insisted, based on the reorganization and recombination of perceptual processes, then we might expect Gibson's flow dynamics to reemerge as part of the organizing template for higher mental processes" (p. 70). Hunt (1995) argues that consciousness is a capacity involving direction, choice, and synthesis of nonconscious processes, exemplifying the deep structure of a kind of intelligence that directly reuses and reorganizes the structures of perception. Spatial abilities are the framework needed for its full development (Hunt, 1995, p. 46). A number of theorists have contributed to our understanding of the visual–spatial basis of thought.

   Arnheim's (1969, 1974) view that abstract visual imagery is the deep structure of verbal and nonverbal conceptual thought is based on his work in aesthetics. He states that felt meanings of visual art (whether naturalistic or abstract-expressionist) are most immediately conveyed by the abstract "visual dynamics" or "skeleton of forces" embedded in the painting at the most basic level of figure/ground differentiation. Using stroboscopic exposures, Arnheim showed that rapid oscillations did not provide enough time to identify specific objects in a painting. Rather, its most basic physiognomic or expressive structure was a looming fundamental dynamic shape. For Arnheim, visual dynamics are "felt" as much as they are seen. Some artists agree. Kandinsky (see Knight, 2001) describes content as the inner element, the emotion in art, while form, the external element, must serve as its embodiment.

   Some research has linked shapes with emotions. Bang (1991) has shown that predominantly horizontal line dynamics tend to convey stability and calm, verticals are more exciting and upward striving, and diagonals convey greater tension. Arnheim believed that abstract diagrams and imagery were important to scientific discovery and Shepard (1978) documented that physical scientists think in spontaneous geometric dynamic imagery. As Hunt argues (1995, p. 174), "the apparent lack of communication in abstract dynamics alone shows that they reflect primarily the inner and microgenic processes of felt meaning and less the conventional, culturally dictated codes for referential pointing." In other words, geometric shapes and abstract drawings may permit insights by virtue of the fact that they contain felt meaning without referential constraints.

   Arnheim's analysis suggesting that fundamental shapes convey felt meaning, not detailed perceptual realism, has important implications for constructing media designed to encourage the development of consciousness. This perspective stands in contrast to VR and VG designers, who traditionally place great importance on realism. Players also rate realism (of sound, graphics, and setting) as an important characteristic of VGs (Wood *et al.*, 2004), and new products to enhance realism are popular, such as the optical head tracker, allowing the gamer to use slight head movements to look around the game environment. Early VGs contained simple shapes due to the limitations of displays. With improved graphics, available details increased and this made pattern recognition easier. Further advances have resulted in more complex environments and more complex games requiring players to master considerable learning during repetitive play. VR designers also had early display quality problems, and a link between sensory fidelity and performance was a common assumption not always achieved in practice. Biocca (1996) has suggested that, to affect performance, virtual design might selectively highlight relevant cues, effectively simulating how we think rather than simulating reality. To do this, we need to identify metaphors for thinking.

Arnheim states that only geometric dynamics are sufficiently complex, precise, and ultrarapid enough to be a primary medium of thought. He asserted that "the perceptual qualities of shape and motion are present in the very acts of thinking" (Arnheim, 1969, p. 118). He continues that they are the medium in which thinking itself takes place. For Arnheim, ultrarapid geometric–dynamic imagery is basic to all thought and he provided many examples of drawings reflecting individuals' understandings of abstract verbal concepts such as time. As Hunt notes, such drawings demonstrate that the logic of semantic relations can be translated into abstract forms, but they lack referential pointing. Arnheim argued that referential pointing is the main function of language while abstract dynamic imagery reflects the inner and microgenic processes of felt meaning. That is, for Arnheim, visual–spatial metaphor is the basis of abstract thought, an idea that was further developed by Lakoff and Johnson.

For Lakoff (1987) and Johnson (1987), basic perception provides "basic level structures" as well as "image schemas." These more abstract forms are regularly occurring embodied patterns of experience, including container, center–periphery, source–goal, up–down, and balance Conceptual structure becomes meaningful because abstract spatial metaphors are kinesthetically embodied. According to Lakoff (1987), image schemas are as basic to the self-referential conceptualization of human experience as they are to the representations of the structures of the external world.

Hunt (1995, p. 175) notes that Lakoff and Johnson both treat image schemas as amodal rather than synesthetic. (See Hunt's Ch. 7, "Synesthesia: The Inner Face of Thought and Meaning," for a fuller discussion.) He argues that there must be a step beyond the manifestation of these structures in movement that is needed to raise them to the status of organizing spatial metaphors, simply because movement structures (path, near–far, etc.) are also organizing behavior principles for nonsymbolic creatures. This missing step is "their abstraction for symbolic use by means of cross-modal translations and transformations" (p. 175). As cross-modal emergents, they would be more complex than simple synesthesias and "would be the fundamental structures out of which representational semantics and syntax could emerge, on the one hand, along with the more structurally intricate patterns of abstract conceptual thought and spontaneous presentational states, on the other" (p. 175). Hunt points out that Arnheim and others suggest that the concept of openness of consciousness could not be thought, let alone realized as felt meaning, without the metaphors afforded by the perception of sky, space, and glowing light or luminosity. "The openness of space constitutes the closest metaphoric approximation to the categories that representational self-reference can ever fully encompass—consciousness, self, and time" (p. 209). Hunt (2004a) further argues that heightened self-awareness is based on the forms of consciousness itself and becomes visible through the embodiment of synesthetic metaphors derived from more abstract properties of nature. For example, ecstatic states can be induced in individuals who are "suitably open to their kinesthetic embodiment and resonance" with the contemplation of "light, wind, fire, and flowing water, the heights and depths of ravines and mountains, etc." (Hunt, 2004a, p. 20).

Hunt distinguishes a more impersonal experience or presence such as the glow of luminous open space becoming, with cross-modal translation, the metaphor for the openness of time. Vital presence is a more personal experience that not only emerges at a symbolic level, but is a basic structure of perception involving both orientation toward horizontal openness and the propriolocation of specific position within the array. Similarly, Almaas (1986) distinguishes two aspects or poles of essence: first, presence–openness or "felt transcendence," that is more impersonal and based on the experience of openness and space, and second, a more personal sense of presence or "I am." Almaas also tells us what consciousness feels like: It is essence—filled with a flowing substance and opening out into an expanded sense of spaciousness. The two aspects of presence point to an interesting issue for media creators. The personal sense of presence is a more representational self-referential awareness, one subordinated to the instrumental set (Hunt, 1995), the presence often found in VGs and VRs. The more impersonal presence appears as spontaneous imagery arising in an expressive symbolic medium and whose facilitating content, suggested by Arnheim, is geometric shapes and nature. This presence is more intuitive and linked to a medium conducive to inferencing.

Hunt (1995, p. 213) argues that presence–openness is "not some sort of psychological process, but an existential fact. We really *are* here...." Presence–openness is the basic organization of perception itself; thus, it is not created but rather revealed by processes of symbolic self-reference." As Hunt (1995, p. 244) summarizes: Space, time, causality, and self are codetermined and inseparable aspects of a single seamless ecological array. This may help us understand the task of media creation—how to present visual dynamics in a comprehensible sequence, a time–space continuity, of Gibson's nested spaces where occluded objects become visible while visible objects disappear as we move and behave.

In his discussion of time as flow, Hunt points out that psychological moments synthesize into longer periods of felt continuity similar to James' streams of consciousness (James, 1890). There are various media techniques that can help us achieve flow or introspection or other states that may develop consciousness. For example, the resulting editing of the sound and visuals of the 1996 film *The English Patient*[3] can induce a hypnogogic state in some viewers. Instead of high stimulation common to action VGs, Suedfeld developed a reduced environmental stimulation technique (REST) that used a chamber or capsule as environment and found that mood improved and arousal was reduced (Suedfeld *et al.*, 1985–6). This technique enhanced scientific creativity (Suedfeld *et al.*, 1987) and produced more pleasant and intense autobiographical memories (Suedfeld & Eich, 1995). Perhaps the low stimulation encouraged spontaneous imagery.

Design features of media are implemented to achieve particular effects. The mimetic ideal is necessarily the goal for some mediated environments, such as simulators for pilot testing, but other considerations direct the creation of the wide variety of media. What choices might facilitate participants' development of consciousness? Detailed realism does not seem the direction to go. Geometric shapes, open horizons, and opportunities for inferencing have been suggested. Gibson points to navigation, orientation, and nested places that support these activities. Active exploration is associated with the development of flow in both VGs and VRs. However, this type of flow is described as an optimal level of experience that the player wishes to maintain (Choi & Kim, 2004), and thus seems more similar to personal presence and instrumental set. However, a few VG studies have linked play variables with indices of consciousness development (Chou & Ting, 2003; Gackenbach, personal communication, Nov. 2005; Gackenbach & Preston, 1998; Nery & Preston, 2005) and VGs have been developed using biofeedback techniques to allow us to explore media events using breath and voice, etc. (See http://www.wilddivine.com for a game designed to elicit a meditative state.) We need more media that permit navigation free from the usual instrumental controls like joysticks. Once we have identified the appropriate visual and spatial–navigational metaphors, there may be many kinds of mediated environments that we can create to provide sufficient opportunities for the development of consciousness, and existing media provide prototypes.

Space and navigation involve eye movement and/or self motion. Still images permit visual exploration of a section of a scene and, therefore, may facilitate development of consciousness even if they do not permit motion. Kandinsky's Composition 8 is known as his masterpiece and consists of geometric shapes with

---

[3] *The English Patient*, 1996, received 9 Oscars including double Oscars to Walter Murch for sound and film editing, John Seale for Cinematography, and Stuart Craig/Stephanie McMillan for Art Direction, making it a visually stunning film. More information is available at the Internet Movie Data Base (http://www.imdb.com/)

perspective and occlusions. When shown this painting, some of my students report that it refers to music, to abstract problem solving, etc. That is, it permits inferencing. Others had difficulty making meaning. Abstract impressionist painters have provided us with a rich and varied landscape to explore the idea that image schemas are synesthetic metaphors, as suggested by Hunt (1995). Some art was created to intentionally represent transcendence[4] (e.g., the work of artist Gordon Onslow Ford, based on his "line, circle, dot" theory, described in Bogzaran, 2003). If Arnheim is correct, that fundamental shapes convey felt meaning, pictures, composed of lines and shapes, should be translated or transformed crossmodally, for symbolic use. Perhaps, as Hunt suggests, individual differences come into play. Those higher in absorption or openness-to-experience may be more willing or better able to infer meaning of abstract stimuli. In 1974, Stein published a physiognomic cue test, consisting of line drawings and two interpretations of each. For example, a line drawing:\\\/// had a rating scale with end points labeled sunrise/sunset – slanted lines. He observed wide individual differences in the degree to which subjects were willing to endorse higher inferential labels.

Installation artist, Gary Hill, in his 1998 exhibition (viewed at Montreal's Musée d'Art Contemporain), created a variety of environments. In one installation that was completely pitch black so that participants had no visual information, sounds were played. Participants tended to sway, and focus on proprioceptive information. Some experienced dizziness or disorientation in the installation and disequilibrium upon exiting. Another installation contained several television screens placed in a line, a few feet apart. Each TV showed a film of a snake that appeared to move from one TV screen to the next in a slow undulating fashion that seemed to mesmerize viewers. What appeared on screen one, moved to screen 2 (and so forth) at a pace consistent with the time it would take to cross the distance between TV sets, and eventually the head would be on one screen, tail on another and the body on some intervening screens. The undulating movement of the snake and the slow pace of the sequence seemed to induce a hypnogogic state in some observers, while others seemed to visibly relax. Slow pace is typically found in dramatic media since it is thought to provide time for a viewer to access deeper and/or personal meaning. In contrast, fast pace requires viewers to attend to rapidly changing perceptual information and this increases arousal and excitement. Degree of narrative structure is also important, because less structure or instrumental set, including more nonlinearity and greater ambiguity, elicits more inferencing by viewers (see Blanchard-Fields *et al.*, 1986). Popular media are typically high structure to nudge viewers toward the producer/director intended interpretations.

With faster computers, advanced graphical software and other technological innovations have come a multitude of individuals and groups experimenting with media space and developing ingenious virtual environments. For example, at the

---

[4] For example, see (http://www.lucidart.org)

University of Illinois, the NCSA Visualization and Virtual Environments Group has developed CAVE, a virtual research environment with true stereoscopic capabilities for researcher–data interaction. Use of 3-D in movies has extended to TV with a November 2005 episode of *Medium* broadcast in high definition 3-D, using technology developed by Sensio Montreal.

Char Davies[5] has developed virtual spaces that incorporate many of the principles and ideas of perception identified by Gibson as well as self-awareness and image schemas described in the consciousness literature. She created Osmose and Ephémère as bodily experiential works (Davies, 2004). They are described as a "mode of access to an ephemeral yet embodied experience" of self in place. Participants wear a head-mounted display and walk through a virtual environment, where real-time motion tracking is based on breathing and balance.

"As a means of subverting the conventional VR aesthetic of hard-edged-objects-in-empty-space," Davies used semi-transparency and translucency visuals, where one can see through more than 20 layers simultaneously. Both content and form are important. For example, Klee (1973) describes content as the impetus for form, but it is form that is process-oriented as in genesis, growth, and essence. Davies states that her intent was to create an all-enveloping flux and flow. Here, "the usual perceptual cues by which we objectify the world — simply disappear, dissolved into an ambiguous enveloping spatiality of soft, semi-transparent, intermingling volumes of varying hues and luminosities." According to Davies, this creates a perceptual state where one becomes acutely aware of one's own embodied presence inhabiting space. This is akin to the heightened self-awareness that, as Hunt (2004a) suggests, becomes visible when more abstract properties of nature become embodied in synesthetic metaphor.

Davies also designed her virtual spaces to counter the medium's bias toward control. To navigate within Osmose and Ephémère, the individual breathes in to rise, out to fall, and alters one's center of balance to change direction. Making the immersive experience dependent on the intuitive visceral processes of breath and balance deliberately countered conventional ways of navigating and interacting in virtual space. Davies argues that relying on hand-based devices such as joysticks, pointers, or data gloves, tends to "reinforce an instrumental, dominating stance toward the world." This is an important design issue because Hunt and Almaas both have linked instrumental set to the more personal, representational sense of presence rather than the expressive, presentational presence of consciousness. Davies also points out that the experience of breathing in to rise and out to fall facilitates a convincing sensation of "floating," and the sensation of floating tends to evoke euphoric feelings of disembodiment and immateriality, which "we intentionally amplify through our enabling the participant to see through and virtually float

---

[5] Char Davies' Osmose premiered at the Musée d'Art Contemporain de Montréal in 1995, and Ephémère premiered at the National Gallery of Canada (Ottawa) in 1998. Davies website (includes articles) is at (http://immersence.com)

through everything around them." As Davies notes, "the effect for the immersant is of floating within a world which is neither wholly representational (i.e., recognizable) nor wholly abstract, but hovering in between."

For Davies, Osmose is a space for exploring the perceptual interplay between self and world, that is, a place for facilitating awareness of one's own self as consciousness embodied in enveloping space. The first virtual space encountered in Osmose is a three-dimensional orientation space. With the immersant's first breaths, this grid gives way to a clearing in a forest which gives access to a dozen "world-spaces." These spaces were based primarily on metaphorical aspects of nature, including: Clearing, Forest, Tree, Leaf, Cloud, Pond, Subterranean Earth, and Abyss. "Immersants" use their own breath and balance to journey within these worlds or hover in ambiguous areas in between.

Ephémère is also grounded in "nature" as metaphor and uses recurring archetypal elements of root, rock, and stream, but it is extended to include body organs, blood vessels, and bones. Unlike Osmose, Ephémère has three hierarchical levels: landscape, earth, and interior body. The ever-changing river is the only constancy and provides a nonlinear means of navigation through the three realms, in addition to that of the immersant's breath and balance. When the immersant "surrenders to the pull of its flow, it metamorphosizes [sic] from river to underground stream or artery/vein and vice versa."

Davies (2004) reports that between 1995 and 2001, more than 20,000 people have been individually immersed in the virtual environments Osmose and Ephémère, and many people experience a heightened awareness of self-presence, describing their experience in euphoric terms or as the sensation of consciousness occupying space. Individual differences in openness-to-experience remind us that presence–openness is a dimension not a point. High absorbers, because they prefer stimulus conditions that encourage focus on internal events (see Roche & McConkey, 1990; Tellegen & Atkinson, 1974), may readily embrace media that are open or ambiguous.

Hunt (1995) has argued that image schemas are synesthetic metaphors derived from abstract properties of nature (p.175). It is not enough for them to be manifested in movement, but rather they need to become spatial metaphors by means of cross-modal translations and transformations. Cross-modal emergents may be easier to achieve with moving audiovisual images, especially those with open horizons and geometric shapes. However, we will need to develop many mediated environments representing differing points on the continuum. Popular media are designed to elicit the director-intended message from a wide audience, and those who initially are uncomfortable in mediated situations without a strong instrumental set may begin with more structured media before trying more open experiences. As technological advances continue and media creators seek innovative ways of expressing felt meaning, especially spatially embodied environments, we may soon be able to identify the contents and formats best able to encourage the development of consciousness in people with differing skills, abilities, and preferences for media engagement.

REFERENCES

Almaas, A. (1986). *Essence*. York Beach, ME: Samuel Weiser.

Arnheim, R. (1969). *Visual thinking*. Berkeley & Los Angeles: University of California Press.

Arnheim, R. (1974). *Art and visual perception*. Berkeley & Los Angeles: University of California Press.

Ashton, M., Lee, K., Perugini, M., Szarota, P., de Vries, R., Di Blas, L., Boies, K., & De Raad, B. (2004). A six-factor structure of personality-descriptive adjectives: Solutions from psycholexical studies in seven languages. *Journal of Personality and Social Psychology, 86,* 356–366.

Bang, M. (1991). *Picture this: Perception and composition*. Boston: Little Brown.

Bartlett, F. (1932). *Remembering*. Cambridge: Cambridge University Press.

Biocca, F. (1996). Intelligence augmentation: The vision inside virtual reality. In B. Gorayska & J. Mey (Eds.), *Cognitive technology: In search of a human interface* (pp. 59–75), Amsterdam: Elsevier.

Biocca, F., & Rolland, J. (1998). Virtual eyes can rearrange your body. Adaptation to visual displacement in see-through head-mounted displays. *Presence, 7,* 262–277.

Blanchard-Fields, F., Coon, R., & Mathews, R. (1986). Inferencing and television: A developmental study. *Journal of Youth & Adolescence, 15* (6), 453–459.

Bogzaran, F. (2003). Lucid art and hyperspace lucidity. *Dreaming, 13,* 29–42. Available at http://www.lucidart.org

Bolivar, V., Cohen, A., & Fentress, J. (1994). Semantic and formal congruency in music and motion pictures: Effects on the interpretation of visual action. *Psychomusicology, 13,* 28–59.

Bryant, J., & Vorderer, P. (2006). *Psychology of entertainment*. Mahwah, NJ: Erlbaum.

Bullerjahn, C., & Güldenring, M. (1994). An empirical investigation of effects of film music using qualitative content analysis. *Psychomusicology, 13,* 99–118.

Bush, V. (July, 1945). As we may think. *The Atlantic Monthly,* pp. 101–108.

CAVE (URL). Available at http://cave.ncsa.uiuc.edu/

Cheung, B., Money, K., Wright, H., & Bateman, W. (1995). Spatial disorientation-implicated accidents in Canadian Forces, 1982–92. *Aviation, Space and Environmental Medicine, 66,* 579–584.

Chion, M. (1990). *Sound on screen* (edited & translated by C. Gorbman, 1994). New York: Columbia University Press.

Choi, D., & Kim, J. (2004). Why people continue to play online games: In search of critical design factors to increase customer loyalty to online contents. *Cyberpsychology & Behavior, 7,* 11–24.

Chou, T. J., & Ting, C. C. (2003). The role of flow experience in cyber-game addiction. *CyberPsychology & Behavior, 6*(6), 663–675.

Cohen, A. (1999). The functions of music in multimedia: A cognitive approach. In S. Yi (Ed.), *Music, mind and science* (pp. 52–68). Seoul Korea: Seoul National University Press.

Cohen, A. (2000). Film music: Perspectives from cognitive psychology. In J. Buhler, C. Flinn, & D. Neumeyer (Eds.), *Music and cinema* (pp. 360–377). Hanover, NH: Wesleyan University Press published by University Press of New England.

Cohen, A. (2005). How music influences the interpretation of film and video: Approaches from experimental psychology. In R. A. Kendall & R. W. Savage (Eds.). *Selected Reports in Ethnomusicology: Perspectives in Systematic Musicology, 12,* 15–36.

Cohen, A., & MacMillan, K. (2004). Music influences absorption in motion pictures. Preprint of article in preparation.

Cranson, R. W., Orme-Johnson, D., Gackenbach, J., Dillbeck, M. C., Jones, C. H., & Alexander, C. (1991). Transcendental meditation and improved performance on intelligence-related measures: A longitudinal study. *Personality and Individual Differences, 12,* 1105–1116.

Cutting, J., & Vishton, P. (1995). Perceiving layout and knowing distances: The integration, relative potency, and contextual use of different information about depth. In W. Epstein & S. Rogers (Eds.), *Perception of space and motion* (pp. 69–117). San Diego, CA: Academic Press.

Csikszentmihalyi, M. (1990). *Flow: The psychology of optimal experience.* New York: Harper & Row.

Davies, C. (2004). Virtual space. In F. Penz, G. Radick, & R. Howell (Eds.), *SPACE in science, art, and society* (pp. 69–104). Cambridge: Cambridge University Press. Available at http://www.immersence.net

Gackenbach, J., & Bosveld, J. (1989). *Control your dreams.* New York: Harper & Row.

Gackenbach, J., & Preston, J. M. (1998). Video game play and the development of consciousness. Tucson III: Towards a Science of Consciousness, Tucson.

Gibson, J. J. (1954, 1994). The visual perception of objective motion and subjective movement. *Psychological Review, 61,* 304–314. Reprinted: *Psychological Review, 101* (2), 318–323.

Gibson, J. J. (1971). The information available in pictures. *Leonardo, 4,* 27–35.

Gibson, J. J. (1966). *The senses considered as perceptual systems.* Prospect Hts., IL: Waveland Press.

Gibson, J. J. (1979). *The ecological approach to visual perception.* Boston: Houghton-Mifflin.

Gombrich, E. (1993). *Art and Illusion.* London: Phaidon.

Grodal, T. (2000). Video games and the pleasure of control. In D. Zillmann & P. Vorderer (Eds.), *Media entertainment: The psychology of its appeal* (pp. 197–214). Mahwah, NJ: Erlbaum.

Hann, J., Armstrong, K., & Preston, J. M. (2005). *Factors in participant enjoyment of apparent-motion media.* Canadian Psychological Association Meeting, Montreal.

Heeter, C. (1992). Being There: The subjective experience of presence. *Presence, teleoperators, & virtual environments, 1,* 262–271.

Hunt, H. T. (1989). *The multiplicity of dreams: Memory, imagination, and consciousness.* New Haven, CT: Yale University Press.

Hunt, H. T. (1995). *On the nature of consciousness.* New Haven, CT: Yale University Press.

Hunt, H. T. (2004a). *Lives in spirit: Precursors and dilemmas of a secular western mysticism.* Albany, NY: State University of New York Press.

Hunt, H. T. (2004b). *Mysticism, madness, and the nature of spiritual suffering: Entrancing, diminishing, and realizing true ecological self.* Lives in Spirit Conference, Brock University, St. Catharines, Ontario, Canada.

Hunt, H., Gervais, S., Shearing-Johns, S., & Travis, F. (1992). Transpersonal experiences in childhood: An exploratory empirical study of selected adult groups. *Perceptual and Motor Skills, 75,* 1135–1153.

James, W. (1890). *The principles of psychology.* 2 vols. New York: Dover.

Johnson, M. (1987). *The body in the mind: The bodily bases of meaning, imagination, and reason.* Chicago: University of Chicago Press.

Kellogg, R., & Gillingham, K. (1986). United States Air Force experience with simulator sickness, research, and training. *Proceedings of the 30th Annual Meeting of the Human Factors Society, 1,* 427–429.

Kennedy, R., Berbaum, K., & Lilienthal, M. (1997). Disorientation and postural ataxia following flight simulation. *Aviation, Space, and Environmental Medicine, 68,* 13–17.

Kennedy, R., Lane, N., Berbaum, K., & Lilienthal, M. (1993). Simulator sickness questionnaire: An enhanced method for quantifying simulator sickness *The International Journal of Aviation Psychology, 3,* 203–220.

Kennedy, R., & Stanney, K. (1996). Postural instability induced by virtual reality exposure: Development of a certification protocol. *International Journal of Human–Computer Interaction, 8,* 25–47.

Klee, P. (1973). *Pedagogical sketchbook.* London: Faber.

Knight, T. (2001). Either/or -> And. *Proceedings.* 3rd International Space Syntax Symposium, Atlanta, GA. Available at http://undertow.arch.gatech.edu/homepages/3sss/proceedings.htm

Kraft, R., Cantor, P., & Gottdeiner, C. (1991). Light and mind: Understanding the structure of film. In R. Hoffman & D. Palermo (Eds.), *Cognition and the symbolic processes: Applied and ecological perspectives* (pp. 351–370). Hillsdale, NJ: Erlbaum.

Lakoff, G. (1987). *Women, fire, and dangerous things: What categories reveal about the mind.* Chicago: University of Chicago Press.

Lang, P. (1995). The emotion probe. *American Psychologist, 50,* 372–385.

Laurel, B. (1991). *Computers as theater.* Boston: Addison-Wesley.

Lipscomb, S., & Kendall, R. (1994). Perceptual judgment of the relationship between musical and visual components in film. *Psychomusicology, 13,* 60–98.

Lombard, M., & Ditton, T.V. (1997). At the heart of it all: The concept of presence. *Journal of Computer Mediated Communication, 3.* Lombard, M., Reich, R., Grabe, M., Campanella, C., & Ditton, T. (1995). *Big TVs, little TVs: The role of screen size in viewer responses to point-of-view movement.* Paper presented at the International Communication Association Meeting, Albuquerque, NM.

Marshall, S., & Cohen, A. (1988). Effects of musical soundtracks on attitudes toward animated geometric figures. *Music Perception, 6,* 95–112.

Maslow, A. (1962). *Towards a psychology of being.* Princeton: Van Nostrand.

McCrae, R., & Costa, P. (1997). Conceptions and correlates of openness to experience. In R. Hogan, J. Johnson, & S. Briggs (Eds.), *Handbook of personality psychology* (pp. 825–845). San Diego, CA: Academic Press.

Minsky, M. (1980). Telepresence. *Omni,* June, 45–51.

Mou, W., Biocca, F., Owen, C., Tang, A., Xiao, F., and Lim, L. (2004). Frames of reference in mobile augmented reality displays. *Journal of Experimental Psychology: Applied, 10,* 238–244.

Neisser, U. (1976). *Cognition and reality.* San Francisco: Freeman.

Neisser, U. (1991). Two perceptually given aspects of the self and their development. *Developmental Review, 11,* 197–209.

Nery, R., & Preston, J. M. (2005). *Video Games: Psychological Factors and Performance.* Paper presented at the Canadian Psychological Association Meeting, Montreal.

Panofsky, E. (1988). *Meaning in the visual arts.* London: Peter Smith.

Preston, J. M. (1998). From mediated environments to the development of consciousness. In J. Gackenbach (Ed.), *Psychology and the Internet: Intrapersonal, interpersonal and transpersonal perspectives* (pp. 255–291). New York: Academic Press.

Preston, J. M. (2005). *Virtual action space: Foreshadowing outcomes in mediate environments.* International Communication Association Meeting, New York, NY.

Previc, F. (1998). The neuropsychology of 3-D space. *Psychological Bulletin, 124* (2), 123–164.

Pylyshyn, Z. (1984). *Computation and cognition: Toward a foundation for cognitive science.* Cambridge: MIT Press.

Reed, E. S. (1988). *James Gibson and the psychology of perception.* New Haven: Yale University Press.

Reeves, B., & Nass, C. (1996). *The media equation: How people treat computers, television, and new media like real people and places.* Stanford, CA: CSLI Publications; New York: Cambridge University Press.

Regan, E., & Price, K. (1994). The occurrence and severity of side effects of immersion virtual reality. *Aviation Space and Environmental Medicine,* June, 527–530.

Roche, S., & McConkey, K. (1990). Absorption: Nature, assessment, and correlates. *Journal of Personality & Social Psychology, 59,* 91–101.

Sensio Montreal (URL). Available at http://www.sensio.tv/

Shepard, R. (1978). Externalization of mental images and the act of creation. In B. Randhawa & W. Coffman (Eds.), *Visual learning, thinking, and communication* (pp. 133–189). New York: Academic Press.

Sheridan, T. B. (1992). Musings on telepresence and virtual presence. *Presence, teleoperators, & virtual environments, 1,* 120–126.

Siegel, R. (1979–80). Dizziness as an altered state of consciousness. *Journal of Altered States of Consciousness, 5,* 87–104.

Slater, M., Usoh, M., & Steed, A. (1994). Depth of presence in virtual environments, *Presence, teleoperators, & virtual environments, 3,* 30–144.

Smith, J. (1999). Movie music as moving music: Emotion, cognition, and the film score. In C. Plantinga & G. Smith (Eds.), *Passionate views: Film, cognition, and emotion* (pp. 146–167). Baltimore, MD: Johns Hopkins University Press.

Spadafora, A., & Hunt, H. (1990). The multiplicity of dreams: Cognitive–affective correlates of lucid, archetypal, and nightmare dreams. *Perceptual and Motor Skills, 71,* 627–644.

Stein, M. (1974). *Communication and line drawing test.* Behavioural Publications Inc.: New York.

Steuer, J. (1995). Defining virtual reality: Dimensions determining telepresence. In F. Biocca & M. R. Levy (Eds.), *Communication in the age of virtual reality* (pp. 33–56). Hillsdale, NJ: Lawrence Erlbaum.

Suedfeld, P., Ballard, E. J., Baker-Brown, G., & Borrie, R. A. (1985–1986). Flow of consciousness in restricted environmental stimulation. *Imagination, Cognition, and Personality, 5,* 219–230.

Suedfeld, P., Metcalfe, J., & Bluck, S. (1987). Enhancement of scientific creativity by flotation REST (Restricted Environmental Stimulation Technique). *Journal of Environmental Psychology, 7,* 219–231.

Suedfeld, P., & Eich, E. (1995). Autobiographical memory and affect under conditions of reduced environmental stimulation. *Journal of Environmental Psychology, 15,* 321–326.

Swartz, P., & Seginer, L. (1981). Response to body rotation and tendency to mystical experience. *Perceptual and Motor Skills, 53,* 683–688.

Tellegen, A., & Atkinson, G. (1974). Openness to absorbing and self-altering experiences ("absorption"), a trait related to hypnotic susceptibility. *Journal of Abnormal Psychology, 83,* 268–277.

Thayer, J., & Levinson, R. (1983). Effects of music on psychophysiological responses to a stressful film. *Psychomusicology, 3,* 44–52.

Turkle, S. (1984). *The second self: Computers and the human spirit.* New York: Simon & Shuster.

Vitouch, O. (2001). When your ear sets the stage: Musical context effects in film perception. *Psychology of Music, 29,* 70–83.

Vorderer, P. (2000). Interactive entertainment and beyond. In D. Zillmann & P. Vorderer (Eds.), *Media entertainment: The psychology of its appeal* (pp. 21–36). Mahwah, NJ: Erlbaum.

Witmer, B., & Singer, M. (1998). Measuring presence in virtual environments: A presence questionnaire. *Presence, 7,* 225–240.

Wood, R., Griffiths, M., Chappell, D., & Davies, M. (2004). The structural characteristics of video games: A psycho-structural analysis. *Cyberpsychology and Behaviour, 7,* 1–10.

Zahorik, P., & Jenison, R. (1998). Presence as being in the world. *Presence, 7,* 78–89.

Zillmann, D., & Vorderer, P. (2000). *Media entertainment: The psychology of its appeal.* Mahwah, NJ: Erlbaum

World Wide Brain: Self-Organizing Internet Intelligence as the Actualization of the Collective Unconscious

Ben Goertzel
Novamente LLC and Applied Research Laboratory for National and Homeland Security
Virginia Tech, National Capital Region
Arlington, Virginia

Introduction
AI and the Internet
Symbiotic Internet Intelligence
  in Philosophical and Psychological Perspective
Self and Morality in the World Wide Brain
References

INTRODUCTION

Anyone who has had the privilege to give birth, or to watch someone else give birth, knows what a wonderful, exciting, magical event it is. And this is so even when, as in the birth of a human, the organism being born has very little new about it—it is "just" a replication, with variations, of already existing creatures. How much more tremendous and dramatic, then, is the birth of an entirely new kind of intelligent organism—a new kind of consciousness, extending and, in some regards, improving on our own?

The World Wide Brain—a hybrid human–digital intelligent network, spanning the globe and carrying out information processing different in extent and nature from anything that has come before—is as yet little more than a dream and a little less than a reality. It is coming into being, bit by bit, each year. This process of emergence is, as all Net-aholics know, a wonder to behold, and growing more wondrous all the time.

I do not make this comparison lightly: The Internet as it exists today is comparable, I suggest, to the mind of a very young child—a child who has not yet learned to think for herself, or even to distinguish herself from the outside world. What we will see over the next couple decades is the growth and maturity of this infantile mind. My goal in this chapter is to give a perspective for viewing

Psychology and the Internet: Intrapersonal, Interpersonal, and Transpersonal Implications

this coming evolution, the future history of the electronic organism we call the Net; and to use this perspective to sketch some projections as to what this future may hold.

This is an exploration in which human psychology and sociology interact in a fascinating way, with the psychology of an emerging, nonhuman organism. It is an exploration in which mundane technical issues such as groupware and server–server communication software rub up against concepts from transpersonal psychology, such as the Collective Unconscious and the Hierarchy of Being. It is, in short, an exploration that not only transcends disciplinary boundaries but pushes the boundaries of human thought itself.

THE FUTURE HISTORY OF THE NET

Over the next decade, I believe, we will see the evolution of the Net into a full-fledged, largely autonomous, globally distributed intelligent system. As this occurs, we will see this Internet artificial intelligence (AI) network wend itself further and further into human affairs, yielding a synergetic, symbiotic global intelligent system, incorporating machine and human intelligence into a single continuum of thought, a human–digital global brain.

This vision of a global Web mind is related to several other visions of the digital future. For instance, many futurists have envisioned a future Net populated by artificially intelligent entities, interacting in virtual worlds. This vision was portrayed most memorably by William Gibson in his entertaining and influential novel Neuromancer (1994). While this is a reasonable idea, and it does not contradict my own thinking in any way, it is different from what I am projecting here, which is that the Net itself will become a global intelligent system—a World Wide Brain.

On the other hand, a number of others thinkers—most famously, roboticist Hans Moravec (1990)—have envisioned that humans will eventually "download" themselves into computers, and will lead bodiless digital lives. This is also related to, but different from, the idea of a global Web mind; the two ideas synergize in a fascinating way.

Initially, the global Web mind will exist as an entity physically separate from human beings: We will interact with it via our computer terminals, and perhaps more creative interface devices such as virtual reality (VR) headsets. This first phase is in store maybe 5 to 20 years down the line, and it is the main focus of my thinking at present. The increasing integration of human activity with World Wide Brain operations may ultimately occur via body-modifying or body-obsolescing technologies a la Moravec, or it may occur without them, through the advent of more sophisticated noninvasive interfaces. One way or another, though, I conjecture, it will fuse the global Web.

The change that is about to come as a consequence of the emergence of the global Web mind will be a very large one—comparable in scope, I believe, to the emergence of tools, or language, or civilization. What will distinguish this change from these past ones, however, is its speed. In this sense, those who are alive and young today are very fortunate. They will be the first human generation ever to witness a major change in collective humanity with a time span of only a single human lifetime, instead of the dozens or hundreds it has taken before.

This chapter treats these developments on several different levels, First, I discuss the nature of mind and intelligence in the context of complex systems science—a newly emerging interdisciplinary body of knowledge that provides a framework capable of comparing intelligence across different physical substrates (e.g., brains and computers). Then, to make the idea of Internet intelligence more concrete, I briefly discuss the Webmind Internet AI (artificial intelligence) software that I helped developing at IntelliGenesis Corporation in the late 1990s, which was aimed at creating "Intranet brains" or "Webmind units" serving as knowledge management systems for businesses and other enterprises, and linking these intranet brains together into a "society of mind" or proto-World Wide Brain (see Goertzel, 2001, for a more extensive discussion of Webmind). I also discuss my current, related work with the Novamente AI system (Looks et al., 2004). Finally, with these important, relatively mundane details under our belts, I turn to the more philosophical and transpersonal side of things, exploring the general human implications of the emergent Internet intelligence that this sort of AI software and other software will make possible.

MIND AS A COMPLEX SYSTEM

My foundation for thinking about Internet intelligence and its relation to human intelligence is the "Psynet model of mind," presented in a series of academic books published over the last 5 years: *The Structure of Intelligence* (Goertzel, 1993a), *The Evolving Mind* (Goertzel, 1993b), *Chaotic Logic* (Goertzel, 1994), and *From Complexity to Creativity* (Goertzel, 1997). According to the Psynet model, trying to program AI on past generations of computers has been essentially futile, because such computers have not had adequate random-access memory. Intelligence, as an emergent property, can only come out of a large, complex, self-organizing system. It does not have to do with any special programming tricks; rather, the special "core twist" of intelligence lies in the way a complex system, skilled at recognizing patterns in its environment, can turn inward and recognize patterns in itself, creating circles and spirals of constructive self-recognition. But this self-organizing self-recognition at the core of intelligence cannot be imitated in a simple logical system; it has to emerge from the statistical chaos of a large system whose parts are working independently yet interacting. You can't fake it!

But current computers, with up to 512 megabytes of RAM on a PC board or up to 5 gigabytes of RAM on an engineering workstation and processors on the order of 500 megahertz, finally provide the power needed for significant real-time self-organization and emergence. Furthermore, the efficient connectivity provided by the intranet and the Internet transforms computer networks into vast, distributed machines containing more power than any individual computer and mirroring the distributed, asynchronous dynamics of the brain far better than any modern motherboard or chip. In short, we have finally reached the stage where emergent intelligence is potentially realizable via computer, and the next generation of Internet AI software will aim to exploit this new opportunity.

THE COLLECTIVE UNCONSCIOUS CONCRETIZED

The main point, however, is not any particular engineering or software innovation. At worst, if the market makes poor software decisions, or if the rate of engineering progress unexpectedly decreases, the advent of global Net intelligence will be slowed by a few years or a decade. The point is the process of self-organization that is occurring, of which all cognitive scientists and Internet software engineers are a part.

This process of self-organization is a dramatic change of culture and consciousness. Computer and communication technology is one of the shining successes of modern Western culture, of the rationalist worldview that has pushed previous mythically and magically focused worldviews into near obsolescence. One of the biggest failures of modern Western culture is the widespread sense of anomie and alienation that it has brought, along with greater individuality and freedom. We have, one might say with a certain dramatic exaggeration, won our freedom but lost our souls! From this view, it is not merely ironic but profound that Net technology offers the possibility of bringing back that unity that was taken from us with the advent of Western rationalism. The World Wide Brain is a kind of global human unity, spawned from the products of alienated culture. Evolved away from the group spiritual experiences that used to bring us in touch with the human "collective unconscious," we are creating technology that revives this collective unconscious in digital form.

The World Wide Brain is not merely an emerging AI, separate from human beings. It is an emerging intelligence, arising from human information and human interactions. It is human communication come to life. We are not merely creating AI, we are creating an artificially intelligent crystallization of the common, collective patterns of the global human mind. This is a new adventure, something that does not merely bring us back to the spiritual unity of past modes of culture, but brings us on to new frontiers that we can barely even imagine. The universe is ever-expanding, not only physically but informationally. What we are seeing is yet another manifestation of the endless quest of the universe to bring new patterns out of itself. In the final section, I explore this aspect of Internet intelligence from the perspective of transpersonal psychology, viewing the emergence of the World Wide Brain in terms of the archetypal Hierarchy of Being.

AI AND THE INTERNET

One way that the development of an intelligent Internet may come about is through the development of artificial intelligence programs and their deployment on the Internet, in a way designed to increase the intelligence of the network as a whole, as well as particular machines on the Net. This is an area I've worked in extensively myself, via the design and development of two different AI systems: Webmind (Goertzel, 2001) and Novamente (Looks *et al.*, 2004). The Webmind system was under development from 1997 to 2001 at IntelliGenesis Corporation, a corporation that I founded and helped manage until its dissolution in April 2001. The Webmind system was never deployed across the Internet due to a collapse of its funding sources, and not all parts of the system were fully implemented and tested. Since 2001, I have been involved with the development of Webmind, Novamente's successor. However, here I will talk about Webmind more than Novamente because Webmind had more of an explicit Internet focus. Novamente is just as capable of being used in an "Internet intelligence" context but that has not been the focus of the project thus far.

The Webmind AI design embodied an understanding of intelligence as self-organizing, asynchronously distributed, and emergent, and provides one concrete vision of how a World Wide Brain could be made to emerge from existing hardware and software. From the user's perspective, Webmind was intended as a general system for posing and answering questions regarding digitally stored information. It was meant to deal, potentially, with information of any kind, although, just as humans require eyes to perceive sights and ears to perceive sounds, Webmind would have needed appropriate "perceptual methods" for processing each type of information into its own internal data structures. Its architecture was that of a massively parallel network, a population of many different static and dynamic agents continually recomputing their relationships with other agents, and acting on other agents in accordance with these relationships. The mix of different types of agents, and the amount of resources allocated to each, determined the emergent structure of the internal network, and hence the intelligence and functionality of the system.

Webmind was designed to run efficiently on powerful stand-alone computers, and in an ideal world, would have run best on a supercomputer with multiple processors and tremendous amounts of random access memory. In the context of contemporary computing hardware, however, it turned out to be most cost-effective to run Webmind over a network of computers, in which case its sophisticated server–server communication methods allowed its internal network structure to harmonize with the connectivity structure of the computer network.

The Webmind design was not tied to any particular programming language, operating system, or hardware architecture; however, the actual implementation of Webmind was based on the Java programming language and was mostly tested on the Linux OS. Java was chosen for Webmind because it is cross-platform, because it supports easy networking across intranets and the Internet, and because its strongly object-oriented structure was so natural for representing the various agents making up Webmind's internal network. It also had the practical advantage of relatively low development time, which was important given the intrinsic complexity of the Webmind system. Some fairly serious performance problems arose from the use of Java, however, which is why in my current large-scale AI work I have reverted to the older language C++.

The essence of Webmind's intelligence resided in the portion of its code called the "Psynet," which embodied a logical/conceptual model of artificial cognition going beyond the Webmind system in particular. A Psynet is a self-organizing network of information-carrying agents. Information is incorporated into the Psynet via the creation of agents embodying that information. The architecture of a Psynet is relatively simple because the intelligence of the system is allowed to emerge from distributed interactions among the population of agents, rather than being imposed by specific reasoning rules or knowledge representation structures. The Psynet represents the minimum of structure required to lead to the adaptive emergence of useful information structures embodying data items. In short, the data stored in the Psynet is allowed to discover its own structure, within given constraints, rather than having structure imposed on it by rigid, preconceived rules. The design of the Psynet package was based on a mathematical theory called the "psynet model of mind," which I developed in a series of four books and numerous research papers over the period 1993–1997 (Goertzel, 1993a, b, 1994, 1996, 1997).

Agents within the Psynet are of three types: static, relational, and mobile. Static agents may represent temporal data, but are static in the sense that they have a continued existence, maintained by the Psynet itself. Relational agents are not known directly to the Psynet but are held by other agents, representing relations between that agent and other agents. Mobile agents are like relation agents, but change frequently with time; they represent the learning of relationship by the Psynet's static agents. The Psynet supports many different types of static agents, tailored for particular purposes.

Static agents are also called "nodes," whereas relational agents are also called "links," a terminology that connects the internal structure of the Psynet with the external structure of the Internet and intranets in many useful ways. However, this language should not distract one from the fact that static and relational agents are much more substantial that the nodes and links found in some other AI architectures (e.g., neural networks). A node within the Psynet is nothing like an individual neuron in the human brain, but might be more fairly compared with a neuronal group within the brain (consisting of 10,000–100,000 neurons tightly connected and oriented toward a single purpose). Psynet nodes cover a wide range of scales, from individual words to entire texts, data files and database records, categories of text, categories of words, trends of change over time in collections of data or collections of nodes, and so on. Most abstractly, there are nodes corresponding to other Psynets with which there is interaction, and nodes modeling aspects of the Psynet itself, for purposes of adaptation and self-improvement.

The construction of nodes that refer to collections of other nodes is of particular importance. These nodes are called "concepts," and they provide a Psynet with a hierarchical structure, complementing its primary associative structure. The superposition of hierarchical and associative structure is called a "dual network structure" and is essential for the emergence of intelligent activity and link patterns.

Learning in the Psynet takes place in five ways:

1. The recognition of patterns in data stored in individual nodes, which is carried out by methods in the Info package
2. The recognition of relationships among nodes, which is carried out by mobile agents
3. The creation of new nodes representing collections of relations among other nodes ("concept formation")
4. The spreading of activity around the Psynet in complex, possibly chaotic patterns, representing spontaneous, emerging focusing of the network's attention
5. Directed introspection, in which the Psynet poses a series of queries to itself.

A query into the Psynet results in the creation of a new node, a "query node" that creates new mobile agents, which travel about within the Psynet and create new links for the query node. The answer to a query is given in terms of the relationships found by this agent-swarming process. The query node is stored for future reference, along with any user feedback regarding the perceived quality of the response to the query. The Psynet's introspection process involves continually querying itself, using queries based on queries it has been posed in the past, and particularly queries on which it has performed badly: In this way, it continually produces new knowledge in the areas in which it has proved deficient and fills in gaps in its performance.

The final and, in some ways, most interesting part of the Psynet is its mechanisms for server–server interaction. An individual Psynet is, potentially, an autonomous AI system. In practice, however, greater intelligence may be achieved by networking Psynets together in various ways. In the Webmind design, Psynets were intended to interact with Psynets running on other Webmind servers in several different ways:

1. They could query other servers, as if they were clients of that server.
2. They could send agents to visit other servers and gather information.
3. They could exchange detailed information about their internal processes with other servers, on a frequent basis.
4. They could swap sections of their memory with other servers in a group, to optimize functioning of the group as a whole.

Each server contained in it a list of the other Webmind servers that were allowed to interact with it in each of these ways. A collection of Webmind servers that interacted with each other was a "Webmind unit." Elements of a Webmind unit were less like humans participating in a society than like different lobes or hemispheres within a single brain. On the other hand, Webmind servers belonging to different organizations were generally be able to interact with each other only via the first two methods or via the first method alone. There is a gradation between "social" and "intra-brain" interaction here, as opposed to the rigid division between individual and society that we experience as humans.

Finally, the social network of a Psynet plays an important role in guiding its introspections. A Psynet thinks about—queries itself about—those topics that it judges to be most important at present, as judged by several criteria: trends it has recognized in itself, trends it has recognized in its social group, and trends in what its users and peer Psynets have identified as its deficiencies. The degree to which a Psynet pays attention to the opinions of another Psynet is determined in an intelligent manner, based on its experience with that Psynet's and other Psynets' opinions, according to an algorithm drawn by mathematical models of human social interaction.

Webmind was designed to be used to solve many problems that are fairly self-contained, detached from the flow and organization of human affairs, such as "Find me information about crazed Third-World dictators; What do the trends in Japan say about the U. S. stock market?" Things become yet more interesting, however, when one envisions the same sorts of questions being asked regularly within an organization, about processes and structures within that organization. Instead of the stock market, one may have productivity statistics from various divisions of a company; and instead of newspaper articles, one may have reports generated within the company, e-mails sent within the company, etc. If Webmind were installed on the company's intranet, then real-time queries regarding relationships between textual, numerical, and other data to do with the enterprise can be posed by (and answered by) any employee with computer access at any time. Webmind's intelligence was intended to be integrated with the social intelligence of the organization and the individual intelligence of the employees.

As a consequence of the deployment of software like this, the social dynamics of the different Psynets residing in different parts of an organization's intranet would grow to reflect the social dynamics of the individuals using those parts of the intranet. For instance, each Psynet would respond most effectively and rapidly to queries involving information that it stores locally; but the information that a certain Psynet within a Webmind unit stores might change over time, depending on user needs and internal Psynet dynamics. Thus, while providing easy access by all users to all information at all times, Webmind was designed to nudge the information at the readiest disposal of individual humans and divisions in certain directions, based on its inferences and its own emergent understanding. An AI system deployed like this would do more than just provide an understanding of structures and processes; it would be a participant in processes, in the formation of emergent human and informational structures.

And finally, as various AI units in various organizations exchange nonproprietary information, in the interest of increased mutual intelligence, an AI system of this nature would be a participant in the formation of human and informational structures on the global scale. This is an exciting new vision of AI, in the business context and beyond—not AI as something separate from humanity, providing us with answers to our questions, but AI as something interacting symbiotically with humanity, participating in our communications, goals, and social structures and processes.

This kind of vision made sense to me in 1997 when I founded IntelliGenesis Corp., and it still makes sense to me now, even though that company failed for financial reasons. The Internet has developed dramatically since the late 1990s, yet it has not advanced all that far in the distributed-intelligence direction, and I think this is more for economic reasons than for fundamental reasons. My current AI project, Novamente, is also based on the general Psynet approach, but we are not initially taking an Internet focus. Rather, the current plan is to achieve a high level of intelligence on a Novamente system running on a fairly small, localized computer network—and then approach the question of Webmind-style broad-scope distributed processing. I remain confident that this kind of distributed Internet intelligence is the future of the Internet, though the precise path by which the Net will get there is not entirely clear.

SYMBIOTIC INTERNET INTELLIGENCE IN PHILOSOPHICAL AND PSYCHOLOGICAL PERSPECTIVES

Let us now shift gears from the immediate and commercial to the prospective and philosophical. Imagine the Internet, a few years from now, the home of an advanced, self-organizing AI system, spanning tens of thousands of intranets worldwide. Such a system would be an independent, intelligent entity on its own, interacting with humans and incorporating human workflow and question asking and answering behavior into its own intelligent dynamics. It would weave the process of collective social inquiry and individual human mental inquiry into a digital fabric of a texture guided by its own processes of intelligent self-organization.

This view of the future of the Net is reminiscent of the archetypal idea of the "global brain," which first started appearing in the 1970s. In Russell's (1995) book on the Global Brain, for example, computer and communications technology are assigned only a minor role, and it is argued that human society is reaching a critical threshold of size and complexity beyond which it will enter the realm of true intelligence, and human consciousness will give rise to a higher level of collective consciousness. Russell's hypothesized suprahuman intelligence might be called a "global societal mind," as distinct from the global Web mind that is my central topic of interest here. Both the global societal mind and the global Web mind, however, are specific manifestations of the general concept of a "global brain"—an emergent, distributed worldwide intelligence.

Russell ties the global brain in with new-age, consciousness-raising practices. By meditating and otherwise increasing our level of individual consciousness, he suggests, we bring the awakening of the global brain closer and closer. When there is enough total awareness in the overall system of humanity, humanity itself will lock into a new system of organization, and will become an autonomous, self-steering, brainlike system.

Speaking generally, one can envision the global Web mind as leading to a global societal mind a la Russell in two different ways. First, we might actually become part of the Web in a physical sense. This could be accomplished either by downloading ourselves into computers, by the fabled "cranial jack," or by some kind of true VR interface. Or it could be done by incorporating our existing bodies into the Web via newfangled sensory and motor devices. Imagine brains as websites, and modem/cell phones inserted directly into the sensory cortex! Or, second, we might become part of the Web via our actions, without any extra physical connections. This is already happening, at least among certain sectors of the population. As more and more of our leisure and work activities are carried out via the Internet, more and more of our patterns of behavior become part of the potential memory of the global Web mind. Webmind or Novamente or similar software, implemented widely and used intensively across intranets, could lead to this effect quite easily.

The global Web mind and the global societal mind, then, are not really such different things at all. If a global Web mind comes about, it will clearly link humans together in a new way, leading to some kind of different and more intelligently structured social order. This is one flavor of global brain. On the other hand, if a global societal mind comes about, communications technology such as the Internet will doubtless play a huge role in its formation. This is another flavor of global brain. The question is, will there be an intelligent Web interacting with humans in a subtle way, or will there be an intelligent societal system incorporating the Web, human beings, and all their interactions. What kind of global brain will we actually see?

In fact, Russell's (1995) book is only the best known of a host of independent discoveries of the concept of a global superorganism over the past few decades. Joel de Rosnay, for one, has published several books in French on the notion of a "cybionte," or cybernetic superorganism. His earliest, *Le Macroscope*, was published in 1975; *L'Homme Symbionte* (de Rosnay, 1996) updates the concept with discussions of chaos theory, multimedia technology, and other new developments. Valentin Turchin (1997) laid out in *The Phenomenon of Science* an abstract, cybernetic theory of evolution, and used it to discuss the concept of an emerging, metahuman "superbeing." His crucial concept is the "metasystem transition," a term for the process of a phenomenon that previously was a whole suddenly becoming a part. For example, the cell, which has its own systemic unity, its own wholeness, becomes a part when it becomes part of the human organism. There is a metasystem transition between cells and organisms. There is also a metasystem transition between computers and networks; one's PC at home is a natural whole, but the networked PC of the year 2010 will be something quite different, in that most of its software will require interaction with outside computers, and most of its behaviors will be incomprehensible without taking into account the network outside it. And with services like Google Desktop and the advent of online multiplayer games like World of Warcraft, it is clear that we are already partway there.

Currently, humans are whole systems, with their own autonomy and intelligence, and human societies display a far lesser degree of organization and self-steering behavior. But, according to Turchin, a transition is coming, and in the future there will be more and more intelligent memory, perception, and action taking place on the level of society as a whole. Turchin's vision is one of progressive evolution; as time goes on, one metasystem transition after another occurs, passing control on to higher and higher levels. One of Turchin's most active contemporary followers is Francis Heylighen, of the Free University of Brussels. Heylighen believes that the Web will be the instrument that brings about the metasystem transition, leading from humanity to the metahuman superorganism. The PrincipiaCybernetica website, which he administers, contains an extensive network of pages devoted to superorganisms, metasystem transitions, global brains, and related ideas. Together with his colleague John Bollen, he has also experimented with ways of making the Web more intelligent, by making its link structure adaptive, in the manner of a neural network.

THE GLOBAL BRAIN STUDY GROUP

Heylighen has done a comprehensive worldwide search for literature on the global brain, and posted the results at Principia Cybernetica. Recently, Heylighen has also assembled an e-mail "Global Brain Study Group" mailing list (see http://pespmcl.vub.ac.be/GBRAIN-L.html, for details). Membership on the mailing list was initially restricted to those individuals who have published something (on the paper or online) on the notion of emerging Web intelligence, but has now been expanded to anyone who is willing to write a brief introductory essay explaining their interest in the Global Brain. (A complete record of the dialogue may be found at http://www.fmb.mmu.ac.uk:80/majordom/gbrain/.) So far, rather than debating the merits of different approaches to making the Web intelligent, the discussion group seems inevitably to veer toward the philosophical—toward the questions of what the global Web brain will be like and how it will relate to human beings, individually and collectively.

The most striking thing about the discussion on the Global Brain Study Group list is not a presence but an absence—the absence of serious disagreement on most issues regarding emerging Web intelligence. Everyone who has thought seriously about the global Web brain, it seems, has largely come to the same conclusions. The Web will become more self-organizing, more complex, and eventually the greater intelligence of its parts will lead to a greater intelligence of the whole. Human beings will be drawn into the Web intelligence one way or another, either by mind-downloading or virtual reality, or simply by continual interaction with Web brain-savvy technology. In this way, human society will begin to act in a more structured way—in a way directed by the global Web mind, which recognizes subtle emergent patterns in human knowledge and creates new information on the basis of these patterns.

A brief stir on the Global Brain Discussion Group was made by the appearance of a brief satirical piece in *Wired* magazine in mid-1996, called *The Human Macro-Organism as Fungus* (online at http://www.hotwired.com/wired/4.04/features/viermenhouk.html). This article is an interview with a fictitious scientist named Dr. Viermenhouk, who parodies Heyligen by taking the absurdist line that the global superorganism is already here. Here is an excerpt of the interview:

> Interviewer: …Heylighen …
>
> Viermenhouk: … walks around all day with a printer port up his ass. I've seen the pictures. He's obsessed with a direct neural interface. His concept of a metabeing, a single unitary organism, hinges on us physically plugging into a "super-brain." He's missing the point. We already have…. Cells don't communicate through direct physical connections; they use electrical interfaces. The neural cells in our skulls communicate through an intricate chemical dance. To expect a macroorganism to develop differently from a multicellular organism is foolish.
>
> Now that we monkeys are part of a greater being, the connection we share is through symbol. Human language, with all of its limitations, is sufficiently complex to support the information-transfer needs of an organism never seen before on Earth. You don't need wires up your butt. Just look at the symbols on your screen. Click on that hypertext link. Send that e-mail. Be a good little cell.
>
> And Heylighen's bizarre notion that this metabeing is an improvement—delusion! Individual humans are intriguing, sensual, spiritual creatures. The human macroorganism is more of a fungus. A big, appallingly stupid fungus. It only knows how to eat and grow, and when all of the food is gone, it will die. It has all the charm and wit of something growing in a dark corner of your basement. Adds a whole new dimension to the concept of human culture.

This writer's notion of the superorganism as a fungus is humorous, but it also conceals a serious point. Yes, the fictitious Dr. Viermenhouk is wrong; the superorganism is not here yet, at least not in full force. But when it is here, will it necessarily be a boon to humanity? Or will it, indeed, be a fungus, a parasite on humans, sucking the life-blood from human-created technology for its own purposes?

Heylighen himself appears to have taken the parody in good cheer. But not all global brain advocates have been so charitable. Valentin Turchin, for one, was deeply annoyed. In a message posted to the Global Brain Study Group2, he stated that he thought the "fun" of the article actually conveyed a genuine outrage by the idea of direct brain links—a relatively common view which Turchin himself had run into before, and with which those who seriously explore this field must be prepared to deal.

Turchin believes that the global brain will have deep, positive, profound human meaning. That it will provide a way of bridging the gaps between human beings and fusing us into a collective awareness—something that spiritual traditions have been working on for a long time. From this point of view, direct brain–computer links should not be viewed as tools for escape from human reality, but rather as gateways to deeper connections with other human beings. And, from this point of view, Williams' remarks are destructive, pointing the readers of *Wired* away from something genuinely valuable—they are about as funny as someone going into schools and teaching children that vegetables are bad for your teeth.

It is not only the fictitious Dr. Viermenhouk, however, who has a negative attitude toward the global brain. Related fears have been voiced by Peter Russell himself, who started a thread in the Global Brain Study Group on the striking topic: Superorganism: Sane or Insane. Russell says[1],

I first explored the notion of superorganisms in my book "The Global Brain"—written back in the late seventies before the Internet really existed. There I showed that, from the perspective of general living systems theory, human society already displays 18 of the 19 characteristics of living organisms (the missing one is reproduction—we haven't yet colonized another planet, although we have the potential to) …
The interesting question for me is not whether a global brain is developing. It clearly is. But will this growing global brain turn out to be sane or insane? If civilization continues with its current self-centered, materialistic worldview, it will almost certainly bring its own destruction.
I have long been fascinated by the striking parallels between human society and cancer. Cancers have lost their relationship to the whole, and function at the expense of the organism—which is insane, since a successful cancer destroys its own host. This is what we appear to be doing, and very rapidly. Our embryonic global brain would seem to have turned malignant before it is even fully born.
I believe the reason for our collective malignancy comes back to individual consciousness. We are stuck in an outdated mode of consciousness, one more appropriate to the survival

---

[1] All quotes from the Global Brain Study group are archived at ⟨http://www.fmb.mmu.ac.uk/majordom/gbrain⟩. Reprinted with permission of the authors.

> needs of pre-industrial society. Thus the real challenge is for human consciousness to
> catch up with our technology. We need to evolve inwardly before any of our dreams of
> healthily-functioning global brains can manifest.

This is more intelligently and respectfully stated than Williams' parody, but in the end, it is somewhat similar. Instead of fungus, we have cancer—a far better metaphor, because cancer cells come from within, whereas fungus comes from outside. Russell believes that we are on a path toward the emergence of the global brain, and that the Web is just one particular manifestation of this path. But, observing that we humans ourselves are riddled with neurosis and interpersonal conflict, he wonders whether the collective intelligence that we give rise to is going to be any better off.

On one hand, Russell believes that the global brain will go beyond individual human consciousness, with all its limitations. In response to a post of mine, questioning whether the Internet might eventually develop a sense of "self" similar to that of human beings, he responded as follows:

> The question is whether this superorganism will develop its own consciousness—and
> sense of self—as human beings have done.
> Back then [in "The Global Brain"] I argued that there were close parallels between the
> structure and development of the human brain, and the structure and development of
> the global telecommunication / information network, which suggested that when the
> global nervous system reached the same degree of complexity as the human nervous
> system, a new level of evolution might emerge. But it would be wrong to characterize
> this new level as consciousness. It would be as far beyond consciousness, as we know
> it, as our consciousness is beyond life, as a simple organism knows it. So I don't think
> discussions as to whether the global social superorganism will develop a self akin to ours
> are that relevant.

Despite this conviction that the global brain will be far above and beyond human consciousness and human mental dynamics, however, he is worried that the flaws of individual human consciousness may somehow "poison" this greater emergent entity, and make it fatally flawed itself.

Responses to Russell's pessimistic post were mixed. Gregory Stock (1993), for instance, took issue with Russell's generally negative judgment of the psychology of the average modern human. A biologist, Stock views human selfishness and shortsightedness as biologically natural, and believes that modern society and psychology, for all their problems, are ultimately wonderful things. Russell's book *MetaMan* (1996) treats contemporary technological society as a kind of superorganism, and views this superorganism in a very positive light. In his book, he says:

> Turchin (1997), on the other hand, agrees substantially with Russell's pessimistic view
> of human nature and its implications for the mental health of the superorganism. He
> believes, however, that it may be possible to cure human nature, at the same time as
> developing new technologies that extend human nature, overcoming its limitations. We
> need to evolve inwardly before any of our dreams of healthily functioning global brains
> can manifest.

Yes. This is why the Principia Cybernetica project came into being. Our goal is to develop—on the basis of the current state of affairs in science and technology—a complete philosophy to serve as the verbal, conceptual part of a new consciousness.

My optimistic scenario is that a major calamity will happen to humanity as a result of the militant individualism, terrible enough to make drastic change necessary, but, hopefully, still mild enough not to result in total destruction. Then what we are trying to do will have a chance to become prevalent. But possible solutions must be carefully prepared.

More positive than Turchin or Russell, though less so than Stock, the physicist Gottfried Mayer-Kress expressed the view that, perhaps, the global brain itself [AU3] might represent the solution to the problems of individual human consciousness, rather than merely transplanting these problems onto a different level:

> I thought a coherent world civilization was what we expect to emerge from a GlobalBrain....
>
> For example, on a global scale it is still cheaper for most nations to choose to pollute the environment and waste energy. In a GlobalBrain world China would recognize that it is better not to introduce large-scale individual transportation (cars) and Brazil would find it better for its own economy not to destroy the rainforest.

Regarding the "cancer" metaphor, Meyer-Kress observes that even an "embryonic global brain" would be a coherent global structure and thereby directly contradict the basic definition of cancer. I would see the cancer analogy more as the global spread of a drug culture. Essentially, Mayer-Kress's point is as follows: Saying that humans are "individualistic" is the same as saying that humans represent the "top level" of a hierarchy of systems. An individualistic system is just one that has more freedom than the systems within it, or the systems in which it is contained. Cells within individual organisms are individualistic only to a limited extent; they are behaving within the constraints of the organism. Cells that make up single-celled organisms, on the other hand, are far more individualistic; they have more freedom than the systems of which they are parts.

The global brain, according to Mayer-Kress, is almost synonymous with the decrease of human individualism. We will still have individual freedom, but more and more, it will be in the context of the constraints imposed by a greater organism. And so, in this view, Russell's idea that the global brain might inherit the problems caused by human "self-centeredness" is self-contradictory. The global brain, once it emerges, will be the top-level system and will be individualistic—but, as Russell himself notes, the nature of its individualism will be quite "inhuman" in nature.

Mayer-Kress, in this post, did not address the question of whether the global brain would be sane or insane in itself; rather, he defused the question by breaking the chain of reasoning leading from human neurosis to global brain neurosis. In my own reply to Russell's message, on the other hand, an attempt was made to take the bull by the horns and answer the question: What would it even mean for a global Web brain to be insane?

About sanity or insanity. Surely, these are sociocultural rather than psychological concepts. However, they can be projected into the individual mind due to the multiplicity of the self. An insane person in a society is someone who does not "fit in" to the societal mindset, because their self-model and their reality-model differ too far from the consensus. In the same vein, if one accepts the multiplicity of the individual self (Rowan, 1990), one finds that in many "insane" people, the different parts of the personality do not "fit in" right with each other. So the jarring of world-models that characterized the insane person in a culture is also present within the mind of the insane person. Because, of course, the self and mind are formed by mirroring the outside!

What does this mean for the global brain? View the global brain as a distributed system with many "subpersonalities." Then, the question is not whether it is sane with respect to some outside culture, but whether it is sane with respect to itself (a trickier thing to judge, no doubt). Do the different components of the global brain network all deal with each other in a mutually understanding way, or are they "talking past" each other?

A key point to remember here is that the global brain can be, to a large extent, real-time engineered by humans and AI agents. So that, if any kind of "insanity" is detected, attempts can be made to repair it on the fly. We are not yet able to do this sort of thing with human brains, except in the very crudest ways (drugs, removing tumors, etc.).

The belief I expressed in this post is that the sanity of the global Web brain is an engineering problem. By designing Web software intelligently, we can encourage the various parts of the global Web brain to interact with each other in a harmonious way—the hallmark of true sanity. The various neuroses of human mind and culture will be in there—but they will be subordinate to a higher level of sanely and smoothly self-organizing structure.

The biggest potential hang-up, in this view, is the possibility that forces in human society may intervene to prevent the software engineering of the Web mind from being done in an intelligent way. Perhaps it may come about that a maximally profitable Web mind and a maximally sane Web mind are two different things. In this case, we will be caught in a complex feedback system. The saner the Web mind, the saner the global brain of humanity, the less likely the forces of greed will be to take over the Web mind itself.

One thing is noteworthy about this particular thread on the Global Brain Study Group: In spite of our disagreements on details, everyone in the Study Group seems to concur that a healthy, sane global brain would be a good thing. An alternative view was given by Paulo Garrido in a message on the Principia Cybernetica mailing list, forwarded by Heylighen to the Global Brain Study Group. Garrido made the remark that if human society becomes an independent organism in and of itself, we should kill it. This is because it would logically limit the freedom and individuality of its components—us as individuals—just as a multicellular organism limits the freedom and individuality; it would increase our survival and comfort, and leave us with no reason to live.

Garrido's remarks, though somewhat paranoid in tone, are well thought-out and represent a natural human fear. Are we all going to be absorbed into some cosmic organism, to lose our human individuality, our freedom, our sense of individual feeling and accomplishment? After all, does computer technology not represent the ultimate in dehumanizing technology?

The difficulty, of course, is that freedom is difficult to assess. Every major change in the social order brings new freedoms and eliminates old ones. And the relative "goodness" of one thing or another is not an objective judgment anyway—standards of morality vary drastically from culture to culture.

THE GLOBAL BRAIN AND HUMAN PROGRESS

By way of comparison, it is interesting to ask the "for good or for ill" question of the computer itself. The answer, in this case as in the case of the global Web brain, is not 100% clear.

What, one might ask, has the computer contributed to economic productivity? It is generally assumed that computers have improved our efficiency, but there are no good figures in existence to prove this. In fact, the most literal reading of the economic figures tells you that computers have had a bad influence on productivity. True, economic measures are always suspect, and it is particularly difficult to measure productivity in the service sector, which is where computers have had the greatest impact. But is seems quite plausible to me that the economists are right, and that computers, rather than increasing the productivity of most businesses, have largely had the effect of replacing one kind of work with another, one kind of employee with another.

And then one might ask, what has been the computer's total contribution to culture and the quality of life? Most of us who use computers regularly will probably answer "Huge! Computers have improved our lives tremendously!" After all, how dull life would be without e-mail; how tedious writing was before word processors; how nice my son finds World of Warcraft on a rainy (or sunny) day; how useful is Excel for the small businessperson, Mathematica for the scientist, etc. And there is no denying these positives, but even so, there are other ways in which the cultural influence of computers has been terribly negative. Computers are, in one view, the ultimate conclusion of a century-long trend toward the impersonalization of business transactions.

How many times have you heard someone remark that in the old days, there was a personal relationship between the businessperson and the customer. There was an element of caring there, and not merely "caring" in the economic sense of caring about retaining someone's business. Business transactions were human interactions. This is a cliché, but like many clichés, it is deeply true. Anthropologist Marvin Harris (1987), in his book *Why Nothing Works*, coined the word "dis-service" to refer to the manifold inconveniences caused to modern Americans by computerized inventorying and billing systems, and other technological and organizational developments that divorce business transactions from genuine human interactions. He points out the tremendous number of hours wasted, and the huge amount of stress caused in trying to rectify the misunderstandings caused by the dehumanization of business.

Computers have given us e-mail, word processing, and lots of cool games and useful tool for working. They have given us ATM machines, safer airplane fights, and cars with superior performance (though not necessarily lower repair bills, as anyone who has ever had to replace their car's "main computer" can attest). But, by contributing to the cultural trend toward depersonalization, they have also taken from us; they have taken a million little opportunities for genuine, rich, physical/mental human interaction. As with any other "advance," there has been a tradeoff.

Computers are a good example because of their obvious relatedness to the global Web mind, but, in fact, the same issues arise with any technological innovation, even civilization itself. Are we, one may ask, better off than our Stone Age predecessors? Some say yes, some say no. Some say that our ancestors worked only 2 hours a day, hunting and gathering, and spent the rest of the time enjoying each other and the world around them. No routine stress, no neurosis. There was genuine pain and suffering in times of cold or hunger or illness, true, but we civilized folk have not exactly eliminated these problems; and we have evolved our own specialized physical difficulties: AIDS, herpes, lung cancer. In fact, modern diseases did not spread significantly until sedentarism replaced nomadism as a standard style of life.

The interesting thing about the ambiguous value of technological innovations, however, is how little it seems to matter, in practical terms. Progress, it seems, can never be resisted, and once it has been made, it can never be permanently retracted. These are heuristic laws of cultural development, to which we have seen no major exceptions in human history so far. There is an ebb and flow to human affairs, but there is also, in the long term, a powerful overall movement toward greater social complexity and greater technological and intellectual sophistication.

No one, today, is going to go back to using a typewriter to write. In the United States today, only a few old or poor people use typewriters. Few middle-class parents are going to let their children grow up without computers; and in another decade, nearly every household will have some sort of networked computer in it, just as nearly every household today has a television. Most probably, the computer and the television will become a single appliance. And no one, today, is going to go back to living in the Stone Age manner. Modern technology is too seductive. It makes me sad to witness the collapse of the few remaining Stone Age cultures, in such places as central Africa, the Amazon jungle, Papua, New Guinea, and outback Australia. But one cannot, in good faith, tell the citified Aboriginals of Western Australia: "No! Go back to the desert! Hunt and gather!" Because one knows that one would do the same exact thing in their shoes. And why not?

The truth is that new technologies appeal to human nature. We like to have more, to see more, to do more. We like to extend our capabilities. Once we see the possibility of climbing up a little higher, we want to go there. We like to be more efficient and "cooler." And furthermore, as biologist Gregory Stock (1993) (a member of the Global Brain Study Group) has argued in *MetaMan*, this kind of attitude is not a quirk of our particular neurochemistry, it is a natural consequence of our intelligence. An intelligent organism is, by its very nature, constantly seeking more, constantly striving to exceed itself. It is possible for intelligent organisms to get locked into relatively stable, steady-state systems, such as aboriginal culture, which remained basically the same for around 50,000 years. Such a steady-state system channels the need for growth and expansion in specific directions, while restricting it from other directions. But even so, the intelligent mind is always striving in all possible directions, and as soon as a new direction becomes apparent—be it computers, civilization, or the global brain—the intelligent mind will seek it out.

Valentin Turchin (1997), like many other systems theorists, speaks of an inevitable rise toward more and more complex forms of life. He applies this principle to the emergence of life from inorganic matter, to the emergence of human intelligence from basic life forms, and to the emergence of the global superorganism from humanity. What this philosophy is doing is merely positing the universe itself as an intelligent system. Turchin is saying that the universe, like the human mind, cannot resist a new innovation, a better, more efficient way of doing things. It may glide along for a while in a steady state, but eventually the new idea will occur, and then it will be irresistible. The universe, like the mind, has an eye for intricate new patterns.

And so, one sees that the global Web brain will be good in some regards, and bad in some regards, but the one thing I believe most strongly is that it will be irresistible. It will have its good and bad points, and it will also help to get rid of some of the bad points of the technologies that support it. For instance, the depersonalization of business interaction, brought on by the computer, will disappear in the wake of new kinds of computer-mediated human-to-human interaction. In the long run, the voices calling to kill the global brain will be no more dominant than the voices calling, right now, to kill civilization and return to the jungle. The heuristic law of progress, the uniters' tendency to build up hierarchies of emergent patterns, is stronger than the human race itself.

WEB SPIRITUALITY

In discussing the philosophy of the global Web mind and the global brain, one is always dancing around the edges of the notion of spirituality. The notion of a global brain has strong religious overtones. There is something very deeply moving about the idea of an overarching mind that embraces individual human minds, melding them into a greater whole. In fact, when phrased in appropriate ways, the global societal mind begins to sound almost supernatural, like some kind of divine overarching being.

Whatever one's religious or nonreligious proclivities, these spiritual overtones in the concept of the global brain are genuine and important, and should not be mocked or ignored. For, whatever one's opinion of its ultimate meaning, spirituality is a part of the human experience, and will continues to be as we move into a new era of digital being. First of all, where the Web and spirituality are concerned, it is impossible not to mention the work of mid-twentieth-century theologian Teilhard de Chardin. Teilhard's evolutionary, information-theoretic spiritual philosophy has reminded many people of modern communications technology, so much so that some have cited his work as a premonition of the Internet.

Teilhard de Chardin prophesied that our current phase of being, in which individual humans live independent lives, would eventually be replaced with something else—something more collective and more spiritual, something focused on information and consciousness rather then material being. He coined the word *noosphere* or *mind sphere* to refer the globe-encircling web of thought and information that he thought would arise at the end of our current phase of being.

Teilhard de Chardin was a Jesuit priest, and his ideas, for all their radicalism, emanate straight from the essence of Christianity. His vision is plainly an extension of the conventional Catholic notion of Judgment Day, a day on which history ends and the angels descend from Heaven; the good are brought up to Heaven and the rest plunged down to Hell. What de Chardin offers is a more refined Catholic eschatology, a subtler vision of the spiritual future, with a focus on information rather than on good versus evil. The subtlety of his vision was not appreciated by the fathers of the Church, who forbid de Chardin to publish and even exiled him to China. Thus, his major work, *The Phenomenon of Man* (de Chardin, 1994), was only published after his death.

"Man," according to Nietzsche (1991), "is something that must be overcome." Nietzsche saw humans as stepping-stones between beast and Superman. Teilhard de Chardin, on the other hand, saw humans as stepping-stones between beast and global Mind. The justification for humanity as it is, he declared, lies in what humanity is going to evolve into: a collective, electric mental organism, transcending the boundaries between individuals and the boundary between mind and body. A cosmic, intelligent, reflective entity, transforming information within itself with perfect efficiency. Teilhard de Chardin spoke of progress, of evolution, of an inexorable, natural movement from simple material forms toward more and more sophisticated, abstract forms—from the mundane toward the spiritual. At the end of the line, he proposed, was the omega point—the emergence of a spiritually perfected global brain or noosphere.

What is the relation between the noosphere and the Net? Some would say the two are virtually identical. Jennifer Kreisberg (1995), writing in *Wired* magazine, put the case as follows:

> Teilhard imagined a stage of evolution characterized by a complex membrane of information enveloping the globe and fueled by human consciousness. It sounds a little off the wall, until you think about the Net, that vast electronic Web circling the Earth, running point to point through a nervelike constellation of wires....

Teilhard saw the Net coming more than half a century before it arrived. He believed this vast thinking membrane would eventually coalesce into "the living unity of a single tissue" containing our collective thoughts and experiences.

I suspect that this overstates the case—but not by a great deal. It is more imprecise than fundamentally incorrect. In truth, although the metaphors that Teilhard de Chardin conceived for talking about his noosphere do mesh well with the Web, the Internet itself does not fulfill his prophecy nor will the emergence of the global Web brain. But when the global Web brain advances to Phase Two, and humans are incorporated into the globally distributed intelligence matrix, then, at this point, Kreisberg's statement will be better justified, and one will have a digital system somewhat vaguely resembling a Teilhardian "mind sphere."

The first key point that Kreisberg glosses over is that Teilhard did not foresee that humans would create a superintelligent mind-sphere; he foresaw that humans would become one. What is required in order to even approximately fulfill Teilhard's dream is, therefore, for humans to become part of the global brain, the intelligent Web. His vision more closely approximated a global societal mind than a global Web mind. It is important not to fudge the distinction between these two different things: Phase One, the emerging global Web mind, and Phase Two, the Russellian possibility of a human-incorporating global bio–digital intelligence.

Even a global societal mind, however, is a long way from Teilhard's (de Chardin, 1994) idea of the end of the world, the wholesale internal introversion upon itself of the noosphere, which has simultaneously reached the uttermost limit of its complexity and centrality. The end of the world, the overthrow of equilibrium, detaching the mind, fulfilled at last, from its material matrix, so that it will henceforth rest with all its weight on God-Omega. Ultimately, the global Web mind may indeed detach mind from its material matrix; and it may indeed represent a "phase transition," if not an "uttermost limit," in the complexity of the global network of human information. But anyone who believes all this will bring divine perfection is being foolish. New advances always bring problems along with solutions. The Net bears some resemblance to Teilhard's vision, but Teilhard's vision was of the mind-sphere as a panacea, and that, one can be sure, the future Net will not be. At bottom, like all transcendental eschatologies, Teilhard's vision is a bit of a cop-out. By telling us perfection is just around the corner, it relieves us of the responsibility of seeing the perfection within the obvious imperfection all around us.

In the end, perhaps the most striking aspect of Teilhard's thought is the way it conjoins spirituality with information and communication. This, rather than his glittering portrayal of future utopia, is really what brings Teilhard so close to Internet technology. Many other theologians have written their own eschatologies, their own versions of Judgment Day. But Teilhard dispensed with the mythical symbols normally used to describe such events and replaced them with very abstract, almost mathematical notions. In doing so, he roused the ire of the Catholic church, and he also—quite unwittingly—helped to bring spirituality into the computer age.

The other theological thinker who is crucial for understanding the Web—though rarely, if ever, mentioned in this context—is Carl Jung. The Web provides a whole new way of thinking about Jung's concept of the collective unconscious, a realm of abstract mental forms, living outside space and time, accessible to all human beings, and guiding our thoughts and feelings. And it gives new, concrete meaning to his concept of archetypes—particular mental forms living in the collective unconscious, with particular power to guide the formation of individual minds (Jung, 1955).

The concept of the collective unconscious has never achieved any status within scientific psychology; it is considered too flaky, too spiritual. Science, perhaps rightly, perhaps (as Card, 1996, argues) wrongly, has no place for an incorporeal realm of abstract forms, interacting with individual minds but standing beyond them. The global Web mind, however, will actually be an incorporeal—or at least digital—realm of abstract forms, interacting with individual minds, but standing beyond them.

Some of the "archetypal forms" that Jung believed we absorb from the collective unconscious are basic psychological structures: the Self, the Anima/Animus (the female and male within), the Shadow. Others are more cultural in nature: the First Man. Some are visual: the right-going spiral, signifying being "sucked in"; the left-going spiral, signifying being "spewed out." But the most basic archetypes of all, in Jung's view, are the numbers. Small integers like 1, 2, and 3, Jung interpreted as the psychological manifestation of order. In fact, Jung suggested that all other archetypes could be built up out of the particular archetypal forms corresponding to small integers. This is a strikingly computeresque idea; it is a "digital" view of the world, in the strictest sense. So we see that Jung's thought, for all its obscurity and spirituality, was at bottom very mathematical; he viewed the abstract structures of the mind as emanating from various combinations of numbers. He viewed the collective unconscious as a digital system.

The global Web mind will fulfill Jung's philosophy in a striking and unexpected way; it will be a digital collective unconscious for the human race. For, after all, the memory of the global Web mind is the vast body of humanly created webpages, which is a fair representation of the overall field of human thought, knowledge, and feeling. So, as the global Web mind surveys this information and recognizes subtle patterns in it, it will be determining the abstract structure of human knowledge (i.e., determining the structure of the human cultural/psychological universe. This is true even for the global Web mind as an independent entity; and it will be far more true if, as human beings integrate more and more with the Web, the global Web brain synergizes with humanity to form a global digital/societal mind.

Specifically, the most abstract levels of the global Web mind will bear the closest resemblance to the collective unconscious as Jung conceived it. These levels will be a pool of subtle, broad-based patterns, abstracted from a huge variety of different human ideas, feelings, and experiences, as presented on the Web, and this body of abstract information will be active. Initially, it will be involved in creating new links on the Web, in creating new Web content, in regulating various real-world and virtual activities based on this content. As it grows more pervasive, it will become involved in an interactive way with human thoughts and feelings themselves. In other words, precisely as Jung envisioned, the digital collective unconscious will be involved in forming the thoughts, feelings, and activities of human beings' individual consciousness.

But what, in the end, are we to make of these parallels between Teilhard, Jung, and the Net? Obviously, Carl Jung did not foresee the Internet and the global Web mind, any more than Teilhard de Chardin did, just as engineers and scientists who designed the Internet did not have any intention of realizing the spiritual ideas of these philosophers.

The situation is well understood in the language of Jungian psychology; what has happened is that the philosophers and the engineers and scientists have tapped into the same emerging cultural archetype. The philosophers have interpreted the global interconnected web in terms of the human meaning of the archetypes and the collective unconscious; the engineers and scientists, on the other hand, have made these archetypes physical and concrete. We humans, as a race, are forever trapped between philosophy and engineering/science—not a bad place to be trapped at all. We are on the very wonderful course of using engineering and science to fulfill our deepest philosophical and spiritual longings.

SELF AND MORALITY IN THE WORLD WIDE BRAIN

In closing, I will draw together some of the technical and philosophical ideas already presented to briefly consider a question posed to me by Jayne Gackenbach, the editor of this volume: Will the World Wide Brain be moral? Will it have a sense of ethics? This question is a good entry into the general question of the self-psychology of the emerging global Web brain.

Conscience is experienced by humans as a "voice inside," giving recommendations as to which actions are right or wrong. Judgments of right and wrong vary a great deal from culture to culture, family to family, and person to person, and seem to depend strongly on early childhood experience. Since the global Web mind's early childhood experience will be rather different from that of a human being, there is certainly reason to question whether any consciencelike phenomenon will emerge.

In the Webmind AI design, there was a Java class called Self, which was an integral part of the system, and whose role was to continuously record what a system is doing, for the purposes of adjusting the system's numerous parameters and guiding the system's introspection (self-querying) processes. According to the animist view of consciousness I have advocated (Goertzel, 1997), this class, like the brain processes regulating human attention, should not be thought of as the location of "raw experience," but rather as the "vortex" within the system at which raw awareness, the primal ground of being, achieves its greatest effect on the world of concretized pattern. The Novamente AI system uses a different approach, in which there is no Self explicitly programmed in, and self-understanding is expected to emerge, but the basic concept is the same.

An AI system may be explicitly programmed to seek behaviors that please its human users, serving their needs as best possible, and also to seek behaviors that please the other AIs with which it is interacting. In this sense, an individual machine or cluster of machines running an AI may have a conscience. The specific contours of an individual AI's conscience will be different from one AI to another, based on experience and adaptation, but this is only to be expected. Asimov's Three Laws of Robotics, which in his science-fiction stories were wired into robots preventing them from doing harm to humans, would be difficult to implement in the context of an emergent, self-organizing intelligence. It is easy to hard-code restrictions preventing an AI from sending commands to the Pentagon instructing bombs to be dropped, but not so easy to prevent it from taking actions indirectly causing humans harm; it is for these cases that conscience must use its own intuition, which adapts over time, sometimes well, sometimes poorly.

We have also seen that various AI systems may interact socially. Most simply, each one may query others for information, and will need to know which others are the best to ask for which types of information. Each one may give the others advice on yet others, and each one must judge the reliability of each other one's advice on each particular topic. This fairly simple concept of adaptive information sharing leads to an Internet AI version of the Collective Unconscious, different from the human Collective Unconscious that emerges from the sum total of human data on the Net. There will be a collection of shifting patterns regulating the interaction within the collective AI unity, dimly perceived by any individual AI mind, but providing a ground for intersubjective creativity.

However, the interaction between AI minds will be more intense than social interaction between humans, in that different AIs will actually be able to exchange "brain lobes" (collections of knowledge, emotion, opinion, etc.). This social information exchange has no overseeing inner eye, no potential conscience as such, because it is a fundamentally heterogeneous, decentralized process.

An additional twist on these observations is obtained by noting that physical reality for many future AIs may basically consist of the Internet itself, and the computers on it. Some AIs may be embodied in physical robots or simulation worlds, but all may not be. Furthermore, the statistical average patterns of the social interaction of AIs will determine patterns of network traffic, ultimately the laying down of new cable, and so on. The physical substrate is, in this sense, going to be molded by the social dynamics, a mirror of how, according to quantum physics, the collective perceptions of the macroscopic systems in the universe lead to the creation of a concrete universe from the underlying microscopic world of uncertainty, the carving out of a mutual path through multiple-universe space.

We thus arrive at the puzzling observation that there may be no global conscience for the World Wide Brain, because of the distributed, multiowner nature of the Internet (i.e., because of the very feature that has led to the Internet's explosive growth). The inner eye of conscience has to have the ability to look into and change each part of the system it interpenetrates. For example, if a particular part of the global brain is made up of software owned by company X, then company X would have to agree to give the inner eye of conscience access to their software, trusting that the inner eye was going to improve it for the good of the whole mind. This goes against the corporate competitive ethic, needless to say.

What this discussion points up, above all, is the way the Net blurs the line between the individual and the social. Whereas for us there is a sharp division between individual mind and social mind, for the intelligent Net, there will be more of a continuum. There will be a panoply of overlapping and disjointed inner eyes, a pandemonium of consciences, overlapping and interfering with each other in a much more intimate way than is possible in human intercourse.

Speculatively, one might conjecture that society is less moral than the individual precisely because it has no inner eye, no overall stream of consciousness. However, the disorganization and immorality of society may be necessary for the organization, focus, and morality of the individual. The Net, by avoiding the rigid distinction between immoral society and the moral individual, may avoid many of the problems that have plagued human history, but will surely experience new problems all its own. Consciousness existing in such an environment of constantly shifting boundaries will probably suffer less from the human tendency toward excessive reification and rigid boundary drawing, but may fall into the opposite error more often.

And what will happen to human consciousness, interlined with such a system, a system that blurs the boundaries of the individual and the social? The only reasonable conclusion is that human consciousness will also lose some of its rigidity in such matters. As, in general, the consciousness of those organisms with which it interacts; so, as humans interact with self-organizing Internet AI systems in the workplace and at home, they will cease to act as if the individual and social were rigidly separate domains, and will begin to actualize the collective unconscious more explicitly in their individual thoughts and doings.

Joan Preston (Chapter 11, this volume) has discussed the process by which computer interfaces, of the standard and VR type, gradually become "transparent" through repeated use and through similarity in various respects to ordinary human environments. What we are discussing here is something related but perhaps more profound; the increasing transparency of the human self, as the transpersonal aspects of mind become much more directly manifest in physical reality. Selves are now the boundaries that divide mental patterns from each other, but in a world of symbiotic human/AI mind, this will no longer be the case, at least not as strongly as it is now. The transparency of computer interfaces between one human and another, and between humans and the collective-unconsciousness-embodying intelligent Net, engenders a deeper kind of transparency. Morality, which is based on "compassion," the reaching out of feelings from one self to another, will take an entirely different guise, as the self boundaries that give morality meaning become more fluid and multileveled.

REFERENCES

Card, C. (1996). The emergence of archetypes in present-day science, and its significance for a contemporary philosophy of nature. *Dynamical Psychology Electronic Journal*, Retrieved Nov. 1, 2005, from ⟨http://goertzel.org/dynapsyc/⟩

de Chardin, T. (1994). *The phenomenon of man*. New York: Borgo Press.

de Rosnay, J. (1996). *L'homme symbionte*. NY: Harper & Row.

de Rosnay, J. (1975). *Le macroscope*. NY: Harper & Row.

Gibson, W. (1994). *Neuromancer*. New York: Ace Books.

Goertzel, B. (1993a). *The structure of intelligence: A new mathematical model of mind*. New York: Springer-Verlag.

Goertzel, B. (1993b). *The evolving mind*. New York: Gordon and Breach.

Goertzel, B. (1994). *Chaotic logic: Language, thought, and reality from the perspective of complex systems science*. New York: Plenum Press.

Goertzel, B. (1996). Subself dynamics in human and computational intelligence. CC-AI: The Journal for the Integrated Study of Artificial Intelligence, Cognitive Science, and Applied Epistemology, 13(2–3), 115–140.

Goertzel, B. (1997). *From complexity to creativity*. New York: Plenum Press.

Goertzel, B. (2001). *Creating Internet intelligence*. New York: Plenum Press.

Harris, M. (1987). *Why nothing works*. Washington, DC.: Touchstone Press.

Jung, C. G. (1955). Synchronicity: An acausal connecting principle. In Collected works of C. G. Jung, Vol. 8 (2nd Ed.): *The structure and dynamics of the Psyche*. Princeton: Bollingen Series, Princeton University Press.

Kreisberg, J. (1995). A globe, clothing itself with a brain. Wired Magazine, Issue 3. 06 June 1995.

Looks, M., Goertzel, B., & Pennachin C. (2004). Novamente: An Integrative Approach to Artificial General Intelligence. Proceedings of the AAAI Symposium on Achieving Human-Level Intelligence through Integrated Systems and Research. Washington, DC

Moravec, H. (1990). *Mind children.* Cambridge, MA: Harvard University Press.

Nietzsche, F. (1991). *The passion of the Western mind.* New York: Ballantine Books.

Rowan, J. (1990). *Subpersonalities, the people inside us.* Routledge.

Russell, P. (1995). *The global brain awakens.* New York: Global Brain Inc.

Stock, G. (1993). *MetaMan.* New York: Simon and Schuster.

Turchin, V. (1997). *The phenomenon of science.* New York: Columbia University Press.

CHAPTER 13

The Internet and Higher States of Consciousness—A Transpersonal Perspective[1]

Jayne Gackenbach
Department of Psychology
Grant MacEwan College
Edmonton, Alberta, Canada
Jim Karpen
Maharishi University of Management
Fairfield, Iowa

INTRODUCTION

The chapters in this book explore a range of aspects of the Internet[2], from its impacts on our sense of self through explorations of new social realities to its possible role in establishing a more tightly coupled field of intellectual and social interaction,

---

[1] The version of this chapter which appeared in the 1998 edition of this book included as coauthor Gregory Guthrie of Maharishi University of Management.

[2] Here, we use the term "Internet" to refer to a complex interconnected array of electronically mediated forms of communication including, among others, cell phones, video games, and MP3 players, since the distinctions among them are becoming increasingly vague.

Psychology and the Internet: Intrapersonal, Interpersonal, and Transpersonal Implications

perhaps viewed as a global brain (see Chapter 12). All of these help us to understand what this new entity means, and what its impact and future will be. Similarly, in this chapter, we view the same goal but through a different lens: that of consciousness.

This topic has been addressed from a range of angles, including the subdisciplines of psychology, business, sociology, human factors, artificial intelligence, and complexity theory. However, the approach here is that of transpersonal psychology, and the focus is on the individual subjective experience of what has been termed "higher states of consciousness" and how an increasingly electronically mediated world might affect the development of such states of being.

Transpersonal psychology takes as its domain a range of experiences often considered outside the realm of normal experience—the mystical and transcendental. In this chapter, we seek to understand aspects of the connection between the Internet and higher states of consciousness, which have been thought to be foundational to the mystical experience. We broach the question of whether the Internet and the experience of virtual reality can stimulate some facet of the experience of higher consciousness. And we consider whether the mesmerizing nature of electronically mediated experiences, including the Internet, is possibly due to characteristics that resonate with an innate appreciation of an underlying unity of existence.

Higher states of consciousness (HSC) were long considered to lie outside the discipline of psychology, in part because the experience was rare and subjective and often unreliably intermittent. But in the last 30 years, a growing body of research is documenting the existence of and the neurophysiological signatures of these states. We begin by characterizing higher states of consciousness, based on the sorts of subjective reports that appear in a range of indigenous traditions, looking briefly at the pioneering compilation of these reports by Bucke (1969). We then survey some of the research in this area, including the studies by Travis *et al.* (2002) on individuals experiencing cosmic consciousness, the work by Lutz *et al.* (2004) on Buddhist meditation, and the research by Newberg *et al.* (2001) on the neurophysiology of spiritual experience. We then consider a hypothesis by Alexander *et al.* (1990) about the sorts of "cultural amplifiers" that can lead to the experience of HSC. This sets the stage for looking at the possibility of whether the Internet, as the latest in a long series of forms of mediated communication, can be such a cultural amplifier.

Next, we consider the relationship between technology and cognition with the ideas of Sternberg and Preiss (2005). We report in detail studies by Gackenbach and colleagues (Gackenbach & Preston, 1998; Gackenbach, 1998, 1999, 2005, in press; Gackenbach & Reiter, 2005), following on the ideas introduced in Preston's chapter (see Chapter 11) on virtual reality as a facet of the Internet and the correlation of this experience with the experience of lucid dreaming. This research focuses primarily on video game as one of the most dominant and immersive aspects of virtual reality (VR) immersion.

The chapter concludes by briefly considering the coevolution of technology and consciousness in an attempt to understand the ultimate significance of the

Internet and speculates that the appeal of the Internet and its like may lie, in part, in its resonance with latent experience of HSC endemic to the human mind.

OTHER APPROACHES TO CONSCIOUSNESS

Introductory psychology texts use simple definitions, such as "consciousness is your awareness of external and internal stimuli" (Matlin, 1995, p. 134) and focus on the role of attention. Although early psychology focused on the problem of consciousness, it went out of favor as an area of inquiry until revived by cognitive and transpersonal psychologists. These two subdisciplines of psychology, unfortunately, share few thinkers, journals, departments, or other more formal areas where researchers might discuss their mutual fascination with the problem of consciousness. A few notable exceptions exist, such as the consciousness studies department at the University of Arizona and its biannual meetings titled "Toward a Science of Consciousness" (http://www.consciousness.arizona.edu).

Additionally, there have been some attempts to more broadly understand consciousness by integrating a variety of disciplinary perspectives (e.g., Hunt, 1995). In fact, interdisciplinary approaches to the study of consciousness are increasingly becoming recognized as necessary in order to truly comprehend the nature of consciousness. In his Vedic science (Maharishi, 1994), a unique formulation of a science of consciousness emerging from the Vedic tradition in India, Maharishi Mahesh Yogi also provides such an integrated approach. While based in a direct subjective definition[3] and approach to the science of consciousness, it also derives relevant models of the dynamics and properties of Western disciplines from this perspective, including unified field models of physics (see Orme-Johnson *et al.* (1990) on the field effect of consciousness).

HUMAN CONSCIOUSNESS AND ITS DEVELOPMENT

Consciousness is a challenging and ephemeral concept. Historically, it has been approached from a range of contexts, and with equally diverse definitions. Alongside a cognitive science perspective of consciousness are those developed in transpersonal psychology, which "has gradually crystallized as the discipline involved in the study of transformations of consciousness especially those associated with the various meditative traditions, as potential expressions of the maximum

---

[3] An approach which is consistent with qualitative explorations to a phenomenon in which the experience itself must be addressed in its totality from the perspective of the experiment. Such qualitative perspectives are thought, at their best, to complement more traditional reductionist, quantitative methods of inquiry and to add to the understanding of personal experience.

synthesis and integration open to consciousness" (Hunt, 1995, pp. 3–4). We base our framework on the empirical research and have adopted specific meanings for a range of terms. Consciousness here simply means awareness. HSC means the experience, perception, and appreciation of a reality, as a result of developmental processes.

Perhaps one of the first psychological researchers to catalog the experience of higher states of consciousness was Bucke (1969) in the classic work *Cosmic Consciousness*, which was originally published in 1901. He described three levels of consciousness: Simple Consciousness, which refers to the awareness experienced by animals; Self Consciousness, which refers to the experience of awareness that people typically have; and Cosmic Consciousness, which refers to a heightened perceptual experience that has been reportedly experienced by individuals in many different cultures around the world. Of Cosmic Consciousness, he writes,

> Cosmic Consciousness is a third form which is as far above Self Consciousness as is that above Simple Consciousness. With this form, of course, both simple and self consciousness persist.... The prime characteristic of cosmic consciousness is, as its name implies, a consciousness of the cosmos, that is, of the life and order of the universe.... There are many elements belonging to the cosmic sense besides the central fact just alluded to. Of these a few may be mentioned. Along with the consciousness of the cosmos there occurs an intellectual enlightenment or illumination which alone would place the individual on a new plane of existence—would make him almost a member of a new species. To this is added a state of moral exaltation, and indescribable feeling of elevation, elation, and joyousness, and a quickening of the moral sense.... With these come what may be called a sense of immortality, a consciousness of eternal life, not a conviction that he shall have this, but the consciousness that he has it already. (pp. 2–3)

The latter part of Bucke's book then collects dozens of historical instances across a range of cultures of individuals who had this experience, based on historical documents, religious texts, and the writings of such individuals.

One obvious question is whether these individuals were simply aberrant or whether these experiences are available to everyone, given the right conditions. Empirical research over the past 35 years is answering this question. For instance, in the past decade, research by Newberg is suggesting that the human brain is hardwired for religious experience. (A summary of the research can be found in d'Aquili & Newberg, 1999, and in a book written for a more popular audience by Newberg *et al.*, 2001.) In a new field sometimes referred to as "neurotheology," Newberg and colleagues have studied the relationship between brain function and mystical or religious experiences. Using a SPECT (single photon emission computed tomography) machine, their research has included study of the neurophysiological basis of mystical experience during the practice of Tibetan Buddhist meditation and the act of prayer by Franciscan nuns. Not only do these subjects report the type of experience described by Bucke, a sense of timelessness and unification with God, but this research offered neurophysiological correlates to such experiences.[4]

In particular, one of their findings examined an area of the brain they call the orientation association area (OAA), which is involved in an individual's distinguishing himself from other objects. As the monks and nuns in the study engaged in the deepest experience of meditation or prayer—which they experienced as a oneness with the universe or a universal spirit—there was reduced activity in the OAA. Self wasn't distinguished from nonself. The researchers concluded that spiritual experience is based in human biology. This suggests that everyone has the capacity for this experience and that given the right cultural circumstances (herein referred to as "cultural amplifiers"), this sort of transpersonal or mystical experience is available to all.[5]

In other recent research on meditation, Lutz and collaborators (2004) have used EEG and functional magnetic-resonance imaging (fMRI) to study the neurophysiological states associated with Buddhist meditation and mindfulness meditation. The practice of Buddhist meditation results in high-frequency gamma waves and brain synchrony, along with an unusually high degree of brain activation in the left prefrontal cortex, a region of the brain associated with happiness and positive thoughts and emotions. The researchers conclude that meditation involves temporal integrative mechanisms and may induce short-term and long-term neural changes. These few studies are a small sampling of the research on HSC.

INTEGRATIVE PROGRAM OF RESEARCH INTO DEVELOPING HIGHER STATES OF CONSCIOUSNESS

Some of the earliest and most extensive research has been done on practitioners of Transcendental Meditation (TM), as taught by Maharishi Mahesh Yogi, in part because there is simply a large pool of subjects conveniently available in the United States who have been trained with a uniform set of meditation procedures. This research program began in the late 1960s, with documentation

---

[4] In addition to this work on a spiritual practices resulting in states of consciousness often associated with the mystical is the work of Persinger (see, for instance, Persinger, 2003). His group has developed a technique of inducing a wide variety of altered states of consciousness including those that have been identified as "higher" using the alteration of magnetic fields through the use of a helmet. The point here is to not pass on the validity or lack thereof of such work but to note that experimental manipulation resulting in states of consciousness alterations is well under way using technologically mediated devices.

[5] This research has been criticized as being reductionist, and writing in *Zygon* (2001), Newberg gives a useful overview of this field and examines the difficult issues involved in interpreting the results.

of physiological and neurophysiological changes during TM meditation practice. Research in the past 10 years now also includes subjects whose long-term practice has resulted in permanent and measurable subjective, psychological, and neurophysiological changes.

We will look in more detail at this area of research because of the large body of studies and because of the useful theoretical framework developed by Alexander and collaborators (Alexander *et al.*, 1987, 1990), which was extrapolated from the teachings of Maharishi (1966). Alexander used this eastern perspective to inform his western psychological developmental model, showing that the growth of higher states of consciousness is a natural phenomenon available to all. He characterized the use of cultural amplifiers as a mechanism for facilitating this development.

We use terminology from Maharishi (1966) to describe HSC, where "pure consciousness" means the substrate from which all things arise and of which individual consciousness is a local expression. "Transcendence" is the process of going beyond ordinary reality and experiencing the source of consciousness. Although we view these terms as distinct concepts, historically, psychology has clumped them together under the general terms "mystical or transcendent experience." Mystical experience generally means either a transitory or permanent experience of these qualities of an HSC. These qualities have traditionally been defined and described in a variety of ways. In review of the work on the mystical experience, Lukoff and Lu (1988) acknowledged that the "definition of a mystical experience ranges greatly" (p. 163). Maslow (1969) offered 35 definitions of transcendence, a term often associated with the mystical experiences. There is now a large body of empirical work on higher states of consciousness. In the late 1970s, researchers began to systematically and empirically define consciousness and its state using a range of assessment instruments. Lukoff (1985) identified five common characteristics of mystical experience that could be operationalized for assessment purposes:

1. Ecstatic mood, which he identified as the most common feature
2. Sense of newly gained knowledge, which includes a belief that the mysteries of life have been revealed
3. Perceptual alterations, which range from "heightened sensations to auditory and visual hallucinations" (p. 167)
4. Delusions (if present) have themes related to mythology, which includes an incredible diversity and range
5. No conceptual disorganization; unlike psychotic persons, those with mystical experiences do NOT suffer from disturbances in language and speech.

In a more recent review of assessment vehicles, MacDonald and Friedman (2002) note that a categorization of spirituality instruments has emerged. Included in this list is what they call an "Experiential/Phenomenological Dimension" which includes mystical scales, peak experience scales, among others. They note about the state of the literature, especially in terms of its relationship to health and well-being, that, "it is in such disarray that the discovery of cogent trends is challenging. The task is made significantly more difficult by the fact that there is not a formally developed nomological net of humanistic and transpersonal constructs" (p. 114).

Therefore, the work of one group who have a uniform theoretical basis, an assessment instrument, and methodologies for both developing and examining HSC is a good choice to focus upon in any such inquiry. Alexander *et al.* (1990) is one such group. They begin by pointing out that to say of these states that they are "mystical" is a misnomer, for they transcend ordinary thinking in no more mystical a way than abstract thinking transcends motor behavior in infancy. They make a point of explaining that this experience of "transcendental consciousness" is the same one that the world's mystics have often spoken of with these common features: "universally available ... discontinuous with ordinary modes of cognition ... more developed ... personally meaningful" (p. 308). The point of transcendental consciousness is the "direct experience of the ultimate ground state of mind, pure consciousness" (p. 309). Whereas, historically, most researchers on mystical experiences consider them isolated or infrequent experiences with little if any theoretical "goal," this group was one of the first (see also Wilber, 1987) to describe them in the context of a general model of development (Alexander *et al.*, 1990), with their permanent establishment in an individual as a sign of the first higher state of consciousness. Furthermore, they point out that "during any developmental period, when awareness momentarily settles down to its least excited state, pure consciousness can be experienced" (p. 310). In terms of incidence, they quote Maslow, who felt that in the population at large fewer than one in 1,000 have frequent "peak" experiences so that the "full stabilization of a higher stage of consciousness appears to be an event of all but historic significance" (Alexander *et al.*, 1990, p. 310).

Another important methodological point regarding the body of work is that virtually all researchers studying the teachings of Maharishi Mahesh Yogi are very careful to distinguish the practice of meditation from the experience of pure consciousness, explaining that the former merely facilitates the latter. This point is pertinent to our thesis in this chapter that there are other such practices, or cultural amplifiers, which can have similar, if less powerful, outcomes. They also go to great pains to show that their multiple correlations of health and well-being are stronger to the transcendent experience than to the entire practice of meditation (for psychophysiological review, see Wallace, 1987; for individual difference review, see Alexander *et al.*, 1987; for theoretical review, see Alexander *et al.*, 1990; for educational reviews, see Dillbeck & Dillbeck, 1987; Nidich & Nidich, 1987, 1990; for a recent compendium of developmental applications, see the special issue of *Journal of Social Behavior & Personality*, 2005, Vol. 17, Issue 1). This large body of research surpasses any other in transpersonal psychology; thus, it is beyond the scope of this chapter to review it. Although there is a large meditation literature (reviewed in Murphy & Donovan, 1988, and in second edition Murphy *et al.*, 1997), few other research groups go to such pains to distinguish the practice of meditation from the experience of transcendence. For instance, in Murphy and Donovan's summary of research on subjective reports associated with meditation, there was little if any distinction between the practice of meditation and the state of consciousness. There is an awareness that experiences that are described as ineffable, blissful, exciting, etc. occur during these practices, but tying these subjective experiences to a specific period or practice is rarely done. The result is that the research literature on these states, excepting that of the group previously noted, is, in a sense, still at a shotgun stage. In fact, Murphy and Donovan's review lacks a theoretical integration. Further, the TM research is consistent with research on meditation in other traditions; thus, it cannot be argued that the effects are local to only one practice.

PHYSIOLOGICAL AND PSYCHOLOGICAL MARKERS OF HSC

The latest phase in the research on HSC has been the establishment of physiological and psychological markers for HSC. While early research largely focused on markers *during* the practice of meditation, researchers are now studying experienced practitioners who report an ongoing experience of HSC. Initially, this research was done on subjects during sleep (Mason *et al.*, 1995), but technological advances have made it possible to study subjects in waking activity.

Travis *et al.* (2002) have studied a group of 17 subjects experiencing cosmic consciousness as a result of Transcendental Meditation and compared them to two control groups. These subjects had been meditating an average of 25 years, and were selected based on self-reports of their experiences of transcendence along with activity and on interviews to determine the validity of their experiences. The goal of the research was to find the distinctive EEG patterns of the Cosmic Consciousness group during activity compared to the control groups. It compared the EEG of 17 persons experiencing Cosmic Consciousness with that of 17 persons who had been meditating an average of 8 years and who primarily experienced transcendence during Transcendental Meditation and also with 17 persons who didn't practice Transcendental Meditation.

The research found that people experiencing Cosmic Consciousness show distinctive EEG patterns during activity that suggest the maintenance of transcendence with waking processes. Specifically, Travis looked at the brain's "preparation response" during a simple task and a complex task, that is, the brain's activity immediately preceding a mental task. High frontal EEG coherence distinguishes the practice of the Transcendental Meditation technique from just sitting resting with one's eyes closed, and Travis found that high frontal EEG coherence was lowest in the nonmeditating group during tasks and highest in the Cosmic Consciousness group. This high frontal coherence is significantly correlated with a wide variety of mind–body characteristics, such as emotional stability, decreased anxiety, inner orientation, increased creativity, increased intelligence, and decreased neuroticism (see, for example, Dillbeck *et al.*, 1981; Dillbeck & Araas-Vesley, 1986; Nidich *et al.*, 1983). In sum, the sort of brain wave characteristics, such as alpha coherence, previously associated with the experience of a universal self during Transcendental Meditation have been found to be maintained at all times—even during deepest sleep—in those who are experiencing Cosmic Consciousness.

Although the TM group offers a certain internal consistency, many of their findings are not inconsistent with other researchers studying HSC. For instance, a study by Lazar *et al.* (2005) showed permanent changes in brain physiology as a result of Buddhist Insight meditation. The research was done on 20 subjects who were very experienced in this type of meditation. Compared to matched controls, the subjects showed increased thickness in cortical regions related to sensory, auditory, and visual perception, as well as internal perception. These regions included the prefrontal cortex and right anterior insula. These areas of the brain are involved in decision making, working memory, and brain–body interactions.

Together, these studies suggest that research is now documenting the existence of higher states of consciousness, such as those described by Bucke. The measurable changes in brain function support the idea that these individuals have an ongoing experience and perception that is different from the norm.

In summary, the research and theory discussed previously, both soft and hard, suggest the existence of higher states of consciousness and that these can be seen, given the right circumstances, as a natural development beyond the formal operational stage previously thought to be an endpoint. These higher states are characterized by, among other things, the experience of universality and boundlessness, of a transcendence of space and time, and of a heightened sense of well-being. These are not vague, subjective experiences, but rather are empirically defined levels of functioning (Alexander *et al.*, 1987). In Alexander's view, they can be developed through a specific meditative practice that allows the mind to go beyond thought to a thoughtless state that is the experience of pure consciousness—that is, consciousness without an object of perception. This state of transcendental consciousness is not an end in itself but a means of systemically developing the permanent experience of higher states of consciousness. He acknowledges that other postrepresentational techniques or cultural amplifiers from other cultures may have traditionally had the same end. We now consider the question of whether a cultural amplifier might include electronically mediated communications vehicles such as the Internet.

TECHNOLOGY AND COGNITION

As technologies have evolved into the dynamic, powerful, and expressive vehicles of today, these expressions are increasingly becoming active participants in our learning and growth process. Literacy, TV, computer games, the Internet—all play a role in shaping how we think. Technology is never innocent—we develop it and use it, and in turn it shapes us. The Internet can function as an alternate, supplemental, or amplifying vehicle for our experience of the world and our participation in it. Technology allows one to have experiences far beyond what are supported by the normal human physiology.

In the preface to *Intelligence and Technology*, Sternberg and Preiss (2005) examine the implications of technology on cognition. When technology is broadly conceptualized as "the building of artifacts or procedures—tools—to help people accomplish their goals" (p. xvii), then the influence of technology on human development is as old as humanity. More recent implications range from redefining writing and calculations to improved spatial skills. Specifically, they note that "writing relates progressively less to the cultivation of expression on paper and more to effective computer use … this change restructures the writing process as planning and reviewing with word processors involves more cognitive effort than does working in longhand" (p. xiii). In mathematics, the use of calculators and computers allows more time for complex problem solving rather than engaging in endless computation. Higher levels of nonverbal problem solving in the specialized cognitive ability of visuo-spatial information processing are also emerging in children who play video games.

A main issue in providing such experiences is the ability to more tightly couple our internal perceptual interpretation systems with the computational and/or technological systems that provide the augmented or synthesized input data. There are many such possible arrangements; from purely synthesized environments as in a computer game, or in data or model visualization from a mathematical system, to instrument-augmented perception systems. With advances in sensor technology and improved human interfaces, such VR systems are becoming an increasingly common part of industry, research, and entertainment systems.

Not only do such systems augment perceptual capabilities, they can couple significant input processing and analysis and image enhancement to normal experiences. Imagine an inspector wearing a set of goggles that allows him to see in the infrared spectrum, and which measures dimensions and status of the viewed system and compares to original specifications in its internal memory, and gives a visible warning and indicator of a virtual arrow pointing at any irregular component with the details of the problem. Such experiences are far beyond the level of daily life, and the ability to have such experiences expanded in space, dimension, scale, and richness is possibly parallel to the qualities of enhanced experiences associated with the development of higher states of consciousness. At the very least, it is becoming increasingly obvious that technology is altering mental functions (Sternberg & Preiss, 2005).

An example of the interaction of such technological augmentations and their effects on mental functions at the least, and on the development of consciousness at the most, is the relationship between video game play and the emergence of experiences thought to be related to consciousness development. Based on the cognitive science (mental model) understanding of our sense of self in the world, it has been pointed out that our perception of reality is a construction, a best guess. VR, and especially full immersive VR, potentially offers practice in maneuvering around in, as well as being in, "artificial" or perhaps "alternative" realities (discussed in the VR literature as "telepresence"). It may well be that such VR practice would translate into more accurate state recognition in dreams, which may be an indication of consciousness development

As noted earlier, an elemental aspect of consciousness is attention. Green and Baveller (2003) found that habitual electronic game players experience improved visual attention. Visual attention needs to be divided in order to play video games and Subrahmanyam *et al.* reported that skilled video game players had "better developed attentional skills than less skilled players" (2001, p. 15). Basically, in order to navigate through the VR of a video game landscape, you have to divide or broaden your attention across the landscape in order to anticipate rapid changes in the situation. Maynard *et al.* (2005) reviewed the attention and video game play literature. They found that experimental manipulations with attention as the dependent variable resulted in improved attention among those assigned to the video game playing condition. But the type of game can affect the outcome. One study finding was that a battle game was better at improving attention than was Tetris, a puzzle game. "Video games make it possible for the first time to actively navigate through representational space," comments Greenfield (Greenfield & Cocking, 1996, p. 91).

Psychological absorption is another, broader measure of attention, and is the psychological equivalent of VR presence as explained in Chapter 11 in this book by Preston. Capacity for absorption can be thought of as a capacity for total attentional involvement. Relatedly, Glicksohn (1993–1994; Glicksohn & Barrett, 2003) has found a positive relationship of absorption to alternative experiences of consciousness such as hallucinatory experiences (Glicksohn & Barrett, 2003) and anomaly in subjective experiences (Glicksohn, 1993–1994). When addressing any effects of technology, and especially VR, on consciousness it's important to consider the role of absorption or presence.

Funk *et al.* (2003) point out that although absorption in computer game play is often reported, it is seldom studied. Psychological absorption in gaming has been examined by Glicksohn and Avnon (1997–1998), who found that some of their subjects reported experiences during video game play indicative of altered states of consciousness[6] (e.g., drifting, flying, or changes in visual or auditory perception). These subjects also showed significant increases in absorption associated with video game play relative to subjects who did not report such consciousness alterations

---

[6] Although aspects of altered states of consciousness are reported in the development of higher states of consciousness, they should not be considered equivalent but rather related.

during video game play. Wood *et al.* (2004) found that rapid absorption into games was rated as highly important by gamers. As noted, Preston (Chapter 11) reviewed the research on absorption and VR immersion, which is most commonly experienced in video game play, concluding that those who score high on psychological absorption

> evaluate information in a distinct way that links it to self. This strongly implies that, regarding vision, audition, touch and balance, information to more modalities increases absorption. Multimodal stimulation creates a greater sense of presence in immersive VR. Immersive VR has the potential to offer low absorbers access to altered states of consciousness like those which high absorbers experience and also has the potential to offer to us all access to a higher level of consciousness.

Other elements of consciousness have been reported as a result of video game play. For instance, Voiskounsky *et al.* (2004), Chou and Ting (2003), and Choi and Kim (2004) note a relationship between video game play and the experience of "flow" as conceptualized by Csikszentmihalyi (1990), which, in turn, can be conceptualized as related to psychological absorption. Voiskounsky *et al.* found flow evidenced by players in a multi-user domain role-playing game while Chou and Ting examined self-reports of flow on a scale they developed among the "membership of virtual communities devoted to Internet games" (p. 666). Using the same scale developed by Chou and Ting, Gackenbach and Reiter (2005) found in preliminary analysis that frequent game players reported more flow experiences along several dimensions than did infrequent players while playing video games. Choi and Kim report flow as a quality associated with continued online Korean gamers.

THE INTERNET AS A CULTURAL AMPLIFIER—VR AND LUCID DREAMING

Some preliminary research now suggests that the experience of virtual reality does promote at least one experience thought to have some relationship to the development of HSC—lucid dreaming. The term *lucid dreaming* is variously defined. Maharishi Vedic Science characterizes it as the ongoing experience of an inner wakefulness, an experience of an absolute, unchanging field of existence that is continuous in waking, sleeping, and dreaming. In regard to dreaming, it is this inner wakefulness that is present during the dreaming. Gackenbach (1991)[7] distinguishes between lucid dreaming as an active dream wakefulness and witnessing dreaming as more removed and uninvolved from the dream activity but still fully aware that it is a dream. Tibetan Buddhism also speaks of lucid dreaming. In a meeting between

---

[7] This distinction was conceptualized based upon conversations with Charles Alexander (1987, 1990), a major researcher, and theorists following the model of Maharishi's Vedic Science.

the Dalai Lama and western researchers, he pointed out that, "The main purpose of dream yoga in the context of tantric practice is to first recognize the dream state as dream state" (Varela, 1997, p. 129). Researchers tend to view lucid dreaming as the experience of being aware that one is dreaming while the dream unfolds (Gackenbach & LaBerge, 1988).

As noted earlier, Blackmore (2003) points out that our sense of self in the world or our perception of reality is a construction, a best guess. Lucid dreaming is another such construction with a different set of input variables from those experienced while awake. Virtual reality (VR), and especially fully immersive VR, potentially offers practice in maneuvering around in, as well as being in, "artificial" or perhaps "alternative" realities. The felt sense of VR's perceived reality is termed in the VR literature as *telepresence*. Witmer and Singer (1998) found that high presence in VR occurred with increases in involvement, control, selective attention, perceptual fidelity, and mimicking real world experiences. All are aspects of video games. Relatedly, Gee (2005) notes that the qualities of successful video games include:

1. Projective Identity (part game character, part self)
2. Trajectory (gaming space, career space, history—like life, you are living it but don't attend to overarching story of your life)
3. Thematic Abstraction (the basics of the game are given and you elaborate upon it)
4. Affordances (various features in the game world which elaborate upon our brain's built-in tendency to react to the world in terms of actions that can be taken).

PREVIOUS RESEARCH INTO VIDEO GAME PLAY, CONSCIOUSNESS, AND DREAMS

Despite the immense popularity of video games, there has been very little research examining the effects of video game play on dreams, an altered form of consciousness through which first indications of HSC are thought to emerge. Players of the puzzle-type game called Tetris reported intrusive, stereotypical, visual images of the game at sleep onset (Stickgold *et al.*, 2000) and Bertolini and Nissim (2002) recognize fragments or characters from the video games in the material of children's dreams. They conclude that due to this radical change in children's play patterns, they must now incorporate video games into their child therapy practice.

In a series of research and scholarship begun in 1998, Gackenbach and colleagues (Gackenbach & Preston, 1998; Gackenbach, 1999; 2005; in press; Gillispie & Gackenbach, in press; Gackenbach *et al.*, 1998; Preston, 1998, in press; Preston & Nery, 2004) have discussed the theoretical basis and some empirical evidence for expanded consciousness experiences occurring among frequent video game players. These observations from players point to the proposed association between lucid dreams, video game play, and the development of consciousness (McLean, 2005):

- "I don't always remember my dreams when I wake up," … "When I do, though, they're extremely lucid."
- "I've had lots of dreams where I've seen it in first and third person," … "It's like, 'Oh, wow, now I'm a player in Halo.'"
- "You almost zone out," … "Your mind just goes on autopilot and you just become one with the system …. Sometimes, you can't believe the moves you're making."

Gackenbach and Preston (1998) posted a questionnaire to 56 Usenet groups focusing on video game play, four Usenet groups focusing on dreams, and about 10 Usenet groups with "teen" in the title but not erotic content. Those selected for the video game group were discussion groups and well-known video game groups. The questionnaire was also sent to former students and colleagues of Gackenbach who might be interested in the topic.

The questionnaire gathered demographic information, video game habits and preferences, and dream and related phenomena, habits, and experiences, including four sleep experiences—lucid dreaming, nightmares, night terrors, and archetypal dreams. Also asked about were three waking experiences (out-of-the-body experiences, mystical experiences, and precognitive experiences). A couple of months later a slightly elaborated version of this questionnaire was placed on the Internet as a form. In this new version, questions regarding dizziness during video game play were added.

Response to the first posting, which requested an e-mail return of the questionnaire, was 41 individuals. Another 50 people filled out the online form as of late April 1998. The majority were men (69%) with an average age between 30 and 39. A series of factor analyses were computed. The first factor analysis looked at all of the variables, except the dizziness ones, for all subjects. Of the seven factors, four involved a mixture of video game and consciousness variables. In factor 2, a lack of mystical experiences was associated with frequent play per week, a lot of types of games played and longer years playing as well as starting and peaking young. For factor 5, playing frequently during the week was associated with low dream recall, use of prayer, and low archetypal dreams. Factor 6 showed a relationship between few dreams recalled per month and playing with friends. For factor 7, long play sessions and lots of games played were associated with meditation and mystical frequency. This factor analysis showed mixed support for the major hypothesis that video game playing would be associated with experiences indicative of the development of consciousness.

Subsequent factor analyses included the dizziness variables based upon Siegel's (1979–1980) speculation that dizziness is a form of play behavior in which we seek to alter our state of consciousness. Although it tends to have negative connotations or consequences, dizziness may be experienced as a positive condition. When it is not accompanied by sickness symptoms, dizziness may include sensations of floating and euphoria. In the two factor analyses involving dizziness, both the positive (lucid dreaming link) and negative (night terrors link) aspects of dizziness and nausea were observed. The positive state is associated with indices of internal control while the negative is related to external control. The findings are consistent with related research where field independence and spatial abilities were found to be related to lucid dreams (Gackenbach & Bosveld, 1989; Gackenbach *et al.*, 1985).

Continuing with this research, some years later Preston and Nery (2004) examined several measures thought to be related to video game play skill as well as several related to the development of consciousness. Participants (n = 22) filled out the same questionnaire as the one used by Gackenbach and Preston as well as a test of psychological absorption and one of spatial orientation. They then did a pretest balance task by walking along a balance beam. Balance scores were recorded. After playing 2 video games for 10 minutes each, they did the balance post-tests and the spatial orientation test again. This brief video game play session improved both balance and spatial performance. Thus, a short-term effect of video game play (priming spatial orientation) was observed. As noted earlier, such spatial skills are associated with lucid dreaming.

They also found, as with the first study, several factors which loaded a combination of the video game playing variables with the development of consciousness variables. Specifically, they found that psychological absorption, self-reported nausea during video game play, and number of spiritual experiences were positively associated. Another factor loaded the length of play with spiritual experiences but a showed negative association to meditation.

Gackenbach (2005a, b) recently hypothesized that various indicators of the development of consciousness would show a relationship to video game play. Two self-report studies were shown. The first asked a few questions about video game play and consciousness development in classrooms using an electronic data collection device while the second study asked the same and related questions in more detail online.

The in-class questionnaire data analysis showed no overlap of conceptual areas of the questionnaire in a factor analysis; thus, video game groups were identified and compared on various transpersonal variables with appropriate covariates (i.e., dream recall and motion sickness while playing video games). The three dream variables showed differences in the expected direction; that is, there were more lucid dreams, more dream control, and more observing dreams for the high video game group of players.

However, results on the other transpersonal variables, mystical experiences and psychological absorption, did not support the hypothesis. Specifically, the low video game play group reported higher scores on the mystical scale, while there were no group differences on absorption. Gackenbach notes that a couple of things need to be considered regarding these two scales. First, the higher scores on the mystical scale were indicative of less disagreement with the items rather than agreement with the items regarding mystical experiences. Second, the absorption items were items culled from the same scale, and were rated higher than the mystical items. So, despite the lack of group differences, these students were more favorably disposed to agree with items that tap psychological absorption and appear to not have the "mystical" overtones in the wording.

Following the in-class data collection, a longer version of the questionnaire was posted to various websites, but especially to one that lists psychology experiments, for 6 months from late 2004 through May of 2005. In order to follow the procedure set up in the first set of analyses, video game groups were again formed using the various video game measures. This included a few more video game play indices than those available in class. The video game ANCOVAs used the same covariates as the first study, with the addition of interest in, and experience with, meditation, which showed video game group differences. Contrary to the in-class data collection, online the three dream variables, lucid, control and observer dreams, showed no group differences.

The other transpersonal variables also showed no group differences. Given this general lack of results on variables similar to the in-class data collection, a ceiling effect for the video game playing groups was suspected and subsequently demonstrated.

Finally, video game players from 1998 were compared to those from 2005 (online data only). Not surprisingly, video game players today started younger, play more, and have fewer negative side effects (e.g., less motion sickness while playing) than those in 1998. However, in terms of the transpersonal variables, most showed no generational difference. Specifically, there were no differences in dream recall, lucid dreaming, nightmares, archetypal dreams, mystical experiences, and interest in, and experience with meditation in the 7 years separating the two groups. There were differences in the reported incidence of night terrors, OBEs, and precognitive experiences as well as in interest and experience with prayer. The 2005 group had fewer of each experience than did the 1998 group except for prayer. The 2005 group had more interest in and experience with prayer than did the 1998 group. Again, we are presented with a mixed picture.

In their most recent study, preliminary analysis replicated the findings for lucid dreaming and observer dreaming being more common among frequent game players than among infrequent players (Gackenbach & Reiter, 2005). This was again controlling for dream recall and motion sickness reported during video game play and defining video game play along five video game variables. They also found, contrary to previous work, a higher reporting of mystical experiences by frequent gamers when prayer and motion sickness were controlled. Finally, as noted earlier, they found most of the subscales of Chou and Ting's (2003) flow during video game play scale, except for the addiction subscale, as higher for frequent gamers. Supporting the development of consciousness hypotheses of this group is also their finding of fewer negative dream types for frequent than for infrequent gamers. As this research progresses, the picture may be less mixed than the early findings indicated. But much remains to be examined.

A related caution is that of Subrahmanyam *et al.* (2001), who point out that most studies on attention and other related cognitive variables as related to technology use measure short-term effects while few look at the long-term implications, which is the focus of this group of studies. Subrahmanyam *et al.* note that, "Computer hardware and software evolve so quickly that most of the published research on the cognitive impact of game playing has been done with the older generation of arcade games and game systems" (p. 13). Thus, marginal effects with less sophisticated systems may show larger and more long-term effects as the apparatus improves. This caveat is important to note in reporting the relationship of video game play to dream forms and other indicators of the development of consciousness.

To conclude, although there does seem to be some relationship between selected transpersonal variables and video game play, the exact nature of this relationship remains to be teased out. It is perhaps as much a mistake to lump puzzle game players in with first-person shooter game players as it is to lump lucid dreams in with mystical experiences. Hunt (personal communication, June 13, 2005) has suggested that the emergence of these attributes thought important to the transpersonal perspective might all correlate at lower levels but at the higher levels break out. This is shown in Fig. 1.

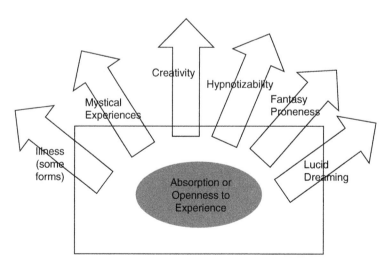

Figure 1   Hunt's Model of Parellel Lines of the Development of Consciousness. All correlate at lower levels but then break out as separate skills, experiences or states of being at higher levels.

In other words, correlations may be confusing, or simply lump together to some degree, at the lower levels of consciousness development. They might only emerge as unique factors at the higher levels. Others have viewed these transpersonal variables in a more hierarchical perspective with, for instance, lucid dreams preceding the mystical states (Gackenbach, 1991; Gackenbach & Bosveld, 1989). In either case, parallel lines of development or hierarchical development, various amplifiers may be able to bring out those attributes associated with the development of consciousness. Those most often examined include meditation, but also the use of drugs, dream recall, enhanced self awareness, flow experiences, and now perhaps video game play. It may be that another way the technological matrix will interact in deeply profound ways with the wet brain matrix will be in the wiring of neural networks to create new and unknown outcomes.

However, this does not imply that technological augmentation of experience, whether playing video games or Internet-mediated interactions and expanded experiences, is a significant approach to the development of HSC. What it indicates to us is that all possible experiential methods, including these, have the capacity for increasing development of our self-knowledge, and this is always an element of the development of consciousness. What we see is that our consciousness grows automatically. This automatic response creates as an artifact technological vehicles that extend its experience, and may also help augment the range and growth of consciousness. This may result in a circular loop of self-augmentation, literally, via technology.

THE COEVOLUTION OF TECHNOLOGY AND CONSCIOUSNESS

In the first edition of this book, this chapter was titled "The Coevolution of Technology and Consciousness." Upon rereading, the chapter, hurriedly stitched together under deadline, seemed flawed. Hence, the new approach in the current chapter.

Still, the idea of the coevolution of technology and consciousness may have some merit. One can't help but have a sense of destiny regarding the Internet—that there is a rapid movement toward a sort of global brain, as discussed in Chapter 12. The Jesuit philosopher Teilhard de Chardin, writing in the mid-twentieth century, described what he saw as the emergence of a "noosphere," a sort of vast intelligence encircling the globe, a sphere of human thought—a transhuman consciousness emerging from interacting human thought. He envisioned an endpoint for this process, an omega point, in which there is an emergence of a new reality. It's hard to observe the rapid development and not have a sense that we are witnessing a mechanism facilitating the emergence of this noosphere.

This teleological perspective of de Chardin, that evolution has a direction, is increasingly being argued these days. Darwin himself held a teleological perspective (see discussion in Himmelfarb, 2005), but as his ideas were developed in the twentieth century, evolution came to be understood as change, with no sense of a development toward a "higher" order. Wright (2000) uses game theory to argue that life has a direction and that biological evolution has led to complex, intelligent animals, which, in turn, set the stage for cultural evolution and the creation of complex societies. Today's global society, with its global Internet, is simply the logical end to a process that began millions of years ago.

In addition, the mechanisms of the emergence of complexity are increasingly being understood. Kauffman (1995) has studied the instances of spontaneous order in nature, and has shown that this phenomenon is much more widespread than originally thought. And he argues that complexity itself triggers self-organizing systems. (See Johnson, 2001, for a popular overview of the new science of emergence theory.)

Other research (summarized in Surowiecki, 2004) is suggesting how a collective intelligence enabled by a mechanism such as the Internet makes possible more accurate information than that offered by even the best individual experts. He describes, for example, how electronic markets can mediate the collective thinking of individuals to arrive at accurate forecasts of events. This suggests that there are readily observable instances of intelligence, manifested by a complex system of mediated communication, that go beyond individual intelligence.

In a sense, the notion of the coevolution of technology and consciousness could be seen as simply the simultaneous emergence of complexity, with complex human intelligence creating technologies for mediated communication and, in turn, these technologies facilitating even greater complexity—a point of the previous version of this chapter. To what end is obviously not yet clear, but the authors tend to envision a sort of spiritual awakening. And the increasing interest in meditation, yoga, and other disciplines, along with the increased research on the nature of consciousness, is also a manifestation of a spiritual awakening.

While it's hard to imagine what we are evolving toward or what may emerge, it may be interesting to use as a model the evolution of higher states of consciousness. Maharishi Vedic Science takes a very teleological perspective on this process, as indicated earlier, saying that human consciousness evolves to higher states. And these states themselves may be instances of emergent order, as EEG research on those who practice TM shows unusual coherence in their brain wave patterns (Travis *et al.*, 2002).

Maharishi Vedic Science hypothesizes that the experiences of those in higher states, such as cosmic consciousness, don't simply represent an individual who has cultivated some innate propensity of the brain. Rather, the hypothesis is that the individual is simply experiencing what he really is, and what the universe really is—a universal field of intelligence. The experience is not an intellectual understanding but a perception. Consciousness in Maharishi Vedic Science is seen as nonlocal rather than being an epiphenomenon of brain processes. The experience of this nonlocal consciousness is natural but typically shrouded. Techniques such as meditation culture the brain's optimal functioning so that one gradually becomes aware of this nonlocal facet of consciousness.

And those who experience this universal consciousness or universal intelligence from whatever tradition, as Bucke (1969) showed, typically have the same sort of subjective experience: of timelessness, immortality, connectedness with everything, infinity, of identification of one's self with something larger than one's self.

If one were to speculate on what may emerge, it may be this sort of universal awareness. And this universal awareness is innate, not just because research has shown that the human brain has this capability, but also possibly because this is the ultimate reality. This ultimate reality is within and without—everywhere/always/nonlocal to self and brain, and it's only a matter of waking up to it.

It's easy to imagine that part of the appeal of the Internet may lie in the fact that it gives a glimpse of this state. This might be one reason for its extraordinary, universal, and incontestable appeal. Its adoption and use has exploded in a way that's virtually unparalleled in history. The adoption of literacy proceeded at a snail's pace, and it wasn't until the industrial revolution that universal literacy became a goal, thousands of years after the technology was developed. The electronic media were adopted much more rapidly, with the Internet's having the distinction of being the mass medium that was adopted the fastest. An oft-cited fact that was first presented in a research report by Mary Meeker, a managing director at Morgan Stanley, which compared the adoption of radio, TV, and the Internet (Morgan Stanley, 1997, pp. 2–2, 2–6). The researchers found that it took 38 years for radio to be adopted by 50 million users in the United States, 13 years for TV to be adopted by that many, and 5 years for the Internet to reach that level of usage. What is it that is so appealing? We propose that the foregoing description of HSC may provide some insight.

The notion here is that higher states are experienced as being connected, of infinity, of universality, of an expanded sense of self, and the Internet (and, to some extent, other electronic technologies) also gives a feeling of connectedness, of an infinite amount of information, of a universal entity that one taps into. One could suggest that people readily take to the Internet because it resonates with something deep within themselves.

It is indeed a successful and uncommon technology that can sustain this initial thrill, even in the presence of significant learning curves, system complexity, and cost obstacles. The Internet is wildly popular despite these obstacles, and its popularity is only growing. While one can cite the vast amounts of specific information available through it, the popularity of the Internet seems to go beyond this. It seems to lie in the thrill of being connected. There is a sense of plugging into an almost universal entity, a sense that one can access virtually anything, can communicate effortlessly with other people across space and time. The developed terminology of "surfing" the Internet clearly reflects this feeling: that somehow accessing things through the Internet is not a trudge to the library, but a joyride through some vastly richer and more charming terrain.

To summarize, we suggest the existence of higher states of consciousness and briefly note research that seems to document these higher states. We suggest that these states are innate and need only to be developed. Further, this chapter tries to understand the role of the Internet and mediated communication in affecting neurological functioning as evidenced by the experience of lucid dreaming in game players. And finally, we speculate that ultimately, the trend is toward an emerging global entity, of which the Internet is an instance, and that the end is the experience of unity consciousness, the highest state of consciousness as described by Maharishi Vedic Science, and the ultimate nature of existence.

REFERENCES

Alexander, C., Boyer, R., & Alexander, V. (1987). Higher states of consciousness in the Vedic psychology of Maharishi Mahesh Yogi: A theoretical introduction and research review. *Modern Science and Vedic Science, 1*(1), 89–126.

Alexander, C. N., Davies, J. L., Dixon, C. A., Dillbeck, M. C., Ortzel, R. M., Muehlman, J. M., & Orme-Johnson, D. W. (1990). Higher stages of consciousness beyond formal operations: The Vedic psychology of human development. In C. N. Alexander & E. J. Langer (Eds.) *Higher stages of human development: Adult growth beyond formal operations*. New York: Oxford University Press.

Bertolini, R., & Nissim, S. (2002). Video games and children's imagination. *Journal of Child Psychotherapy, 28*(3), 305–325.

Blackmore, S. (2003). *Consciousness: An introduction*. London: Oxford University Press.

Bucke, R. M. (1969) *Cosmic consciousness: A classic investigation of the development of man's mystic relation to the infinite*. New York: E.P. Dutton.

Choi, D., & Kim, J. (2004). Why people continue to play online games: In search of critical design factors to increase customer loyalty to online contents. *CyberPsychology & Behavior, 7*(1), 11–24.

Chou, T. J., & Ting, C. C. (2003). The role of flow experience in cyber-game addiction. *CyberPsychology & Behavior, 6*(6), 663–675.

Csikszentmihalyi, M. (1990). *Flow: The psychology of optimal experience*. New York: Harper & Row.

d'Aquili, E. G., & Newberg, A. B. (1999) *The mystical mind: Probing the biology of religious experience*. Minneapolis: Fortress Press.

Dillbeck, M. C., & Araas-Vesely, S. (1986). Participation in the Transcendental Meditation program and frontal EEG coherence during concept learning. *International Journal of Neuroscience, 29*, 45–55.

Dillbeck, S., & Dillbeck, M. C. (1987). The Maharishi technology of the unified field in education: Principles, practice, and research. *Modern Science and Vedic Science, 1*, 383–432.

Dillbeck, M. C., Orme-Johnson, D. W., & Wallace, R. K. (1981). Frontal EEG coherence, H-reflex recovery, concept learning, and the TM–Sidhi program. *International Journal of Neuroscience, 15*, 151–157.

Funk, J. B., Buchman, D. D., & Jenks, J. (2003). Playing violent video games, desensitization, and moral evaluation in children. *Journal of Applied Developmental Psychology, 24*(4), 413–436.

Gackenbach, J. I. (1991). A developmental model of consciousness in sleep: From sleep consciousness to pure consciousness. In J. I. Gackenbach & A. Sheikh (Eds.), *Dream images: A call to mental arms*. New York: Baywood.

Gackenbach, J. I. (1998). Video game play and the development of consciousness. Available at http://www.sawka.com/spiritwatch.

Gackenbach, J. I. (1999, July). Video Game Play and the Development of Consciousness as Measured by Some Dream Experiences. Paper presented at the annual meeting of the Association for the Study of Dreams, Santa Cruz, CA.

Gackenbach, J. I. (2005, June). Video Game Play and Dreams: A Replication & Extension. Paper presented at the annual meeting of the International Association for the Study of Dreams, Berkeley, CA.

Gackenbach, J. I. (in press). *Video game play and lucid dreams: Implications for the development of consciousness.* Dreaming.

Gackenbach, J. I. (in preparation). Transpersonal implications of telepresence resulting from being online. Manuscript accepted for inclusion in a special issue of the *Journal of Computer Mediated Communication Special Issue on Religion on the Internet.*

Gackenbach, J. I., & Bosveld, J. (1989). *Control your dreams.* New York: Harper & Row.

Gackenbach, J. I., Guthrie, G., & Karpen, J. (1998). The coevolution of technology and consciousness. In J. I. Gackenbach (Ed.), *Psychology and the Internet.* San Diego: Academic Press.

Gackenbach, J. I., Heilman, N., Boyt, S., & LaBerge, S. (1985). The relationship between field independence and lucid dreaming ability. *Journal of Mental Imagery, 9,* 9–20.

Gackenbach, J. I., & LaBerge, S. P. (Eds.). (1988). *Conscious mind, sleeping brain: Perspectives on lucid dreaming.* New York: Plenum.

Gackenbach, J. I., & Preston, J. (1998, April). Video Game Play and the Development of Consciousness. Poster presented at the third biannual meeting of the Science of Consciousness, University of Arizona, Arizona.

Gillispie, J. F., & Gackenbach, J. I. (in press). *Cyber.rules: Negotiating healthy Internet use.* New York: Norton.

Gee, J. (2005, June). Learning is the Engine that Drives Good Video Games. Invited address to the biannual meeting of Digital Game Researcher Association, Vancouver, BC.

Glicksohn, J. (1993–1994). Rating the incidence of an altered state of consciousness as a function of the rater's own absorption score. *Imagination, Cognition, and Personality, 13*(3), 225–228.

Glicksohn, J., & Avnon, M. (1997–1998). Explorations in virtual reality: Absorption, cognition, and altered state of consciousness. *Imagination, Cognition, and Personality, 17*(2), 141–151.

Glicksohn, J., & Barrett, T. R. (2003). Absorption and hallucinatory experience. *Applied Cognitive Psychology, 17*(7), 833–849.

Green, C. S., & Baveller, D. (2003). Action video game modifies visual selective attention. *Nature, 423,* 534–537.

Greenfield, P. M., & Cocking, R. R. (Eds.). (1996). Interacting with video. Advances in applied developmental psychology (vol. 11). Norwood, NJ: Ablex Publishing Corp.

Himmelfarb, G. (2005). Monkeys and morals. *The New Republic, 233*(4,743), 33–37.

Hunt, H. (1995). On the nature of consciousness: Cognitive, phenomenological, and transpersonal perspectives. New Haven: Yale University Press.

Jackson, D. N. (1993). Dynamic spatial performance and general intelligence. *Intelligence, 17*(4) 451–460.

Johnson, S. (2001). *Emergence: The connected lives of ants, brains, cities, and software.* New York: Simon & Schuster.

Kauffman, S. (1995). *At home in the universe: The search for the laws of self-organization and complexity.* New York: Oxford UP.

Lazar, S., Kerr, C. E., Wasserman, R. H., Gray, J. R., Greve, D. N., Treadway, M. T., McGarvey, M., Quinn, B. T., Dusek, J. A., Benson, H., Rauch, S. L., Moore, C. I., and Fischl, B. (2005). Meditation experience is associated with increased cortical thickness. *Neuroreport, 16*(17):1893–1897.

Lukoff, D., & Lu, F. G. (1988). Transpersonal psychology research review topic: Mystical experience. *The Journal of Transpersonal Psychology, 17*(2), 155–181.

Lukoff, D. (1985). The diagnosis of mystical experiences with psychotic features. *The Journal of Transpersonal Psychology, 17*(2), 155–181.

Lutz, A., Greischar, L. L., Rawlings, N. B., Ricard, M., & Davidson, R. J. (2004). Long-term meditators self-induce high-amplitude gamma synchrony during mental practice. *Proceedings of the National Academy of Sciences, 101*(46), 16369–16373.

Maharishi Mahesh Yogi (1966). *The science of being and art of living.* Fairfield, IA: MIU Press.

Maharishi Mahesh Yogi (1986). *Life supported by natural law.* Fairfield, IA. MIU Press.

Maharishi Mahesh Yogi (1994). *Vedic knowledge for everyone, Maharishi Vedic University, Introduction.* Fairfield, IA: Maharishi Vedic University

Maslow, A. (1969). *Towards a psychology of being.* Princeton: Van Nostrand.

Mason, L., Alexander, C. N., Travis, F. Gackenbach, J., & Orme-Johnson, D. (1995) EEG correlates of "higher states of consciousness" during sleep. *Sleep, 24,* 152.

Matlin, M. W. (1995). *Psychology (2nd Ed.).* Fort Worth: Harcourt Brace College Publishers.

Maynard, A. E., Subrahmanyam, K., & Greenfield, P. M. (2005). Technology and the development of intelligence: From the loom to the computer. In R. J. Sternberg & D. D. Preiss (Eds.), *Intelligence and technology: The impact of tools on the nature and development of human abilities* (pp. 29–53). Mahwah, NJ: Erlbaum.

MacDonald, D. A. & Friedman, D. A. (2002). *Assessment of humanistic, transpersonal and spiritual constructs: State of the science. Journal of Humanistic Psychology, 42*(4), pp. 102-125.

McLean, A. (2005, Feb. 12). Sweet dreams for gamers: Video games prompt more lucid dreams, says Grant MacEwan prof. *Edmonton Journal,* retrieved Feb 12, 2005, from http://www.canada.com/edmonton/ edmontonjournal/news/culture/ story.html?id=9d1c053b-16e5- 4f1e-ad7c-f893509c952c

Morgan Stanley U. S. Investment Research (1997) The Internet Retailing Report New York: Morgan Stanley. Available at http://www.morganstanley.com/ institutional/techresearch/inetretail. html? page=research

Murphy, M., & Donovan, S. (1988). *The physical and psychological effects of meditation.* San Rafael, CA: Esalen Institute.

Murphy, M., Donovan, S., & Taylor, E. (1997). *The physical and psychological effects of meditation: A review of contemporary research with a comprehensive bibliography, 1931–1996.* San Francisco: Institute of Noetic Sciences.

Newberg, A. B. (2001). Putting the mystical mind together. *Zygon, 36*(3), 501–507.

Newberg, A. B., d'Aquili, E., & Rause, V. (2001). *Why God won't go away: Science and the biology of belief.* NY: Ballantine.

Nidich, S. I., & Nidich, R. J. (1987). Holistic student development at Maharishi School of the Age of Enlightenment: Theory and research. *Modern Science and Vedic Science, 1,* 433–470.

Nidich, S. I., & Nidich, R. J. (1990). *Growing up enlightened.* Fairfield, IA: MIU Press.

Nidich, S. I., Ryncarz, R. A., Abrams, A. I., Orme-Johnson, D. W., & Wallace, R. K. (1983). Kohlbergian cosmic perspective responses, EEG coherence, and the Transcendental Meditation and TM–Sidhi program. *Journal of Moral Education, 12*(3), 166–173.

Orme-Johnson, D. W., Alexander, C. N., & Davies, J. L. (1990). The effects of the Maharishi technology of the unified field. *Journal of Conflict Resolution, 34*(4), 756–768.

Persinger, M. A. (2003). The sensed presence within experimental settings: Implications for the male and female concept of self. *Journal of Psychology, 137*(1), 5–16.

Preston, J. (1998). From mediated environments to the development of consciousness. In J. I. Gackenbach (Ed.), *Psychology and the Internet* (pp. 255–291). San Diego: Academic Press.

Preston, J. (in press). From mediated environments to the development of consciousness II. In J. I. Gackenbach (Ed.), *Psychology and the Internet (2nd Ed.).* San Diego: Academic Press.

Preston, J. & Nery, R. (2004, November). *Video game play, spatial skills, balance, and consciousness experiences.* Unpublished manuscript.

Siegel, R. (1979–80). Dizziness as an altered state of consciousness. *Journal of Altered States of Consciousness, 5,* 87-104.

Sternberg, R. J., & Preiss, D. D. (2005). *Intelligence and technology: The impact of tools on the nature and development of human abilities.* Mahwah, NJ: Erlbaum.

Steuer, J. (1995). Chapter 3: Defining virtual reality: Dimensions determining telepresence. In Frank Biocca & Mark Levy (Eds.), *Communication in the age of virtual reality (pp. 33-56).* Hillsdale, NJ: Erlbaum.

Stickgold, R., Malia, A., Maguire, D., Roddenberry, D., & O'Connor, M. (2000). Replaying the game: Hypnagogic images in normals and amnesics. *Science, 290*(5490), 350–353.

Subrahmanyam, K., Greenfield, P., Kraut, R., & Gross, E. (2001). The impact of computer use on children's and adolescents' development. *Applied Developmental Psychology, 22*, 7–30.

Surowiecki, J. (2004). *The wisdom of crowds: Why the many are smarter than the few and how collective wisdom shapes business, economies, societies, and nations.* New York: Doubleday.

Travis, F., Tecce, J., Arenander, A., and Wallace, R. K. (2002). Patterns of EEG coherence, power, and contingent negative variation characterize the integration of *transcendental* and waking states. *Biological Psychology 61*(3), 293–320.

Varela, F. (Ed.). (1997). *Sleeping, dreaming, and dying: An exploration of consciousness with The Dalai Lama.* Boston: Wisdom Publications.

Voiskounsky, A. E., Mitina, O. V., & Avetisova, A. A. (2004). Playing online games: Flow experience. *PsychNology Journal, 2*(3), 259–281.

Wallace, R. K. (1987). The Maharishi technology of the unified field: The neurophysiology of enlightenment. Fairfield, IA: Maharishi International University Press.

Wilber, K. (1987). The spectrum model. In D. Anthony, B. Ecker, & K. Wilber (Eds.), *Spiritual choices.* New York: Paragon.

Witmer, B., & Singer, M. (1998). Measuring presence in virtual environments: A presence questionnaire. *Presence, 7*(3), 225–240.

Wood, R. T. A., Griffiths, M. D., Chappell, D., & Davies, M. N. O. (2004). The structural characteristics of video games: A psycho-structural analysis. *CyberPsychology & Behavior, 7*(1), 1–10.

Wright, R. (2000). *Nonzero: The logic of human destiny.* New York: Pantheon.

INDEX*

* Lowercase "t" and "f" indicates that entry can be found within a table or figure.